W9-DEP-257

THE SIN OF SLOTH

THE SIN OF SLOTH:

ACEDIA

IN MEDIEVAL THOUGHT AND LITERATURE

SIEGFRIED WENZEL

THE UNIVERSITY OF NORTH CAROLINA PRESS
CHAPEL HILL

Manufactured in the United States of America
Library of Congress Catalog Card Number 67-17027
Printed by the Seeman Printery, Durham, North Carolina

To my parents

PREFACE

Attention to the medieval notion of *acedia* or "spiritual sloth" has in recent decades experienced a surprising revival. Not only has it been the cornerstone in the exploration of certain works by Petrarch and Albrecht Dürer and in our evaluation of their significance for the history of Western sentiment, but the word itself has become quite fashionable among the literati. Critics of life and literature from Josef Pieper and T. S. Eliot to Harvey Cox and John Ciardi have used it in their analyses of poetry and of humanistic ethics. Papers such as the London *Times* and its *Literary Supplement*, the *Christian Century*, even the *Saturday Evening Post*, have accommodated the term in their pages. Contemporary novelists are eager to explore sentiments which their critics then tell us are modern—and amoral—forms of the medieval vice; dictionary-makers have decided to include the word in their volumes; and the student of *acedia* can always count upon finding literate ears receptive, even at a cocktail party.

Yet in spite of this revived interest in *acedia*, the medieval history of the concept has never been fully studied and presented. A few articles or essays exist which have attempted to survey the notion historically, from Bishop Francis Paget's noteworthy "Introductory Essay concerning Accidie" to articles of varying quality in a number of encyclopedias.[1] Often the term has received incidental attention in studies on monasticism,[2] mysticism,[3] folklore,[4] psychology and sociology,[5] or literature.[6] More directly concerned with it are investigations of the seven deadly sins, and it is especially Morton W. Bloomfield's study of this scheme which presents the fullest historical account of the vice.[7] A unified monograph, however, which would gather as much information as possible and at the same time disentangle the strands of *acedia*'s rather confusing development, has so far not been written.[8]

To fill this gap is the purpose of the present study. I intend to pursue the history of the concept of the sin of sloth from its beginnings in the fourth Christian century to the end of the Middle Ages. The following pages deal essentially with the history of an idea. But a word of caution is necessary. From the outset of my investigations it has been clear to me that in studying the concept of *acedia* historically one must carefully direct one's attention to the word itself and exclude consideration of texts which portray a sentiment that may look very much like *acedia* but which do not use the term. Such a procedure might appear unduly pedantic, yet it alone can guarantee some success in explaining the diversity and confusion that is found in the concept during the later Middle Ages. Thus, the chapters that follow deal primarily with the meaning of a word. Yet they are more than a purely semantic study, inasmuch as the history of *acedia* was intimately connected with, and dependent upon, the milieu in which the term was meaningfully employed, becoming itself molded by larger changes in doctrine, intellectual as well as practical preoccupations, and society.

The sources for this study—consonant with the nature of its subject—are predominantly theological or religious writings. I have not systematically canvassed imaginative literature yet have given attention to the use of *acedia* in works by four important poets (Chapter VI). On the other hand, I have, after some deliberation, excluded the fine arts altogether, chiefly because the documentary value of medieval and early Renaissance sculpture and painting for a study of this nature is very restricted, especially when compared with the wealth of detail furnished by written documents. In addition, a survey of the iconography (in the strict sense) of *acedia* should be preceded by a comprehensive cataloguing of the extant monuments, an enterprise which lies beyond my present task and resources. I hope that what information is offered here, particularly in Chapter V, may prove a useful basis for such a survey and for further iconographical analysis of given works of art.

For information on many of the figures, movements, and periods dealt with here, I am greatly indebted to standard works or specialized monographs. In several cases I have acknowledged such sources in the notes, but I have not made a consistent effort to provide comprehensive bibliographies; such lists would have required space out of proportion to their direct usefulness for this study. The translations which appear in the text are my own unless otherwise stated. Biblical references as to book, chapter, and verse are to the Latin Vulgate text, but the titles of biblical books are given in English as they appear in the Douai version.

The system of documentation I have adopted is of necessity somewhat complicated and demands some explanation. (*a*) References to and quotations from works in manuscript are always fully identified. A list of manuscripts consulted and used will be found on pp. 259-60. (*b*) References to and quotations from works available in print are, both in the text and in the notes, nearly always identified in very short form (the exceptions being references to printed sources used only once or twice in my text, which are then fully identified). A given passage from a medieval work that has been printed will be identified by author, title of the work (or the title alone if the work is anonymous or if it is customary to cite the work by title, as is the case with *Handlyng Synne*), and chapter and/or paragraph. This identification is then followed in parentheses by a standard-form reference to the page (or, the volume and page) where the respective passage can be found in the editions I have used. The reader will find a list of editions used in my "List of Printed Sources" on pp. 253-58. Sometimes the edition used forms part of a series (such as EETS, GCS, SATF). In this case the "List of Printed Sources" uses a standard abbreviation explained in the section "Abbreviations" on pp. 203-4. For example:

Bonaventure, *Breviloquium*, II, 10 (IV, 393)—the given passage is found on p. 393 of vol. IV of Bonaventure, *Opera omnia* (Quaracchi, 1882-1902).

Jacob's Well, 18 (p. 102)—the given passage is found on p. 102 of *Jacob's Well*, ed. A. Brandeis, in vol. 115 of the Original Series issued by the Early English Text Society (London, 1900).

(*c*) References to printed sources which appear in one of the well-known collections of medieval texts are identified in a fashion similar to (*b*), but here the collection is identified by an abbreviation followed by reference to volume and page (or column). For a list of such abbreviations, see pp. 203-4.
For example:

Evagrius, *De oratione*, 75 (PG 79:1184)—the Evagrian passage appears in col. 1184 in vol. 79 of Migne's *Patrologiae Cursus Completus, Series Graeca.*

Councils, II, 1059—the respective passage appears on p. 1059 of vol. II of Powicke and Cheney, *Councils and Synods*, etc.

My greatest debt in undertaking this investigation is to Morton W. Bloomfield. Not only has his work on the seven deadly sins made such a book possible, by tracing a path through the immense field of medieval literature and outlining the works and areas to be explored, but I am also profoundly grateful to him for initially directing my studies and later encouraging them in many ways. I also wish to acknowledge my gratitude to the American Council of Learned Societies for a fellowship; to the Smith Research Fund of The University of North Carolina at Chapel Hill for a small grant for manuscript preparation; to the Alumni Annual Giving funds of The University of North Carolina at Chapel Hill, administered by the University Research Council, for a grant to aid in publication; to the trustees and staff of the British Museum and of the Bodleian Library for allowing me to make use of manuscript material in their holdings; to the library staff at The University of North Carolina at Chapel Hill and at Duke University for their help; and to my departmental chairmen at The Ohio State University and at The University of North Carolina for their tolerance and encouragement. My most deeply felt thanks are to my wife, whose care has given me much freedom for scholarly work, and to my parents, without whose personal sacrifices this study would not have been possible.

CONTENTS

THE SIN OF SLOTH

I

ORIGINS

As it happens with many other elements in medieval culture, the quest for the origin of the idea of sloth leads back to a far distant past whose shapes are many-colored and rather blurred in their contours. Sloth is such a universal experience that one will find it analyzed and condemned whenever man's reflection on his nature has reached a fairly subtle stage. More specifically, the concept as it was developed during the first Christian centuries seems to have more or less obvious roots in such diverse milieus as the Bible and its Jewish and Christian commentators, various Jewish and Christian ascetic movements, Gnosticism, Hellenistic psychology (particularly Stoic, Epicurean, and Neoplatonic moral doctrines), and even the myths of Babylon and the East.

Fortunately, in none of these is there anything very much like the idea with which this book is concerned. For the historian of the medieval sin of sloth the task of uncovering its origins is considerably easier than appearances might suggest, for two reasons: first, because sloth was singled out from a host of moral defects and made a chief vice or, as it came to be called, a deadly sin; and second, because the concept appears under a very peculiar technical name—*acedia* or *accidia*[1]—, which furnishes a convenient key with which to unlock the door to its past. The very word, unmistakably Greek in form and always a linguistic foreigner in the Latin and vernacular literatures of the Middle Ages, points to a precise milieu and period at which the medieval idea of sloth was born: that of the Egyptian desert monks near Alexandria in the fourth century. One can be even more precise and name a literary figure who—although this has not been fully recognized—holds a position of prime importance in the history of the seven deadly sins and of sloth: Evagrius Ponticus.

Born in 346, Evagrius became an acclaimed preacher in Constantinople but withdrew from the dangers of the capital in 382 and lived from then until his death (399) among the hermits of Mount Nitria and the Desert of Cells. There he became a disciple and close friend of Macarius, important and influential for his teaching and writings on mysticism. Evagrius himself was highly educated. He had studied under Basil the Great and Gregory of Nazianzus and had read Clement and Origen, whose doctrines are widely reflected in his own works. The connection with Origen actually proved detrimental to his fame: after his life, in the sixth century, Evagrius was several times condemned with Origen, and many of his writings were lost or circulated, for centuries, under different names. It is only in our age that his real significance in the history of Christian asceticism and mysticism has been rediscovered, so that Bousset could call him "the beginner and creator of genuine Christian mysticism."[2]

The community of monks to which Evagrius had withdrawn was part of a cluster of hermit colonies gathered at Nitria and Scete and the "Desert of the Cells" some forty to sixty miles to the southeast of Alexandria. In these deserted places the monks lived in separate huts, far enough from each other so as not to disturb their neighbors, yet close enough to gather for common worship on the Sabbath. They were mostly simple, uneducated Egyptian peasants; intellectuals such as Evagrius or Arsenius were exceptional among them. Their spiritual program was fairly simple and lacked the regulated organization of the cenobitic life. Yet their spiritual life was intense, with a strong emphasis on ascetic practices, and it found literary expression in a variety of forms. The richest and most direct witness of their ideals, practices, and experiences is Evagrius, whose works antedate other gnomic collections and descriptive accounts by at least a generation.

Today, Evagrius' writings lie scattered under different authors' names (mostly Nilus, but apparently also Origen) and in a variety of languages: his original Greek as well as Armenian, Syriac, and Latin. Authorities still disagree on the attribution of a few treatises, but a basic *corpus Evagrianum* has been established which enables us to gain a clear and full picture of Evagrius' teaching—or at least reporting—of the "wisdom of the desert."[3] These works furnish the first full picture of *ἀκηδία,* the temptation which later became the sin of sloth. One description presents it in the following way:

> The demon of ἀκηδία, also called "noonday demon," is the most oppressive of all demons. He attacks the monk about the fourth hour and besieges his soul until the eighth hour. First he makes the sun appear sluggish and immobile, as if the day had fifty hours. Then he causes the monk continually to look at the windows and forces him to step out of his cell and to gaze at the sun to see how far it still is from the ninth hour, and to look around, here and there, whether any of his brethren is near. Moreover, the demon sends him hatred against the place, against life itself, and against the work of his hands, and makes him think he has lost the love among his brethren and that there is none to comfort him. If during those days anybody annoyed the monk, the demon would add this to increase the monk's hatred. He stirs the monk also to long for different places in which he can find easily what is necessary for his life and can carry on a much less toilsome and more expedient profession. It is not on account of the locality, the demon suggests, that one pleases God. He can be worshipped everywhere. To these thoughts the demon adds the memory of the monk's family and of his former way of life. He presents the length of his lifetime, holding before the monk's eyes all the hardships of his ascetic life. Thus the demon employs all his wiles so that the monk may leave his cell and flee from the race-course.[4]

Additional traits of the temptation are scattered in other Evagrian works.[5] They all characterize it as psychic exhaustion and listlessness caused by the monotony of life and the immediate surroundings or by the protracted struggle with other temptations; occasionally, this boredom also bespeaks a soul that is still too much attached to sensual pleasures. Its effects are dejection, restlessness, hatred of the cell and the monk's brethren, desire to leave and seek salvation elsewhere—the latter temptation often suggested under the appearance of charity. In the end ἀκηδία causes the monk either to give in to physical sleep, which proves unrefreshing or actually dangerous because it opens the door to many other temptations, or to leave his cell and eventually the religious life altogether. Hence, it can quite rightly be called the most dangerous as well as "the most oppressive" of all temptations.

On the other hand, the monk who endures hardships and successfully combats tedium and depression grows in strength and gains immeasurably. The chief remedy against ἀκηδία is to practice endurance and patience. Under no circumstances must one flee one's cell. Insistent prayer, reading, the recitation of psalms, and shedding tears are helpful practices. So is the remembrance of, and meditation on, relevant verses from Scripture: Evagrius himself compiled for the monks a large number of such "spiritual weapons" against ἀκηδία and the other main temptations.[6] As to inner dispositions, the thought of one's death and of heavenly rewards will renew one's hope and thus repulse the demon. And finally work by hand is the great external remedy practiced and taught by all the experienced fathers.

The name given to this special form of boredom was not invented by the monks. Ἀκήδεια or ἀκηδία,[7] literally "lack of care, *incuria*," had a long history in Greek literature, from a work attributed to Hippocrates down to Hellenistic writers, although it apparently had never been in frequent use. Cicero used the noun once in its Greek form, but the precise meaning is not clear from the context.[8] The same is true of its connotations in classic Greek in general: they are vague and often even ambivalent. "Lack of care" can mean a negative as well as a positive state: carelessness or freedom from sorrow, and both uses are attested. A second meaning is "weariness, exhaustion, apathy," which in at least one passage is connected with the moral endeavors of Stoic philosophy. Lucian (second century A.D.) has the skeptic inquirer enlighten his Stoic friend: "So it is to get into the neighborhood of Happiness . . . that you toil like this, wearing yourself away, letting this great portion of your life slip from you, while you are sunk in dullness (ἐν ἀκηδίᾳ) and wakeful weariness."[9] But we can be certain that ἀκηδία in non-Christian usage was not a *terminus technicus,* nor was the concept it stood for ever subjected to analysis or detailed description.

More important for the later history of the word is its appearance in the Septuagint.[10] Our knowledge of the supposed seventy or seventy-two translators and their background is minimal, but it is plausible to think that they were familiar with the term from their contact with Hellenistic culture in the Near East, specifically Alexandria. The term occurs nine times in the Septuagint, as a noun or as the derived verb ἀκηδιᾶν or ἀκηδιάζειν, and translates several different Hebrew roots. Its general meaning is faintness, weariness, anguish. One of these passages should be singled out because of its later importance as a bridge between the still very vague meaning of ἀκηδία in the Septuagint and its eventual application to a specific temptation. It is verse 28 of Psalm 118: "My soul has slumbered because of ἀκηδία" (ἐνύσταξεν ἡ ψυχή μου ἀπὸ ἀκηδίας).

Since the Septuagint was *the* universally known and commonly used biblical text among early Christians in the East, it is reasonable to think that it, rather than pagan authors, transmitted the term to early Christian writers.[11]. Yet for two or three centuries ἀκηδία hardly appeared in patristic literature at all. It does not occur in the New Testament. The *Shepherd of Hermas* uses it once, in the sense of "sloth, negligence" caused by excessive attention to worldly business.[12] It is only in several passages attributed to Origen (d. 253-54) that the term appears more often and with a meaning that is more relevant to its later history. The *Philocalia,* a florilegium of Origen's sayings, declares: "If [Scripture] be read and not understood, the hearer sometimes grows listless [verb ἀκηδιᾶν] and weary."[13] Similarly, a homily on the Gospel according to Luke counts ἀκηδία among temptations like sleep and cowardice: "Mark and Luke say that 'He was being tempted during forty days', which is, in those days [the devil] tempted Him from afar by means of sleep, ἀκηδία, cowardice, and such temptations."[14]

Some more information about the nature of this temptation can be derived from various scholia and comments on the Psalms which have survived under Origen's name. Of great importance is Ps. 90:6: "His truth shall compass thee with a shield: thou shalt not be afraid of the terror of the night. Of the arrow that flieth in the day, of the business that walketh about in the dark, of invasion, or of the noonday devil." A scholium to this verse states, "They say that 'the noonday demon' is the demon of ἀκηδία."[15] And a longer comment explains: "The 'noonday demon' he calls ἀκηδία or negligence. This attacks some people. Now and then they suffer this attack when the mind is broken by love of pleasure, when the heart grows slack and is weighed down by fleshly love, when it grows weary [ἀκηδιάσῃ] on account of the works of piety and grows old on account of its pains with regard to [the pursuit of] virtue."[16] Equally important is the already-mentioned verse: "My soul slumbers on account of ἀκηδία" (Ps. 118:28). A commentary ascribed to Origen deals with the Greek variant readings for "slumbers" and then explains:

> The Psalmist says, "I have come close to death, making small account of the evils which press upon me. But you, confirm me in your promise!" [This state occurs] when the assault of sin weakens our rational control [λογισμός] and produces ἀκηδία.

> But the latter causes sleep, and sleep causes death. . . . The Psalmist says that when the soul has fallen into ἀκηδία, anguish and grief, it loses its vigilance and falls into sleep, which is denounced by the verse: "Do not admit sleep to your eyes nor slumber to your eyelids!"[17]

The same idea is expressed in a scholium found with Origen's name in a Vienna manuscript: "The continuous assault of sin often weakens the strength of one's rational control [or, thoughts] and prepares the athlete to give up and thus causes what is called ἀκηδία. When the soul has grown slack, it admits sleep. But sleep leads to death."[18] Finally, the temptation of ἀκηδία is again seen in connection with the assault of demons and, at the same time, related to the Platonic parts of the soul. A commentary on Ps. 139:3 explains:

> Through our thoughts the demons wage war against us when they arouse in us, now desires, then irritation, and on another occasion both furor and concupiscence in the same person. From this arises the temptation that is called "perplexed mind." But this one occurs only at the time of ἀκηδία, while the other [temptations] come at certain intervals, one succeeding upon the other. But no [other] evil thought follows upon the thought of ἀκηδία on that [same] day: first, because it lasts a long time; second, because it contains wellnigh all evil thoughts in itself.[19]

A similar psychological description of the temptation is given more succinctly in another scholium on Ps. 118:28: "Ἀκηδία is a movement of long duration in the irascible and the concupiscible parts: the former being irritated by present objects, the latter being desirous of future ones."[20]

In these passages, the term ἀκηδία denotes spiritual listlessness and slackened attention which may be caused by weariness from the prolonged assault of other temptations (mostly, fleshly thoughts) or by plain boredom. This meaning is certainly very close to the temptation described by Evagrius, and it may seem as though Evagrius, who as is well known depended much on Origen's thought, had received his notion of ἀκηδία, too, from the great Alexandrian theologian. Yet the attribution of the quoted works to Origen is weakened by serious doubts. The quoted comment on Ps. 139:3 occurs elsewhere under the name of Evagrius,[21] and the *Selecta in Psalmos* on the whole has been shown to differ in doctrine, terminology, and style from Origen's other works and, instead, to be frequently identical with Evagrius' writings.[22] The same can be said of the quoted homily *In Lucam*.[23] And the third work of relevance, the *Philocalia,* though having the greatest claim to containing Origen's own words, was compiled as late as a century after his death (viz., in 356) by Basil and Gregory of Nazianzus, who by that time had been in direct contact with the Egyptian desert fathers. Thus, Origen's position in the history of ἀκηδία is uncertain and questionable.

In the quoted passages attributed to Origen, ἀκηδία is hardly at all connected with early monasticism, but as we move closer in time to Evagrius this connection becomes quite pronounced. Bishop Athanasius (*ca.* 357), in his biography of St. Anthony, the founder of Egyptian monasticism, includes ἀκηδία in a series of inner disturbances which, as St. Anthony explained in an address to his monks, result from "the attack of the evil ones"[24] and uses the derived verb ἀκηδιᾶν to denote carelessness in the practice of asceticism.[25] Less specifically, Athanasius' commentary on the Psalms declares that ἀκηδία fills man's soul when he sees the power and tyranny of attacking demons, or when God delays His gifts; and like the *Selecta in Psalmos* Athanasius equates ἀκηδία with the noonday demon of Ps. 90:6.[26] At approximately the same time, St. Basil (d. 394) also used the term in reference to the monastic life. His *Regulae fusius tractae* ("Detailed Rules") recommend variation in prayer and psalm-singing, "for the mind often suffers ἀκηδία and is distracted because of monotony,"[27] and the *Sermo asceticus* mentions "ἀκηδιασμός in psalm-singing" among the faults for which, at the end of the day, the monks are to search their consciences.[28] Basil's relatively tolerant attitude toward boredom in the performance of spiritual exercises, incidentally, is characteristic of the saint. In another work he even goes so far as to allow the monk an occasional emergence from his cell, "for often the ἀκηδία which besets the soul is dispelled by going out."[29] 'Ακηδία, therefore, designates a mental or spiritual weariness and boredom which the monk has to overcome,[30] a sentiment that can likewise be found in various homilies by St. John Chrysostom.[31]

In the last group of writings the connection of ἀκηδία with monasticism is quite explicit. A homily attributed to Macarius, one of the most venerable monks in the desert of Scete and teacher of Evagrius, explains: "Often comes the hour when the grace of the Lord allows Satan to make war on him [viz., the monk]. He rouses against him the passions of evil and brings on him sleep, ἀκηδία, languor, and many other [passions] which it is impossible to enumerate."[32] In similar fashion, Nilus, an early fifth-century abbot of a monastery near Ankara, writes of ἀκηδία as the temptation of monks to grow slack and desist when they are attacked by "the spirits of evil."[33] Hence Nilus recommends persevering in battle like a high-minded soldier, "for even those who have been wounded by the enemy, as long as they will not grow weary [verb ἀκηδιᾶν] of the hardships of penance . . . will finally triumph."[34] In other letters he enjoins persistence in prayer[35] and hope and piety to one in whose heart the demons have cast ἀκηδία and sorrow.[36]

To these letters, ascetic treatises, and saints' lives must be added another literary genre in which, during the fifth century, the temptation of ἀκηδία appears with firm contours and a meaning that is identical with the phenomenon described by Evagrius. These are stories about the monks who lived in the deserts near Alexandria, stories that reflect the life and teaching of the desert fathers with a high degree of immediacy. The first important collection of such stories is by Palladius, bishop of Helenopolis, who before his consecration had lived for twelve years among the monks near Alexandria and had been a personal disciple of Evagrius. His *Historia Lausiaca* (420) is "a series of biographical sketches of the monks whom he had known."[37] Another florilegium of anecdotes and ascetic sayings, the *Apophthegmata,* was written down somewhat later in the same century but clearly reflects traditions of a hundred years earlier.[38] Both collections together contain about a dozen passages in which the noun ἀκηδία or the verb ἀκηδιᾶν appear with meanings that parallel the description by Evagrius. It is the temptation[39] of getting bored with the religious life[40] and the cell;[41] it usually befalls the beginners in the ascetic life;[42] it is the worst temptation[43] and urges the monk to flee the cell[44] or to forsake the religious life entirely.[45]

Our survey thus shows that the term ἀκηδία underwent a considerable rise in importance and restriction in meaning some time before, approximately, A.D. 400. From a rather inconspicuous place in the vocabulary of classical and Hellenistic Greek it was raised to the dignity of denoting one of the main temptations in the Christian ascetic life, a dignity which it should retain up to the Renaissance and beyond. And from its association with a variety of vague, even ambivalent meanings, ἀκηδία came to be a *terminus technicus.* This semantic change was completed by the time Evagrius wrote his treatises. We must now determine precisely what Evagrius' place in the history of ἀκηδία was.

Obviously, Evagrius did not himself discover spiritual sloth. The temptation of boredom and dejection that he described is presented as common to those who had withdrawn to the desert for a more intensive religious life. Nor did Evagrius take the idea from a book: his writings and other contemporary *sententiae* and anecdotes have an air of experienced reality that is not very frequently found in later medieval ascetic and moral literature. Nor was Evagrius the first to apply to this spiritual phenomenon the ancient name of ἀκηδία. All available evidence points to the currency of the word and the phenomenon in the milieu in which Evagrius lived and wrote: the hermits of Lower Egypt during the second half of the fourth century. It is the desert fathers of Nitria and Scete who must be credited with the "discovery" of *acedia*.

How much their spiritual experience and vocabulary depended on earlier or contemporary theologians of first rank is now extremely hard to discern. Because of textual confusion, we cannot be sure whether Origen used the concept ἀκηδία at all. The Cappadocian fathers who employed the word had themselves been influenced by Egyptian monasticism: St. Basil, for example, had visited the Egyptian monk colonies in his youth, and his *Regulae fusius tractae* depend greatly on Eustathius of Sebaste, who had been brought up among Egyptian monks. On the other hand, ascetic authors who wrote of ἀκηδία in the century following A.D. 350 usually had been in direct contact with desert monasticism. Athanasius lived among the Egyptian hermits during one of his numerous exiles from Alexandria and admittedly wrote the *Life of Saint Anthony* as a portrayal of the customs and ideals of the desert monks. Macarius and Nilus, finally, are important representatives of desert spirituality, yet it is at the moment impossible for us to say how much their thought or individual experience may have influenced Evagrius, as the attribution of their works is very uncertain. It seems, therefore, safe to affirm that ἀκηδία was a concept that belonged to the common experience and tradition among the desert fathers.

However, in contrast to Macarius, Nilus, the *Historia Lausiaca*, and the *Apophthegmata*, Evagrius presents a picture of ἀκηδία that is considerably more detailed, more comprehensive, and more systematic. He must be claimed as the first writer who has given a full analysis of the temptation. Thus, the experience he describes was not exclusively his own; and the word he used for it had had a long history, in which earlier Christian writers may have prepared the path it was to take in the desert; but Evagrius' work marks the moment when the temptation of boredom with the cell and spiritual dejection was fully grasped and analyzed and when the term ἀκηδία, after a gradual semantic change, became permanently attached to it as a technical term of Christian asceticism.[46]

The history of the word before Evagrius does not, however, fully explain why this particular term was used in preference to ἀμέλεια (negligence), ῥαθυμία (sluggishness), δειλία (cowardice, the evil opposed to the cardinal virtue of fortitude), or ἀργία (idleness)—terms of much greater frequency in didactic literature. To find an explanation we must return to Evagrius' analysis and examine the larger context in which the temptation is presented.

The first peculiarity that strikes the reader is that Evagrius speaks of ἀκηδία as an evil spirit. Not only the longer description quoted above, but numerous shorter sayings refer to the vice as "the demon of ἀκηδία" (τὸ τῆς ἀκηδίας δαίμων) or "the spirit of ἀκηδία" (τὸ ἀκηδίας πνεῦμα).[47] The same is true of other chief temptations that befall the monk. In fact, the fight against demons looms so large in the teachings of the desert fathers that it forms a basic and quite distinctive trait of their spirituality. Already in the *Life of St. Anthony* the hero is seen in constant battle against evil spirits, whose immediate aims and tactics change with Anthony's growing saintliness. In his brilliant exposition of early Christian demonology, Jean Daniélou[48] has shown the gradual development of this complex trait and disentangled the various strands—Iranian, Hellenistic, Gnostic, and Judeo-Christian—which have mingled in it. At its root lies the dualistic conception of good and evil spiritual powers which can lead man's soul the way of goodness to salvation, or the way of evil to destruction. This idea of the two ways appears especially in the *Manual of Discipline* from Qumram[49] and in the early Christian *Shepherd of Hermas* (before A.D. 150),[50] where good thoughts and evil thoughts are attributed to the agency of a good and a bad angel in man's soul. The *Testament of the Twelve Patriarchs* (end of second century B.C., with later Christian additions) develops these ideas a step further by attributing individual vices to single demons. It speaks of the "seven spirits of deceit": the spirit of fornication, of insatiableness, of fighting, and so forth.[51] Origen, who knew the *Testament* and referred to it explicitly (*In Josue,* XV, 6), accepted the doctrine and can be credited with transmitting it to the desert fathers.

The battle with demons may have been one of the reasons why the Egyptian monks chose the desert for their dwelling, because it was popularly considered the proper habitat of evil spirits. But this seems to have been at best a minor reason. Primarily, the desert offered the opportunity par excellence for the detachment and solitude which are deemed essential to an advanced spiritual life. The whole ascetic movement we are considering[52] was characterized by the idea that the exodus (ἀναχώρησις) from towns and villages into the desert—the farther, the better—was a necessary condition for reaching the higher stages of perfection. The hermits' conception of perfection and their approach to it is neatly outlined in this passage from Evagrius:

> Asceticism consists in that you do not, in any way, take your fill of bread, water, and sleep; that you promptly resist any disturbing thought [λογισμός], whatever it be, with firmness and wisdom, asking God for it; that you devote yourself diligently to reading, prayer, the office, conversation with God and remembrance of Him; that you do not lend your mind to vagrant thoughts. This is the highest degree of perfection: that your thought be never detached from God; each time it separates itself from Him, bring it back![53]

This elementary blueprint of the spiritual life is at first sight, of course, not peculiar to Egyptian monasticism until one realizes that its last sentence was, by Evagrius and his companions, taken most literally. To them, life in God meant thinking of Him without the slightest interruption. Behind this spiritual ideal, sometimes praised or frowned upon as "Greek intellectualism," lies the concept of ἀπάθεια,[54] the freedom from disturbing passions, obtained through rational control over one's senses, desires, feelings, and memory. The term is of Stoic descent and was appropriated for Christian moral theology by Clement of Alexandria. "Passions" (πάθη) are affections of the irrational part of man's soul, which originate in sense impressions or in memory and are often accompanied by pleasure. It is the duty of reason to judge them and to separate the good from the harmful ones. As long as reason is incapable of thus keeping constant watch, man's soul remains in a state of imperfection, for reason is then subjected to the ebb and flow of affections, which tyrannize it and keep it in a state of turmoil—the master has become a slave. It is precisely this imperfection which the desert fathers tried to overcome. Their goal was a state of peace (ἡσυχία) in which the πάθη were kept under the unswerving control of reason. The question whether this state is identical with perfection or only preparatory to it was answered differently by different writers, and Evagrius' teaching seems not to be entirely consistent on this point. But the central position of ἀπάθεια as the ideal of the desert monks' ascetic endeavor is a clearly established and common doctrine. Evagrius himself declared, "the Kingdom of Heaven is the ἀπάθεια of the soul, with a true knowledge of the things that exist."[55]

The "evil thoughts" arising from the πάθη and disturbing the inner peace are, in Evagrius' works, consistently called λογισμοί. They are the object of the monk's watchfulness and spiritual fight. What, then, is their relation to the demons? Λογισμός and δαίμων are often used indiscriminately, but it is clear that the λογισμοί are the tools or "weapons"[56] used by the demons as instruments of temptation: "the demons war against the soul by means of the λογισμοί."[57] Except for rare occasions, the demons themselves remain invisible and not directly accessible to human experience, whereas the λογισμοί are and thereby form, so to speak, the raw material with which the ascetic has to deal on his way to God. This relation between πάθη, λογισμός, and δαίμων is brought out very clearly in the following *sententia* by Maximus the Confessor: "From the passions [πάθη] embedded in our soul the demons seize opportunities of stirring up in us impassioned thoughts [ἐμπαθεῖς λογισμούς]. Then, warring upon the mind through them, they force it on to consent to sin. When the mind is overcome, they lead on to the sin of thought; and when this is completed, they finally carry it prisoner to the deed."[58] Temptation and moral evil is, thus, the result of a combination of an external agent and a disposition in human nature. Hence the seeming contradiction in calling ἀκηδία, sometimes an (objective) spirit or demon, and sometimes a (subjective) "evil thought" or a "movement of the soul" (cf. the scholium to Ps. 118:28 from *Selecta in Psalmos,* quoted earlier).

This twofold reference, to a demon and to an evil thought, ἀκηδία shares with other chief temptations. In Evagrius' writings one finds several detailed descriptions of the "eight evil thoughts" against which the monk has to fight. This system of eight chief vices was first recorded and perhaps even established by Evagrius himself. The ultimate origins of the scheme,[59] however, are much more difficult—if at all possible—to discern. Two main theories have been proposed, in varying forms, which would explain why certain vices were organized in a scheme of eight or, later, seven. The astrological theory, represented among others by Professor Bloomfield,[60] sees in the sin list a remnant of the Babylonian myth of the Soul Journey, according to which man's soul, after death, has to pass a series of demons who are connected with specific sins (such as pride, fornication, greed, and the like) and who judge the soul with regard to that particular sin. These demons are sometimes connected with the seven planets. Hence the suggestion that a system of seven vices must have existed in pre-Christian times (although not a single complete series of sins which is clearly connected with this myth has been preserved). The main difficulty in accepting this hypothesis is the difference in numbers: there is not the slightest doubt that Evagrius thought and wrote of *eight* evil thoughts (not sins, incidentally).[61]

In contrast, often in averred opposition to the astrological theory, a number of scholars have suggested that Evagrius' scheme is based upon similar lists in non-Christian moral philosophers. Especially the combination of the four Stoic affects (hope or desire, fear, pleasure, and sorrow or pain) with the four cardinal vices (folly, cowardice, intemperance, and injustice) offers itself as a tempting model or even source. Early Christian writers such as the author of the *Shepherd of Hermas* and Origen did indeed use series that betray Stoic models and look somewhat like the Evagrian scheme. But modern attempts to combine elements existing in such earlier writings into a scheme which could be thought of as a predecessor of the Evagrian sin list have invariably led to a great deal of juggling of terms and to numerous tours de force, which weaken the argument considerably.

Finally, two scholars have approached the problem with the more refined and careful method of singling out the various constituents of the, after all, rather complex phenomenon, and of paying closer attention to specifically Christian thought processes. Irenée Hausherr[62] claims that the sins themselves are already mentioned in the New Testament, and that their names occur all in Origen, even in sin lists that are fairly static though not as systematic as Evagrius'. These evils are not called πάθη or κακίαι, as they were among Stoics and Neoplatonists, but λογισμοί because of the διαλογισμοί, "evil thoughts," of Matt. 15:19. Their number of eight derives from Origen's interpretation of Israel's fight against the seven Canaanite peoples after their leaving Egypt (thus yielding seven plus one combats), which would agree with the words of Jesus that the evil spirit, driven out of the soul and finding it empty, returns with seven other spirits (again, seven plus one; Matt. 12:43-45). All the elements—generic term, individual names, and number—were therefore furnished by Origen and the Bible, whereas Evagrius merely arranged the λογισμοί in his order of eight.

In contrast to Hausherr, A. Vögtle does not deny a possible influence of non-Christian thought and practices (such as the Pythagorean examination of conscience) but stresses the influence of biblical exegesis and the original contribution of the desert fathers in establishing this particular list. He sums up his findings:

> With the support of traditional topoi of biblical exegesis and of the general doctrine about vices, especially the catalogues of vices, the practical-ascetic needs of Egyptian monasticism led to establish the scheme of eight vices; this was first only an elementary summary for purposes of daily examination of conscience and of instruction, but was eventually and gradually—especially after the rise of monastic literature—, elaborated after the model of the profane doctrine about the affects [i.e., with a discussion of the psychological origins of vices, their κρίσις (classification, definition), and their therapy].[63]

This view does of course not deny a possible survival of Babylonian myths among early Christians or their possible influence on Egyptian or later schemes of chief vices. But it emphasizes that the evidence we have points to the monks of Nitria and Scete and to Evagrius as the creators of the scheme which was to become the seven deadly sins. How original Evagrius' personal contribution in this respect was is hard to tell. The *Historia Monachorum* praises him as "a wise man and skilled in words, who had a competent understanding of the λογισμοί" (XX, 15). On the other hand, Cassian speaks of the doctrine of eight chief vices as a common tradition among the desert monks. The literary historian Gennadius is undecided: Evagrius, he says, wrote eight books "against the temptations of the eight chief vices which he either was the first to observe or learned from those who were the first."[64] At the present state of our knowledge, we have, again, to be contented with stating that Evagrius "was the first to enunciate the teaching clearly."[65]

Probing into the background of the sin scheme contributes little to our knowledge of the origins of sloth beyond reinforcing the conclusions we have already reached from the history of the word. In the various sin schemes that have been suggested as models for the Evagrian list, I have found nothing which in nature and importance would equal ἀκηδία. Horace's famous series of vices contains *inertia*;[66] Servius' account of the evil gifts of the planets speaks of the *torpor* the soul receives from Saturn;[67] several Stoic and Neoplatonic schemes include δειλία (cowardice), the opposite of fortitude;[68] and finally the Qumram *Manual of Discipline* lists "the slackening of hands in the service of righteousness" among the vices that pertain to the spirit of iniquity.[69] But these are at best vague analogues. With the possible exception of the last mentioned, none of these vices has the spiritual implications of ἀκηδία, and none of them is ever made the subject of close scrutiny and description. How different is the position of ἀκηδία in the teaching of Evagrius: Here it is a clearly defined temptation with a firm place among a series of main vices. It even occupies a place of pre-eminence among the eight evil thoughts: not only is it described as the most violent of them, but it becomes identified with the noonday devil of Ps. 90:6. As we have noticed, the *Selecta in Psalmos* and Athanasius' commentary made the identification first: "The 'noonday devil' is said to be the demon of ἀκηδία,"[70] and this interpretation remained well known to the very end of the Middle Ages.[71] Its rationale is easy to grasp: in the Egyptian desert the temptation of boredom and weariness came usually around noon. The very association with the series of grave dangers enumerated in Psalm 90 speaks for the singular concern with which the desert fathers regarded this temptation.

Why such an important vice received a seemingly insignificant name can perhaps be elucidated with reference to another psalm passage. In the Septuagint version Ps. 118:28 states: "My soul slumbers on account of ἀκηδία." Very probably this verse reminded the monks of the danger they experienced in being tempted to grow listless and to give up. The spiritual meaning of "sleep" is pointed out in various scholia to this verse. The *Selecta in Psalmos* explains: " 'slumber' is the neglect on the part of the rational soul of the virtues and of the knowledge of God"; and Origen declares, "the soul, when slackened, admits sleep; but sleep leads to death."[72] One must in this connection recall the powerful connotations of "sleep" in the Hellenistic world during the first Christian centuries. In the myths and speculations of the Gnostics, for example, it stands for the state of the human soul after its fall from heaven, when it is poisoned by and enmeshed in the evil world.[73] "Sleep," in this sense, refers to a basic type of human existence and implies the loss of knowing what man's nature and his goals in this life are.[74] Much of this *Lebensgefühl,* no doubt, penetrated into early Christian teaching; it is enough to remember St. Paul's call: "Now it is high time to wake out of sleep: for now is our salvation nearer than when we believed" (Rom. 13:11). It is not impossible that this existential slumber, the unresponsiveness to or neglect of the highest spiritual good, was experienced by the Egyptian monk in the specific form of weariness at noon, boredom with the cell, and the temptation to walk out and quit. Very likely Psalm 118 suggested the authoritative name for it.

In the two or three centuries after Evagrius ἀκηδία continued to be mentioned and described by Greek writers in the East, usually in ascetic treatises. Here and there a writer added a little touch of his own to the characterization of the vice. Cyril of Alexandria, for example, in an Easter homily mentions that miracles bring back hope to the mind that is depressed by ἀκηδία.[75] Other monastic authors, such as the monk Antiochus or John Climacus in the seventh century, give long descriptions of the vice, which are mostly borrowed from the earlier desert fathers.[76] But there are no innovations. By and large, in the East the characterization of the vice remained static.

Not so in the West, where the transmission of the concept immediately led to changes. John Cassian,[77] born between 355 and 365, entered a monastery in Bethlehem and there became thoroughly acquainted with the cenobitic life. About 386 he traveled in Egypt and visited the hermit colonies of Nitria and Scete. There he came to know Evagrius and his teaching, which was to have the greatest influence upon Cassian's later literary work. The condemnation of Origenism in 400 and the concomitant persecution of its followers drove him from Egypt. After other expulsions from Constantinople and Rome he finally landed in France, where, in the second decade of the fifth century, he founded several monasteries at Marseilles.

For these young monastic communities Cassian wrote two treatises on the spiritual life, the *De Institutis Coenobiorum* (published about 425) and the *Collationes Patrum* (426-428). The former is a description of the monastic life as Cassian had known it from Palestine and Egypt and includes many of the religious ideals and techniques he had observed. Books V-XII of this work treat the eight chief vices. Cassian's second work, the *Collationes,* deals with similar subjects, pretending to be a report of "conferences" with the most famous desert fathers. This work is directly derived from the monk stories and the gnomic literature of the desert. In contrast to Evagrius, Palladius, and the *Apophthegmata,* however, Cassian's writings have a more systematic and artistic—in short, literary—quality.

Book X of the *Instituta,* entitled "de spiritu acediae,"[78] gives the classic description of the vice:

> Our sixth combat is with what the Greeks call ἀκηδία, which we may term weariness or distress of heart. This is akin to dejection, and is especially trying to solitaries, and a dangerous and frequent foe to dwellers in the desert; and especially disturbing to a monk about the sixth hour, like some fever which seizes him at stated times, bringing the burning heat of its attacks on the sick man at usual and regular hours. Lastly, there are some of the elders who declare that this is the "midday demon" spoken of in the ninetieth Psalm.[79]

It instils in its victims abhorrence of the place, disgust of the cell, and contempt for the brethren. The monk becomes disinclined to any work within the cell. He deems his life spiritually useless and imagines that he could make better progress elsewhere. If he does not leave the place, he might even forego his salvation. The slackness of his body, hunger, and the heat make him unquiet and confused in mind. He begins to think it better to go out and perform some deed of mercy: visiting the sick or bringing comfort to a brother. Then the monk either sinks into slumber or leaves his cell and looks for consolation in other people's company. If flight becomes a habit, the monk will soon give up his profession altogether (*Inst.*, X, 2-6). His chief weapon against *acedia* is manual work, which Cassian discusses in the remaining chapters of this book (X, 7-25). The discussion is based on the example and the teaching of the Apostle Paul—"verus ac spiritalis medicus"—, especially on his injunctions to the Thessalonians (I Thess. 4:9-11; II Thess. 3:6-15).

Cassian's dependence on the Egyptian desert monks and especially on Evagrius is evident from the tenor of his whole work. In addition, scholars have frequently pointed out verbal identities between the two writers.[80] Although Cassian's description of *acedia* itself is not noticeably different from Evagrius', it contains several features which indicate a continued reflection upon the concept. A tendency toward clarity and precision can be seen in his translating the Greek term and then using the new phrase as a fixed formula (*anxietas sive taedium cordis*).[81] More pronounced, however, is his desire to classify and systematize, which led to the introduction of various new aspects into the eight-vices scheme that were to have a long history in subsequent theology. Thus he tabulated the effects (*genera*) of the vices and established a list of virtues which replace the vices after their expulsion from the human heart. *Acedia* leads to either sleep or flight from the cell;[82] and its opposite virtue is *fortitudo,* strength or courage.[83]

The eight vices are divided up in several ways. Unfortunately, Cassian here is not as explicit and complete as one could wish. He first speaks of two kinds of vices: natural ones such as gluttony, and non-natural ones (*extra naturam*) such as avarice. The distinction seems to be based on the notion that certain vices spring from instincts that are absolutely essential to man's life, and that hence the desire for food can never be eradicated; this at least is the later medieval position. Another way of distinguishing between vices is by the manner in which they come about: some cannot be put into practice without co-operation of the body (gluttony and lechery); others can so indeed (pride and vainglory); a third group receives its causal impulse from outside (avarice and wrath), whereas the last two vices (*acedia* and sorrow) "are born from inner movements."[84] From this somewhat confusing scheme Cassian derives the distinction between *vitia carnalia* and *spiritualia,* although he does not yet distribute all eight between them (*Coll.,* V, 4). Finally, sorrow and *acedia* take a special place insofar as they—needing no external impulse—are proper to solitaries and to the desert hermits.[85] That *acedia* in the form we have so far become acquainted with is a temptation peculiar to desert monks (i.e., hermits) was already realized by Evagrius, who put it in a group of five vices against the three others (gluttony, wrath, and lechery) which beset "those who live under the rule of others."[86]

A somewhat different division sets off pride and vainglory against the other six vices (*Coll.*, V, 10). These six, Cassian says, "are linked to one another by a genetic relationship [*cognatione*] and, as it were, concatenation [*concatenatione*], so that each rises out of an abundance of its predecessor." *Acedia* springs from sadness, which in its turn arises from wrath, and so forth. The series and its order also furnish the plan of attack against all vices: one must eradicate *acedia* first and then proceed in right order to sadness, wrath, and so on, until one comes to lechery. This idea of a genetic concatenation[87] of the vices became very important in later theology, as did the connection of *acedia* with sadness and with wrath.

Perhaps the most important result of Cassian's endeavors to classify is the establishment of a fixed progeny of each vice, that is, of a series of faults which arise from the chief vices. Thus, "from *acedia* [are born] idleness, somnolence, rudeness, restlessness, wandering about, instability of mind and body, chattering, inquisitiveness" (*de acedia* [*nascuntur*] *otiositas, somnolentia, importunitas, inquietudo, pervagatio, instabilitas mentis et corporis, verbositas, curiositas*; *Coll.*, V, 16). These progenies seem to be a product of Cassian's own thought; at least, there are no models or analogues in previous monastic writers. On the other hand, an influence of biblical models is possible. For the offspring of *acedia* the two passages which Cassian himself uses as St. Paul's teaching on "this sickness which arises from the spirit of *acedia*" (*Inst.*, X, 7)—I Thess. 4:9-11, and II Thess. 3:6-15—are very suggestive. In Cassian's exegesis *inquietudo, curiositas,* and *otiositas* are explicitly related to the Apostle's words;[88] *importunitas* is implied in one verse;[89] and *pervagatio, instabilitas,* and *verbositas* may be brought into connection with another.[90] One might add the combination of *otiosae, verbosae,* and *curiosae* of I Tim. 5:13. Such combinations of faults in St. Paul's letters are very likely to have determined Cassian in selecting certain terms for his progeny.

The long section in which Cassian interprets the Pauline passages (*Inst.*, X, 7-16) is even more important in another respect. The purpose of the whole section is to impress upon Cassian's monks the necessity of manual labor, as the authority of the Apostle has shown it in words and by his own example (*Inst.*, X, 17-18). Work by hand was also, as we have seen, practiced and recommended as a help against depression by the Egyptian monks. But their main remedy against ἀκηδία was to keep the cell, to practice endurance, to nourish supernatural hope, and so on. In the *Collationes* Cassian similarly recommends cultivating fortitude and keeping the cell (V, 23 and XXIV, 5). In contrast, the *Instituta* speaks only of manual work. This difference in Cassian's conception is easily explained by what he himself states about the purposes of the two works: the *Collationes* treats of the monk's "inner dispositions," whereas the *Instituta* is concerned with the external regulations given to a monastic community in need of a rule.[91] The cenobitic life as Cassian established it at Marseilles, in contrast to the more individualized form of life followed by the hermits of Nitria and Scete, demanded a firm order imposed on the whole community. Here the idler constituted a much graver spiritual danger to the whole than among semi-hermits. In addition, it was basic to the cenobitic life that the monastery be a self-sustaining unit for whose support the individual monk had to contribute his share.[92]

The long discussion of manual work in connection with *acedia*, therefore, represents an important step in the history of the vice: we witness the concept in the process of being transferred from the desert to the monastery. The change of habitat is accompanied by a shift of emphasis in the nature of *acedia* itself, which is also reflected in *Instituta* X. The vice which Cassian with the help of St. Paul strikes at is not really dejection or boredom but simply idleness (*otium* or *otiositas*). Here idleness is not merely included in the progeny of *acedia* (as in *Coll.*, V, 16)—it occupies at least seventeen out of twenty-five chapters devoted to the vice, and once the two terms are even verbally equated: "somno otii vel acediae" (*Inst.*, X, 21).[93] The reasons for this insistence on the dangers of idleness are, of course, the same that determined Cassian's treatment of manual work.

Cassian's importance for the history of *acedia* is, then, twofold. He handed on the concept from the Egyptian tradition to the West but not without adapting it to a new and different form of asceticism. At the same time he reflected on and tried to elucidate its nature by clarifying its place among the other chief vices. These two tendencies—adaptation to new situations, and theological and psychological analysis together with a more solid systematization—continued to be at work throughout the Middle Ages. They were responsible for much that the following chapters will relate.

II

TRANSFORMATIONS

Cassian's introduction of the sin list to western Europe was followed, more than a century and a half later, by the establishment of a new and different series of chief vices. This was the work of Gregory the Great, last of the Latin Fathers of the Church, the great pope who never lost his nostalgia for a monk's solitude. In his symbolic exegesis of the Book of Job, Gregory speaks of *seven* chief vices (*principalia vitia*) that spring from the root of pride. *Acedia* is not among them, nor is there anything synonymous in the series.[1] Did Gregory simply drop it and thereby reduce Cassian's eight to seven? The question must be answered in the negative because Gregory arrived at his list by various changes other than mere omission.[2] Moreover, his sin of grief or sorrow (*tristitia*) contains traces that are strongly reminiscent of *acedia*. Unfortunately, in the chapters devoted to the seven vices Gregory did not discuss each as elaborately as Cassian and Evagrius had done. The only indication of what the vices meant to Gregory can be found in the progenies he attached. The following are the offspring of *tristitia* and *acedia* according to Cassian and to Gregory:

Cassian		Gregory	
Tristitia:	*rancor*	*Tristitia:*	*malitia*
	pusillanimitas		*rancor*
	amaritudo		*pusillanimitas*
	desperatio		*desperatio*
			torpor circa praecepta
			vagatio mentis erga illicita
Acedia:	*otiositas*		
	somnolentia		
	importunitas		
	inquietudo		
	pervagatio		

instabilitas mentis
et corporis
verbositas
curiositas

The juxtaposition shows that three of Gregory's terms (*rancor, pusillanimitas, desperatio*) correspond verbally with three "daughters" of Cassian's *tristitia.* On the other hand, Gregory's *torpor circa praecepta* and *vagatio mentis erga illicita* parallel several members of Cassian's *acedia,* such as *otiositas, pervagatio, instabilitas mentis et corporis, curiositas.* Hence it is possible, if Gregory knew Cassian at all, to think of his *tristitia* as a combination of traces from both the *tristitia* and the *acedia* of the Cassianic-Evagrian scheme of eight vices. The new concept should, however, be considered, not as the result of a simple fusion, following the mathematical rule that two and two make four, but rather as a new creation from parts of the old vices.

Why did Gregory do this? It is of course possible that he was not familiar with the word *acedia* at all. Indeed the word seems to appear only a single time in his works. The *Commentary on the First Book of Kings* mentions it within a series of six vices and their respective remedies: "Thus also the vice of *acedia,* that is, weariness of heart [*taedium cordis*], is driven away if one always thinks of the heavenly goods."[3] For a long time the *Commentary* has been regarded as spurious or as a revision of Gregory's oral deliveries on I Kings, made by Abbot Claudius.[4] Recent stylistic and thematic analysis, however, has led to the conclusion that the work is authentic, with only rare "personal touches" introduced by Claudius.[5] This conclusion has, in its turn, raised strong expressions of doubt.[6] But whether or not the *Commentary* is genuinely Gregory's, the fact remains that, to say the least, *acedia* had no important place in Gregory's vocabulary.[7] On the other hand, we can be reasonably sure that Gregory knew Cassian's works and hence must have been acquainted with the term.[8]

In order to explain the disappearance of *acedia* from the sin list it has been suggested that Gregory's mystic delight in number symbolism led him to substitute seven vices for the traditional eight.[9] Although the saint's overwhelming concern with allegory and symbolism can of course not be denied, it is all too easy for modern scholars to overestimate his fascination with mystic numbers.[10] In addition, Gregory's preference for the septenary does not really elucidate our problem, for the scheme of seven vices was not arrived at by mere omission of one vice; and even if the process had been so simple, why should Gregory drop *acedia*? It is evident that we must look for deeper, more rational motives than the play with numbers.

Dom Robert Gillet, in discussing the genesis of Gregory's sin list, suggested that Gregory did not mention *acedia*, either because he did not distinguish it clearly from *tristitia* or because, on the contrary, he perfectly grasped its pathological character and, therefore, considered it as lying outside the realm of morals.[11] The idea that *acedia* was looked upon as no more than a physical or psychic disturbance is an attractive suggestion but does not prove much since we have no evidence that Gregory or his contemporaries indeed held this view.[12] More light on the possible reasons for fusing *acedia* and *tristitia* in Gregory's system is shed by Dom Gillet's other suggestion, the conceptual affinity of the two vices. In the description which Evagrius and Cassian gave, these vices share a good many symptoms. Such effects as dejection and sorrow, absence of the wonted elation in spiritual exercises, impatience in work and devotion, wrath against the brethren, and despair of ever reaching one's spiritual goals, are all common to both *tristitia* and *acedia*. In the following extract, for example, it is almost impossible to tell which of the two is portrayed: "[The vice] does not allow it [the mind] to say its prayers with the usual gladness of heart, nor permit it to rely on the comfort of reading the sacred writings, nor suffer it to be quiet and gentle with the brethren; it makes it rough and impatient in all the duties of work and devotion" [Cassian, on *tristitia*].[13] Cassian's description of *acedia*, as we saw earlier, begins with: "This is akin [*affinis*] to *tristitia*" (*Inst.*, X, 1), and the psychological affinity of the two states is brought out in various other contexts (*Coll.*, V, 3, 9, 10). The idea appears again in Cassian's concatenation of vices: *acedia* is engendered by *tristitia* (*Coll.*, V, 10).[14] Finally, a Greek apothegm attributed to Mother Syncletica goes so far as to equate sinful *tristitia* verbally with *acedia*.[15]

While the two vices were thus felt to be closely akin, an ambiguity in the concept of *tristitia* itself may have further contributed to their eventual fusion. St. Paul had already distinguished between a positive (*tristitia secundum Deum*) and a negative kind of sorrow (*tristitia saeculi*), the one leading to penance and salvation, the other to death (II Cor. 7:10). A careful distinction between the two is made by ascetic authors whenever *tristitia* is defined. Cassian, for example, characterizes the good kind of sorrow as that which arises from remorse for one's sins or the desire for perfection, whereas sinful sorrow results from the frustration of worldly desires.[16] Only the second kind is of course morally evil. But sadness which results from unfulfilled carnal desires obviously has its roots in other vices, such as greed or gluttony, lust or pride—in any vice, as a matter of fact.[17] Should then *tristitia saeculi* not be considered as the psychological effect of vices in general, rather than as a separate capital sin? Here the Evagrian-Cassianic sin scheme, which set up *tristitia* as a separate *vitium principale,* enters into open conflict with Greek psychology and ethics: Aristotle had taught that pleasure and sorrow (λύπη) were the two states to which all passions led,[18] and this doctrine had become a widely accepted tradition by Gregory's time. Whether or not the Church Father was aware of, or even troubled by, such logical clashes, whether or not he attempted a reconciliation, I cannot tell. Neither his mentality nor the sources of his philosophical equipment have as yet been satisfactorily explored. It is generally assumed that his thought depended largely on St. Augustine, but a careful analysis of details like the present one reveals much originality. It is quite possible that Gregory's awareness that *tristitia* designated one psychological effect of many vices as well as (in Stoic teaching) one of the four main affects led him to fuse it with the Evagrian *acedia* (by including in it traits like *pusillanimitas, torpor,* and *vagatio mentis*) in order to preserve its status as a separate vice. That he continued to call it *tristitia*[19] was unfortunate, however, and brought the whole difficulty again to the forum of discussion among the Schoolmen.

There is, however, a motive of a different order which furnishes a better and more direct explanation of Gregory's changes than any of the reasons so far discussed. The ἀκηδία of Evagrius and Cassian was admittedly a temptation peculiar to "solitaries and . . . dwellers in the desert" (*Inst.*, X, 1). In the West, however, the monastic life differed fundamentally from the ascetic ideals and techniques current among the Egyptian hermits, and this difference is sufficient to explain what happened to *acedia* in Gregory's hands.[20] The temptation as it had been defined by Cassian was apparently felt to be either not frequent or not oppressive enough to merit inclusion among the "chief vices." This is at least the explanation implied in a treatise attributed to Hrabanus Maurus.

Discussing *acedia* at great length, the author points out the various changes made by Gregory in the sin list. About *acedia* he says: "This vice, however, the holy Doctors of the Churches of God did not list among the eight chief vices,[21] but placed under the name of *tristitia*. . . . In contrast, the holy Fathers of Egypt, Palestine, and the Orient . . . stated that *acedia* was indeed one of the eight chief vices—for that reason namely, that this passion has been experienced to a greater extent by monks and solitaries and is a grim and frequent enemy of those who live in the desert."[22]

Various environmental factors, such as climate and landscape, undoubtedly had some influence, but it is mostly the entirely different conception of monasticism that was responsible for this change. A glance at the *Regula Benedicti* can show this readily. Even if the *Regula* did not gain its unique position until later, and even if Gregory may not have known it at all,[23] it can safely be taken as representative of monastic ideals that were current in the sixth century and after, ideals to which Gregory was most intimately committed. Unlike their brethren of Nitria and Scete, Western monks did not live alone but in well-regulated communities. Their ἀναχώρησις, though still accompanied by physical withdrawal from the world, consisted primarily in a more abstract and spiritualized "movement": the relegation of the will of the individual monk into the hands of his abbot. Absolute obedience to the head of the monastery as Christ's representative is the basic principle of Benedictine monasticism: "so that by the work of obedience you may return to Him from whom you had withdrawn through the sloth of inobedience."[24] This obedience takes form in complete submission to a Rule. The monk's individuality is merged in an order that regulates practically every minute of his day with a series of appointed activities: spiritual exercises and manual work, private meditation and "public" liturgical worship. Hence, the monk is not continuously thrown upon his innermost thoughts. 'Απάθεια, brought about by unremittingly watching the movements of one's mind, is not Benedict's ideal of perfection. Boredom with the religious life will, of course, continue to plague the monk, but it will no longer be the specific kind described by Evagrius, so heavily fraught with noonday heat and desert solitude.

To these important differences one must add a specific contrast in the respective attitudes toward sleep. Among the Egyptian desert monks, sleep was a necessary evil, to be tolerated as little as possible. For Benedict, it is a requirement of human nature which must be fulfilled to satisfaction. Hence his monks are to sleep, not on the floor but on beds (*Regula*, XXII, 1). In summer, during the hot hours after noon, they are allowed to rest on their beds—precisely at the time when the demon of *acedia* used to strike the Egyptians![25] Moreover, the monks sleep in a common dormitory: the individual is never cut off from his neighbors as strictly as he was at Nitria and Scete. Two older monks are appointed to look out for a "*frater achediosus* who indulges in idleness or fables and is not intent upon his reading, and thus not only is useless to himself but also distracts others" (XLVIII, 17-18). If one is found to be unwilling or incapable of meditation, he is given some other work to do, even on Sundays (XLVIII, 23). With the community thus watching over the individual, solitude can hardly ever become so oppressive as to engender the frightening temptation of ἀκηδία described by Evagrius.[26]

If the omission of *acedia* from the list of chief vices indeed indicates Gregory's refusal to consider, not merely the name, but the notion itself as worthy of the exalted position of "leader" of many other vices, the Church Father must be credited with changing and adapting the sin list to the ideals and techniques of Western monasticism. One may go even further and point out that although the *Moralia* was written at the instance of Gregory's own monastic community, the analysis of ascetic psychology and the system of ethics it develops really apply to a Christian life of perfection of much larger scope. Though this cannot be proven beyond doubt, it is possible that the disappearance of *acedia* from Gregory's list of chief vices was due to the future pope's concern with Christian morals in general.[27]

If Gregory's sin list had at once and completely replaced Cassian's scheme, our history of the concept of *acedia* would come to an end here. But despite Gregory's enormous influence on medieval thought, his system of seven vices did not win the day without a long and confused struggle, and then the victory was but a compromise: Gregory's seven principal vices became the seven "deadly sins," but his *tristitia* was replaced by Cassian's *acedia*. Until this solution was achieved, in the twelfth century, the two schemes lived side by side, sometimes even in works by the same author.[28] Actually, in this intermediate period, even a third scheme can be found which apparently stems from Isidore of Seville. It lists eight vices, but they are the Gregorian ones (with *tristitia*) plus *superbia,* which in Gregory's original series stood as "queen" and "root" of the seven *principalia vitia* outside the series itself.[29] The eventual identification of *tristitia* with *acedia* was already foreshadowed at the end of the eighth century when Bishop Theodulf of Orléans, in a series of instructions given to his parish priests, spoke of the third *principale vitium* as "acedia sive tristitia."[30] In the twelfth century the verbal identification became quite frequent and appeared in the theological works of Hugh of St. Victor and Peter Lombard (after 1139; "acidia vel tristitia").[31] As the latter's *Sententiae* became the textbook for Scholastic theologians,[32] the position of "*acedia*" in the series of capital sins was assured. Although "*tristitia*" still occurred on occasion as the name of the respective chief vice in later medieval works of theology, the standard term remained *acedia* or *accidia.*

Why should the term—despite its foreign appearance, its connection with a strange, restricted form of monasticism, its rare occurrence outside the Cassianic sin list—have ousted the more homely *tristitia,* which bore the authority of a Church Father? The main reason undoubtedly is the *de jure* and *de facto* connection of Cassian's works with Benedictine monasticism and, through it, his influence on penitential practices, which spread from the British Isles to France and the rest of Europe. Cassian's teachings continued to live in the monastery, and there, apparently, the term *acedia* was felt to be too useful to be discarded.

St. Benedict in Chapter 73 of his *Regula,* and Cassiodorus in the program he drew up for his monks at Vivarium,[33] prescribed explicitly that the *Instituta* and the *Collationes* be read by their monks. It was especially Cassian's analysis of the eight chief vices that recommended his work so highly, whose reading, in the words of an early twelfth-century Benedictine abbot, "brings diligent readers fruit of immense usefulness."[34] Even as late as the fourteenth and fifteenth centuries, Cassian's account of the contemplative life continued to form a major source for mystic and devotional writings,[35] while during the flowering of Scholasticism his scheme of chief vices was looked upon as a sacred tradition which systematic theologians had to come to terms with.

In this monastic tradition *acedia* preserved the traits described by Cassian. However, insofar as we can tell from surviving texts, this continuity was by no means simple and static. I have elsewhere analyzed the use of *acedia* in writings of the period from 700 to 1200 in greater detail and shown that the meaning of *acedia* seemingly changed as different writers and periods placed different emphases on one or the other aspect contained in Cassian's description.[36] Thus, in general, writers through the eleventh century saw in *acedia* primarily physical phenomena of idleness and somnolence, whereas in the following century spiritual authors laid greater stress on its inner phenomena of mental slackness, lack of fervor, tedium, and the like.

A good example of the earlier view is Peter Damiani (1007-1072), who equated *acedia* with drowsiness[37] and physical weariness which the monk has to overcome in his ascetic practices of waking and praying. To Peter, *acedia* meant the temptation of closing eyelids, which must be vigorously fought by the monks: "The coming of dawn, at which time *acedia* falls upon us more heavily, must find us upright and busy with reciting the Office."[38] The unrelenting fervor of an old monk is praised, "because never did the weariness of *acedia* press down his eyes."[39] The vice recurs in two episodes of saints' lives written by Peter Damiani, which bespeak so well the strange harshness of their author's own character. St. Romuald, at the beginning of his saintly career, could hardly read and had a very hard time in keeping up with his teacher when they recited the Psalter: "He could hardly unravel the notation of his verses syllable by syllable, and this strain of his eyes gave him an intolerable affliction of *acedia*."[40] In consequence of which Romuald not only suffered eye strain but also got flogged on the head by his austere but not very perceptive mentor. Another saint, Rodulphus, had to struggle with *acedia* alone. He would overcome it by tying ropes to the ceiling of his cell, putting his arms through, and singing the psalms thus in hanging position.[41]

Peter Damiani's conception of *acedia* as physical drowsiness gave way to a much more spiritualized view of the vice in the twelfth century. This was the golden age of treatises on the "inner life" in which the theory and practice of contemplation blossomed into a new brilliancy with such masters as St. Bernard, his Cistercian followers, and the Victorines. This revival of interest in the psychology of the spiritual life, which had been fairly dead since the days of the desert monks, the Church Fathers, and Cassian,[42] also affected *acedia* in the sense that in the works of twelfth-century spiritual writers (and of their contemporary systematic theologians as well) the word overwhelmingly refers to a state of mind.

This shift in "monastic" *acedia* is well demonstrated by two writers who both speak of restlessness and flight from the cell as an effect of *acedia.* The first lived in the early eleventh century and repeated in substance a remark of Cassian's: "There are two kinds of *acedia.* One drives the monk to be lazy in the service of God [*ad opus Dei*] and to fall asleep; the other makes him roam hither and thither and encourages him to flee the company of the brethren with whom he lives."[43] In comparison, "rest" and restlessness as used by Aelred of Rievaulx (1110-1167) appear much more spiritualized: "Those who aspire to the contemplation of spiritual things need quietude [*quies*] above everything else. But *acedia* assails quietude and tries to render the mind restless."[44] "The spirit of *acedia* totally overturned my state of tranquility, and by inflicting in me horror of solitude and hatred of quietness forced me to yield to inordinate roaming, a sign of fruitlessness and danger."[45] The implication that *acedia* is an internal state of the mind appears also in a passage by St. Bernard, where the vice is clearly distinguished from physical weariness: "Is anyone strongly disturbed, languishing either from some bodily discomfort, from some worldly affliction, or from *acedia* of the spirit and slackness of the mind?"[46] Bernard's pupil Isaac of L'Étoile likewise speaks of monks who are "outwardly resting from useful work, and inwardly lazy and *acediosi.*"[47]

In these writers the term *acedia* is frequently found in close conjunction with such nouns as *tristitia, taedium, fastidium,* and *tepiditas,* and we shall see that these terms also appeared in a variety of definitions that were furnished by twelfth-century systematic theologians, definitions later taken up, harmonized, or rejected by the Schoolmen.[48] The many passages where *acedia* occurs in the company of such terms make it clear that during the twelfth century monastic *acedia* meant spiritual slackness, weariness and boredom with religious exercises, lack of fervor, and a state of depression in the ups and downs of spiritual life. Novices are especially exposed to this affliction: "However strong the devotion of those recently converted from the world may be, they nevertheless suffer frequently from the vice of *acedia.*"[49] But the vice is apt to assail the monk throughout his religious life and manifest itself in the form of spiritual lukewarmness.

Tepidity in spiritual pursuits, of course, is quite dangerous because monks who pray or read without much fervor are open to other temptations. Isaac explains that when the devil sees them "acediosos ac tepidos," he approaches and, sensing their "interior defectus," shows them false goods in which they erroneously hope to find relief: "He who dares not approach a strong, constant, and fervent monk, but only watches him from afar, comes with evil intentions to a monk who is *acediosus* and idle. . . . When the tempter notices a mind that is listless in the joy of God, he invites it to avarice."[50] An old saying of the desert fathers had compared the spiritually tepid to a pot of lukewarm milk on which the flies settle readily—a simile that among later writers became a favorite image for *acedia*.[51]

Yet lack of fervor and absence of spiritual comfort are not necessarily sinful. Rather, they accompany the normal fluctuations of the spiritual life in which, according to St. Bernard, one progresses "now more sluggishly, now more joyfully." The important thing is that the monk should not desist: "When you feel yourself affected by torpor, *acedia*, or tedium, do not therefore lose confidence or desist from your spiritual strife."[52] Isaac of L'Étoile describes the same state thus: "Sometimes I rejoice . . . in joy and praise; . . . at other times I am fearful and weep, wrapped in darkness and full of bitterness, and languish in such a great distress of weariness and *acedia*."[53] And Richard of St. Victor writes of *acedia*:

> To the good it often happens that they now are warmed with spiritual consolations and then filled with bitterness, that they now abound with grace and then suffer from *acedia*. But they have learned from Scripture that temptation is a trial, and they consider the oppressive attack of *acedia* a temptation, because the flesh struggles against the spirit and wants to be equal to, or even better than, the heart. . . . [But God] alleviates and partly heals the sickness of *acedia* which the mind suffers from lack of grace.[54]

Medieval writers on the spiritual life were well aware that this form of *acedia* resulted from slackening attention and man's inability to sustain concentration and to engage in one and the same activity for any prolonged period. The homely wisdom of "All work and no play makes Jack a dull boy" had occurred already to St. Basil,[55] and twelfth-century authors continued to keep it in mind. Aelred, for example, wrote to a recluse: "If the psalms become burdensome, change to reading; if this begins to bore you, get up for prayer; when you are tired of these activities, take up some manual work, so that by healthy alternation you may refresh the mind and drive away *acedia*."[56] And St. Bernard had earlier praised Abbot Suger of St. Denis for improving his monastery's spiritual discipline so that now "the variation in holy observances expels tedium and *acedia*."[57]

Nevertheless, the best protection against this vice is constant watchfulness. Isaac of L'Étoile developed this exhortation in a somewhat strained but very moving sermon on the episode of Christ's sleeping in the Apostles' boat while the storm raged (Matthew 8): "And as he fell asleep, a great storm arose."[58] Isaac interprets the episode as an image of those religious who, in false security, let Christ fall asleep in their souls and become mentally slack ("intus desides et acediosi"). But with a storm Christ shakes them out of their "*acedia*, which leads to the flow of evil thoughts, like an inner and unbearable tempest." "Woe to you if Christ sleeps in you! The wind wakes, the sea wakes, the storm and waves of evil thoughts wake, and thousand tides of temptation come upon you, if only He is asleep in you. . . . Therefore let us be vigilant, brethren, let us be vigilant above all against the plague of *acedia*!"[59]

Isaac's admonition is, to my knowledge, a unique instance in twelfth-century literature of a whole sermon's being devoted to *acedia*. As a matter of fact, the term itself occurs much less frequently in the ascetic literature of the twelfth and of preceding centuries than one would expect. The patient reader will frequently come across references to negligence, slackness, dejection, and so on, but will find the word *acedia* only at very long intervals on his laborious way. Instead, different terms are used, such as *desidia*, *segnities*, *torpor*, *tepiditas*, *taedium*, *fastidium*, and others. A good example is the following passage by Adam Scot, a twelfth-century Carthusian monk, which is often thought of as a classic description of monastic *acedia*:

> Oftentimes, when you are alone in your cell, a certain inertia, a dullness of the mind and disgust of the heart seize you. You feel an enormous loathing in yourself. You are a burden to yourself, and that internal joy you used so happily to experience has left you. The sweetness that was in you yesterday or the day before has turned into great bitterness; the stream of tears with which you used to be bathed so abundantly has totally dried up. The spiritual vigor in you has withered, your inner calm lies dead. Your soul is torn to pieces, confused and split up, sad and embittered. When you try to appease her, you cannot do it. Your reading does not please you; prayer brings no sweetness; you cannot find the customary sweet showers of spiritual meditations. What need to say more? There is not the least

> spiritual joy and cheerfulness in you. You are ready and quick to jokes, funny stories and idle talk, but quite slow and lazy to be silent and to take up something useful or some spiritual exercise. O what a miserable change in your enterprises![60]

The terms Adam Scot employs are *inertia, languor spiritus,* and *taedium cordis*—but not *acedia.* What accounts for this reluctance to use it?

There are, I believe, two different reasons. One is that perhaps Adam Scot did not consider the state of spiritual dryness described in the quoted passage as quite synonymous with *acedia.* This applies also to similar descriptions given by St. Bernard and his followers and raises the whole problem of the relation between *acedia* and spiritual dryness, which will be discussed in Chapter III.[61] The other reason is more of a linguistic nature. In the Latin West, the word *acedia* was not backed by the biblical authority it had in the East. Jerome's Vulgate version does not contain the noun; the important verse 28 of Psalm 118 was translated as "dormitavit anima mea prae *taedio.*" Likewise, the other three Fathers of the Latin Church (Augustine, Ambrose, and Gregory), as far as I can tell, did not use *acedia.* Only Benedict employed the term (in the form of the derived adjective) a century after Cassian had given it to the West, when he spoke of the "frater achediosus."[62] The word therefore lacked that literary authority which for medieval authors carried the greatest weight, and I believe it is for this reason mainly that *acedia* never became fully acclimatized in the general Latin vocabulary.

Nevertheless, the word continued to live as a *terminus technicus* for the peculiar chief vice described by Cassian and maintained itself against the Gregorian *tristitia.* The tenacity with which monastic authors clung to it can be seen in a case of strange duplication in the discussion of the capital vices by a follower of Hugh of St. Victor. Here the capital vice itself is called "tristitia seu acedia" and defined as, "an anguish of the mind that is perturbed by the frustration of its desire through something contrary, or, the weariness [*taedium*] to perform a good deed well."[63] The definition obviously links the Evagrian-Cassianic *tristitia* (the effect of thwarted carnal desires) with *acedia* (weariness of life). "Acidia" [*sic*] then appears a second time in the progeny of the sin, as one of its seven branches: "sorrow or weariness or overwhelming bitterness of the spirit, born of a very great distress of the soul. By it, spiritual joy is quenched, and the mind is, as if by the beginning of despair, overthrown in itself."[64] Whether the writer attempted to harmonize different traditions[65] or was carried away by a mistaken etymology (*acidia* from *acidus*)[66]—his treatment, I believe, reveals the firm hold the term had on theological minds of the twelfth century.

Since the continuity of *acedia* was assured by the connection of Cassian's teaching with monasticism, it is no wonder that until about 1200 *acedia* should have remained primarily a monastic vice, that is, one which attacked chiefly religious who devoted themselves to the contemplative life. From Cassian to twelfth-century treatises the statement recurs again and again that *acedia* mostly vexes monks or contemplatives.[67] But in this long period *acedia* was not totally restricted to the monastery. In several writings of the Carolingian period, the concept became adapted to the moral life of laymen and thereby assumed features which tended to widen its meaning of "boredom with the cell," which it had held in Evagrius and Cassian, to something like "negligence in the fulfillment of spiritual duties." The change came about very gradually—like all innovations by very slight shifts in emphasis—and was to dominate the popular conception of *acedia* fully only in the thirteenth century (see Chapter IV). But its beginnings and early course can be seen clearly enough in four works of the eighth and ninth centuries, all written for the instruction of Christians who lived in the world.

The first is the *Scarapsus* by St. Pirminius, Apostle of the Alamanni (710-724). A kind of missionary's handbook, it expounds the main points of Christian faith and morals to an obviously unsophisticated lay audience. In its second part Pirminius enumerates the Cassianic eight chief vices (II, 13) and cites several biblical passages by which each vice is condemned. When he comes to *acedia* (II, 14), Pirminius does not repeat the term but instead says: "May no-one give himself to idleness, because it is written: 'The soul of him who does not work suffers hunger' [Prov. 19:15]. And again: 'Idleness is an enemy to the soul.'[68] And the Apostle says, 'If any will not work, neither let him eat' [II Thess. 3:10]."[69] *Acedia* is here apprehended as synonymous with idleness (*otiositas*), and a few paragraphs later Pirminius equates the two terms explicitly: "May he who was *acediosus*, which is idleness, work with his own hands or do good in some craft, whereby he himself can live and give to others for the sake of eternal glory. For it is written . . . [four quotations]" (II, 27).

Alcuin, too, wrote a treatise on vices and virtues for a noble layman (*ca.* 799), in which he instructed him in Christian morals for those who live in the world. Alcuin's description of *acedia* is fairly derivative and, like Cassian's, stresses that this vice "primarily drives monks from their cells into the world, and throws them from a life according to the Rule into a gulf of vices." Yet the description contains some features of its own which show a changing emphasis: Alcuin uses different terms in the progeny of *acedia,* of which "laziness in good work" (*pigritia operis boni*) for "idleness," and "tepidity in working" are especially interesting.[70]

Alcuin's progeny appears again in *De institutione laicali* by Jonas of Orléans (d. 843). This work is addressed to Count Mathfredus of Orléans and purposes to show him "how you and other married folk should live to please God."[71] It deals at length with virtues and vices, including the Cassianic chief ones. The description of *acedia* follows Cassian and Alcuin, but Jonas explicitly includes laymen in the victims of the vice: "The sixth vice is *acedia,* that is idleness, of which Solomon says, 'idleness is an enemy to the soul'. . . . Many clerics and laymen suffer from this plague and yet hardly know their failing."[72]

The slight changes to be observed in Alcuin's and Jonas' accounts became more pronounced in *De ecclesiastica disciplina* by Hrabanus Maurus, written 842-847.[73] The work is addressed to Bishop Reginald and purposes to instruct him in what he should teach his recently converted flock: "We shall take pains to show . . . how these Christians ought to be instructed in Catholic dogma and reformed by the discipline of the Church; how they who have become soldiers of Christ ought to fight with the virtues against the vices and persevere, to their life's end, in striving for a good life."[74] For these Christians in the world, *acedia* bears the following features:

> The eighth and last poison [*virus*] of the eight principal vices is *acedia.* From it arises languor of the mind and a harmful sluggishness, which renders man useless to any good work and pushes him to his destruction. Wherefore it is written: "Idleness is the enemy of the soul," which the devil, hostile to all good, engenders in man through the mentioned disease [*morbus*] of *acedia*; so that he injuriously causes man to be listless and exert himself the least in good works. For *acedia* is a plague which proves to be of much harm to those who serve God. The

> idle man grows dull in carnal desires, is cheerless in spiritual works, has no joy in the salvation of his soul, and does not become cheerful in helping his brother, but only craves and desires and performs everything in an idle fashion. *Acedia* corrupts the miserable mind which it inhabits with many misfortunes, which teach it many evil things. From it are born somnolence, laziness in good deeds, instability, roaming from place to place, lukewarmness in work, boredom, murmuring and vain talks. It is defeated by the soldier of Christ through reading, constancy in good deeds, the desire for the prize of future beatitude, confessing the temptation which is in the mind, stability of the place and of one's resolution, and the practice of some craft and work or prayer, and the perseverance in vigils. May the servant of God never be found idle! For the devil has greater difficulty in finding a spot for temptation in the man whom he finds employed in some good work, than in him whom he encounters idle and practicing no good. . . . Such then is the Christian who, when he arises in the morning from his bed of drunkenness, does not engage in any useful work, does not go to church to pray, does not hasten to hear the word of God, does not make an effort to give alms or to visit the sick or to help those who suffer injustice: but rather goes hunting abroad, or stirs quarrels and fights at home, or devotes himself to the dice or to useless stories and jokes while his food is being prepared by hardworking servants.[75]

In this "character" of a slothful man, which is the most "advanced" portrait of a layman's *acedia* I have found that was written before the thirteenth century, the vice is once more equated with idleness and has become a failure that all Christians may be guilty of. In essence it is no longer boredom with the cell or with monastic practices but slackness and negligence in performing spiritual deeds. The specific reminiscences of Egyptian monasticism which had resounded in Cassian's account and could still be heard in the teaching of Alcuin and Jonas are here toned down or wholly omitted. Such faults of monastic or clerical *acedia* as sluggishness in reading and prayer are now accompanied by imperfections that are peculiar (even if not restricted) to the life of noblemen outside the monastery: dicing, hunting, and unbecoming jokes at times hallowed for religious observances.

In the view of Hrabanus Maurus, thus, *acedia* when applied to laymen evidently meant plain idleness, that is, not being occupied in profitable enterprises. The other works for laymen show the same equation with idleness, and in this they did not stand alone. Contemporary *libri poenitentiales*, i.e., handbooks for hearing confession and imposing penances, often included the Cassianic chief vices, and when they did so indicated penances for only three specific aspects of *acedia*: idleness, somnolence, and instability.[76] This reduction of Cassian's concept and its eightfold offspring was undoubtedly due to the practical purposes of these writings, because the confessor had to deal with concrete, external faults rather than inner attitudes. One can give a remedial punishment for standing idle, being late for services, sleeping during prayer, roaming outside the monastery, but not for boredom and listlessness.

We should not overlook, however, that such external faults were no inventions of the *libri poenitentiales* or of Carolingian theologians but had already occurred in the description of *acedia* given by Cassian. As a matter of fact, through several chapters of the *Instituta* (X, 7-25) *acedia* is quite clearly taken to mean idleness, and on one occasion Cassian even identifies the two verbally: "whoever is overcome by the sleep of idleness or *acedia* . . ." (*quisque somno otii vel acediae superatus*; *Inst.*, X, 21). I believe this emphasis on idleness made it all the easier for men like Pirminius and Hrabanus to extend *acedia* to the layfolk.

To the transformations of our concept caused by the different nature of Western monasticism and by the concern for the moral struggle of Christians in general, we must now add another change, which came with the psychological analysis of the sin scheme and of the individual vices. By the middle of the twelfth century the Gregorian list of seven, but with *tristitia* now called *acedia*, had been generally accepted as part of moral theology. Although the series of seven capital sins has never become a matter of dogma, medieval theologians were inclined to accept it at least as a sacred tradition of the Church's teaching. With the Scholastic movement the great endeavor of rational analysis of matters of faith—*fides quaerens intellectum*—seized the seven vices, too. The Scholastic analysis of *acedia* specifically will have our attention in the next chapter. Here we shall examine the results of the analysis with regard to the whole scheme, results which of course affected *acedia*, too. The main problem which faced twelfth- and thirteenth-century theologians in this respect was to find a rationale for the Gregorian list: why *seven* chief vices? and why these particular ones?[77] In the following I shall briefly sketch various answers given by major theologians. The account does not aim at completeness, nor do I suggest that the development was necessarily as straight and linear as the following paragraphs imply. Unfortunately, a good many documents of primary relevance to the history of the sins in the Scholastic period still await the patient labors of unearthing, classifying, dating, and editing. However, I believe the general lines of the development emerge with sufficient clearness, and the ensuing presentation follows the course of chronology and literary dependency.[78]

Cassian, as we saw, taught that six of the eight vices were linked to one another by some kind of psychological concatenation so that one flowed naturally from the other in the order he had established, from gluttony to *acedia* (*Coll.*, V, 10). Gregory applied the same idea to all seven vices (*Moralia*, XXXI, 89). In the later Middle Ages the best and most original advocate of this psychological concatenation was Hugh of St. Victor (d. 1141), whose main work, *Summa de sacramentis christianae fidei*, has been called "the first dogmatics of great style produced in Europe."[79] Hugh defines "vice" as a spiritual infirmity or disease: "Vices are corruptions of the soul, from which, unless they are restrained by reason, sins (that is, acts of unrighteousness) arise. When consent is given to the temptation of a vice, an act of unrighteousness occurs, which is called sin."[80] He believes the series of seven capital or chief vices is based on scriptural authority, but in reality he quotes the Gregorian list with the changes which by his time had become standard.[81] The seven vices are linked in this fashion: "Ex iis tria hominem exspoliant. . . . Superbia aufert homini Deum, invidia proximum, ira seipsum; acidia flagellat spoliatum, avaritia flagellatum ejicit; gula ejectum seducit, luxuria seductum servituti subjicit."[82] The psychological concatenation, reflected in the rhetorical catena of Hugh's terse Latin, is explained in another work in the following way:

> Pride is the love of one's own excellency, when the mind loves its goodness for its own sake, that is, without Him from Whom it has received the good. . . . And thus it happens that it cannot possess what it has in a useful way if it does not love it in Him from Whom it has come. For as every good is truly from God, thus no good may be possessed in a useful way apart from God. . . . Whoever knows only the good he himself possesses, must needs love the good that is in him. Now, when he sees in someone else some good which he does not have, then his own im-

perfection torments him the more bitterly, the less he loves Him in Whom every good exists. And thus always envy follows upon pride: for he who does not direct his love to where all goodness is [fix his love upon the origin of all goodness] is grieved the more by someone else's good the more he prides himself of his own. . . . But this corruption, once it has begun, does not stop here. As soon as envy has sprung from pride, the wretched mind brings forth wrath out of itself. It becomes enraged at its own imperfection, because it cannot, in charity, be joyful at another's good. And thus even what it possesses begins to displease, because the mind perceives in someone else what it cannot have. Therefore, since the mind has tried in its pride to possess apart from God what it could possess only through charity in God, it now loses its neighbor through envy and its own self through wrath. Now, as there is nothing left from which the miserable mind [*conscientia*] could receive joy, it is dashed upon itself through grief.[83]. . . After pride, envy, and wrath, therefore, which despoil man, comes immediately sorrow, which scourges him in his nakedness. Upon it follows greed, which throws him out after the scourging; for after losing his inner joy he is compelled to seek comfort outside. Then gluttony approaches, which seduces him in his exile; through the natural appetite this vice tempts the mind that stands open to external goods and entices [allures] it to engage in excess. Finally, lust comes and by violence brings the seduced mind into its slavery [its servitude.][84]

Hugh expresses the same idea in a second image, the spoiling of the vessel of the heart or soul. "The rational soul in its health is a strong and sound vessel without any corruption. When the vices enter into it, they spoil [*vitiant*] and corrupt it in this way: through pride it becomes blown up, through envy it dries out, through wrath it cracks, through *acidia* it breaks, through greed it is scattered about, through gluttony it is stained, and through lust it is trodden under foot and reduced to clay."[85] Although in this metaphor the psychological concatenation is not brought out as clearly as in the first passage, the verbs forcefully express the downward progression of the soul through the successive effects of the seven vices upon her. Thus, in Hugh of St. Victor's teaching the vices are brought into an order of succession, but no attempt is as yet made to explain why there should be seven or why these particular ones should be the "heads, beginnings, or origins of all other" vices.[86]

Though Hugh's discussion contains brilliant analyses and original images, it still represents older traditions and can, thus, only serve as a point of departure with which we may compare later analyses of the vices in order to determine the nature of the changing conceptions. Within roughly a decade after *De sacramentis* was written, two works picked up Hugh's idea of concatenation and the image of the despoiling of man: the *Summa sententiarum*,[87] which had a great influence on following authors, and the *Ysagoge in theologiam*. The latter work indicates the general direction which the analysis of the vices would take. After its author has discussed the sequence of Gregory's seven vices, he adds: "Pride and greed are related to injustice; grief[88] and envy to weakness; wrath, gluttony, and lust to immoderation."[89] In other words, he divides the seven vices between the opposites of the (three) cardinal virtues, which he discussed earlier in his treatise (p. 78). This means an attempt is made to reconcile the seven vices with, or to elucidate them by, an element of psychological theory which originated in distant classical Greek thought.[90] Such an attempt by the anonymous author of *Ysagoge* was, of course, neither original nor unique. We noticed before that Cassian had divided up a number of vices among the (Platonic) three parts of the soul and that in this he had followed similar divisions made by Evagrius.[91] In the Carolingian period Alcuin made a somewhat original contribution by assigning the Cassianic eight vices to the three parts of the soul and their respective powers, from whose "corruption" the vices originate in this fashion:

concupiscentia—*gastrimargia, fornicatio, phylargiria;*
ira —*tristitia, acedia;*
ratio —*superbia, cenodoxia.*[92]

But Alcuin's and similar attempts remained rather sterile, failing to lead to any deeper psychological penetration of moral behavior. This remained the task of the twelfth and thirteenth centuries. The *Ysagoge*, then, only marks the continuation, or perhaps, resumption, of analytical endeavors which had gone on for centuries, however half-heartedly.

Perhaps it is advisable to recall the two basic models of the soul and its functions which the Middle Ages inherited from classical Greek psychology and which, despite manifold changes and combinations, always remain discernible in the systems of medieval thinkers.[93] One is the Platonic division of the soul into three parts or layers, each with its own mode of cognition and volition and its chief virtue:

reasonable part (λογιστικόν, *rationale*)	—prudence,
irascible part (θυμοειδές, *irascibile*)	—courage or fortitude,
concupiscible part (ἐπιθυμητικόν, *concupiscibile*)	—moderation.[94]

The fourth "cardinal" virtue, justice, Plato held to be common to all three parts. In contrast, Aristotle developed a system of five "powers" or faculties of the soul, according to the various observable activities of living beings. These powers are:

1. Vegetative: nutritive, augmentative, generative;
2. Sensitive: the five external and the internal senses;
3. Locomotive;
4. Appetitive:
   (a) sensitive appetite or sensuality, with two species: irascible and concupiscible;
   (b) intellective appetite or will;
5. Intellective.[95]

Cognition and volition here are complex processes which involve the action of several powers. An act of will, for example, would include sensory perception (2), a reaction of the sensitive appetite combined with some passion or affect ultimately either painful or pleasurable (4a), deliberation and consent of reason (5), and finally volition proper (4b). The "powers of the soul," then, are vehicles of such functions as nutrition, growth, sensory perception, desire, and the like. Once this predominantly "functional" psychology of Aristotle's *De anima* became fully known in the West,[96] Christian theologians seized it avidly for a new and more profound analysis of moral behavior and of actual sin. In this trend, the seven vices also had to be brought into relation with the inner mechanism of volition, and a brief analysis of some major works of the three decades between, roughly, 1240 and 1270 will show us how Aristotelian psychology finally helped to find a rationale for the seven vices.

In the early part of the thirteenth century Alexander of Hales, using the characteristic methods of Scholastic argumentation, elaborated a scheme in which the capital sins[97] are still related to the three parts of the soul (*vires animae*), as they were by Alcuin. *Acedia,* the "weariness of the inner good" (*taedium boni interioris*), is classified as the sin which hinders the act of desiring the good and thus belongs to the concupiscible part. *Cupiditas, luxuria,* and *gula* likewise belong to the *vis concupiscibilis,* whereas *invidia* and *ira* hinder the functions proper to *vis irascibilis.*[98] This scheme, however, did not satisfy Alexander. In contrast, he based the seven sins on the threefold division of human nature into *spiritus, anima,* and *corpus. Anima* here refers to the soul insofar as it has some connection with the body; *spiritus* is "the very essence of the soul without relation to the body." The acts of *spiritus* are to desire spiritual good and to detest spiritual evil ("spiritual" in the sense of "proper to the spirit," not necessarily religious). If *spiritus* desires or detests its objects immoderately (*inordinate*), sin occurs. Hence, two capital sins are proper to *spiritus*: pride (the immoderate desire for one's own excellence) and envy (the immoderate aversion to excellence in someone else). Similarly, *anima* is the seat of three capital sins, according to its three different powers. The concupiscible part desires what is good for the body; from this desire comes greed. The irascible part rises against what is bad or harmful for the body; from it comes wrath. And the third part, the operative power ("vis ordinans ad opus") shuns what is difficult or wearisome; from it the sin of *acedia* arises. To the body, finally, belong the alimentative and the generative functions; their misuse is gluttony and lust.[99] It is quite clear that in this conception the seven capital vices result from misuse of the powers of the soul, even though Alexander of Hales does not state this notion as a general principle.

It is equally evident that for the Aristotelian three souls (vegetative, sensitive, and rational) Alexander has substituted the more Christian-sounding *spiritus, anima,* and *corpus* (cf. I Thess. 5:23). He actually concludes his treatment of the sins with a reference to Gregory's division of the vices into five spiritual and two carnal ones, with which his own scheme clearly agrees if one concedes that Gregory took the word "spiritus" *sensu lato,* including Alexander's *anima.*[100] Albertus Magnus in his commentary on Peter Lombard's *Sentences* follows Alexander closely but bases the sins on the simpler division of human nature into *spiritus* and *caro.* To the former belong pride, envy, *acedia,* and wrath. The other three vices are not treated in this article. One wonders whether, if Albert counted greed among the carnal vices, he realized his deviation from Gregory's teaching and stopped short. But more important for the Scholastic analysis and for our interest in *acedia* is the fact that Albert introduced the notion that the seven vices are distinguished "in reference to the general principles which move the appetite."[101]

Albert himself did not develop this notion further but left this task to his pupil, Thomas Aquinas, to whose discussion we shall turn presently.

The possibility of deriving the seven vices from man's appetitive power and dividing them according to principles found there is fully worked out in the *Compendium theologicae veritatis,* a work formerly attributed to Albertus Magnus but in reality written by Hugh Ripelin of Strassburg. Hugh discusses a large number of ways in which sins are divided. As the last division he mentions that of the seven capital vices, which he says is based on "the act of the person who desires" (*actum hominis appetentis*).[102] The rationale of the individual vices is explained in the following manner: "Vice" is, first of all, a disorientation of our will. This can be twofold: either a desire for things that we ought not to desire, or an aversion against things we should not flee from. In the first case, Hugh distinguishes three kinds of good according to which the misguided will can err: internal good, whose improper desire is vainglory (pride); external good, related to greed; and an inferior good, also called "delectable." The delectable good itself is of two kinds: the first belongs to the conservation of the individual and is, if immoderately desired, the object of gluttony; the second belongs to the preservation of the species and is the object of lust. On the other hand, when our will is disordered because it shrinks from what it should not flee, the movement can be threefold, according to the three parts of the soul. If the will flees from some good because the instinct of our rational part is perverted, the result is envy. Wrath and *acedia* are similarly related to the irascible and the concupiscible part respectively.[103]

Hugh Ripelin is thus able to lead the Gregorian vices back to a disorder or disorientation of the human will. Yet his system still has something logically unsatisfactory about it, especially since it introduces the three parts of the soul again, but also because of the basically dualistic conception of separate good and evil objects of the will.[104] These difficulties are avoided in Thomas Aquinas' mature thought. He, too, accepts the principle that good moves the appetite to pursuit, whereas evil moves it to flight. But this double movement is not responsible for different vices; it belongs logically to each vice. For example, the immoderate pursuit of one's own excellence is the vice of pride; but pride is equally responsible for the immoderate flight from any evil, anything harmful that is directly opposed to one's excellence. The same can be said of gluttony, lust, and greed, the four vices being differentiated by the three kinds of good as in Hugh Ripelin (except that Thomas calls them the good of the soul, the good of the body, and external good).

From this mode, in which good and evil move the appetite directly, however, Thomas distinguishes a second mode, by which good and evil move the appetite indirectly. This situation occurs when one flees some evil but in so doing also flees some good to which the evil was attached. For example: our appetite naturally shrinks from what is hurtful to our own existence, and if it does so immoderately, we suffer from pride. Now, our excellence may be threatened by some good in another person. Our appetite naturally shrinks from the harm but at the same time also shrinks from the good which is accompanied by the small harm to ourself. This, precisely, is envy. Wrath and *acedia* can be explained in a similar fashion. The latter is the shrinking from one's own good (or, as Thomas also expresses it, sadness about one's spiritual good) because of the *labor corporalis*, the effort and pain that goes with its attainment.[105]

In Thomas' system the seven capital vices thus become part and parcel of the moral behavior—or misbehavior—of man. Thomas' psychology of moral conduct rests upon the simple but grand confrontation of the will (which in Thomas' psychology comprises *appetitus rationalis, irascibilis,* and *concupiscibilis*) with the world of its objects. The traditional seven vices here derive from the very interaction between the two: objects move the appetite, the appetite responds in a certain way, certain kinds of responses are capable of leading to moral evil, or sin, if consented to. The vices are ultimately differentiated not by parts of the soul or objects of human desires but with respect to "certain fundamental modes of moving the appetite."

We could continue to investigate the ways in which other Scholastic theologians—predecessors, followers, rivals of Thomas—tried to establish the rationale for Gregory's vices. But I think our selection has already more than sufficiently shown the trend in which Scholastic reasoning elucidated the traditional scheme. The relatively simple idea of psychological concatenation has given way to a profound analysis of man's moral acts in which the vices lie at the roots of his appetitive faculty. They are differentiated in accordance with various modes in which the appetite is moved and with different kinds of objects. This transformation or deepening of the entire vice scheme by means of psychological analysis affected the concept of *acedia* in a way quite parallel to that of the changes or adaptations mentioned earlier. In the *Summa theologiae* of Thomas Aquinas *acedia* is a general, universal form of moral misconduct. From "boredom with the cell" through "negligence in performing spiritual deeds" it has reached the abstract, psychologistic stage of "aversion of the appetite from its own good because of bodily hardships that accompany its attainment," losing in the process all accidental references to a specific social class, geographical area, or form of religious life.

III

THE SCHOLASTIC ANALYSIS

Beyond establishing a psychological rationale for the seven chief vices, the probing of Scholastic theologians eventually turned upon the notion of *acedia* itself and endeavored to elucidate its nature and position in man's moral life with greater precision. To be sure, the vice was never the subject of a theological controversy like those about predestination, free will, the sacraments, or the nature of original sin. In the strictly theological literature before the second quarter of the thirteenth century, *acedia* hardly ever gained more than passing mention: I know of no early *quaestio disputata* or *quodlibet*[1] that deals exclusively with this concept, and the many commentaries written on Peter Lombard's *Sentences* follow the Master's example in treating the capital vices merely as a group. But in the theological *summae* of the thirteenth century *acedia* received an attention considerably greater and more original than that paid to it by theologians of previous ages. The *summae* of Guillaume d'Auxerre (1220-1225), Alexander of Hales (1241-1245), Albert the Great (after 1270), and Thomas Aquinas (1270-1272)[2]—to mention only the most outstanding documents of Scholastic thought on our subject—devote entire chapters to *acedia* which, in modern editions, run to at least three or more printed pages.

In order to examine the essence and aspects *acedia* had in Scholastic theology, I have chosen to follow the treatment which Thomas Aquinas gave of the vice, not only because of his almost immediate position of authority in the Church, but also because of the tighter formulation and structure of his section on *acedia* and the greater degree of integration and originality which mark his work. However, Thomas' thought does not stand in a vacuum, and what characterizes the Scholastic conception of *acedia* appears as well in the works of the other writers mentioned above.

Thomas discusses *acedia* twice: in the earlier *Quaestio disputata de malo* and in the *Secunda secundae* of his *Summa theologiae*.[3] Although the earlier treatment is longer and occasionally uses a slightly different terminology, the two agree in substance and in the various arguments. Thomas takes up the questions whether *acedia* is a sin, whether it is a special vice, whether it is a mortal sin, and whether it is one of the (seven) capital vices. In the course of debating these four questions, he discusses the definition of the vice, its essence, the virtue to which it is opposed, the rationale for the traditional progenies of the vice established by Cassian and by Gregory, and the harmony between the two series.[4]

The definition of *acedia* which Thomas adopts as the foundation of his whole treatment is *tristitia de spirituali bono*: the sorrow about, or the aversion man feels against, his spiritual good. "Sorrow" is here understood as the negative reaction of man's sensitive appetite to an object which is either truly evil, or evil only in appearance but good in reality. The latter reaction constitutes *acedia* properly speaking. Man's true good—the objects and values to which human nature according to the right order of Creation is oriented and in which alone it finds its fulfilment and ultimate happiness—is the spiritual good. But this good may appear to man as an evil, and he consequently can experience an aversion to it. Since this aversion is contrary to the right order, it constitutes sin. Sometimes even a genuine evil can cause sinful spiritual aversion or sorrow: namely, when this sorrow becomes immoderate: "Also the sorrow about a true evil is bad according to its effect, if it depresses man so much that it makes him withdraw entirely from a good deed."[5] This secondary aspect of *acedia* which Thomas mentions in this article reflects, of course, the Cassianic vice of *tristitia*, immoderate grief. In the following articles, however, Thomas does not think of *acedia* as including immoderate grief about the loss or the absence of (temporal) goods.

If *acedia* is thus conceived as, essentially, the aversion against the spiritual good when it appears to man as evil, the question arises whether this aversion is not common to all vices.[6] The glutton, for example, takes excessive delight in food and drink; to him the virtue of sobriety—observing a rational measure in the quantity of his food, its quality, and the time of eating—necessarily appears as an evil; hence he will experience an aversion against the spiritual good of sobriety or, in Thomistic terminology, "tristatur de abstinentia cibi."[7] Is this aversion the same as *acedia*, which was defined as "tristitia de spirituali bono"? If so, *acedia* is not a special vice but merely a consequence of all other vices, since all vices consist in the twofold movement of the appetite of turning toward an apparent good which is really evil (excessive delight in food) and of turning away from an apparent evil which is really a good (the rational measure in food and drink).

Thomas counters this objection by pointing out that *acedia* has a special object which clearly distinguishes it from the other vices. This is not the common spiritual good contained in all the virtues, but rather the spiritual good which lies above them, the *bonum divinum*. *Acedia*, therefore, more accurately means the sorrow or aversion against God himself and the things that are directly related to Him. It is the opposite of the joy in the divine good that man should experience. Thus, *acedia* is indeed a special vice, and is opposed to spiritual *gaudium*, which is an aspect of the theological virtue of *caritas*.[8]

But when and why, one may ask, does the spiritual or divine good appear to man as evil? Thomas gave two different answers to this question, which at first sight may appear contradictory. In his discussion of the rationale for the seven vices (in *Prima secundae*) he declared that *acedia* was an aversion against spiritual good "because of the bodily labor attached to it."[9] In other words, man loathes religious exercises and the practice of virtues because such activity opposes the natural tendency of his body toward rest. This reason for *acedia* was a common view among theologians before St. Thomas.[10] But the Angelic Doctor was apparently not satisfied with it because in his discussion of *acedia* itself (in *Secunda secundae*) he states, "*acedia* is not a special vice in so far as it flees the spiritual good because this is wearisome or annoying to the body or impedes its delight."[11] Although shrinking from bodily efforts that are necessary for the acquisition of spiritual good still is an ingredient of *acedia*, Thomas now realizes that this alone does not make *acedia* a special vice, distinguished from others like gluttony or lust. What constitutes its essence more precisely is the fact that it relates to an object of its own, the *bonum divinum*, as we have seen earlier. The distinction is fully drawn in *De malo*:

> The work of any special virtue, then—let us say, of chastity—, can be lovable and delectable in two ways. First, according as it is a work of that virtue, and this way is proper to chastity. Second, according as it is related to the divine good, and in this way it is proper to charity. We must say, then, that the sorrow about this special good which is the internal and divine good

> makes *accidia* a special sin; just as the love of this good makes charity a special virtue. This divine good, however, can induce sorrow in man because of the opposition between spirit and flesh, for—as the Apostle says in Galatians 5:17—"the flesh lusteth against the spirit"; and thus, when carnal desire rules in man, it is disgusted by spiritual good as by something contrary to itself, just as a man who has a corrupted sense of taste loathes wholesome food and feels sorrowful about it when he ought to take such food. Such sorrow and loathing or disgust of the spiritual and divine good is *accidia*, which is a special sin.[12]

Acedia is thus apprehended as inappetence, as lack of desire for God and cheerlessness in activities that relate to Him directly (prayer, meditation, and the like), a consequence of the fact that after the Fall man's spirit is burdened by his flesh.

After clarifying the nature of the vice, Thomas turns to the question of its sinfulness: is *acedia* a mortal sin?[13] Here one must again keep in mind that *acedia* refers, not to all kinds of sorrow, but only to the sorrow about the divine good. The words of Christ, "My soul is sad, even unto death" (Matt. 26:38), or of the Apostle Paul, "[Let us conduct ourselves] as sorrowful yet always rejoicing" (II Cor. 6:10), do therefore not apply to the question under consideration. "Tristitia" in these two and similar cases means sorrow about temporal evils, not about the divine good.[14] In contrast, true *acedia* is by definition a mortal sin, since it opposes the virtue of *caritas* and its special aspect of spiritual joy. But it must be considered that this sin is not always "perfect" or completed. Its beginning is an aversion of man's sensitive appetite against the divine good. This aversion per se is not a mortal sin; it becomes such only if reason gives its full consent. Therefore, saintly persons frequently experience movements of *acedia* without however falling into mortal sin.

Finally, Thomas considers the question whether *acedia* is a chief vice.[15] According to an earlier definition, the *vitia capitalia* are vices which give rise to others by being their final cause. This would mean that *acedia*, the sorrow about the divine good, is a chief vice insofar as it is responsible for many morally wrong actions which man will commit in order to avoid or repel the aversion he experiences against what seems to him an evil. Such actions are of two kinds: some are taken in order to avoid objects or occasions that may cause aversion against the divine good; others, in order to find delight elsewhere. To these two kinds of actions can be reduced the various vices which Gregory the Great had established as the "daughters of *acedia*." Flight from man's spiritual end is despair. Flight from the means that conduce man to his spiritual end occurs in the vices of pusillanimity (shrinking from spiritual hardships which accompany the practice of the evangelical counsels) and of *torpor circa praecepta* (shrinking from fulfilling what is demanded by common justice, i.e., the Commandments). Such flight sometimes leads to a sort of inner fighting against the causes of aversion. Thus, to fight against persons who, by word or example, lead men to spiritual goods is the nature of *rancor*; while the same inner fight against the spiritual goods themselves is called *malitia*. Finally, the second kind of action—to seek delight in external goods because "inner" or spiritual goods are loathsome—is represented by *evagatio circa illicita*.

After finding a rationale for Gregory's "daughters of *acedia*," it is an easy thing to show how Gregory's progeny agrees with those of *acedia* and *tristitia* in Cassian's system. *Pusillanimitas* and *desperatio* are the same in both lists. Gregory's *malitia* is nearly synonymous with *acedia*. As to the rest, the following equation is self-evident:[16]

Cassian:		Gregory:
amaritudo	is an effect of	*rancor*
otiositas *somnolentia*	correspond to	*torpor circa praecepta*
importunitas mentis *curiositas* *verbositas* *inquietas corporis* *instabilitas*	correspond to	*evagatio mentis circa illicita*

This brief and somewhat barren exposition of Thomas' mature thought on *acedia* calls for some comment and interpretation. First, the definition of the vice as *tristitia de spirituali bono*. By the middle of the thirteenth century, Scholastic theologians had developed a variety of definitions for *acedia* which basically agreed in considering the vice as a kind of inappetence, of aversion to spiritual good or spiritual deeds. This aversion was expressed in such terms as *torpor, taedium, fastidium,* or *tristitia,* each used in definitions which had become more or less traditional.[17] The desire to harmonize varying traditions—a chief aspect of Scholastic theology—

compelled the Schoolmen to seek logical connections between these ideas. Thus, Alexander of Hales thought that in essence *acedia* was a kind of *tristitia,* whereas the definitions with *taedium* and *torpor* referred to particular aspects of the vice: viz., negative attitudes toward the (spiritual) good insofar as this, respectively, has already been conferred upon man or is still to be attained.[18] Such an attempt to harmonize three or more conceptions is still visible in Thomas Aquinas' mature treatment;[19] but in contrast to Alexander and to Albert the Great he built his discussion of the vice more firmly on only one definition—*tristitia de spirituali bono* (or *de bono divino*) —at which, as we have seen, he arrived by carefully distinguishing *acedia* from other vices.

Thomas' conception of *acedia* as a form of *tristitia* is the culmination of a semantic and intellectual development which had taken place for at least a century and a half. We noticed earlier that during the twelfth century the two terms were equated to designate the respective chief vice as "acedia seu tristitia."[20] But this equation was more than a verbal trick employed to reconcile two different traditions; it affected the very essence of *acedia.* For from the early twelfth century on, the noun *acedia* suddenly came to mean sadness or grief of some form or another. The earliest writer of this period in whose works I have found this phenomenon is Guibert, abbot of Nogent-sous-Coucy (d. 1124). In commenting on Osee 5:12, "I am unto Ephraim as a moth . . . ," for example, he writes: "God becomes 'unto Ephraim as a moth' when our mind in the midst of temptations languishes through heavy attacks of *accidia*; for that man is eaten up by a moth, as it were, who on account of grieved anguish [*moeroris angustia*] is quickened by no zeal of reading or prayer but, as the psalm says, 'their soul loathes all food' [Ps. 106:18]."[21] Guibert evidently understood *acedia* as *moeror* (grief) or as evil *tristitia* (cf. his relating *acedia* with the moth, a standard image for *tristitia*)—a fact borne out by other passages in his works.[22] Very similarly, *acedia* meant "spiritual sadness" in the vocabulary of Richard of St. Victor.[23]

Parallel to the usage of spiritual writers, the vice was frequently defined as some form of *tristitia* by systematic theologians. For example, in his great *Summa de sacramentis fidei,* Hugh of St. Victor wrote: "*Acidia* is a sadness [*tristitia*] born of a confusion of the mind, or, weariness [*taedium*] and immoderate bitterness of the mind; through it spiritual joy is quenched and the mind is overthrown in itself, as it were by the beginning of despair."[24] Writers of lesser stature than Hugh occasionally identified *acedia* as *tristitia hujus saeculi* (cf. II Cor. 7:10),[25] a tradition still reflected in St. Thomas.[26] And we must also mention that the equation even entered the important dictionary by Huguitius of Pisa, written about 1200.[27]

Yet the most influential identification of *acedia* with *tristitia* put forth in the twelfth century occurred in a translation of a Greek work, made about 1150 but not fully exploited for the analysis of the vice until a century later. The Greek theologian John of Damascus (eighth century) had, in his *De fide orthodoxa*, gathered and handed on a rich treasure of patristic as well as non-Christian Greek thought. Among other things, he furnished a classification of the passions, for which he used older, ultimately Stoic, schemes. The passage which was particularly influential on the Scholastic analysis of *acedia* is John's division of the passion *tristitia* (λύπη) into four species: sorrow which produces speechlessness (ἄχος), depressing sorrow (ἄχθος), envy, and mercy.[28] *De fide orthodoxa* became fully available to Latin theologians after it was translated about 1150 by Burgundio of Pisa.[29] In this version the relevant passage appears as follows: "Tristitiae vero species sunt quatuor: accidia, achos, invidia, misericordia. Accidia igitur est tristitia aggravans, achos vero est tristitia vocem auferens, invidia vero est tristitia in alienis bonis, misericordia vero est tristitia in alienis malis."[30] It is hard to say precisely what determined Burgundio to choose "accidia" for John's "depressing sorrow" (beyond possible considerations of pseudo-etymology, see below, p. 54). But his formula "acedia est tristitia aggravans" eventually entered Scholastic discussions of the vice and finally, as can be seen in Thomas Aquinas, became the philological tool to connect Cassian with Gregory and with Aristotelian psychology. The formula appeared in the analysis of *acedia* as early as the 1220's, in the *Summa aurea* by Guillaume d'Auxerre (where it is rejected, fol. 90v), and later became a favorite definition with Alexander of Hales, Albert the Great, and Thomas Aquinas.

Here a curious inconsistency must be noted. Albert in his treatment of *acedia*, and Thomas in the earlier discussion of the passions,[31] equate *acedia* not with *tristitia aggravans* but with *tristitia vocem auferens* (or *amputans*), the Greek ἄχος. Thomas attributes this definition to "Gregorius Nyssenus," a name which stands for Nemesius, owing to a common confusion among the Schoolmen. Nemesius was a bishop of Emesa in the fourth or fifth century and wrote a discussion of the passions, in his treatise *On the Nature of Man,* which became the direct source for John of Damascus. Nemesius' classification of sorrow is the same as that mentioned above. But in the twelfth-century translation, also made by Burgundio, the relevant passage appears thus: "Tristitiae vero sunt species quator: achos, achthos id est acedia, anxietas, invidia, misericordia. Acedia vero est tristitia vocem amputans; anxietas vero est tristitia aggravans. . . ."[32] I am unable to say what light this inconsistency in Burgundio's work throws upon twelfth-century translations of Greek authors or the use which Scholastic theologians made of them. Although it gave the Schoolmen one more occasion to harmonize different traditions, the whole matter is of minor importance for us except that it suggests a small insight into the working of Scholastic minds with respect to *acedia.* One suspects that both ἄχος and ἄχθος were translated as *acedia* partly because of the similarity in sound or spelling. There is at least one important witness to the Scholastic belief that *acedia* was etymologically related with ἄχος. Albert the Great wrote: "[John of Damascus] says that *acedia* is *tristitia aggravans* because, on account of the hardship in acquiring the good, one becomes heavy [*aggravatur*] and weak in pursuing the good. In everybody, however, the depressing weakness sharpens the voice [*acuit vocem*], as is evident in all sick people; and from such depression is derived the noun *acedia* in Latin: because ἄκος [*sic*] in Greek is the same as "depressing the voice" [*vocem aggravans*]."[33]

It must be immediately added, however, that Albert's derivation is a curiosity in medieval theological literature. Customarily, the etymology of *acedia* is explained from either *acidus,* "sour," or *cadere,* "to fall." Whereas the latter is rare,[34] the former is the standard derivation. A representative passage states succinctly: "*Accidia* is named after the sourness of the mind [*ab accedine animi*] and the bitter will, in accordance with Proverbs 10, 'As vinegar [*acetum*] to the teeth, and as smoke to the eyes, so is the sluggard [*piger*] to them that send him.' "[35] It seems that this pseudo-etymological explanation from Latin roots was a product of the Scholastic period; by the thirteenth century, ordinary theologians had evidently lost awareness of the Greek origins of the term and its true etymology.

To define *acedia* as a species of *tristitia* has, of course, implications that go beyond merely preserving one or two elements of theological tradition. In Scholastic psychology, *tristitia* was one of the chief passions. Already Aristotle had traced a system of passions in the *Nicomachean Ethics,* which the Schoolmen adopted and developed further.[36] According to Thomas Aquinas, *tristitia* signifies the painful reaction of man's sensitive soul to any evil which is present (not anticipated), be it a wound, lack of food, the loss of a friend, or frustrated expectations. But the meaning of *tristitia* extends even further: It is one of the two basic affects (joy and sorrow, or pleasure and pain, *gaudium* and *tristitia*) to which all eleven passions can be reduced as their final affective states. In other words, *tristitia* is the very fundamental reaction of man's sensitive nature to draw back from anything that presents itself as evil, whether the object is present or anticipated, real or imagined, easy to flee or hard to overcome. In the view of St. Thomas, *acedia* of course refers to a very special kind of such a negative reaction of the appetite; but in this analysis the theological vice is thus very intimately linked to the deepest roots of man's affective and volitive life.

If the vice is firmly rooted in Aristotelian psychology, its trunk and branches, nevertheless, breathe the air of Christian ethics. It is aversion against man's *spiritual* good, against the divine good itself. Because of the dignity of its object (the *bonum divinum*), *acedia* actually occupies a very high rank among the chief vices. This exalted position, so to speak, is also reflected in the virtue to which, according to the Schoolmen, it is opposed; the joy which man should experience in loving God and serving Him. *Acedia* is the negation of *caritas,* the greatest Christian virtue. This opposition, common among the Schoolmen, deviates somewhat from earlier, traditional views. The Egyptian desert monks had opposed *acedia* with the virtue of patience or endurance (ὑπομονή).[37] Cassian, on the other hand, considered the opposite of *acedia* to be strength, *fortitudo,*[38] and this view remained standard in Western theology until the Scholastic period, whereas in popular catechetical teaching it continued to be the favorite one to the end of the Middle Ages. The rival of *acedia,* however—Gregory's *tristitia*—had always been the vice opposed to spiritual joy (*gaudium* or *spiritualis laetitia*).[39] Thus the gradual equation of Cassian's *acedia* and Gregory's *tristitia* is also reflected in the fate of their respective opposite virtues. Hugh Ripelin's *Compendium theologicae veritatis* still maintains this distinction: "This vice [*acedia*] has two names. . . . In so far as it is called *tristitia,* it is opposed to the spiritual joy that is in spiritual exercise; but in so far as it is called *acedia,* it is opposed to fortitude, which consists in attacking what is arduous, and in enduring what is contrary."[40] But Thomas Aquinas' firm conception of *acedia* as a species of the passion *tristitia* does away with Hugh's notion of two different aspects or even vices in the one capital vice. Here the opposite of the vice becomes unmistakably the virtue which is logically contrary to spiritual sorrow: *gaudium,* a major effect of *caritas.*

For Cassian and his predecessors these oppositions were remedial ones, that is, a certain virtue was "opposed" to a certain vice as its remedy. Thus, "patience heals *acedia,*" or, "fortitude will build up whom *acedia* has laid in ruins."[41] Quite in contrast, Scholastic theologians consider such oppositions a matter of logic. Since *acedia* is a species of *tristitia,* it has to be contrary to the latter's opposite, *gaudium*—a relation already set up in Aristotle's system of the passions.[42] Furthermore, *acedia* opposes spiritual joy (or *caritas* itself) because they are opposite attitudes toward the same object: the divine good, which man can either love and feel joyful about, or loathe and feel disgusted at.

During the high Middle Ages, the idea of opposing individual vices and virtues had become part of larger speculative attempts to find correspondences between the various series of seven members, or *septenae,* which had been established as elements in traditional theology.[43] The capital vices were thus related not only to the chief virtues but also to the seven gifts of the Holy Ghost, the seven petitions of the Lord's Prayer, and the seven blessings of the Sermon on the Mount. As one might expect, unusually fertile minds would find further correspondences with the seven planets[44] and other heptads.[45] The greatest impulse in these endeavors came from Hugh of St. Victor, in the twelfth century, who was apparently so fond of them that he developed the correspondences between five septenaries several times in his works.[46] In his system, *acedia* appears related to the petition for daily bread: "Because sorrow [*tristitia, seu acedia*] is weariness of the mind with sadness: when the mind, through being somehow wasted away and embittered by its vice, does not desire the internal good and, as all vigor lies dead, is cheered by no desire for spiritual food. In order to heal this vice we should, therefore, pray the Lord's mercy that He Himself, in

His wonted goodness, may provide our soul, as it languishes in its weariness, with inner nourishment."[47] The conception of *acedia* as spiritual inappetence is consistently developed. Not only is the vice cured by the petition for daily bread but it is opposed by Christ's blessing of those who hunger and thirst for righteousness and consequently, the virtue of *justitiae satietas*. Finally, the healing power for it comes in the gift of fortitude.[48]

Such equations, however, did not meet the logical requirements of thirteenth-century Schoolmen, and of Hugh's five septenaries only three are consistently considered in Thomas' *Summa theologiae*: the virtues, the vices, and the gifts of the Holy Ghost. Moreover, these elements occur in different combinations. Thus, for reasons we have seen earlier, in the *Secunda secundae, acedia* is related to *caritas* and to the gift of *sapientia*. But Thomas establishes another relation, which seems to have been a more serious problem with theologians of his period: the relation of the seven vices or capital sins with the Ten Commandments. At first sight it may seem strange to us that the vice of *acedia* should be condemned by the Third Commandment, but upon closer inspection the connection reveals itself as quite logical. Thomas explains that the commandment about the sanctification of the Sabbath, "in so far as it is a moral precept, commands the mind's rest in God" (*quies mentis in Deo*).[49] We must remember that in the Aristotelian doctrine of the passions, *quies* is the affective state in which the will enjoys the possession of some good; in other words, *quies mentis in Deo* is synonymous with *gaudium de bono divino*.[50]

These relations of *acedia* with the Third Commandment, with the gift of *sapientia*, and most of all with *caritas*, bear out the fact that in Thomas' theological system the vice—because of its object—occupies a place of high dignity. This is manifest, too, in the very order in which *acedia* appears in Thomas' ethics. The second part of his ethics (*Secunda secundae*), dealing with moral acts in particular, is constructed on the sequence of the seven chief virtues, from faith to moderation. In this scheme, the seven chief vices are not treated in a group (as they would have been by Thomas' predecessors) but appear scattered in their respective places as opposites to individual virtues. As a matter of logical consequence, *acedia* is the first capital vice to be discussed. It opposes *caritas*, more precisely the joy man ought to experience in contemplating the divine good, and precedes envy, which negates the joy man ought to experience in contemplating the good of his neighbor.

The exalted position of *acedia* indicates that to Scholastic theologians the vice meant more than simple laziness. We have found that in several Carolingian moral treatises for laymen and in penitential handbooks the vice came to mean spiritual idleness or negligence in performing one's duties to God, and we shall see later that, contemporary with the Scholastic analysis, the same conception was to dominate popular literature on the vices. Even Schoolmen occasionally identified *acedia* with *pigritia*,[51] for which they found support in Prov. 10:26, the passage cited earlier in connection with the supposed etymology of "acedia" (". . . sic piger iis qui miserunt eum in viam").

But in marked contrast to this trend, for Thomas Aquinas the essence of *acedia* is not laziness or indolence. He draws a firm and clear distinction between the two when he differentiates *acedia* from the common unwillingness to make spiritual efforts because of the hardships these entail for the body. This distinction is implied in Thomas' discussion of *acedia* as a special vice which we noticed earlier. Moreover, *pigritia* or *segnities* is to him a quite different psychological phenomenon: not sadness or aversion, but a species of fear. In Aristotelian terms, laziness is man's flight from action because he is afraid to make the necessary effort.[52] Hence, *pigritia* and *acedia* belong to entirely different main passions.

This distinction seems to me so important because it reveals clearly that in Thomas' later conception the essence of *acedia* does not *primarily* derive from the fact that man lives in a body. For him (and for the major Schoolmen in general) the vice is essentially not an inordinate yielding to the body's desire for, or need of, physical rest. The old division of the chief vices into carnal and spiritual ones does probably not make much sense in Thomas' system; but it is evident that his notion of *acedia* agrees with, and perhaps has drawn the consequences from, Cassian's suggestion and Gregory's explicit statement that this vice is to be counted among the *vitia spiritualia*.[53]

On the other hand, the scholastic *acedia* is by no means unrelated to the body. This is manifest, first of all, in the very definition of this particular vice as *tristitia*, i.e., as a species of a passion. In

Aristotelian-Thomistic thought, the passions are characterized as "movements" of the soul accompanied by certain changes in the body. "If this physiological element did not exist, we would be dealing with a pure sentiment of a totally spiritual and voluntary order, but not with a passion."[54] The passions, therefore, more than any other phenomenon of human experience, are constant reminders of the essential unity of man's body and soul. They are, of course, basic to the affective life in general and hence to all the virtues and vices. But the scholastic preference for defining *acedia* as *tristitia aggravans* seems to emphasize more strongly than is the case with other vices the close relation between this vice and a passion.

Passions, however, vary in strength and combination according to the individual constitution of human beings. Some men will consequently be more disposed to *acedia* than others, and in some individuals *acedia* may spring from such a strong, peculiar disposition that it is a physiological defect rather than a vice. Many Scholastic thinkers thus recognize that occasionally *acedia* is caused by an imbalance of the humors or by disease. Thomas Aquinas does not discuss this aspect,[55] but other Scholastic theologians do include some remarks on it in their treatments of the vice. John of Wales (d. 1285?), for example, distinguishes between a natural cause of the vice and various contingent causes; the former is the cold and moist disposition.[56] Other writers cite the melancholy humor as a cause of *acedia*. Guillaume d'Auvergne, for example, says: "This vice is sometimes increased and strengthened by the melancholy humor or vapor."[57] The presence of a "natural" cause like melancholy also lessens the sinfulness of the vice. "In this respect [*acedia*] is not the greatest sin nor incurable, because it occurs in many people who are disposed to it, as the melancholy. Hence, it often arises from the infirmity of *melancholia* or another weakness, and thus is not said to be the greatest sin or incurable."[58]

This realization leads, of course, to the conclusion that some people who suffer from *acedia* are better helped, not by practicing patient endurance, work of hands, keeping the cell, or the like, but by relaxing their concentrated mental efforts, by taking a walk, and perhaps even by dieting.

> Since according to Scripture [Wisd. 9:15] "the body, when it becomes sick, burdens the soul, and the earthly dwelling-place depresses a mind that thinks much," it is necessary for the mind's tranquillity that our human weakness sometimes turn

> away our mind from its attention to inner and outer cares and turn it toward comforts and recreations that are necessary for our body. Because otherwise our spirit becomes anxious, dull, *accidiosus,* sadder than it ought to be, weary with disgust of the good, querulous, and ready to frequent movements of impatience and anger. Therefore the greatest saints sometimes unbent from spiritual cares to comfort, and sometimes loosened their rigorous abstinence and shortened their excessive vigils.[59]

This humanistic attitude of Roger Bacon is shared by the theologian and Bishop of Paris, Guillaume d'Auvergne, who recommends against *acedia,* after divine grace, the human remedies of lightening the burden of work and other exercises and relaxing the bonds of the cloister.[60] Guillaume adds, "Also of great help in this is music," and the same idea occurs a little later in the *Moniloquium* by John of Wales: "It is believed that it helps them [i.e., those who suffer from *acedia*] much to hear music and musical instruments. But these things are to be left to the physicians."[61]

In Scholastic thought, therefore, *acedia* holds an interesting intermediate position between body and spirit.[62] On the one hand, it is—in essence—not physical laziness or shrinking from spiritual exercises because of the concomitant efforts and pains of the body, but rather the spiritual phenomenon of aversion from, or disgust at, what ought to be the object of man's greatest love. On the other hand, it does have some connection with the body, whether it springs from one's complexion or merely from lack of food, or whether (in Thomas' more spiritualized conception) it stems from the opposition between spirit and flesh.

This intermediate position between body and spirit would also distinguish *acedia* from a purely spiritual phenomenon with which it could be most easily confused: spiritual dryness. Christian mystics and theologians have always recognized a variety of psychological states— such as tepidity, desolation, and dryness—which share with *acedia* such symptoms as the absence of devotion, a feeling of being abandoned by God, depression, inner bitterness and coldness, and so forth. Indeed, these common symptoms make spiritual phenomena traditionally designated by different names look so much alike that spiritual writers find it rather difficult to draw satisfactory lines between, for example, desolation and dryness and to establish some kind of relationship between them.[63] However, contemporary theologians insist on keeping *acedia* (or tepidity) clearly apart from spiritual dryness.[64] We may ask whether Scholastic thinkers also recognized a difference and, if so, how they related the two phenomena.

The Scholastic *summae theologicae* do not give us an immediate, direct answer, since they, as a rule, are not concerned with mystical theology or asceticism as such, but with Christian morals in general. To find an answer, we have to analyze a medieval description of spiritual dryness and then relate it to *acedia*. The following is a passage from St. Bernard's sermons on the Song of Solomon, a passage which has been taken as a classical description of spiritual dryness by medieval as well as by modern theologians.

> This barrenness of my soul, this lack of devotion which I suffer. How has my heart become thus dry, how has is curdled like milk, become like a land without water? I cannot even be moved to tears, so great is the hardness of my heart. Psalm-singing does not taste, reading does not please me, prayer does not delight me, the wonted meditation I do not find. Where is my spiritual drunkenness? Where the serenity of my mind, the peace and joy in the Holy Spirit? Thus I am lazy in the work of my hands, sleepy in vigils, quick to become angry, persistent in hatred, rather indulgent with tongue and palate, and rather indolent and dull in preaching.[65]

At first sight, Bernard's description might suggest that he is speaking of *acedia*. Here is the same lack of delight in spiritual exercises and the same laziness and somnolence that flow from it. But closer analysis reveals that Bernard is describing a quite different spiritual malaise. First of all, he calls this psychic state, not *acedia* but *sterilitas animae*—a term he no doubt inherited from Cassian.[66] Secondly, Bernard experiences "this lack of devotion" (*devotionis inopia*) as an absence of the customary spiritual consolations, as God's withdrawal from the soul (see especially the last full sentence of the following quotation); in other words, he is *conscious* of a down in his spiritual life. He is, thirdly, equally conscious of its cause: his own pride, for which he is being punished. The quoted passage actually begins thus: "This weariness of my soul, this slackness of mind, this unwonted idleness of my spirit, which has been in me since yesterday or the day before, is not without cause. I was running well; but lo, a stumbling-block lay in my way: I dashed against it and have fallen. Pride has been found in me, and the Lord has turned away in wrath from His servant. Hence this barrenness . . . ."[67]

Finally—and this is perhaps the most important aspect for our comparison—Bernard is deeply disturbed about this languor of his soul. In marked contrast to the *accidiosus,* the person who suffers from spiritual dryness not only realizes his spiritual deficiency but worries about it. Consider the strong, active yearning for devotion that is expressed in another, much earlier description of *sterilitas mentis*: "While we were groaning and endeavoring to restore ourselves to our former disposition, our mind was unable to do this, and the more earnestly it sought to fix again its gaze upon God, so was it the more vehemently carried away to wandering thoughts."[68] Besides the fact that both Cassian and Bernard call this state *sterilitas* and not *acedia,* it is quite obvious that the two passages, with their intense consciousness and desire for devotion, could not possibly have been spoken or written by a monk suffering from *acedia.*

Nevertheless, we discern that *acedia* and spiritual dryness have an important aspect in common: the lack of devotion, or *indevotio.* This term will help us to understand the relation between the two states as far as the Schoolmen were able to clarify it. In *De malo* Thomas Aquinas meets the objection that *acedia* cannot be sinful because it is characterized by absence of devotion, and to pray with devotion is a gift of grace, outside man's power. Thomas replies that, indeed, devotion comes from God; but at the same time man has the power either to dispose himself to receive this gift, or to hinder its coming: in the latter case, *indevotio* is a sin, because "*indevotio* is not the same as *acedia* but arises from it."[69]

The same causal relation was neatly established in a work written perhaps as early as 1236. This is the *Summa de vitiis et virtutibus* by the Dominican William Peraldus, a handbook which became the model for popular catechetical instruction in Latin as well as in the vernacular languages. Among other things, Peraldus, as it were, "fixed" the standard progenies of the seven vices. In his systematization *acedia* has an offspring of sixteen vices, of which the thirteenth is called *indevotio.* It is related to *acedia* in this way:

> *Indevotio* is a certain spiritual dryness [*ariditas spiritualis*]. . . . This dryness comes from many causes. Sometimes it arises from pride, which is Mount Gilboa, on which neither dew nor rain falls. Hence, Bernard, speaking in the person of one who has lost his devotion, says: "Since yesterday or the day before . . ." [the entire passage from Bernard's sermon quoted above]. Some-

> times, however, this dryness comes from a deficiency of spiritual food. . . . And sometimes from *accidia*.[70]

We can draw the conclusion that in the Scholastic analysis *indevotio*, a major aspect of spiritual dryness, can also be an effect of *acedia*. It is, in other words, the same fruit growing on different trees. Although Scholastic theologians did, apparently, not distinguish between these trees as carefully and explicitly as did the mystic writers of the sixteenth and following centuries, the elements for this later clarification were all present in medieval thought. The basic difference between the two psychic states lies, from the human point of view, in man's attitude toward his experience of spiritual weariness, slackening attention, and diminishing devotion: he can either care and worry about his spiritual state, or not care any more.[71] Theologically speaking, the difference is one between a trial of man's faith and love, ordained by God, purgative, and hence beneficial for man's spiritual ascent; and temptation which, if consented to, leads to mortal sin.[72] Or in other words, it is the difference between lack of taste or delight, and inappetence. The distinction is expressed in classical form by St. John of the Cross:

> It is evident that this disgust and dryness [*sinsabor y sequedad*] do not come from slackness and tepidity [*flojedad y tibieza*]; for, tepidity is characterized by not caring much or having an inner solicitude for the things of God. Therefore, there is a great difference between dryness and tepidity. Because the state of tepidity implies great negligence and slackness in will and mind, without willingness to serve God; but purgative dryness is accompanied by the usual willingness, with concern and sorrow (as I have said) that one does not serve God.[73]

We can now assess what role and importance the Scholastic analysis had for the history of *acedia*. Most salient, of course, is the peace the Schoolmen brought about in the long-standing rivalry between Cassian's *acedia* and Gregory's *tristitia* to designate one of the standard seven capital vices. The reconciliation achieved in Thomas' *Summa theologiae* is no longer the superficial juxtaposition of the two terms that it was in Hugh of St. Victor but has become a harmonization in which the rivals recognize their true natures and relationship. It may very well be that Gregory the Great, when he called the particular vice *tristitia*, was not at all thinking of the Aristotelian-Stoic passion. But the later Middle Ages realized that the difference between the two traditions, Cassianic and Gregorian, had become almost a matter of names alone, that the two concepts meant psychologically and theologically the same, and that Gregory's term *tristitia* might indeed be explained with reference to the Aristotelian passion. Hence, the two concepts could be harmonized by considering *acedia,* which (in Thomas' words) "Gregory more conveniently called *tristitia,*"[74] as a species of the passion *tristitia.* The harmonization was then completed by showing how the different progenies in Cassian and Gregory, too, really referred to the same moral faults.

The establishment of this new definition for *acedia* as "tristitia de bono divino," and its subsequent clarification, is absolutely central to the scholastic analysis of the vice. From it derive, quite logically, the one or two deviations from traditional views that we noticed, such as pitting *acedia* against *caritas* rather than *fortitudo,* or linking it with the Third Commandment. These are, therefore, only minor changes or corrections which we can hardly call innovations, especially when we compare them with the various pre-Scholastic transformations of the concept before 1200. What the Scholastic analysis really contributed to the history of *acedia* was, first, to make a penetrating analysis of the psychology of the vice, and second, to integrate it firmly into a complete and consistent system of moral theology.

We have seen how Thomas Aquinas, with the help of Aristotelian psychology, was able to connect *acedia* with one of the main passions and consequently show very clearly the place and function *acedia* has in man's affective and volitive life. No similar analysis had been even attempted in Christian theology before the thirteenth century. In Chapter II we saw how Scholastic theologians searched for a rationale for the seven vices, and our brief survey ended with Thomas' linking the vices to "certain fundamental modes of moving the appetite," in his *Prima secundae.* It is, however, only in the later *Secunda secundae* that Thomas definitely comes to grips with the true nature of *acedia.* From this analysis the vice emerges as a disorder in man's affective life. At the root of *acedia* lies, not physical exhaustion or a weakening of man's will or intellectual darkness, but a disorientation of his affect or, as we would say today, his emotional life. This view is very nicely expressed by some Scholastic and later writers in the metaphor of the *pes affectus*: how can the *accidiosus* get to heaven, they ask, if he sets forth the foot of his intellect but always drags the foot of his affect behind him?[75] For medieval Christianity *affectus* is, of course, not a matter of sentiment and "feeling" but of will and love resulting in "good works." Hence Peraldus' equating the image of *pes intellectus* with "good intention" and of *pes affectus* with "work."[76] It is easy to see from this detail how the vice of *acedia* could thus become linked to a multitude of neglects and omissions of good works, as it was in the popular catechetical literature. Scholastic theology itself, however, was not concerned with observable faults but rather analyzed their psychological roots.

In addition, Scholastic theologians built—or at least attempted to do so—all the elements of dogma and tradition into a coherent system of theology. Again, for the first time in Christian theology, the nature, aspects, and implications of *acedia* were clarified to such a degree of precision and completeness as to give the vice a logical place in the entire system of moral theology. Not only is its psychological nature defined, but *acedia* is shown to be a mortal sin and a capital vice and is placed in a precise and logical relation to the virtues, to the Decalogue, and ultimately to man's position in a divinely ordered cosmos.

What distinguishes Thomas from his fellow Schoolmen is that his *Summa theologiae*—as a systematic presentation of theology, gathering up the tradition, elucidating it, and fitting it together into a logically coherent structure—is more consistent, more penetrating, more catholic, and more original. Part of its originality reveals itself in the very organization of the *Summa*—a fact which modern historians of Scholastic thought are just beginning to explore more fully.[77] Especially interesting to us in this respect is the plan of *Secunda secundae*, dealing with man's moral life in particular. The literary prototype of Scholastic compendia of theological knowledge, Peter Lombard's *Sentences*, arranges its material in the order of the Apostles' Creed or (which amounts to the same) in the order of sacred history, *Heilsgeschichte*. From a discussion of the nature of God, of the Holy Trinity (Book I), it goes on to treat Creation and the Fall (Book II), Christology (Book III), and the sacraments (Book IV), ending with the Last Judgment. What there is of "moral theology" appears in Book III: the seven (theological and cardinal) virtues followed by the seven gifts of the Holy Ghost and the Ten Commandments. Quite unrelated to this, the psychology of sin is treated in connection with the Fall of Man (Book II), and the seven chief vices are only listed in a few lines, without any further analysis (II, 42, 6). Quite in contrast, Thomas writes first a long treatise on Christian morals in general (the *Prima secundae*), dealing with human acts, the passions, habits, and external forces that influence moral behavior. Next he treats of "moral acts in particular," where he follows the sequence of the seven virtues and builds vices, gifts, and commandments around individual virtues (in the *Secunda secundae*). In consequence, the scheme of the seven capital vices becomes torn apart and the traditional vices are treated in isolation, scattered among a number of other vices not considered "capital." Their place and order in this treatment are, therefore, determined not by Gregory's or Cassian's lists, but by the logical exigency of their nature as seen in opposition to a capital virtue. Consequently, *acedia* appears as the first capital vice treated in the *Secunda secundae,* since it is opposed to *caritas.*

It is important to stress that, as *acedia* appears in opposition to a theological virtue, it is itself a theological vice. Thomas, of course, does not call it this; for the writer of a *Summa theologiae* all vices are "theological." Yet in a narrow sense *acedia* may well be called "theological" because it refers directly to man's relation to God, not to himself or his neighbor or society at large. The object of this vice, so to speak, is the love of God, not the pursuit of virtue, let alone the quest for fame, wealth, or a better society. Despite their reliance on Aristotelian psychology and ethics, the Schoolmen always drew a clear line between Aristotle's vices and the *vitia capitalia* of Christian tradition, rejecting the former and clinging to the latter when they built their system of Christian ethics. A genuinely Aristotelian classification of vices, in which each of the virtues treated in the *Nicomachean Ethics* would be flanked by two vices (excess and lack), is usually ventilated as an objection to Gregory's *seven* capital vices but refuted because of the greater authority of the Church Father.[78] Scholastic writers often make it quite clear that they are aware of a difference, with respect to the *vitia,* between moral philosophy and theology.[79] The same holds true of *acedia* in particular. In the *summae theologicae* the vice is not identified with one of the vices in Aristotle's scheme. Even in Thomas' *Secunda secundae,* which discards the Gregorian scheme of chief vices as a structural principle, *acedia* is sharply distinguished from such (Aristotelian) vices as *negligentia, pusillanimitas, mollities,* or *insensibilitas,* and maintains a position of its very own which is characterized by the vice's special object, the *bonum divinum.* Compare, in contrast, the definition given by Alanus: "*Acedia* is the torpor of the mind by which one either neglects to begin good works or grows weary in finishing them."[80] It is obvious that, in comparison with Thomas' "tristitia de bono divino," the definition by Alanus is wider and more "worldly." Upon further comparison, it is equally obvious that the strong theological hue which *acedia* bears in the mature Scholastic *summae* resulted from a sharper and more comprehensive confrontation of the traditional concept with Aristotle's vices, in reply to the question whether *acedia* was to be held a special vice. The important point is that in the fully developed Scholastic systems of the thirteenth century *acedia* is a genuinely theological vice.

IV

THE POPULAR IMAGE

The analysis which St. Thomas and other Scholastic theologians had made is in many ways the peak in the history of *acedia,* but it does not necessarily represent its most visible aspect. From the summits of speculative theology we must now turn our eyes to the foothills of practical thought and teaching, which stood much more tangibly in the foreground, at least for the majority of medieval Christians. How does the notion of *acedia* which Everyman had differ from the Scholastic conception?

This question takes us from the lecture room to the pulpit and the confessional, because it is in the new public teaching on the vices which began soon after 1200 that we find the popular image of *acedia* fully portrayed. The early thirteenth century witnessed an enormous effort in the Church to reform all its members by removing ignorance and combatting vice, an effort officially proclaimed by Pope Innocent III at the Fourth Lateran Council of 1215-1216, restated by the bishops in their diocesan synods, and carried out to a large extent by the popular mission of the new orders of mendicant friars. This reform movement was mainly directed toward Christians at large, toward the layfolk in towns and villages, and it is this effort to bring traditional doctrine to the grasp of the masses which opened a new phase in the history of *acedia* in which it was fully to emerge as Everyman's vice and to be described with an unprecedented wealth of detail.

The specific relevance of this reform movement for the sin of sloth lies in two areas. First, the Fourth Lateran Council decreed that every Christian must go to confession and receive the sacrament of penance at least once a year (Canon 21); and second, many regional councils of that period ordered their clergy to preach regularly to their flocks on the main subjects of Christian faith and morals.[1] Both charges immediately led to the production of an increasing amount of pastoral literature: instructions on how to administer penance, on what questions to ask of the penitent, on the penances to be imposed; and regular "catechetical handbooks" explaining such matters as the Creed, the Pater Noster, the seven chief sins, the virtues, and so on. "There are so many books and treatises on the vices and virtues and on divers doctrines," complains the translator of the *Orologium sapientiae* in the fifteenth century, "that any man's life, which is so short, would end before he could either study or read them."[2] It is precisely this literature, written between approximately 1200 and 1450, which shows the popular image of *acedia* and thus forms the source for this and the following chapter. As the relevant material is quite vast, often unedited, and frequently even uncharted, I shall restrict the account of popular *acedia* to works written in England and a few treatises that originated in France but became very influential across the Channel (and indeed in all of medieval Europe).

By the year 1200, *acedia* and the other chief vices had been connected with the practice of confession for a good half-millennium. Although here is not the place to review the history of penance and of private confession, a few remarks are necessary in order to elucidate the relation between the sacrament and our concept.[3] Most historians now consider that private penance which could be reiterated during one's life was established on the British Isles during the sixth and seventh centuries. Before that date, in the southern parts of Europe usually the forgiveness of grievous sins could be received only once after baptism, and the reconciliation with the Church had been accompanied by hard and prolonged works of penance and some sort of public ritual. From the sixth century on, however, forgiveness could be obtained privately and more than once. In consequence, sinning Christians (especially laymen) would confess their sins more and more frequently, and hence a religious practice came into existence which eventually spread from Ireland, Scotland, and England to France, Germany, Italy, and the rest of Western Christendom. The practice of frequent confession is attested for England about 670 A.D.,[4] and in Gaul from about 800 on it became the rule to confess at the beginning of Lent.[5] Similarly, confession was deemed to be a necessary preparation for receiving holy communion; hence, it is likely that by the eleventh century it was customary and obligatory in many regions to confess one's sins three times annually.[6] The famous decree of 1215 which obliged every Christian to confess and receive communion at least once a year, then, only established a minimum obligation for all Christians.

Already at an early stage private confession was linked with the seven or eight chief vices. Several French synods of the early ninth century decreed that priests who hear confession should know the chief vices and instruct their penitents in them.[7] It may very well be that this connection of vices and institutionalized confession was responsible for the widening of the concept *acedia* that we noticed in Chapter II. In any case, this connection must have been the main impulse to the development of more and more detailed literary treatments of the individual vices, including *acedia.* For the priest hearing shrift needed a clear guide which enumerated the common moral faults of religious and laymen in an orderly, systematic fashion and which would help him determine the gravity of a particular sin and hence the measure of penance he was to impose. Likewise, educated laymen would eventually request a guide outlining the chief sins in more or less detail, which they could consult in making their examination of conscience before going to confession. Such guides could be, and were, organized on different principles: the Ten Commandments, the seven chief vices, the seven chief virtues, the five senses, and so forth; but beyond any doubt the prevailing scheme was that of the seven vices or "deadly sins," as they now came to be called.[8]

The confessional literature of the Middle Ages which thus grew and reflected various theological and social changes began with the *libri poenitentiales.*[9] These originated in Ireland and England during the sixth and seventh centuries and from there spread to the Continent, apparently carried by Irish and Anglo-Saxon missionaries, such as St. Columban and others. *Libri poenitentiales* are collections of canons that determine a fixed amount of penance ("pénitence tarifée") for certain specified sins, an amount which may vary according to the state of the penitent. The purpose of such fixed penances, however, is not only to give a penalty (in the form of fasting mostly, but also of prayer, sexual abstinence, discipline, and the like) for a spiritual offense, but also to furnish medicine for spiritual diseases or wounds. The latter are the chief vices, and many of the extant penitentials at least mention the series of *vitia capitalia,* following either the Cassianic or the Gregorian list.[10] Where *acedia* appears, the penitentials often specify and chastise three particular aspects: idleness, somnolence, and instability. Thus, the *Penitential of Cummean,* which was composed in

Ireland or Scotland probably during the second half of the seventh century, declares:

Of Languor (*accidia*)

1. The idler shall be taxed with an extraordinary work, and the slothful (*somnolentus*) with a lengthened [?] vigil; that is, he shall be occupied with three or [seven?] psalms.
2. Any wandering and unstable man shall be healed by permanent residence in one place and by application to work. (Bieler, p. 121)

This canon was repeated in expanded form by later penitentials.[11]

For various reasons, among them especially the reform movement to unify and centralize the Church, the eleventh century witnessed an important change in the whole conception of these handbooks for confessors. Now the determination of the amount of penance came to be left to the discrimination of the individual priest, whereas the handbook instead tried to give the principles for the administration of penance and for the judgment of particular cases. Such principles were eventually divided between two different disciplines, theology and canon law. The theologian would clarify such questions as what constitutes sin, the necessity of confession, the power of priests to absolve, and so forth, whereas the canonist was responsible for knowing the ecclesiastical legislation related to moral behavior (especially concerning marriage, holy orders, excommunication, and the like) and applying it to specific cases. This division is, of course, somewhat artificial, but it must be noted that from the eleventh century on canon law had a very profound influence on the theory and practice of penance.[12]

The new orientation led to a more "casuistic" approach in penitential handbooks, that is, to a greater attention to individual faults the confessor was likely to meet. Hence arose the practice of discussing "how the confessor should interrogate his penitent," and the author of a manual would then give a detailed questionnaire for each chief sin. The earliest *summae confessorum* or *de poenitentia*[13]—those by Burchard of Worms, Ivo of Chartres, and Bartholomew of Exeter—merely repeat the decree that the confessor should instruct his penitent in the seven vices, and quote Gregory's list of vices (with *tristitia*) and their "daughters."[14] But at the beginning of the thirteenth century, several penitentials call the respective vice *acedia* and discuss it at greater length, in one form or another.

A good illustration of the new trend is the *Poenitentiale* by Thomas of Chabham, master of theology at Paris and upon his return to England vice-dean at the Cathedral of Salisbury (1214-1230).[15] The purpose of the work is announced in the very beginning: "We shall pass over the subtle theoretical questions concerning penance and instead pursue with great diligence what practical knowledge and behavior is necessary to priests in hearing confessions and in imposing penances."[16] After a quick consideration of the nature of penance, the treatise deals with the subject matter of "what is to be heard in confession, from which the penitent is to be healed and cured, because all confession is medicinal." The subject matter are the seven *criminalia peccata* with their circumstances and a number of "irregularities."[17] In this second part of the treatise, Thomas lists the chief vices in their Gregorian scheme but adds that *tristitia* is also called "*accidia*." He goes on to show that the seven agree with the Ten Commandments and correlates them with the seven petitions, gifts of the Holy Ghost, virtues, and blessings.[18]

The vices, or rather "criminal sins," are discussed a second time in Part VI, which is the longest section and occupies almost half of the treatise. The confessor is once more urged to name the sins to the penitent, because many people do not know all of them. This is especially true of the spiritual sins: "Few people confess their *spiritualia peccata.* For hardly anyone accuses himself of envy, wrath, avarice, *accidia,* or pride. Many have never learned or heard what *accidia* is, and yet they have often sinned by it. . . . Concerning *accidia* the penitent must be given to understand that to be lazy in God's service and to be affected with disgust while doing good works is a mortal sin."[19] Then all seven sins are explained at length, and "*accidia*" once more appears as the sin of serving God with loathing and disgust, "which often springs from laziness and negligence."

Similar instructions on how to hear confession, including a discussion of the chief vices, occur in other penitentials of the same period, such as those by William de Montibus[20] and Robert of Flamborough,[21] as well as in the synodalia and decrees issued by various bishops, such as Alexander Stavensby (bishop of Coventry, 1224-1237), Robert Grosseteste (bishop of Lincoln, 1239?), John Peckham (archbishop of Canterbury, Council at Lambeth, 1281), and Peter Quivil (bishop of Exeter, 1287).[22] The stimulus sent forth by such official decrees led to the composition of a vast number of shorter or longer treatises called *tractatus de poenitentia* or *de confessione* or *modus confitendi,* and so on, which are mostly anonymous and quite repetitious in the way they deal with *acedia.* Much of the canonical material related to confession and penance was eventually collected and systematized in bulky *summae de poenitentia* or *de casibus.* But these later works offer nothing for the "popular image" of *acedia.* The authoritative *Summa casuum conscientiae* by St. Raymund of Pennaforte, for example, only enumerates Gregory's seven "crimina capitalia" with their offspring.[23] Similar works of the fourteenth and fifteenth centuries content themselves with short summaries of what St. Thomas had written about *acedia* in the *Summa theologiae.*[24] For more detailed discussions of the vices we shall have to look elsewhere.

The new orientation in confession and penance illustrated by Thomas of Chabham was only one impact the reform movement had on the history of *acedia* during the early thirteenth century. The other impact came from the urgings of pope and bishops to give the people more regular and systematic instruction in the basic matters of faith and morals.[25] Here again, the nature of the movement and its relevance for *acedia* can best be demonstrated by attention to an early representative treatise, the *Summa brevis* attributed to Richard Wethershed, chancellor of Lincoln (*ca.* 1220-1229).[26]

The work is addressed to priests and purposes to instruct them in the subjects they are to preach to their flocks:

> Mostly you should preach what belongs to faith and morals, namely: the Creed with its twelve articles of faith; the Lord's Prayer with its seven petitions; the gifts of God, in general and in particular . . . ; also the four cardinal virtues . . . and the theological ones; and especially you must preach the seven capital vices. . . . Likewise you should make known the seven sacraments . . . , the two commandments of charity . . . , the ten commandments. . . . And you must preach what the reward of the just in heaven will be, both in body and in soul. And what pains the damned have in hell.[27]

These subjects are then dealt with in the given order, though not too exhaustively. Richard was obviously intent on giving his students a systematized survey of the essentials of Christian religion as the bare bones for their future work in the parishes. To make things easier to memorize, he summed up the main points in terse hexameters, of which one example must be given:

Accidie causas necnon exempla tibi dent:
Spes dilata, labor, dolor ingens, morsque minata—
Sponse, Tobyas, dormitant, Petrus, Elyas.

(fol. 229r)

Which means: *Acedia* may come from one of four causes: delay of the fulfillment of one's hopes, great physical hardship and weariness, immense grief, and the threat of death. These four causes are typified in the biblical figures of the Foolish Virgins (Matt. 25:1ff.), Tobias (who fell asleep, worn out from burying the dead, and lost his sight; Tob. 2:10ff.), the Apostle Peter (probably when he fell asleep in Gethsemane, grieved at the nearing death of his Master; Matt. 26:36ff.), and Elias (falling asleep under a juniper tree and desiring death when he was persecuted; III Kings 19:1ff.).

Another mnemotechnic device employed by Richard Wethershed is more important than his "poetry" and appeared constantly in later works of the same kind. He related each capital vice to a petition of the Pater Noster, a gift of the Holy Ghost, a main virtue, and a blessing from the Sermon on the Mount. *Acedia* thus corresponds with the prayer for daily bread, the gift and the virtue of fortitude, and the blessing of those that hunger and thirst for righteousness.[28] In the words of a later Middle English treatise: "*Panem nostrum quotidianum da nobis hodie.* In þis askynge we prayeþ of þe holy goost þe ȝifte of strengþe þat putteþ awey þe synne of sleuthe and settiþ in þat stede þe vertu of prowes, þat lediþ a man to þe blessidhede of hunger and þirst of rightwisnes and to þe mede þat longeþ þerto, þat is gostliche ful of endeles ioye and likynge."[29] To connect various septenaries in this fashion had come into vogue with Hugh of St. Victor,[30] and although some speculative theologians looked at it rather critically,[31] it remained a favorite device in popular teaching to the end of the Middle Ages. The individual correspondences as Hugh had established them, too, remained authoritative, with only very few exceptions.[32]

Comprehensive treatments of the basic elements of Christian religion, as we had seen them outlined and surveyed in Richard Wethershed's *Summa brevis,* soon multiplied in the thirteenth, fourteenth, and fifteenth centuries, from the *Summula* of Peter Quivil, bishop of Exeter (*ca.* 1287),[33] and the very widespread *Summa rudium* (beginning of the fourteenth century) to John de Burgo's *Pupilla oculi* (1385), written "for the use of simple priests" who could not afford many expensive and more complicated books. Eventually works of this scope and purpose were also written in

English, such as John Mirk's *Instructions for Parish Priests* (*ca.* 1450) and other works to be mentioned presently.

Such manuals for priests, which for lack of a better name I shall call "catechetical handbooks," are not always distinguishable from handbooks of confessional instruction, because confessors were normally urged to instruct their penitents also in the Ten Commandments, the articles of faith, the main virtues, the works of mercy, and so on, with the result that books on "how to hear confession" often include expositions and long sections of questions concerning the Creed and so forth.[34] On the other hand, catechetical handbooks of wider scope frequently have an explicit orientation toward confession, such as the Anglo-Norman *Manuel des Péchés* by William of Wadington, abbreviated and Englished in 1303 by Robert Mannyng as *Handlyng Synne.*[35] Similarly, the *Ayenbite of Inwyt* states in its "Fore-speech" that "this book is written for Englishmen, so that they may know how to confess and make themselves clean of sin in this life" (p. 5). The *Ayenbite* (1340) is a translation of a highly influential French handbook, the *Somme le Roi* by Frère Lorens (1279). The genesis of the latter work and its relation with the very similar *Mireour du monde,* both extant in various redactions, still await satisfactory elucidation.[36] In any case, one or the other French work was translated or adapted into English in various forms and at different times, where they appear as the *Ayenbite, The Book of Vices and Virtues* (fourteenth century), and Caxton's *Royal Book* (1484);[37] such works as *Jacob's Well* (*ca.* 1440), William Nassyngton's *Speculum vitae,* and the prose *Mirror to Lewed Men,* all depend closely on them.

These catechetical handbooks, as well as the instructions on confession, furnish a good deal of material on the popular image of *acedia.* But we must add to them yet another class of works which are more specifically concerned with the vices. These are handbooks and veritable encyclopedias for preachers and confessors, compiling masses of religious and moral knowledge for ready use in sermon and confessional instruction. The first of them—in time and in importance—is the *Summa de vitiis et virtutibus* by the Dominican William Peraldus or Guillaume Peyraut, written before 1250, a book which demonstrably had an enormous influence on practically all subsequent popular literature on the vices, although the work is only vaguely known today.[38]

The first part of the *Summa* (cf. Appendix B) discusses each of the seven capital vices (plus sins of the tongue) at great length.

Section V, "De accidia," in the edition of 1587, comprises twenty-seven chapters, some of them of considerable length. Peraldus discusses three general topics: Reasons for avoiding this vice (Part I, chaps. 1-4); the species of *acedia* (Part II, chaps. 1-17); and remedies (Part III; a fourth part deals with indiscreet fervor, see below). Reasons for detesting *acedia* are provided, first, by a number of examples from nature which teach man to be active and zealous in the service of God.[39] Inanimate things (the sun), plants, animals (the ant), and men—bad as well as good—all provide such examples, and in each case Peraldus can strengthen the example of nature with authoritative passages from Scriptures or the Fathers. Next, Scripture itself "admonishes to work and dissuades from indolence and laziness." A battery of fourteen passages is arranged to make this point. Third, Peraldus affirms that it will be easier to shun *acedia* when one learns "how much this sin displeases God, pleases the Devil, and harms man." Again, Scripture is quoted to demonstrate that God abhors the lukewarm (Rev. 3:15-16) and loves a fervent sinner more than ninety-nine *justi accidiosi* (cf. Luke 15:7). Similar quotations show (indirectly) that this vice provides the Fiend "quiet shelter" (*hospitium quietis*). The harm to which it can bring a man is threefold: it inflicts in him evils of punishment (poverty, vileness, and affliction or pain) and of guilt, and deprives him of all sorts of goods. The latter include man's very faculty to work as well as natural gifts, grace, and heavenly glory. Concerning the loss of natural gifts, Peraldus launches into a lengthy presentation of eight reasons for not wasting time. Then, this initial section, on detesting *acedia,* closes with six more reasons for shunning the vice.

In the second section Peraldus indicates and discusses sixteen "vices belonging to *accidia,*" followed by a final chapter on monastic *acedia.*[40] This list of species of the vice became very important in the further development of the progeny, which will be examined later. Finally, the third section indicates rather briefly the remedies for *acedia,* to which is added a last section "De indiscreto fervore," which is very interesting from a theological point of view insofar as it deals with the vice which consists in an excess of the virtue to which *acedia* is opposed: exaggerated zeal. In other words, Peraldus here followed the Aristotelian conception that a virtue is flanked by two vices. In our case, fortitude is the golden mean between its deficiency, *acedia,* and its superabundance, "indiscreet fervor."[41]

This brief outline of Peraldus' section on *acedia* makes it more than sufficiently clear that in this thirteenth-century Dominican we find a trained Scholastic theologian setting forth the logical and rhetorical tools to assist preachers and confessors in their labors of instructing Christians at large against the chief sins. The entire treatise presents, in highly logical order, the arguments to persuade man to the good life, which is conceived of as a struggle against the vices in order to attain the virtues.

Peraldus' three major concerns: reasons for shunning the vice, specific vices that spring from it, and remedies for it, occur again and again in the literature written for similar purposes. The Franciscan theologian John of Wales, for example, wrote a treatise called *Moniloquium* in the second half of the thirteenth century,[42] in which he purports to teach the "younger preachers" of his order about "vices and virtues, punishment and glory," the four topics that St. Francis had enjoined his brethren to preach "for the edification and usefulness of the people."[43] The twelve chapters devoted to *acedia* deal with the definition of the vice (chap. 1), its causes (chap. 2), its remedies (chap. 11), its evil effects (the Gregorian progeny, chap. 12), and a variety of subjects which show how reprehensible the vice is, how much harm it does, why it should be avoided, and so forth (chaps. 3-10). In contrast to Peraldus, John of Wales has a more "Scholastic" and "humanistic" bent of mind, in the sense that he enumerates a variety of definitions, allows for a "natural cause" of the vice (the cold and moist disposition), and quotes "pagan" authors more frequently (Seneca especially, but also, for example, Ovid, Lucan, Valerius, Junius). But the basic concern of the two authors is the same.

Another work of similar orientation is the fifteenth-century *Destructorium vitiorum* by Alexander Carpentarius.[44] Again, its twenty-two chapters devoted to *acedia* deal with the particular concerns a preacher or confessor would have in studying the vice: its nature (chap. 1), examples which teach that *acedia* must be shunned (chap. 2, a condensation of the first four chapters in Peraldus, whom Alexander acknowledges as "Parisiensis"), the species of the vice (chaps. 3-21), and its remedies. The most interesting aspect of this work from our point of view is that Alexander combines the teaching of Thomas Aquinas with that of Peraldus. This becomes a quite original task where he discusses the offspring. Alexander follows Thomas in explaining the Gregorian progeny and its rationale, but then adds that "to these six species of *accidia* may be reduced many other species which Parisiensis in his *Summa de viciis* . . . mentions, as with the grace of God will become clear *infra*" (fol. 182r). Which it does, more or less. It should be noted that despite the authority Peraldus holds for Alexander, the latter often defines the species and arranges the material in his own way.

Finally, the theological and rhetorical commonplaces on the vices (and other subjects) also appear in religious encyclopedias. The richest source of this type for *acedia* is the *Speculum morale*, attributed to Vincent of Beauvais (d. 1264) but in fact written only in the first quarter of the fourteenth century.[45] The section on *acedia*, which in the quarto edition of 1624 occupies twenty-four pages, comprises material from various sources, including St. Thomas and William Peraldus. In order to facilitate consultation, other writers arranged the traditional material in alphabetical order, creating such encyclopedic handbooks as *Omnebonum* (1350-1360),[46] John of Mirfield's *Florarium Bartholomaei* (end of fourteenth century),[47] and John Bromyard's *Summa praedicantium* (middle of fourteenth century).[48] The last-mentioned work treats *acedia* in six articles, in which one easily recognizes the "basic concerns." The remedies this time are omitted; instead, after short articles on the nature of the vice and its "daughters," where Bromyard bows to the authority of Thomas but arranges things his own way (especially the progeny, which combines rather than identifies the Gregorian with the Cassianic series), Bromyard devotes four articles to the bad effects of the vice and its reprehensibility.

In the three groups of religious-didactic literature—confessional instructions, catechetical handbooks, and handbooks for preachers—the popular image of *acedia* appears in essentially two different forms, which to some extent, though not strictly, coincide with different types of literature. Catechetical handbooks and manuals for preachers usually list a number of "species" of the sin, such as idleness, pusillanimity, despair, and the like, which are each defined and discussed in more or less detail. In contrast, works of confessional instruction usually enumerate particular faults for which *acedia* is responsible. As a result, we encounter on the one hand an abstract, rational scheme of "branches" of *acedia* and on the other a picture of the slothful man, which sometimes reads like a Theophrastian character. Each of these forms of treatment must now be examined in detail.[49]

The establishment of "branches" or "daughters" of each capital vice goes back at least as far as Cassian's *Collationes,* where *acedia* was said to give birth to eight other vices. Gregory adopted the idea and listed a progeny of six vices for *tristitia,* and the two schemes rivaled each other for several centuries until the Schoolmen managed to harmonize the two series. It is basically the Gregorian scheme which was preserved in St. Thomas' analysis, and this is true also of his immediate predecessors as well as of many later authors of theological *summae* and of handbooks for preachers and confessors.[50] But the great and continuing authority of St. Gregory did not prevent medieval theologians from giving *acedia* almost any number of "daughters." We have seen that the early *libri poenitentiales* concentrated on three (Cassianic) species of *acedia.* In later works on the vice—before as well as after 1200—one can find progenies of five, seven, eight, ten, and twelve members. Another illustration of the relative freedom with regard to this particular tradition appears in the fact that, in translating or adapting a Latin source, the adaptors often varied the offspring considerably. St. Edmund's *Speculum ecclesiae,* for example, gives six daughters of "tristitia vel accidia"—essentially the Gregorian offspring, although some names have changed. In vernacular versions of this work I have found four, five, six, and seven "daughters."[51]

The new impetus in the religious life around 1200 brought some innovations in this matter, too. The treatise *De virtutibus et de vitiis et de donis Spiritus Sancti* by Alanus of Lille presents an entirely new offspring of eight members, for which no source has been found so far.[52] The eight "species" of *acedia* are: *Desidia, pigritia, pusillanimitas, negligentia, inprovidentia, incircumspectio, tepiditas, ignavia.* The vices are defined in quite abstract terms. *Incircumspectio,* for example, "is a vice of the mind through which one fails to discern the opposition between vices with sufficient caution, so that, for example, one avoids greed in such measure that he falls into prodigality."[53] Alanus' progeny never became very popular, but it can be found in some penitentials of the thirteenth century.[54]

Another innovation in the offspring of *acedia,* and a much more successful one, was made by Peraldus, who established sixteen "vices belonging to *accidia*": *Tepiditas, mollities, somnolentia, otiositas, dilatio, tarditas, negligentia, inconsummatio, remissio, dissolutio, incuria, ignavia, indevotio, tristitia in divino servitio, taedium vitae, desperatio.* A few of these terms have counterparts in the progenies of Cassian, Gregory, and Alanus, but many more appear here for the first time. As the background of Peraldus' *Summa de vitiis* is completely unstudied, we know nothing about his immediate sources. I venture to suggest, however, that Peraldus himself must be credited with selecting and arranging this progeny. The most likely sources from which he may have selected such aspects of *acedia* are extensive formulas of confession, in which an imaginative penitent accuses himself of all possible sins and faults by simply mentioning a string of abstract nouns. A good example is the *Wessobrunner Beichte* of the eleventh century: "I have sinned in sloth, in tardiness, in softness, in lack of constancy, in ignorance, in imprudence . . . [twenty-four faults in all]."[55]

Whatever its sources, Peraldus' progeny was copied in later treatises[56] and soon adapted and expanded in vernacular handbooks. Both the *Mireour du monde* and Frère Lorens' *Somme le Roi* increased the offspring of *acedia* to eighteen, divided the branches into three groups, and arranged them in an order of increasing gravity. The various Middle English treatises which depend upon the two French works, mentioned earlier, copy or imitate this progeny closely. In all of them, *acedia* is therefore treated in a rather abstract way, with its branches listed and briefly defined. As illustration of this form of popular teaching I shall present the eighteen branches as they appear in *The Book of Vices and Virtues* (*BVV*), and add variations in name or nature of the respective branch as found in Peraldus (P), *Mireour* (*M*), *Somme le Roi* (*S*), *Ayenbite of Inwyt* (*A*), *Jacob's Well* (*JW*), and *The Desert of Religion* (*DR*).[57]

"Slewthe" is, first, defined as, "a werynesse of goode deedes" (p. 26). It causes man to have an evil beginning, a worse "amending," and "an altherworst endyng." These three parts comprise the following vices:

A. Evil beginning.

1. *Tendernesse.* "As whan a man loueþ litle and slakly oure lord, þat he scholde loue brennyngly; and þer-of comeþ þat he is feble and wery and tendre to do any god" (p. 26). This vice is *tepiditas* (P), *tevete* (*M*), *petit amour* (*S*); *A* has no special name for it (loving God "lite and lheucliche," i.e., little and tepidly) ; *JW* calls it "slugnesse," and *DR*, "dasynes of hert."
2. *Tenterhed* or *nessched of herte.* Softness, exaggerated regard

for the comfort of the flesh; *mollicies* (P). *A* calls it "tyene [i.e., vexation] of herte" and (mistakenly) "arȝnesse." *JW* and *DR* consider it as tenderness of the flesh.

3. *Ydelnesse.* Being unoccupied or engaged in vain things; *ociositas* (P), *oiseuse* (*S, M*).
4. *Heuynesse.* This branch of sloth causes man to desire nothing but to lie, rest, and sleep; he may be willing to pursue some worldly activity, but when he is called to serve God, he wants to sleep. If he does pray, it is without devotion and savor. *Pesanteure* (*M*), *pesantume* (*S*); "heuynesse of herte" (*JW, DR*). It corresponds to *somnolentia* (P).
5. *Schrewednesse.* Failure to rouse oneself to repent or call upon God for help when one has fallen into sin or temptation. *Mauvaistie* (*M, S*); "wyckednesse" (*A*), "lythernes of hert" (*JW, DR*). It corresponds to *ignavia* (P).
6. *Pusillanymyte, vnboldenesse.* Fear to begin good work, cowardice in spiritual deeds. This is like being scared by one's dreams and like a child's fear of a snail or of hissing geese (*JW*). *Pusillanimite* (*M, S*); "litol wyl" (*A*), "arwenesse" (*JW, DR*).

B. Branches of sloth which hinder amendment of a bad life.

1. *Vntrewþe.* Having good intentions, but deferring their realization. *Deleaute* (*S*). However: *Delaiant* (*M*), "tarying" (*JW, DR*), the delay in turning to God, in serving Him, which corresponds to *dilatio* or *tarditas* (P).
2. *Rechelesschep.* The opposite to busy, diligent, and attentive action; spiritual negligence. *Negligentia* (P); *nonchalant* (*M*), *negligence* (*S, JW*). *A* here *speaks* of "sleuþe."
3. *Forȝetfulnesse.* Forgetfulness especially in confession, which of course is a grave spiritual danger. *Oubliance* (*M, S*); "forgetyng" (*A, JW, DR*).
4. "Slewþe þat comeþ for defaute of herte and of an yuel wone." This is plain laziness in spiritual works. *Peresche* (*M*), *parece* (*S*); in Middle English variously called "sleuth" (*JW*) and "slawness" (*DR*); *A* calls it "slacnesse" and combines under it branches 4 and 5.
5. *Yuel discrecion, fooly brennyng.* Exaggerated and unwise religious zeal, which can lead to languor and sickness that deprive man of all desire to do good. *Fole ferveur* (*S*). This aspect of sloth is often dealt with by mystical writers.—A

different tradition, represented by *M, JW,* and *DR,* gives as this branch "lacches," which seems to be an increasing laxness in fulfilling religious duties, so that one gradually withdraws further and further from God. See next branch.

6. *Werynesse. BVV* considers this an increasing slackness which leads man to be recreant. *Lachete* (S); "werihede" (*A*). This apparently corresponds to the fifth branch of *M, JW,* and *DR.* These works have here, as their sixth branch, "faylyng," i.e., slackness in service, both religious and secular; *defaillance* (*M*).

C. Branches of sloth that bring man to an evil end.

1. *Vnbuxumnesse.* Disobedience in religious matters, as in performing the penance or other work that has been imposed. *Inobedience* (*M,S*).
2. *Vnsuffraunce, for inpacience.* Unwillingness to suffer reproof, to hear about one's sins, or to accept spiritual advice. *Impacience* (*M, S*); "untholemode" (*DR*).
3. *Grucchynge.* Anger and murmuring at being reproved. *Murmure* (*M, S*).
4. *Anger* and *sorwe.* "So moche þis anger ouergoþ hym, þat what þat euere any good man seiþ hym, or he doþ hym, and al þat euere he hereþ or seeþ, al it teeneþ hym; and þus he falleþ in sorwe" (p. 29). This seems to be spiritual touchiness or oversensitivity; the person who suffers from it becomes inwardly annoyed at anything that goes against his will and, in consequence, falls into dejection (following branch). Different names exist for this vice: *Tristitia* (P), *tristesce* (*M, S*); "zorȝe," leading to "tyene to libbe" (*A*); "heuynes" (*JW*); "dreryness" (*DR*).
5. Self-hatred and desire for death. This dejection follows upon sorrow (preceding branch). It may come from mourning out of measure and includes weariness of life and despondency. *Taedium vitae* (P); langueur (*M*), *annuie de vivre* (*S*); "langure" (*JW, DR*).
6. *Wanhope.* Despair of God's mercy, often leading to suicide. *Desperatio* (P); *desesperance* (*M, S*).

The preceding scheme of branches forms the apogee in the evolution of the progeny of sloth. Not only are the individual vices symmetrically arranged into three large groups, but they follow each other in an order of increasing gravity. This may not be very clear in each individual case, but it is unmistakable in the third section where one vice genetically leads to another and where the slothful soul sinks from religious disobedience to despair and to temporal and eternal death. Such progenies were further developed in the fifteenth century but lost structural tightness and symmetry. As an example of a late medieval progeny of sloth, *The Kalender of Shepherds* might be mentioned. Here the author presents a somewhat amorphous Tree of Vices on which sloth includes seventeen branches with 154 smaller twigs![58]

The second way in which confessional and other handbooks deal with the sin of sloth is by enumerating specific faults for which *acedia* is responsible. This was done in various distinct forms, such as (*a*) questionnaires, (*b*) confessional formulas, and (*c*) descriptions of the effects of the vice.

(*a*) Questionnaires on *acedia* began to appear in the new penitentials and confessional instructions of the early thirteenth century and remained in use to the end of the Middle Ages. Most often found in English manuscripts and treatises is a formula which is commonly ascribed to Robert Grosseteste. It begins with these questions: "[the penitent is to be asked] whether he has neglected to learn the Creed or the Lord's Prayer or to teach them to his spiritual children. Whether he has neglected to pray in due time and place, or to go to church in due time, or has hindered others from going there. Whether he has despised listening to the preacher's word."[59] This formula appears in various redactions and is sometimes followed by a series of sins of sloth committed by heart, mouth, deed, and omission.[60] A fairly long version of it as used by John de Burgo can be found reproduced here in Appendix C. Works in Middle English also made use of this questionnaire, notably John Mirk's *Instructions for Parish Priests*.[61]

(*b*) Confessional formulas ("I have sinned in . . .") were organized on the scheme of the capital vices long before 1200, although the full development of particular faults of each vice was, apparently, again a result of the later missionary movement in the Church. An Anglo-Saxon formula of rather undeveloped shortness appears in several manuscripts and has these details on *acedia*: "I have often sinned through sloth [*asolcennysse*] when I was unwilling to do good or to go to God's house or to take courage to carry out any good work; but I lived my life in sloth for a long time, without good works and good worship."[62] The detailed faults were multiplied in later Middle English formulas[63] until they swelled the sin of sloth to fairly all-inclusive proportions in *The Clensyng of Mannes Sowle* of the late fourteenth century.[64] Also, the questionnaire by Grosseteste was eventually transformed into a confessional formula and appears to be the basis of the versified "Boke of Penance" which is added to the *Cursor mundi* in one manuscript version.[65] The eighteen branches of sloth from the *Somme le Roi*, too, were used in an occasional formula of confession.[66]

(*c*) Descriptions of the effects of sloth cannot so easily be classified, but their common characteristic is to state that *acedia* makes a man grow weary in God's service, unwilling to get up in the morning, fall asleep in church, and so on. Such descriptions occur from the time of Evagrius and his companions on. Medieval handbooks on the sins usually define *acedia* briefly and then go on to specify its effects in precisely this form. Among the innumerable descriptions of this type, in Latin and in the vernacular, the Middle English discussions in *Handlyng Synne* and in the already-mentioned addition to *Cursor mundi* (but in a passage different from that referred to under [*b*])[67] are especially interesting for their wealth of detail.

From these many sources the sin of sloth emerges with the following characteristics.[68] The largest number of defaults concern the two main obligatory religious practices of medieval Christianity: attending church services on Sunday and holy days,[69] and receiving the sacrament of penance. The slothful person is unwilling to go to church. When the bell for matins rings, he decides to stay in bed till later, while a fiend called "Terlyncel" persuades him that going to mass alone is enough.[70] Sometimes the slothful will not go to church altogether because the weather is either too hot or too cold. If they go at all, they are frequently late. Once in church, the slothful hardly know how to occupy their minds fittingly. They are ignorant of the elementary prayers, the Pater Noster and the Creed, and thus "kan nat wurschep Goddys name" (*Handlyng Synne*, l. 4242). The sermon bores them stiff, they think it lasts a hundred years, and they would rather hear the dinner bell than the preaching friar. If the service is drawn out, they become greatly irritated. Otherwise, the slothful often fall asleep in church. This type of sinful slumber was always a very dominant aspect of the traditional notion of *acedia* and occasioned many alarming *exempla*. A worse offense than sleeping, however, is to disturb the service by talking, thus hindering others in their worship. The slothful "jangle" and engage in "harlotry" (idle talk). This must have been a very common occurrence in medieval churches, to judge by the various *exempla* told against it in vernacular documents.

Sloth can manifest itself in a subtler form, too, when it deprives man of spiritual comfort so that he may perform his religious duties but experience no devotion. As a result, priests and laymen pray or perform divine services hastily and omit syllables or entire words. Their lack of devotion and inner joy shows in their sad, cheerless mien.[71] Needless to say, however undevout and negligent a slothful man may be about his religious obligations, he does not lack zeal when it comes to deeds of "ydelnesse." Here he is eager and never gets bored. Instead of properly serving God on Sunday, the slothful person spends his time playing chess or "at the tables." But whether on Sunday or at any other time, too great an attachment to "idle deeds" is a result of sloth and always sinful. *Jacob's Well* gives a long list of games, sports, and entertainments—discussed under the branch "ydelnesse"—which endanger the soul if indulged in to an excess. The particular danger lurking in such occupations is that idleness (*otium*, in the sense of not being occupied with profitable, serious activities) is "enemy to cristen man saule, stepmodire and stamerynge agaynes gude thewes, and witter-wyssynge and waye till alkyn vices";[72] or more poetically, "the ministre and the norice unto vices"[73] who opens the gate to all evil.

After the Sunday obligation, the sacrament of penance is the other major occasion for faults of sloth. The vice causes man to delay shrift till Lent, then till the end of Lent, and finally till the hour of death, which of course is trusting the untrustworthy. At the bottom of such perilous delay lies vain trust in long life or God's mercy (presumption),[74] closely allied with its opposite, despair of God's mercy (wanhope)—themes which were dramatically exploited in allegorical poems and morality plays.

Sloth can make the penitent forget part of his sins and thus produce an incomplete confession. In addition, the slothful are often disobedient to their confessor and do not perform the penance they received or do penance at their own discretion.[75] More widespread, however, is sloth in works of penance in general. This sin is characterized by softness, by too much regard for bodily comfort and ease, by unwillingness to practice mortification. Thus, the slothful person likes to wear soft clothes next to his skin, to take frequent baths, to comb himself often.[76] He loathes to go barefoot, to wear the rough side of clothes on his body, to fast and abstain from dainty food and drink, to kneel on the stone floor for prayers, to suffer cold on hands or feet, and to discipline himself. *Jacob's Well* accuses especially life at courts of such softness. A different form of the same fault is spiritual cowardice: Slothful men will not undertake a pilgrimage because they dread possible sickness on the way; or they may want to give alms, but then reflect that the world is hard and they may easily become poor themselves.

To faults regarding the Sunday observance and the sacrament of penance, our sources add other instances of spiritual negligence. The slothful often lack gratitude for the gifts of God or man. They are negligent in keeping the Church's commandments of fasting and tithing[77] and in fulfilling their vows. Sometimes they are even remiss in matters of faith and practice witchcraft, sorcery, and "charming" (*Cursor*, ll. 28310-11). More important, they neglect to perform the works of bodily and spiritual mercy, such as feeding and clothing the poor and praying for the dead.[78] The *Cursor* adds to these the lack of spiritual zeal for the dying and for unbaptized children (ll. 28326-31).

Another grave aspect of sloth is failure to guard one's mind:

> Quen idel thoght me come and vain
> Wit will i stode þam noght again,
> Bot oft i lete þam on me rene
> To þai me drogh to dede on sine.
> (*Cursor*, ll. 28332-35)

"Keeping one's heart" is particularly difficult, though vital, during prayer; it is an inner disposition especially exposed to attacks from sloth among the religious.[79] Besides being unstable in mind, the slothful fail to control their evil thoughts, such as wrong suspicions and false judgments of others.

The sin also hinders men from fulfilling their professional duties well. It causes priests to speed up and abbreviate their prayers and mass, as we have already observed in discussing faults against the Sunday observance. In addition, it makes them neglect their pastoral duties: "I have been very remiss in the cure of souls. As pastor, I have been negligent in teaching, correcting, and admonishing my parishioners. I have not helped them sufficiently in temporal matters. I have administered spiritual matters to them negligently and have prayed less for them than I ought to."[80] The same text adds various other faults of priests concerned with the sacramental system: singing mass in deadly sin, receiving holy orders "unshriven," and performing religious functions without devotion.

The head of a family may similarly fall into slothful behavior and fail to govern his subjects rightly. It is sloth when parents neglect to chastise unruly children, to teach children and god-children the Lord's Prayer and the Creed, and to care for infants properly. The slothful husband takes insufficient care of his household; he is a bad "leader" of his wife and servants and fails to guide and help with good counsel (*Cursor*, ll. 28264-69). Mirk, for example, has the confessor ask his penitent,

> Hast þow slowe and feynt I-be
> To helpe þy wyf and þy meyne
> Of such as þey hade nede to?
>
> (ll. 1195-97)

Even the absence of love between husband and wife can be due to sloth (*Jacob's Well*, p. 106). Of course, neglect of family duties is not restricted to the husband. The wife also sins when a child dies in her womb through "recheless gouernauns" (*Jacob's Well*, p. 109); and servants are slothful when they do not keep their "covenant" or are not "scharpe and busy" in their work (Mirk, *Instructions*, ll. 1200-1204).

Finally, sloth interferes with the right fulfilment of man's duties towards his neighbors. Many of the faults mentioned can have wider repercussions by providing a bad example to one's "evenchristen" or by directly hindering them from fulfilling their duties. More specifically, the slothful are inattentive to their neighbors' needs or harm them by careless actions. The *Ancrene Riwle* and other treatises mention several faults of this type, such as failing to forewarn other people of an impending evil or loss, or treating carelessly objects that have been lent or committed to one's care (*Ancrene Riwle*, p. 93).

The members of this large and variegated family of sins of sloth are, of course, not all equally grave. They vary in seriousness from attitudes that are not sinful at all to the unpardonable sin against the Holy Ghost, despair. *Jacob's Well* closes its treatment of sloth with a short disquisition on how to judge individual sins. The author distinguishes between, first, mere feelings of dislike that come from man's nature and lessen one's devotion without, however, destroying the love of God or one's neighbor—this is no sin at all; second, lack of desire for, or aversion to, spiritual works, to which some consent is given—this is a venial sin; and third, leaving unsaid or undone what is necessary for the salvation of one's soul or for the salvation of one's neighbor—and this is mortal sin, to which belong despair and suicide.[81]

The essential difference between this "popular image" and the Scholastic concept of *acedia* appears very neatly in one of the canons issued by Alexander Stavensby, bishop of Coventry (1224-1237), where he instructed his clergy on the administration of penance. Alexander wrote: "Quartum peccatum est accidia, que appellatur tedium de bono, quod potest anglice dici ydelnesse in servitio dei."[82] Here a common Scholastic definition of the vice—*taedium de bono*—is rendered in the language of the common folk. The rendering is anything but exact, yet it is absolutely characteristic of what happened to *acedia* when it passed from the lecture room to the confessional.

The shift from a state of mind (*taedium*) to external behavior (*ydelnesse in servitio Dei*) pervades and informs the entire popular image of *acedia,* which emphasizes, not the emotional disorientation of disgust for the divine good, but rather the numerous observable faults which derive from such a state. The *acedia* known to Everyman from the early thirteenth century on can be characterized as neglect in the performance of spiritual duties. As a matter of fact, Alexander Stavensby says, a few sentences after the quoted definition: "This sin may be called negligence in divine works [*negligentia in operibus divinis*]." *Acedia* has become synonymous with spiritual idleness or indolence. Quite in contrast to St. Thomas' view of "aversion against the divine good itself," the essence of this popular form of the sin is weariness, torpor, or plain laziness (*pigritia*)[83] in performing spiritual acts—attitudes which Thomas explicitly rejected when he distinguished *acedia* from other vices. In consequence, the popular image carries a heavy emphasis on the physical and considers *acedia* a bodily vice, a sin of the flesh.[84]

This difference can be discerned already in the names which the vice received in medieval vernacular languages.[85] Bishop Alexander used "idleness in God's service." From the Old English period on a variety of other nouns had been used, such as *asolcennys* (literally, "languor," "sloth," "remissness"),[86] *unlust* ("disinclination," "listlessness"),[87] *sleacmodness* ("slackness of the mind"),[88] and *æmelnes* ("loathing").[89] The Anglicized form *accidie* also appeared occasionally.[90] With the thirteenth century, however, the standard term for the sin became *sloth* (or similar nouns derived from the adjective *slow*),[91] while the former English names virtually disappeared. The changing terminology thus reveals the same shift from mental or spiritual states (listnessness, loathing, slackness of the mind) to qualities of physical behavior (slowness, negligence, idleness). Similar developments took place in other vernacular languages, especially in French and German, where *paresse* (from *pigritia*)[92] and *Trägheit*[93] have become the technical terms for the sin. It is rather remarkable that *acedia* has survived in the active vocabulary of none of the major national languges. Evidently, apart from ecclesiastical Latin, the word *acedia* remained a stranger, a term belonging to the technical vocabulary of clerics. As *Ayenbite* explains: "Sleauþe, þet me clepeþ ine clergie: accidye" (p. 16).

The same emphasis on neglect and idleness regarding spiritual obligations appears in the virtue which popular works often recommend as the antidote to sloth. Owing to the confusion of *acedia* with *tristitia*, the traditional remedy for the vice had been one of two virtues: fortitude or spiritual joy.[94] Either virtue occurs frequently in vernacular literature as the opposite of sloth, with fortitude ("prowesse" or "strength") perhaps being more common because of its place in the traditional septenaries. But besides these two conventional virtues a third one appears as a new antagonist to sloth: *busyness*.[95] It is fairly frequent in Middle English devotional literature and can also be found as a personified figure in allegorical works and medieval drama.[96] Even Chaucer follows this trend: "This firste stok was ful of rightwisnesse, . . . and loved besinesse, Ayeinst the vyce of slouthe, in honestee."[97]

Whether this shift in the view of the sin from *taedium* to idleness and negligence, and of its opposite virtue from spiritual joy or fortitude to busyness, represents a genuine change of the meaning of *acedia*, or merely a shift in emphasis from the psychological cause of the vice to its visible effects, will be further discussed in the final chapter. For the moment, it will suffice to state the obvious: that this shift came as a result of the eminently practical purposes of the literature from which we have extracted the popular image of sloth. Confessional instructions and handbooks for preachers were written to help every Christian recognize every manifestation of sin in his daily actions, to understand and overcome the concrete failures and shortcomings of his moral life. Hence, this literature did not investigate the nature and definition of *acedia* and determine why it should be considered a special vice, a capital vice, and a sin, as the Schoolmen had done, but instead furnished reasons for shunning it by pointing out its harmful effects and, most importantly, listed its numerous manifestations. This practical concern of the literature which grew out of the new missionary movement of the early thirteenth century thus resulted in the proliferation of "branches" and aspects of sloth surveyed above.

The majority of faults springing from *acedia*, as they are specified in questionnaires, confessional formulas, or the descriptions contained in *Handlyng Synne*, *Jacob's Well*, and elsewhere, pertains to *religious* obligations, such as the Sunday observance, the practice of confession, the Ten Commandments, the commandments of the Church, and so forth. Beyond doubt, popular *acedia* was a vice which, first and foremost, led to the neglect of spiritual or religious duties, as can also be clearly seen in the fact that Middle English treatises most commonly qualify the sin as sloth in God's service. Yet the same works include in their discussions of the sin faults that do not concern religious acts or practices in the strict sense. Our portrait of popular sloth listed such "worldly" faults as failure to keep one's oath, to rule the household properly, to love and guide one's wife, to take proper care of babies, to make restitution or return borrowed objects in time,[98] to pay wages promptly, and to serve one's master faithfully. It is not too difficult to relate these to some religious precept, such as the Fourth, Seventh, or Eighth Commandment. Thus, when a treatise on the seven deadly sins says of slothful servants, "Also þe slewful man disseyueth his lord of his catel and þerfor he schal be put out of his herytage of heuene,"[99] this manifestation of sloth is condemned because evidently it violates the Seventh Commandment. In other words, in these cases sloth still means neglect of some religious duty. But the connection with the Ten Commandments is no longer so close in the case of such faults as eating the fruit of other men's hard labor undeservedly,[100] of wasting one's youth in idleness instead of learning a profitable trade (*Handlyng Synne*, ll. 5045-50), of failing to make the proper effort to earn one's bread,[101] or of the entire conception of sloth in the treatise "On the Seven Deadly

Sins," now attributed to Nicholas Hereford (*ca.* 1385).[102] Here the sin is, quite conventionally, first called "slouthe in Gods servise" (p. 142). But in the next sentence Hereford shifts to speaking of "ydelness in servise of God" and then goes on to discuss idleness in the three estates: priests, "gentil men," and laborers (or "comyns"). Sloth therefore seems to mean neglect in the obligations of one's *status* or profession. Evidently, in these passages we find indications that toward the end of the Middle Ages the sin of *acedia* came to include failure in the performance of worldly duties and activities, or in other terms, plain laziness.

For including such "worldly" faults in the sin of *acedia*, the later Middle Ages had a very good theological reason, namely, the notion that, according to Job 5:7, "man is born to work, and the bird, to fly."[103] This verse, and a new theological conception of *labor* or *occupatio*, were frequently included in the longer discussions of *acedia*. From Peraldus on, one of the main reasons why *acedia* is sinful and to be avoided is that the obligation to work forms an essential aspect of man's very nature, implanted by God already before the Fall. The *Speculum morale*, for example, explains:

> God gave the first man a law that he should work, as is said in Gen. 2: "God took man and put him into the Garden of Eden [*in paradiso voluptatis*] to dress it [*ut operaretur*] and to keep it [Gen. 2:15]," that is, in order that work may keep man from falling, or, that by working man may keep Paradise; and as soon as he should stop working through *acedia*, he would lose Paradise. In the same fashion, God gave man a law after his fall, as it were as penance for his first sin, saying, "In toil thou shalt eat of the ground all the days of thy life," and further, "in the sweat of thy face shalt thou eat bread" [Gen. 3:18-19]. This law and this penance is broken by the *acediosi*. (col. 1205)

In late medieval thought, this law of work included physical activity in worldly endeavors and was closely linked to the *status* of medieval society, as is shown by the following extract from a sermon by Thomas Brinton, bishop of Rochester (1373-1389):

> Since man is by nature born to work, the army of Christians, which chiefly consists of three degrees, namely of prelates, religious, and workers, must in hope of the kingdom of God be constantly occupied: either in the works of active life (which are the works of mercy, such as feeding the poor, clothing the naked, visiting the sick and similar things), or in the works of contemplative life (which are praying, keeping vigil, preaching, hearing divine matters, etc.), or in the works of human servi-

> tude (such as digging, plowing, sowing, reaping, and working with one's own hands). In consequence, those miserable idlers who are not usefully occupied in any of these three degrees and hence are unfruitful, deprive themselves by divine justice of the kingdom of God.[104]

Since God has structured human society—or rather, the *ecclesia militans*—in an order of different *status*, each with its own clearly defined duties, failure to fulfil these duties is automatically sinful.

This new appraisal of human or worldly activity, which seems to have come somewhat into the foreground during the fourteenth century,[105] led occasionally to results which look very much like a reversal of earlier positions. A case in point is the word *labor* of the quoted biblical verse. In Gregory the Great's moralization of the Book of Job, *labor* means suffering ("it is quite impossible that man pass through the time of his pilgrimage without sighing") and the sinful enmeshment in transient things of this world.[106] In the later Middle Ages, the term is interpreted as work, as salutary activity of mind and body. The correlated term *quies* underwent a similar change of evaluation, which is amusingly illustrated by the fate that befell an observation made by St. Augustine. In *De civitate Dei* he had written about the Roman worship of gods and goddesses:

> While they offered to all these gods and goddesses solemn and public worship, they should yet have been unwilling to give public acknowledgment to her whom they name Quies because she makes men quiet, but built her temple outside the Colline gate. Whether was this a symptom of an unquiet mind, or rather was it thus intimated that he who should persevere in worshipping that crowd, not, to be sure, of gods, but of demons, could not dwell with quiet; to which the true Physician calls, saying, "Learn of me, for I am meek and lowly of heart, and ye shall find rest unto your souls"?[107]

For St. Augustine, *quies* meant tranquillity, peace of mind. But by the fourteenth century *quies* had become synonymous with laziness, and the Church Father's intention is completely reversed. Peter Berchorius cites the Romans as a noble example against *acedia*: "In Book IV, chapter 16, of *De civitate Dei*, Augustine says that the Romans received into their city many gods whom they believed to impel men into action, and worshipped them among 'public gods'. . . . However, the goddess *Quies* was not received into the city but had her temple outside, for the Romans did not want any god among them who might bring rest or laziness."[108]

The logical stepping-stone between this view of *labor* and the sin of *acedia* was of course *otiositas,* idleness or failure to be occupied. This term had been closely related to *acedia* ever since Cassian and was occasionally mentioned as its synonym. Cassian also included it in the offspring of the vice, and this position it maintained in the progenies developed by Peraldus and the *Somme le Roi.* In the period of 1200-1450, sloth and idleness are often identified, and although longer theological handbooks preserve a distinction between the two, in shorter presentations they often appear as though interchangeable. Thus the quoted canon by Alexander Stavensby renders *acedia* as "idleness in God's service," which a treatise from the early fourteenth century repeats: "Quartum peccatum est Accidia, anglice ydelnesce."[109]

This virtual identity of *acedia* with idleness underlies a good deal of the argumentation in the *Summa de vitiis* by Peraldus. The first section of the treatment on *acedia* furnishes reasons "which may help to detest this vice." Before Peraldus quotes scriptural injunctions and speaks of the evil effects of sloth, he canvasses the whole universe: inanimate bodies, plants, animals, and men, to show that everything in the created world is active and busy to fulfill the purposes for which it was created. The sun rises and sets every day, "and is never lazy, from day to day, winter or summer, to fulfill God's command"; trees grow and bear leaf, flower, and fruit; ants work and gather provisions; all are busy except the *homo acediosus,* who fails to "work" altogether.

Since man is a composite of body and soul, his obligation to be active extends to both parts, whereas conversely the sin of *acedia* affects not only the activity of his spirit in performing religious duties but also the activity of his body in performing religious as well as "worldly" duties. The comprehensive effect of the sin is often expressed in works of instruction from the fourteenth and fifteenth centuries. Thus, a man who does not work, "neyþer bodely ne gostely, is vnskilfully clepid man" (i.e., is called "man" against reason).[110] John Mirk exclaims in a sermon on the Pater Noster: "And þus ȝe schull put away þe foule synne of slouþe þat woll noþer travayll to helpe his body, ny his soule . . . ."[111] And *Jacob's Well* defines the sin in the following manner: "Slowthe is whan þou art vnlusty of þi-self, to seruyn god or þe world, desyring princepally bodyly ese, lothe to travayle, outhir for lyiflode bodyly ouþer for lyiflode gostly" (p. 103).

One can consider this more positive and universal notion of labor as part of what might be termed the Gothic urge to all-inclusiveness, which manifested itself also in other, more general forms in late medieval literature and thus tended to widen the notion of *acedia* to include worldly duties. This tendency can be observed, first, on the level of rhetoric. Peraldus' *Summa de vitiis* again furnishes a good example, not only in itself but also because in this respect, too, it was imitated by innumerable followers. Peraldus warns against *acedia* because it often leads to poverty—and "poverty" is here to be understood literally. In Peraldus' thinking, therefore, the sin must include failure to work diligently for worldly goods. This point appears within the following frame:

Sloth displeases God;
pleases the Devil;
harms man—by inflicting evils;
—by depriving him of goods.

The evils which *acedia* inflicts are those of guilt and of punishment, and it is among the latter that poverty occurs, together with vileness and (spiritual) affliction or pain. Thus, it is not difficult to see that the reason why Peraldus included worldly poverty among the bad effects of the vice is a strong urge to be comprehensive or all-inclusive in demonstrating how bad *acedia* really is. For this persuasive purpose he shows that man is warned by the whole universe, from God (who worked six out of seven days) down to inanimate matter (the sun), and by the evils that befall the slothful in body as well as in soul, in time as well as in eternity.

The tendency to be all-inclusive is revealed in other ways, too. Later confessional formulas, especially, tend to widen sloth to a rather shapeless, comprehensive sin: "I haue synned in slouþe, my Lord God, of þi seruise þat I haue left þat I shulde doo, and þat I shulde haue left I haue doon."[112] A more specific form of growing inclusiveness appears in connection with faults in confession. We noticed earlier that confession and the sacrament of penance were one of the main areas where faults of sloth were committed. But in the following formula the usual defaults by sloth (delay, forgetfulness, and so forth) are increased by faults whose connection with *acedia* is hard to see: "In my confession I have sometimes knowingly held back sins or the circumstances of sins. I have gone to confession under false pretense, that is, in order to be seen by people. I have sometimes lied in confession."[113] It looks as if *acedia* were in process of changing from a sin which included faults in confession to the sin of faulty confession.

A final form of inclusiveness appears in the encyclopedic treatments of *acedia,* such as the work by Peraldus, the *Speculum morale,* or the *Summa* by St. Antoninus of Florence (*ca.* 1440). Here, sub-sins such as idleness, pusillanimity, despair, or lack of devotion are treated at great length and often with an astounding wealth of specific detail. Of course, all this serves a practical purpose, but the reader does reach a point where he asks what the discussion has to do with *acedia.* A good example is Antoninus' treatment of *negligentia,* where he descends to such particular cases as whether barbers may or may not cut hair after sunset on Saturdays. Antoninus is fully aware that only some faults of negligence are due to *acedia,*[114] yet he blithely discusses all of them in this very section. His reason for doing so, obviously, is the fact that *negligentia* has traditionally been an aspect of *acedia;*[115] hence, here is the logical place to discuss it exhaustively. One might conclude that in such late medieval *summae* the scheme of seven capital vices has become nothing but a convenient frame in which to organize the matter of moral theology.[116]

In spite of these tendencies to be comprehensive, to equate sloth with idleness, and to relate it to the late medieval view of *labor,* the sin of sloth came to include astonishingly few worldly faults and beyond any doubt remained a theological concept in the literature surveyed here. The just-mentioned *Summa* by St. Antoninus is a good witness that, even by the middle of the fifteenth century, what we have called the popular image of sloth showed the sin as neglect of strictly religious duties. Antoninus is commonly praised for his modernity, for keeping up with contemporary social and economic changes and modeling his moral teaching on them. Yet his *acedia* is most certainly the traditional concept of Peraldus, Alanus, and Hrabanus Maurus: neglect of spiritual duties because of an inner aversion against the spiritual good.[117] It is true that Antoninus discusses such seemingly "unspiritual" vices as *negligentia, pigritia, otiositas,* and *pusillanimitas* (besides the more "spiritual" ones of *taedium* and *desperatio*). But what he considers in each case are religious, spiritual faults. The problem about barbers, referred to above, is only a very special case of moral decision or legislation posed with regard to the Third Commandment: to sanctify the Sabbath. Similarly, under *pigritia* Antoninus discusses delay in conversion, delay in confession, and delay in finishing good work. The specific faults he mentions in the last section—which at first sight seems to lend itself most readily to the inclusion of worldly faults—turn out to be exclusively religious: failure to carry out vows, to fulfill the imposed penance, to make restitution, and to carry out legacies bequeathed for pious causes for the benefit of the testator's soul.[118]

In other works where we did find worldly faults, such as neglect of professional duties, failure to learn a trade and earn one's bread honestly, misspent youth, and so on, these are by far outnumbered by strictly spiritual or religious faults. If one can at all speak of an extension of the concept *acedia* to include worldly and social duties, at best one finds tentative impulses which never progressed very far.[119] Of course, at present we are considering only the theological literature between 1200 and 1450, and the picture is somewhat, though not radically, different in works of secular wisdom and in genuine poetry, which will be seen in the following chapters. In any case, the evidence so far examined shows that in the popular image the sin of sloth remained sloth in God's service, with "God's service" being occasionally extended to include obligations in this world and to society.

V

THE ICONOGRAPHY OF THE VICE

However variegated and even confusing, the popular image of sloth we have examined in the preceding chapter remains incomplete unless we add to it the rhetorical devices and images by which medieval preachers attempted, not only to instruct, but to move and occasionally to entertain their audiences.

Rhetorical devices have of course always been employed where moral instruction is given. In the history of *acedia*, the Egyptian desert fathers already made full use of them to illustrate the effects of *acedia* and to suggest remedies. Nilus, for example, compared the monk suffering from the inner emptiness and outward instability caused by the vice to a waterless cloud, to a fruit tree too often transplanted, to a dry twig in the desert which every wind moves about. Evagrius collected fifty-seven scriptural passages which might comfort and strengthen his fellow monks in their struggle against the demon of *acedia*. Cassian ended his description with a series of monk stories which later became standard *exempla* against the sin. Gregory the Great also is quite typical of later argumentative and rhetorical practices in the teaching of the vices and virtues. Although he did not use the word *acedia* there, he included a chapter on *pigritia* in his *Regula pastoralis*, where he collected five biblical passages which the preacher should use to show his faithful how Scripture condemns this vice. This technique and the very passages collected became standard in later medieval preaching on *acedia*.[1]

But it is only during the later Middle Ages that such devices of persuasion, the imagery of *acedia*, were collected and organized for the handy use of preachers and confessors. The first work of importance in this respect is the *Summa de arte praedicatoria* by Alanus of Lille. As the title indicates, this treatise furnishes instruction on preaching. It includes a number of chapters on what a sermon should be about, chapters which to some degree are model sermons. One of these is directed "Contra acediam." After a description of the vice (from which I quoted earlier) Alanus piles up a number of relevant biblical passages and examples: "This is the *acedia* which draws back a Christian's hand from the plow, which with Lot's wife looks back toward Sodom, which with Lot dreads to ascend the mountain and with Ruth does not desire to return to the land of Bethlehem."[2] More similes and examples follow, and in the same fashion Alanus treats of the other capital vices. This technique of pastoral argumentation and persuasion was no invention of the Scholastic age, but with the thirteenth century and its upsurge of popular instruction the technique as well as its rhetorical ammunition became organized around certain topics (such as the seven deadly sins), leading in the end to the alphabetized handbooks for preachers, which are true encyclopedias of the commonplaces of popular instruction.

The wealth of medieval *topoi* for *acedia* thus appears mostly in the type of literature that has already revealed to us the popular conception of the vice. To it we must add some specialized *exempla* collections and, eventually, several works that stand on the dividing line between strictly catechetical literature and "imaginative" literature or belles-lettres, wherever this line may be. Of the greatest importance for the iconography of *acedia* is, again, Peraldus' handbook. His "authorities," comparisons, and illustrations occur again and again in the manuals and sermons of later writers, so that the student of medieval *topoi* for the vices and virtues could find no better single source than Peraldus' *Summa de vitiis et virtutibus*. It is indeed a sum of commonplaces, of the preacher's stock-in-trade for the sin of sloth.

Before we can make a more or less systematic survey of the iconography of *acedia*, one difficulty must be pointed out and met. Peraldus attributed to the chief vice sixteen branches, each of which he treated in detail by adducing reasons why such a vice must be shunned and illuminating it with scriptural authorities, exemplary figures, and tales. Thus, his sections on *otiositas* and, especially, *dilatio* are very long and contain much illustrative material. Yet in later alphabetical handbooks the entry on *acedia* may be quite short, whereas many standard commonplaces have been shifted to separate chapters on *otiositas, dilatio, pusillanimitas, desperatio,* and so on.[3] Moreover, additional material may have found its way into the discussion of these now separate vices. Were one to collect the iconographic material contained in all these entries, the result would be an ever-expanding universe of medieval sermon *topoi.* In fact, one would not know where to stop, because from *acedia* one would have to go to *negligentia, pigritia,* and *otium,* and thence to *labor* and *operatio* (see Chapter IV), to *somnus,* to *tempus* (which the slothful shamefully waste), and so on, through practically the whole collection. To avoid such profuseness, I shall restrict myself to material which in later handbooks is explicitly gathered to illustrate *acedia.* I shall, however, consider material which Peraldus included among the branches, because in later treatises it often reappeared as illustration of *acedia* in general.[4]

Outranking all other devices—similes, *exempla,* and personification allegory—in mere quantity are biblical quotations, adduced for or against the vice. Although neither the noun *acedia* nor the adjective *acediosus* occurs in the Latin Vulgate, medieval theologians managed to find an amazing number of biblical passages which "condemn this vice." The connection was, of course, by way of terms used in the definition, description, or progeny of *acedia.* For example, the definition "taedium boni" would remind the theologian of Job's words, "taedet animam meam vitae meae" (Job 10:1), or of the Psalmist's "Dormitavit anima mea prae taedio" (Ps. 118:28). The equation with *otiositas* led to such favorites as "multa enim mala docuit otiositas" (Ecclus. 33:29), or the good wife who "panem otiosa non comedit" (Prov. 31:27), or the iniquity of Sodom caused by "superbia, saturitas panis et abundantia et otium ipsius et filiarum eius" (Ezech. 16:49). Likewise, such aspects of the vice as *pigritia, tristitia, dissolutio, somnolentia* (or *dormitio*), or the need for *labor* and *vigilantia* each drew a number of appropriate scriptural passages. Obviously, a writer such as Peraldus had a biblical concordance, probably alphabetical, at his elbow, which he used freely.

Both testaments furnished their share of theological ammunition of this kind, but of the various books the Old Testament sapiential literature proved the richest arsenal. The Book of Proverbs lent itself best to the preacher's purposes; from it Peraldus collected almost three dozen verses for his section on *acedia.* Ecclesiastes and Ecclesiasticus together are not very far behind. The homely wisdom of "Propter frigus noluit piger arare" (Prov. 20:4), of "De stercore bovorum lapidandus est piger" (Ecclus. 22:2), or of "Mane semina semen tuum, et vespere ne cessat manus tua" (Eccles. 11:16) forms a standard accompaniment to later medieval popular instruction on sloth.

It would be tedious to list all scriptural quotations found in Peraldus' or other treatments of the vice, but four or five passages must be mentioned because, in the discussion of *acedia,* they have no merely ornamental but an argumentative and authoritative function. There is, first, the verse from Ecclesiasticus which uses the derived verb *acediari*: "Ne acedieris in vinculis ejus [i.e., Sapientiae]" (Ecclus. 6:26),[5] and thus warns against slackness in fulfilling the divine precepts.[6] More important is Ps. 118:28 ("Dormitavit anima mea prae taedio"), the verse which had once given the term ἀκηδία authority among the Greeks and had then remained basic to the discussion of the sin among the Latins, despite its noun *taedium* in the Vulgate translation. Cassian was the transmitter and set the tone: "All the troubles of this sickness, blessed David expressed elegantly in one verse when he said, 'My soul slumbers for weariness,' that is, for *acedia.*"[7] Similar explanations occur in later biblical commentaries, devotional writings of Scholastic theologians, and handbooks for confessors.[8]

Equally frequent is the citation of Ps. 106:18, "Omnem escam abominata est anima eorum." "Because sometimes the soul of the good is so much afflicted by this vice that it loathes all food, that is, all spiritual exercise, so that neither prayer, nor reading, nor meditation, nor manual work is pleasing."[9] And as *acedia* produces spiritual nausea in the soul it attacks, so the slothful in their turn nauseate God and are synonymous with the lukewarm of Rev. 3:15-16: "Utinam frigidus esses, aut calidus: sed quia tepidus es . . . incipiam te evomere ex ore meo." The verse condemns primarily *tepiditas,* a major branch of *acedia,*[10] but it is likewise directed against the capital vice itself. According to Caesarius of Heisterbach, "this is said by Christ through St. John to some *accidiosus* who represents all of them."[11]

To these passages, which concern inner dispositions like spiritual loathing and tedium, others may be added that condemn the aspect of indolence and unwillingness to work. Chief among them is the divine injunction after the Fall, "In sudore vultus tui vesceris pane" (Gen. 3:19), already used by Evagrius and ubiquitous in late medieval discussions of sloth. As we saw earlier, this verse together with Job 5:6 ("Homo nascitur ad laborem . . .") was authoritative for the view that work is essential to man's spiritual and physical existence.

Just as often as scriptural quotations are biblical figures and episodes cited to exemplify the vice or to serve as models against it. Again, both the Old and the New Testament furnished an abundance of material. I mentioned earlier that Alanus likened the slothful to Lot who refused to climb the mountain and to Lot's wife who turned back toward sin. The very iniquity of Sodom is a result of *acedia,* or rather of idleness (Ezech. 16:49, referring to Genesis 19). Yet the principal figure from Genesis who is always named in connection with *acedia* is Cain, the impenitent murderer, who with Judas represents the gravest aspect of the vice: despair. Another parallel is found in the history of Israel's wandering in the desert:

> When the Israelites went through the desert by God's command in order that they might reach the Promised Land, they often suffered tedium and sadness on account of their labors, and sometimes even abhorred the manna. Therefore, they were often punished and finally kept from the Promised Land, according to Num. 14. And this signifies the *accidiosi,* who loathe going through the desert of penance or the religious life because of its labors, and who are disgusted with all spiritual things, so that finally they are deprived of everlasting life.[12]

Israel's fight against the Canaanite nations became, from early Christian times on, a standard prefiguration of man's struggle against the seven capital vices, and the seven were often connected with individual nations.[13] Sometimes the vice is also seen in the weary rear guard of Deut. 25:18, who are smitten by Amalech.[14]

Passing to the other historical books of the Old Testament, we find a number of stock exemplary figures for *acedia* whose meaning is obvious: they fell through lack of vigilance or moral and religious slackness. Samson (Judges 16), Sisaran (Judg. 4:17ff.), Holofernes (Judith 13), and Saul in losing his lance and cup (I Kings 26:7ff.), are all types of sinful sleep; while David's adultery (II Kings 11) and Solomon's turning to heathen gods (III Kings 11) demonstrate the consequences of idleness. To this group also belongs Isboseth, another figure of *acedia,* who like Samson, Holofernes, and Sisaran trusted a woman (i.e., the sensitive part of his soul, or reason grown feeble) and relaxed (II Kings 4:5-6).[15] He "was sleeping in his bed at noon, and robbers came and killed him. What else does this mean but that a man who does not rejoice in the praise of God in his time and place, but languishes and sleeps in his bed of laziness, gets killed spiritually? Therefore, this treasure [of grace] must be guarded lest it be taken away by the torpor of *accidia*."[16] The vice renders man incapable of doing any good by maiming his hands and feet, like Adonibezet of Judg. 1:7.

In the Gospels *acedia* is most impressively illustrated in the sleeping Apostles in Gethsemane and the Lord's warning words, "Vigilate et orate" (Matt. 26:36ff.). "By the sleeping disciples are indicated the *accidiosi*, whose inner eyes are heavy with the sleep of indolence."[17] And Peraldus explains that "to wake with the Lord means, following His example to guard against the sleep of *accidia*" (*Summa*, 3.5). Many parables and incidents in Christ's life show the dangers of this vice. The unfruitful tree is condemned to die (Luke 13:6ff.) and the cursed fig tree withers (Matt. 21: 18ff.). Likewise, the *servus piger* who buries his talent (Matt. 25: 24ff.) and the man who comes to the wedding feast without the proper garment (Matt. 22:13)[18] meet damnation. Idleness is, of course, condemned by the parable of the Lord of the Vineyard: "Quid hic statis tota die otiosi?" (Matt. 20:6), while the "sleep of negligence and *accidia*"—of prelates as well as of Everyman—is shown as letting the fiend come and sow tares among the wheat (Matt. 13:24ff.). Similarly, those who "sleep through *accidia* under appearance of devotion" are prefigured in the young man Eutychus who, during St. Paul's preaching, dozed off and fell to death (Acts 20:9ff.).[19]

How displeasing to God the lack of fervor in the slothful is can be seen in Christ's words about the one sinner at whose conversion there is more joy in Heaven than about ninety-nine just (Luke 15:7). "Our Lord places one fervent sinner in front of ninety-nine just who are *accidiosi*," says Peraldus, "exactly as a leader in battle loves a soldier who, having first fled and then returned, presses hard on the enemy, more than him who has never fled nor ever borne himself bravely" (*Summa*, 1.31).

Late medieval preachers continued to see in *acedia* one of the gravest and most diabolical temptations, as the desert fathers had done before, and applied to *acedia* the Lord's words about the unclean spirit who, after he is driven out of man's soul and finds it empty and swept, returns with seven other spirits that are more evil than himself (Matt. 12:43-45).[20] Hence the proverb that sloth or idleness is the mother of all vices[21] and the image of the *accidiosi* as the resting-place of the devil.[22] The parable about the unclean spirit perhaps caused Peraldus and his followers to see *acedia* in two miracles in which Christ drove out devils: the episode of the Gadarene swine (Matt. 8:31ff.) and the healing of the Canaanite woman's daughter (Matt. 15:21ff.). The latter miracle finds a rather strained explanation in a sermon written probably by Peraldus. Here the seven evil spirits of which Mary Magdalen was healed (Luke 8:2) are linked to the seven chief vices. The fourth is then related to Matt. 15:22, "filia mea male a daemonio vexatur," which Peraldus explains by applying the mother-daughter relation to that between reason and will: "This demon belongs to the sin of *acedia*. Reason is like the mother of Will, because her function is to govern it. But the will of an *accidiosus* finds neither savor nor delight in the good, which has to him become sour [*acetosa*], so to speak. Hence it suffers great affliction."[23]

Besides these many examples of *acedia* Scripture also shows models for overcoming the sin. The lives and deeds of the patriarchs and saints, of the Blessed Virgin and, of course, of Christ Himself, were in general held up by the preacher as "examples that will help to detest *acedia*." In particular, the scene where Moses lifted his rod in the battle against Amalech, and his hands as they grew heavy were supported by Aaron and Hur (Ex. 17:9ff.), gives a beautiful illustration of a chief remedy against *acedia*: "For those whose hands are heavy with *acedia* it is necessary to live with men who, by their example, may enlighten them with their doctrine and strengthen them with their prayers" (Peraldus, *Summa*, 3.4). Another exemplary patriarch is Abraham who, when the three angels approached, "*hastened* into the tent unto Sarah . . . and *ran* unto the herd" (Gen. 18:6-7).

Haste and eagerness in God's service are also shown in the life of the Blessed Virgin, who "abiit in montana cum festinatione" (Luke 1:39) to visit Elizabeth upon a mere suggestion made by the Angel. To Mary are applied the words from the praise of the good housewife, "Panem otiosa non comedit" (Prov. 31:27), and Conrad of Saxony says that, "against *acedia* Mary was most indefatigable through her zeal [*sedulitas*]. . . . And since Mary was not *acediosa*, she also was not idle, but kept not only her mind busy in holy meditations and her tongue in devout prayers, but also her hands in good works" (pp. 45, 52).

But the prime example of zeal and fervent devotion is Christ, who "was not lazy but rejoiced as a giant running his way" (Peraldus, *Summa,* 3.5; cf. Ps. 19:5). As an illustration of the weariness and exhaustion He willingly suffered during His life, Peraldus cites John 4:6, "Jesus ergo fatigatus ex itinere sedebat sic supra fontem" (1.142). Of the seven words Christ spoke on the cross, the fourth was especially directed against *acedia*: "The fourthe word that Crist spak here, was when he criede Eloy; and bi this word he puttid out slouthe, whanne he preiede his God now, and confessid in a manere that God dide thus for his good. . . . And sith God lefte Crist in his enemyes hondis, to good of him and his Chirche, what art thou that grutchist aȝens God, to suffre peyne and flee slouthe?"[24]

Two figures from the parables are singled out as anti-types of *acedia,* to teach zeal and vigilance: the housewife who, owning ten drachmas, lost one and searched the whole house for it (Luke 15:8ff.), and the landlord who is constantly on his guard against the digging thief (Matt. 24:43). Finally, in the preacher's exhortation to overcome delay of confession or even despair, two important aspects of *acedia,* the parable of the Prodigal Son (Luke 15:11ff.)[25] and the case of the penitent thief who gains Christ's forgiveness in sharp contrast to the despair of Judas (Luke 23: 39ff.)[26] are often cited as examples of God's readiness to forgive.

The examples and authoritative quotations we have surveyed were taken from the Bible. But occasionally Peraldus and his followers drew such material from other sources, the medieval school authors. As is to be expected, their favorites were Seneca[27] and Ovid, but quotations from Horace, Juvenal, Valerius, and Lucan also occur, though in very small number. A fairly frequent authority against *acedia* (and especially idleness) is Ovid's distich,

> Quaeritur Aegistus quare sit factus adulter?
> In promptu causa est, desidiosus erat,
> (*Remedia amoris,* ll. 161-62)

which was used, not only by Peraldus and later writers, but also by Alanus and Albertus Magnus.[28] Peraldus similarly quotes the Ovidian "Otia si tollas, periere Cupidinis arcus" (*Rem. am.,* l. 139; Peraldus, *Summa,* 2.04); Seneca's "Otium sine litteris mors est" (*Epistulae,* 82, 3; Peraldus, *Summa,* 2.04); and the Horatian

Impiger extremos currit mercator ad Indos
Per mare pauperiem fugiens, per saxa, per ignes.
(*Epistulae*, I, 1, 45, as an authority against *tarditas*;
Peraldus, *Summa*, 2.06)[29]

Another literary device medieval preachers employed with readiness and gusto is the simile. It was often used to compare *acedia* to idle and unprofitable things. Bromyard, for example, likened the vice to fallow ground, stagnating water, and an unused plow, driving home the lesson that exercise is necessary to prevent spiritual decay.[30] Similarly, *acedia* was compared to unused armor that rusts,[31] slow water which can be crossed by serpents,[32] still air that causes people to die or a restful body in which the humors dry up,[33] the bilge water in the bottom of a ship,[34] or a peasant who often sharpens his hoe and a barber who hones his razor but never uses it.[35]

Other figures compare the vice to the indolent behavior of men and beasts: the sluggard who does not rise when it thunders—"but Christ has thundered on the Cross and in His preaching: and He will thunder again on the Day of Judgment"—,[36] or several lazy servants, whom we shall meet again in the *exempla*. The most widespread simile of this kind is that of the cat who wants to catch a fish but does not want to get its feet wet—or, as Chaucer puts it,

For ye be lyke the sweynte cat
That wolde have fissh; but wostow what?
He wolde nothing wete his clowes.
(*House of Fame*, III, 1783-85)[37]

With the lazy cat comes a large host of other animals symbolizing *acedia*. Foremost, of course, is the ass, who—though by no means a fixed image[38]—usually stands for stupidity, ignorance, and laziness.[39] He is especially equated with *acedia* by Hugh Ripelin (in a list of correspondences between the seven vices and animals, sicknesses, and stages in Christ's Passion),[40] *Jacob's Well* ("A slow man is lyche an asse, for an asse louyth weel ese, and is lothe to trauayle, but he be constreynd þerto," p. 103), Hilton's *Scale of Perfection* (II, 14), and many other works.[41]

Although the ass was the standard animal symbol for *acedia*, its rule was by no means exclusive. The famous comparison of the seven deadly sins to animals and their whelps in *Ancrene*

Riwle likens sloth to a bear, a rather unusual comparison, although a somewhat similar one occurs in the fifteenth-century Scottish *Buke of the Governaunce of Princis.*[42] A more common representative of *acedia* is the pig. It was obviously the vice's aspect of heavy sleep that suggested this animal; in Peraldus (*Summa,* 2.03) and Antoninus of Florence (*Summa,* ii, 2) the bestiality of sleep makes man like a pig (under the branch of *somnolentia*), and the same connection appears in a Middle English lyric:

> We loue so slouþe and harlotrie,
> We slepe as swolle swyn in lake[43]

as well as in one of John Mirk's sermons.[44] Dunbar used the animal as the chief simile for sloth in his *Dance of the Seven Deadly Sins,*[45] and another poet, a century and a half later, still echoed the same medieval commonplace when he has a feigned madman in his babbling liken man to a "hog in sloth."[46]

Yet comparison with the pig not only visualizes sluggishness and somnolence but hints at something more dire: Like the hog the slothful are fattened for the devil. A metrical confession declares,

> Sicut porcus, qui servatur
> Ad mactandum, impinguatur
> Per quietem otii,
> Sic quiescens per torporem
> Me nutrivi ad dolorem
> Ultimi supplicii.[47]

Chaucer's Lady Fame again takes up the image, which makes her sound so much like a fishwife:

> Ye masty swyn, ye ydel wrechches,
> Ful of roten, slowe techches!
> (*House of Fame,* III, 1777-78)

In addition to these major figures one can find a whole menagerie of other animals symbolizing *acedia* which occur less frequently than the ass and the pig. M. W. Bloomfield has gathered a variety of them, such as the owl, ape, buffalo, leopard, dormouse, crayfish, stork, snail, and dog,[48] to which even more items can be added. The dog, actually, is a comparatively frequent symbol for the vice. Already Evagrius declared that "the demon of ἀκηδία . . . tears the soul asunder as a dog the fawn."[49] In the later Middle

Ages *acedia* was often compared to a hungry dog who craves for vanities and impurity and lets the flies (of evil thoughts) creep into its ears.[50]

A frequent implement of discussions of sloth is the raven (*corvus*), whose cry "cras, cras" makes him a fitting symbol of procrastination. Hence he appears in Peraldus' branch of *dilatio* and elsewhere.[51] Another slothful bird is the kite, *milvus*, whose name is etymologized as *molliter volans*.[52] Similarly, the tortoise (*testudo*), as one might expect, stands for *acedia*: "A good horse runs farther in one day than a tortoise in a year. Thus a man who is fervent in love makes greater progress in little time than an *accidiosus* or lukewarm person in a hundred years."[53]

A quite different aspect of *acedia* becomes visible in the worm of Prov. 25:20, the spiritual sadness or depression which befalls monks and nuns.[54] "As the worm does harm to the wood and eats and corrupts it, so does *accidia* to the just man, for *accidia* takes away all spiritual good that is in man."[55] Originally, the scriptural verse "Sicut tinea vestimento, et vermis ligno, ita tristitia viri nocet cordi," was indeed applied to *tristitia* rather than *acedia* by Cassian and his predecessors, but later the simile together with *tristitia* entered the progeny of sloth.[56] The idea that inner sadness eats away man's devotion and therefore nullifies the value of his spiritual exercises also underlies the image of the vulture, which is used for *acedia* by Petrus Cantor: "*Accidia*, too, destroys devotion in prayer and psalm singing, as a vulture devouring the sacrifice and driving out charity."[57]

Other animals, such as bat and butterfly (*papilio*), stand for the unprofitable life which results from the vice: "Notice that the butterfly, which flies about but does nothing useful, is the religious in a state of *acedia*."[58] The author of the treatise in which the latter image occurs, the Franciscan Malachy of Limerick, was very fond of animal symbols. He likens the vice not only to the butterfly but also to the thrush and the turtledove (*turdus* and *turtur*, because of their "etymology" of *tardus*), to a snake (who is languid in cold weather, like the *piger* of Prov. 20:4), and to a caterpillar (*eruca*), who first destroys the strength of trees by eating up their foliage, then spins itself into a cocoon for the winter and becomes inactive.

Two more animals are only indirectly connected with *acedia* but appear frequently in vernacular literature. Frère Lorens' and related treatments liken the slothful in their dread to begin hard enterprises to children who are afraid of hissing geese or of the snail when it puts its horns out.[59] And finally we must not forget to mention the two important counter-examples, the ant and the bee. Following the scriptural injunction, "Vade ad formicam, o piger, et considera vias eius" (Prov. 6:6), medieval writers often went to great lengths to moralize the nature of ants in minute detail.[60]

Almost as long as the list of animals[61] is that of diseases to which *acedia* was compared. Paralysis takes the first place, which "unloosens the whole man and renders him useless for any good work."[62] This equation is very common[63] and finds scriptural justification in the various *paralytici* of the Gospels, especially the one at Bethesda who had been sick for thirty years (which signifies those "who always lie close to the Sacrament of Confession and Penance but never care to enter until they come to die," Holcot, to John 5:2ff.) and the man with the withered hand (Matt. 12:10).

But it is not the hand so much which is allegorically affected by *acedia* as it is the foot. Hence preachers often likened the vice to spiritual podagra or the gout. *The Prick of Conscience* makes this disease the punishment for the slothful in Purgatory (ll. 2992-93), and Bromyard declares that "those are affected by podagra who are usually rather slack in things that belong to God, such as sermons and useful enterprises, while they are much faster when it comes to shows and idle occupations" (art. 6). The connection of *acedia* with the feet is quite widespread and occurs in different forms. Primarily, spiritual languor is aptly visualized in slow physical movement. Thus, Dante has *acedia* punished by an incessant running on the fourth cornice of *Purgatorio*. In the same vein, Hilton relates the vice to the feet of his Image of Sin.[64] Secondly, *acedia* is usually linked to the wounds Christ suffered in His feet, an equation which occurs in several Middle English lyrics, as for example:

> Arise up, vnlust, out of þi bed,
> And biholde my feet, þat are forbled.[65]

And lastly, since *acedia* is a disorientation in man's affective life, it could again be expressed by a foot image: In medieval exegesis the foot often stands for *affectus*, or both feet for *intellectus* and *affectus*:[66] "Our spirit has two feet—one of the intellect and the other of the affect, or of cognition and of love—, and we must move both so that we may walk the right way."[67] The *accidiosus*, then, moves his *pes intellectus* but lags behind with *pes affectus* (or *operis*). In metrical form:

Sic et ego intellectu
Passum feci, sed affectu
Sequi differebam.[68]

Other diseases as symbols for *acedia* occur less frequently. Lethargy is sometimes used in a table which relates the seven sins to seven animals, diseases, and aspects of Christ's Passion, which is different from the table that equates *acedia* with paralysis.[69] Like the *lethargus,* the slothful person "always wants to sleep and is nearly dead."[70] Since the *accidiosus* has lost his taste for spiritual things, he might be said to be moribund;[71] and the spiritual drowsiness of the vice probably suggested to Barclay the image of poppy seed.[72] The sin is also likened to a festering blain[73] and, in a fifteenth-century sermon, to the bite of a rabid dog.[74]

A few similes cannot be classed so easily in such groups as idle things, animals,[75] or diseases. Some of them express the idea that the slothful are ready prey to temptations of all kinds and stand quite defenseless. Peraldus likens them to a snowman in front of a fire (*Summa,* 2.02), to a target exposed to arrows, and to a city without walls (2.04). Of similar import is the comparison of the slothful to a lukewarm pot, "for the devil tempts a tepid person with many vices with which he would not dare tempt a fervent man; whence says an authority, 'flies do not sit on a boiling pot' " (2.01).[76] Peraldus uses the pot image somewhat differently when he says that the slothful soul is like a vessel full of dirt (*receptaculum sordium*) because it admits all sorts of evils (2.04).

In this state the slothful provide a comfortable resting-place (*hospitium*) for the devil who can lie in their soul as on a soft couch or featherbed.[77] The idea of companionship with the Fiend produces such images as the devil's ass[78] and the devil's chamberlain.[79] Bromyard uses the latter figure to develop a whole Court of the Devil, in which the *accidiosi* are not only chamberlains but also porters and carriers. The Dominican writer realizes quite well the inherent paradox of the image and adds, "In this respect the government of the devil differs from others. For other rulers can be found who want to employ servants that are proud, lecherous, cruel, greedy, and so on; but hardly do they want idlers" (art. 4).

From the simile we pass to the *exemplum,* the very brief narrative told to illustrate a particular moral. *Exempla* for *acedia* were taken in astonishing number from the life and experience of monks, even in late medieval handbooks which provided instruction for laymen. The chief source for such tales was the *Vitae Patrum*, whose stories go back to the gnomic literature of the Egyptian desert fathers. But later storytellers and collectors, too, furnished a good many tales, from Gregory the Great (*Dialogi*) on to Jacques de Vitry, Étienne de Bourbon, Caesarius of Heisterbach, and others.[80] Occasionally, a late medieval writer also reports stories which he had witnessed himself or received through hearsay.[81]

A number of *exempla* are concerned with the vice directly. When an old hermit is asked how he manages to escape tedium and *acedia*, he answers that he constantly meditates on three letters he has: one is black (his own sins), the other red (the Passion of Christ), and the third golden (future bliss).[82] Meditation on the bliss and the pains to come is recommended also in another, fairly ubiquitous *exemplum*: to a young monk's question, "Why am I afflicted with *acedia* when I sit in my cell?" Abba Achilles replies: "Because you have not yet seen the rest we hope for, nor the pains we fear."[83] Hence the age-old advice to keep one's cell. "Because it is proved by experience that the attack of *acedia* must not be eschewed by flight, but fought by resistance," says Cassian after reporting his own temptation and the advice he received from Abba Moses (*Inst.*, X, 25). This is repeated in the eighth-century *Poenitentiale Bigotianum* and added to by other warnings against *vagatio*, including Abba Antonius' words that monks out of their cells are like fish on dry land.[84] The danger of leaving the cell is vividly brought home in the fourteenth-century *Scala caeli* by Johannes Gobius, O.P., where a monk who thinks he cannot stand his cell any more because of the heat and his weariness is brought to heel by a more circumspect *pater* with a reference to the greater fire that is likely to grow out of *accidia* and *otium* (fol. 6r).

This warning is substantiated in John Herolt's *Promptuarium* by a vision of an *accidiosus* who has to spend forty years in purgatory (No. 14), whereas a worse fate has befallen a woman who was thrown into hell because on holy days she had always left the church before the end of mass.[85] On the contrary, a peasant who was always zealous in serving God and doing good works, but at whose death bad weather broke, is seen by his daughter to live in heaven, whereas his lazy and sinful wife, at whose death the sun shone brightly, has been damned to hell.[86]

A large group of *exempla* enjoin work by hand as the chief remedy against sloth. These stories are nearly all about monks, and many of them go back to the desert fathers, for whom *acedia* was the most dangerous vice. In a vision Abba Macarius saw his monks tempted by the devil. None succumbed save one, and he through sloth.[87] When in the beginning of his eremitic life St. Anthony was plagued by *acedia*, he asked for divine guidance and had a vision of an angel who alternated prayer with handwork, weaving a rope. Anthony followed his example and was saved.[88] Abba Arsenius is reported to have answered to the question in what he trusted, "In that I have fled human company and have kept silence for a long time; but mostly I rejoice that I have worked with my hands."[89] How essential manual labor was to the spiritual welfare of the desert monks is revealed in two stories in which an overly zealous beginner who wanted to be more perfect by giving himself to uninterrupted prayer was, by his companions, rather drastically brought to earth. Abba Silvanus refused to give food to a monk who thought he was above manual labor, and Abba Johannes, who wanted to be like an angel and left his monastery for the desert, was turned away with mockery when he came back.[90]

In order to be always occupied, the desert fathers would go so far as to undo their work: Abba Paulus is famous for burning the palm-leaf baskets he had woven during the year.[91] *Jacob's Well* tells of a hermit who had to fetch his water every day from very far. He decided to build his cell closer to the water. But then he saw an angel counting his steps, each of which was to be fully rewarded; and in consequence he removed his cell five more miles from the well (p. 111). In similar fashion, a prudent clerk who had a servant that was not fully occupied made him carry stones back and forth "so that he might not be unoccupied; for idleness teaches much evil."[92] Idleness, indeed, is to be shunned because, as Abba Pastor said, "as bees are driven out by smoke, in order that one may take away the sweet fruit of their labor, so does bodily rest drive out the fear of the Lord from the soul and all good work is taken away from her."[93] Another wise man pointed to sun, earth, ant, and rooster, to inculcate the same lesson.[94] Man is like the son of a rich landowner, sent out into his vineyard (the soul) to clear it of evil weeds (deadly sins); he must not despair when he sees the greatness and multitude of weeds but go to work and uproot today one weed, tomorrow another.[95]

Some more homely *exempla* show the foolishness of the lazy

who will not act even if they lose their goods and lives. Fairly frequent is the story of a peasant who has fallen into a swamp and cries for help but is too lazy to stir and get out by himself. This tale exists in various forms, one of which replaces the peasant by a charioteer.[96] Other examples of indolence are the servant who, when sent out to see if it is raining, calls a dog into the house and feels if its skin is wet;[97] and a carter who, with his cart stuck in the mud, prays God for help but himself does not lay hand on it.[98] More widespread than these tales, however, is the one about the three sons of Emperor Polonius who vie in laziness for their father's realm. The first is so lazy that he will not draw back his foot from the fire that burns him; the second will not cut the rope with which he is about to be hanged, though he holds a sword in his hand; and the third will not turn away when dripping water falls in his eye.[99] This tale is also found in Gobius' *Scala caeli* but expanded by the addition of two more contestants: one who is too lazy to close his mouth in which he has bread, so that the birds carry it away; the other "sat, and mice came and gnawed off his ears to the brains, so that he was destroyed merely because of his laziness to draw back" (fol. 5v).

Gobius' collection of *exempla* in general shows this Gothic desire to embellish and be comprehensive. Still under "Acedia" he builds up an entire *monasterium godiardorum* (for *goliardorum*?) in which a number of chambers are inhabited by men who allegorically demonstrate all sorts of *acedia*: knights who fall off their horses when they only hear of the enemy, men with bread in their hands eating stones, a sick man too lazy to turn to the healing medicine beside him, scholars who grow more ignorant the more they are taught, and so forth (fol. 6r).

One aspect of *acedia* drew an especially large number of *exempla*: the sinful sleep of religious men and women during divine worship. The most frequently told story of this group concerns a monk who, at the hour of Matins, was always covered with sweat so that, fearing he was sick, he stayed in bed. One night, as everybody else was asleep, he wanted to get up, but to his astonishment found a devil under his bed whispering that he should stay. Of course, the monk was cured for good.[100] Caesarius of Heisterbach, who reports this story, has several others of similar kind,[101] in which his explicit intention is to show that sleep in church is not so much—as many allege—a matter of bodily weariness, as it is the work of the devil. Visions of the Fiend in various animal shapes confirm this, as well as the punishment God deals out to such sinners: A sleeping priest saw Christ turn His back on him, and a somnolent monk was struck dead by the crucifix.[102] The point is also proven by the episode where a group of monks fell asleep during the sermon but were wide awake when the preacher mentioned King Arthur.[103]

As a counter-example to sleep Bromyard points to Saint Charlemagne, who got up every night to pray (art. 5). *De oculo morali* brings a very interesting tale, taken from Hélinand of Froidmont's *Chronicles,* against prelates who cultivate the bed. Hélinand reports his own experience with the bishop of Beauvais whom the monk once tried to rouse for an early mass. The tale is so interesting because of the ready, off-hand way in which Hélinand administers moral instruction to a high-ranking member of the clergy, first pointing to the birds, then citing Scripture, and climactically finishing off with a quote from the commentary of St. Ambrose. It is also interesting for its life-like tone—the bishop's indignant "Go, kill your lice!" and Père Hélinand's witty reply, "Look out, Father, that you don't get killed by the worms," and so forth. The story is not only amusing but also gives a very good insight into the mechanism of informal preaching in the later Middle Ages.[104]

Sinful sleep has its companion vice in "syncopation," the mumbling and curtailing of words in saying mass or the office. In a famous vision a devil by the name of Tutivillus scuttles about with a sack full of clipped and overskipped syllables.[105] A brother of his, like a medieval Screwtape, is busy watching out for similar faults of sloth: He writes idle words spoken in church on a large scroll. On one occasion he has to enlarge the parchment by drawing it out with his teeth but bumps his head heavily against the wall, to the delight of his witness.[106]

Other aspects of *acedia* were illustrated by a smaller number of *exempla.* A "holy father" laments his own lack of fervor when he sees how diligently a street girl cares for her body and clothes, and for the same reason Abba Pambo is driven to tears at the sight of a worldly woman in Alexandria.[107] *Instabilitas* is the theme of a story about a monk who cannot remain quietly in choir,[108] and idle occupations in general are condemned by the story of the importunate minstrel whose noise disturbed a bishop so much in his prayers that one day a stone kills him.[109] *Handlyng Synne,* where the latter story is told against sloth, also gives two *exempla* of the dire consequences of not chastising unruly children properly. One concerns a five-year-old who blasphemed and was snatched away to hell; the other is the biblical story of the two sons of Eli (I Kings 2:22-36; 4:4-18).[110]

The same work tells of an impenitent servant of King Conrad of Mercia who delayed his repentance for too long and, in a vision before his death, saw two angels with a very small book of his good deeds give way before two black devils with a large tome of his evil deeds and fiery knives that cut him to pieces (*Handlyng Synne*, ll. 4361ff.). A similarly gruesome end demonstrating *accidia confessionis* is reported in *Speculum laicorum*, where an impenitent rich man on his death bed gorges himself with his jewels (pp. 29-30).

Caesarius of Heisterbach's *Dialogus miraculorum* contains perhaps the richest collection of *exempla* on *acedia* after Peraldus' treatment and illustrates, besides sinful sleep, a number of aspects which are mostly proper to the monastic life. Spiritual cowardice befalls clerks (a Parisian teacher) and laymen (a knight) who think of entering the monastery but are afraid of the rule of silence or of lice. A more interesting case is that of a parish priest who had joined a regular order but after a year was tempted to return to his parish which he knew to be in unsatisfactory hands—obviously one of the more subtle forms of *acedia* like those the desert fathers described.[111] Other monks are tempted by pusillanimity to leave the monastery or, in some cases, to blaspheme.[112] But the gravest aspect of the vice is the temptation to end one's life. Several religious in Caesarius' stories try, sometimes successfully, to commit suicide because of spiritual dejection, although this also happens to a nun "because of the magic arts of a miserable brother," to a girl who was left by her lover, and to an unsuccessful gambler.[113]

To these stories, which are all set in a Christian milieu, a few authors add one or two *exempla* from the pagan world. For obvious reasons, pagan *exempla* for or against *acedia* are not at all numerous in works of religious instruction, whereas they may be somewhat more frequent in treatises on worldly education, such as the *Epistle of Othea* by Christine de Pisan (where Polyphemus becomes an example of sloth),[114] or true works of literature, such as Gower's *Confessio Amantis* and Dante's *Purgatorio*. A good many religious writers did of course have a penchant for classical culture, at least for those aspects that could be easily moralized in Christian terms. Yet even they do not use many pagan *exempla* for this particular vice. *De oculo morali* brings a story from Macrobius' *Sa-*

turnalia about Emperor Augustus and the lesson he drew from a soldier's skill to hide his great debts (cap. viii). Bromyard repeats the fable of Virgil's gadfly under "Accidia" to show that leisure opens man's soul to the devil: a "certain philosopher" was waked up by the sting of a fly just as a snake was about to enter into him (art. 5). And Berchorius retells a story from St. Augustine, who is reported as having written in *De civitate Dei* that the Romans admitted to, and worshiped in, the city of Rome many gods who were believed to incite men to action. But the Goddess Quies had her temple outside the city walls "because the Romans did not want to have any god amongst them who would bring rest or laziness."[115]

Berchorius thoroughly missed St. Augustine's intention, but his *exemplum* is fairly typical of what virtues fourteenth-century churchmen saw in the noble Romans, virtues that were opposed to medieval *acedia*. Another episode of Roman history, also culled from St. Augustine, furnished an *exemplum* of similar import. It points out the sloth and idleness which resulted when the destruction of Carthage had removed Rome's archenemy and with it the need to keep vigilant and ready in arms. In consequence, ease of life led to wealth, debauchery, and civil wars. I have found this as an *exemplum* against sloth in John of Wales, whose moralizing interest in classical history and literature is well known;[116] in Antonius de Bitonto;[117] and in the *Ship of Fools*.[118]

The divers rhetorical devices so far examined—biblical quotations and exemplary figures, similes, and *exempla*—were also used as integrating elements in a more sophisticated device, the extended allegory. We have, of course, met allegory before in works of instruction, devotion, or speculative theology, such as the brief personification of Pride as the "queen of the chief vices" in Gregory, or the image of the "daughters" that each capital sin has, or the various branches and twigs on the tree of vices, the latter image giving rise to a whole forest of allegorical trees including a separate Tree of Accyde in *The Desert of Religion*. Allegory assumes a more general and important function in the sustained image of the cleansing of the well (of man's soul) in *Jacob's Well*, where it is used as a graphic structural device to hold the various catechetical matters firmly within one frame. Considering this, one might speak of more ambitious allegorical poems, such as Deguileville's *Pèlerinage de vie humaine,* as catechetical handbooks in the form of an allegory, because—like *Jacob's Well* or *The Book of Vices and Virtues*—the *Pèlerinage* contains sections on the Ten Commandments, the Articles of Faith, the seven sacraments, the seven deadly sins, the five works of mercy, and so on, and gives instruction on how to confess one's sins. But here, as in what I have called "extended allegories," the didactic element appears to be secondary to the work of the writer's imagination which has transformed concepts into images and pictures.

These extended allegories present *acedia* within the series of the seven deadly sins, and for these medieval writers devised a number of frame allegories. The general conception which underlies all of them is that of spiritual struggle against obstacles or dangers to man's salvation, inherent already in the teaching of Evagrius, Cassian, and their followers. In the seventh century Aldhelm described the Cassianic eight vices in terms of combat, in which "languid *Acedia* leads the sixth line of battle."[119] This assault on man also occurs in the late thirteenth-century *Songe du Castel,* where seven kings attack the castle of man (l. 159).[120] In the fourteenth-century *Chemin de Povreté et de Richesse* the dreamer is warned against the attack of Paresse on the wrong way (to the left).[121] The *Mirror of the Periods of Man's Life* shows the seven sins approach and tempt Man at various ages of his life,[122] and similar assaults occur in medieval morality plays.

A slightly different battle is that of personified vices against virtues. Prudentius' *Psychomachia,* the archetype of this battle, had used a series of vices different from either Cassian's or Gregory's chief vices, and neither *acedia* nor *tristitia* is among them. But in the first half of the thirteenth century—the period in which so many fruitful allegories appeared in vernacular writings—the theme was freshly developed. Huon de Mery's *Tournoiemenz Antecrit (ca.* 1234) shows the seven vices under Antichrist fight against the virtues under Christ.[123] The theme recurs in Lydgate's *Assembly of the Gods,* where Virtue is attacked by Vice with the help of seven captains, though in this poem the traditional seven deadly sins are quite subordinate in importance. Finally, the armed fight between personified abstractions is sometimes changed to a verbal battle or dialogue. Thus, the *Moralité des sept péchés mortels et des sept vertus,* after some preliminary matter,[124] has each vice dispute with a virtue, leading to the vice's "conversion."

Another frame allegory for the deadly sins is the allegorical marriage: The Devil begets a series of sins whom he marries off to a series of suitors. The late medieval archetype of this allegory seems to have been the theme of the Marriage of the Devil's Nine Daughters, studied to some extent by Paul Meyer.[125] The nine daughters are not the seven chief vices, but in at least one Latin manuscript version the usual "faux service" is replaced by "Accidia," "quam dedit [diabolus] maxime pro omnibus aliis servientibus."[126] The allegory was most profusely developed by John Gower, in *Mirour de l'omme,* where the Devil, after engendering Death upon Sin, marries Death to Sin, who then gives birth to the seven chief vices. These are next individually married to World and have each five children of their own. The marriage of World and the Seven Sins leads to a grand procession, which Gower describes in no less than almost nine thousand lines.

A third frame of great importance is the allegorical pilgrimage. In one form, the pilgrimage to hell or to paradise, the seven vices appear as stations on the way. Jean de Le Mote's *La Voie d'Enfer* (1340) and Rutebeuf's *La Voie de Paradis* (*ca.* 1265)[127] are good examples and contain detailed descriptions of *acedia.* The second form is the pilgrimage of life, best represented in the little-known *Le Chemin de Vaillance* by Jean de Courcy (early fifteenth century)[128] and the famous *Pèlerinage de vie humaine,* written by Deguileville (1330 and 1355) and translated by Lydgate (1426).[129] Here the vices meet Everyman as tempters on his journey to eternal bliss.

Within these various frames the figure of Acedia is characterized in different ways: by description, by monologue, and by dramatic action. Description itself can be of two kinds, which one may call moral and pictorial. In a moral description the sin is characterized by what it does to man, the faults it causes in him, the evils it leads him to. Aldhelm's *De octo principalibus vitiis,* the *Chemin de Povreté et de Richesse, The Desert of Religion,* and Rutebeuf's *La Voie de Paradis* use this method, the first three stressing the conventional offspring of the vice, the last work tending more toward a characterization of a slothful person. Thus, allegories which use moral description are very similar in their treatment of the vice to the more prosaic handbooks and offer little that is of interest for the imagery of *acedia.*

In contrast, pictorial descriptions furnish a good many interesting details. In Huon de Mery's *Tournament of Antichrist* the figure of Peresce (*pigritia*) forms the rear guard in the host of the Fiend. She is asleep, prefers to remain in her pavilion, and never leaves the company of Cowardice, Treason, and Despair. When she rides to battle, she drowses on top of a "restful, slothful elephant," and as soon as Prowess brandishes her lance, she runs away for good (ll. 1174-1220, 2454-55). The procession to battle is more colorfully described in Chapter 75 of Farinator's *Lumen animae.* Here Accidia rides an ass and wears the image of an ape on her helmet (because apes like to eat nuts, but when they find how bitter the shell is, throw it away with the sweet kernel), of a buffalo on her shield (who flops to the ground when he is given a great burden), and of a leopard on her mantle (who easily desists from catching his prey when this proves difficult).

Jean de Le Mote's *La Voie d'Enfer* gives a long description of the Inn of Paresse, which the dreamer reaches in the company of Murder, Despair, and three deadly sins (sts. 87-96). It is a very poor, dirty, ragged place. A fire is burning and has spread to the bedstraw, but Paresse is too lazy to put it out. Her servants are Faintise and Laschetes. When the dreamer is introduced by Pride, she hardly opens her eyes, but she manages to tell the pilgrim how he can get to hell through Sloth and her daughter Nicete (Folly): Never work, even if you are poor; stay away from church, sacrament, and prayer; never fast; and always be close to bed or easychair! Then she serves the pilgrims a mean meal of hard bread crusts, fried turnips, and water, spread on the ground without a tablecloth. Nevertheless, the pilgrim sleeps noisily till next day's dinnertime. Later he sees the result of such a life when Paresse shows him the place where her followers are punished in hell (sts. 175-78): they lie on beds of burning coal in the embrace of devils.

Pictorial and moral descriptions are used side by side in Gower's characterization of Accide and her offspring in the *Mirour de l'Omme.* The sin is the fifth in the marriage pageant. She comes riding slowly on an ass far behind the others, carrying an owl on her fist. By her side is always her bed made of lead. Her aspect is somewhat dull, because she has not had enough sleep (ll. 889-900). Her children are then described in moral terms that are very reminiscent of the picture of a slothful man we had seen earlier in such handbooks as *Handlyng Synne.* As a matter of fact, this long characterization is a texture that combines all the logical and rhetorical devices employed in popular instruction during the later Middle Ages. Gower uses the classification of sins and faults by attributing "daughters" to the chief vices and even creates a more regular pattern in which each sin has the same number of children (five). As just mentioned, he draws "characters" of Somnolence, Laziness (Peresce), Faintness (Lachesce), Idleness (Oedivesce), and Negligence. Within these, he uses a good many of the authoritative quotations, exemplary figures, similes, and *exempla* we have been discussing. To mention only a few that are easily recognized: The biblical injunction to burn a barren tree and St. Paul's words that the idler shall not eat are cited against Laziness (ll. 5569-71; 5455-56). A quotation from Cato appears in the section on Somnolence (ll. 5266-68). As exemplary figures the rear guard of the Hebrews and the plowman who looks back are mentioned (ll. 5653-62, on Lachesce), and in the section on Somnolence a reference to Leviticus appears, which may be an allusion to Isboseth (ll. 5269ff.). Various familiar animal similes occur: the indolent cat (ll. 5395ff.), the snail and the ass (5413ff.), the moth and worm of sadness (ll. 5717-18), and others. Finally, the *exemplum* of the lazy carter who leaves it up to God to pull his cart out of the mud is at least alluded to (ll. 5809ff.).

In all fairness to Gower it must be said that, regardless of its length, his description of the vice is far more readable and less tedious than similar allegories that use the same conventional material. Besides, Gower's total conception of *acedia* bears an interesting accent that makes it slightly different from the concept we had analyzed in the preceding chapter: Religious faults deriving from the capital vice and worldly ones are very neatly balanced. Accide is introduced as the sin who "does no service to either God or the world" (l. 256), and her five children have such a disposition,

> Que pour labour du camp ne vine
> A nul temps serront travaillez,
> Ne se serront abandonnez
> A les prieres ordeinez,
> Comme sont precept du loy divine.
> (ll. 5129-33)

Similarly balanced statements occur again and again in the descriptions of individual daughters. Lachesce, for example, always delays:

> Trestout met en delaiement,
> Et le divin et le mondein.
> (ll. 5615-16)

Gower's *acedia* connotes as much neglect of the proper care for the body as for the soul:

> Car, si Peresce dont vous dis
> Fait l'omme tard et allentis
> Selonc le corps de ce qu'appent
> Au monde, encore plus tardis
> Fuit le corage et plus eschis
> De ce que l'alme proprement
> Duist faire a dieu.
>
> (ll.5533-39) [130]

If Gower's *Mirour* furnishes a good example of characterization by description, another method is primarily used in a Latin allegory contained in British Museum MS. Harley 1294. In this work narrative and description are reduced to a minimum, and the personified vices characterize themselves by monologue. One day Greed meets Lust and says, "Why do I see you walking about so cheerful and happy?" Whereupon Lust explains her character. The same happens when Accidia comes upon the already assembled vices and expresses her eager joy at finding them, with whom she had so urgently wanted to talk. " 'What is it you have to talk about so badly?' they ask her. 'Nothing,' she answers. 'I just want to kill time with some small talk, for I die of boredom unless I spend my day prattling or running about.' "[131] When she is alone, so she goes on to say, she wonders who has put the sun in the sky. Silence is torment to her; staying in one place bores her to death. She hates manual work but lives on prattling (*verbositas*), sleep, and restlessness of body and soul. Listening to rumors and looking at novelties is bliss. Her special disciples, she concludes, are hermits and solitaries, but monks (*cenobite*) do not so easily fall into her hands, since they pass their days with a variety of occupations. "Whereas secular people and those who do not practice any spiritual work, I disdain to attack."

Another example of such self-revelation is the *Moralité des sept péchés mortels et des sept vertus*. In a first appearance with Pride, Accide carries a crucifix, which somewhat upsets her master. But she calms him by declaring that she bears God's image in His derision. She made the children of Israel stray and adore idols in the desert and caused Solomon's fall. She still turns Christians away from doing good by making them stay in bed at mass time and jangle, play, and backbite in church.[132] She has the complexion of Mercury, who is changeable and opposed to firm faith, thus causing unbelief, hypocrisy, and feigning (ll. 391-436). The sin appears a second time in the dispute with *Porueanche* (ll. 1565-1697). Now she is called Pareche. She has to be waked up and then explains her nature in conventional terms, for which she is rebuked in equally conventional fashion. At last, she confesses to a hermit that she has always lived "en accide" (1685) because

> i'aie este trop niche
> Et trop endormie a bien faire.
> (ll. 1692-93)

A less conventional dramatization of the sin is the rather remarkable, though short, fifteenth-century poem, *The Mirror of the Periods of Man's Life* (EETS 24). Here the temptation of Sloth is correlated with various ages of Man. At twenty, Sloth advises Man to take his rest; he is forbidden to be busy, to go to church, and to listen to good counsel (ll. 125-26; 209ff.). In old age, when Pride, Lechery, Gluttony, Envy, and Wrath have left Man, only Avarice and Sloth remain with him (ll. 505ff.), the latter finally in the form of Overhope and Wanhope.

The *Mirror* already demonstrates in part a third method of characterizing the vice: dramatic action. This device was undoubtedly more often employed in late medieval preaching than has been recorded. A good example is preserved in the fifteenth-century *Treatise on the Ten Commandments,* where at the Devil's call the Seven Deadly Sins congregate in a tavern. Sloth comes as "the marshall of that hall" and "looks over all of them and charges Idleness to cheer them up and to sit still, and [see to it] that the cup be not empty."[133]

But dramatic action comes to full life—apart from the moralities, which we shall examine later—only in the great allegorical pilgrimages of the fourteenth and fifteenth centuries. These poems, too, use moral and pictorial description along with dialogue, but in addition they characterize the vice by means of the situation in which it attacks the pilgrim, the action of its companions, the pilgrim's reaction, and so on. It is a commonplace that later medieval allegories owed an enormous debt to the *Romance of the Rose.* This is truer of the pilgrimages than of the other allegorical poems we have mentioned. Here the reader gets a much stronger sense that the poem tries to express the psychological reality of temptation, of vices and virtues in their action within man, just as Guillaume de Lorris had done this in his psychological analysis of love by means of personification allegory. Besides, the two pilgrimages we shall examine have obviously lifted a character from the *Romance* and linked it to *acedia*: Dame Oiseuse, whom we shall meet presently.

Jean de Courcy's *Le Chemin de Vaillance*, a dream vision of some 41,000 lines, shows the author in pursuit of *vaillance*. The second of the four books into which the poem is divided has him encounter the seven deadly sins. After passing the castle of Pride, the mountain of Envy, the hard rocks of Wrath, and the treasures of Avarice, our pilgrim—in the company of the seven daughters of Sapience, who always hover in the background—arrives at the edge of a large bog where the water is still and motionless. In its middle stands a high tower, strong-looking but apparently with no guard on it. Suddenly the pilgrim notices an extremely beautiful damsel, blond-haired, white-necked, and so on, the only disturbing thing about her being her near immobility, like that of a bird in a cage. But Desire sends the pilgrim on to greet her. He notices that she is singing softly and picking flowers to weave some pretty chaplets. As it turns out, her name is Oiseuse, daughter of Paresce, who governs the Tower of Accide. Her father lives in his tower at complete ease, without any care in the world, sleeping as long as he pleases behind closed windows. Her own function is to lead recreant pilgrims to the tower. All this sounds attractive enough to the Pilgrim and he follows Oiseuse, who weaves him a chaplet, though she has to rest twice or three times on the way. As soon as they arrive, Tedicité (i.e., *taedium vitae*) locks the door, and the Pilgrim forgets his quest. He meets Paresce, still asleep, who eventually lets him read his commission from the Devil to guard the bog. He has five servants for this purpose: Debilité, Tedicité, Negligence, Pusillanimité, and Desespoir. Then the Pilgrim gives up his sword and shield, lies down, and the window is closed.

But fortunately his companion Désir has remained outside. He now goes back to camp and fetches Diligence, who comes with five warriors. They carry a flag with a swallow painted on it, "diligente, plaisant[e], et belle," while the evil host flies a banner with the figure of

> ung asne parescheux, pesant,
> Quy tousiours est lent et gesant.
>
> (fol. 160v)

A siege with war engines begins, leading to two lengthy verbal disputes. In the first, Magnanimité confronts Pusillanimité. It is worth noting that the virtue exhorts the vice, not only to the love and service of God, but also to the pursuit of worldly glory.

> Par tulles nous est recite
> Soyes fort contre aduersite
> En vsant de hardy courage
> Ce cera a vostre auantage
> Pour puissance en siecle auoir
> Et la gloirc de dieu auoir
> Pour ce doibs tu hault vouloir prendre
> Sans toy a cuer failly attendre
> Car quy de luy trop fort s'approche
> Viure ne pourroit sans reproche.
>
> (fol. 162r)

Similarly, not only the saints but also "les preux quy conquestoient Pluiseurs regnes ou ilz estoient" are held up as examples against sloth. In view of this argument, Pusillanimité can make no defense. In her place Desespoir rushes in to guard the fort. A second debate begins, now with Esperance, who shows by examples from classical lore that despair leads to suicide,[134] whereas God is always merciful. But her words fall on deaf ears: Desespoir kills herself. At this the Pilgrim, who has apparently been listening, flees from the Tower of Accide. The episode ends with a very long conversation between him and Diligence, who launches into a sermon on Paresce and its evils (including some classical *exempla*[135]) as well as on Diligence (with some more *exempla*[136]), exhorting the dreamer to seek *vaillance seculière* as well as *vaillance divine.* The Pilgrim—finally—repents of his folly and gets ready to meet new perils (as it turns out, Gluttony).[137]

Apart from the images Jean de Courcy has used to characterize *acedia,* and the curious combination of secular and divine values whose pursuit is neglected by this sin, the important element in this poem for our study is the peculiar relation of idleness to *acedia*-sloth. Here the *Chemin de Vaillance* obviously combines two traditions: the old Cassianic idea of *otiositas* being a "daughter" of the capital vice and almost synonymous with it; and the function of Oiseuse in the *Romance of the Rose* as porter to the Garden of Delight, that is, as leader to the life of ease and freedom from cares. The latter function appears even more clearly in Deguileville's *Pèlerinage de vie humaine,* where Idleness and Sloth are farther separated in space and in their roles in the Pilgrim's progress yet preserve the same genetic relation. This is quite clear in the first version of the poem (D I); in the revision (D II) Deguileville made some changes which eventually led to an unclear relationship of the two figures in Lydgate's version (L).[138]

The general plan of the episode with which we are concerned is this: When after lengthy preparations the Pilgrim finally sets out on his journey (L: ll. 10305ff.), he soon comes to a crossroads where the two ways are divided by a hedge (Penance). On the left path sits Idleness, on the right a netmaker called Labor, who constantly makes and unmakes his nets, like a latter-day Abba Paulus. The Pilgrim speaks to both and eventually proceeds on the path of Idleness (under the guidance of Youth, in D II and L). This wrong choice, of course, gets him at once into trouble in the form of the seven deadly sins, whom he now meets seriatim. In D II and L, Gluttony and Venus come first, but in D I the Pilgrim is immediately caught by Sloth (the two other sins attacking him much later). The confrontation with Sloth itself is fairly much the same in all three versions.

Idleness, or rather Oiseuse, appears in D I explicitly as the daughter of Paresse, put by her at the crossroads to lead pilgrims into her snares. Oiseuse foretells the Pilgrim that he shall meet Paresse near by (D I: ll. 6841ff.; D II: fol. xlv, r); and similarly Paresse enlightens him later that it was her daughter Oiseuse's guile that brought him to her (D I: ll. 7243ff.; omitted in D II). In Deguileville's original plan, therefore, the genetic and functional relation between the two figures is quite clear. So is Oiseuse's derivation from the *Romance of the Rose*: She calls herself *portière* (D I: l. 6747) and leads to the same pleasures as her ancestor in the *Romance*. Some additional details of her characterization may be noted: She carries one hand under her armpit[139] while the other plays with a glove (D I: ll. 6524ff.);[140] her "work" consists in trimming herself with comb and mirror and telling fables on Sundays; and she cares very much for the Pilgrim's body, seeing to it that it is free from pain and always well dressed and adorned.

In striking contrast to this lovely creature stands her mother, Paresse or Sloth, hideous, old, bald like a singed cat, her body covered with black down.[141] The Pilgrim wants to escape from the wrong path through the hedge of Penance but stands still in fear and perplexity as he considers its sharp thorns. Then all of a sudden he finds himself bound, sees Sloth, and calls her foul and of low birth. The old hag defends herself: she has been with emperors, kings, bishops, abbots, and so on. Her master is the chief butcher of hell.[142] She causes children (as well as grown-ups) to lie in bed and "sleep, dream, and slumber" (L: l. 13789); she makes the sailor sleep under the mast till his ship is wrecked; and she is responsible for the brambles, nettles, and weeds in one's garden. She has learned the raven's song "craas, craas." Her name is "Slouthe," but she may also be called "Hevynesse" (or Tristesse, in D I and D II),[143] for she is that mill which always turns and never grinds anything "save waste vpon myn owne thouht" (L: l. 13836). She carries an axe in one hand, two ropes in the other, and five cords around her neck. The axe, she explains, is "werynesse off a manhys lyf," i.e., *taedium vitae,* which caused Elias to sleep under the juniper tree. The two ropes, which were not made at Clairvaux, are Sloth and Negligence (or, Negligence and Lacheté or Fétardie, in D I and D II); and the five cords [144] are Hope of Long Life, Foolish Dread, Shame, Papelardie (i.e., hypocrisy), and Despair. With these, Dame Sloth prevents people from confessing their sins, and she now proceeds to tie them around the Pilgrim's neck; the Pilgrim is finally saved only by a white dove sent from Grace Dieu.

One easily recognizes that Deguileville has used a number of iconographic elements from conventional teaching on *acedia* and transformed them into images, or rather into details of the fairly well unified image of Sloth and man's confrontation with the sin. Thus, biblical quotations such as "The sluggard buries his hand in his armpit" (Prov. 26:15, in the Vulgate version) and "I went by the field of the slothful . . . , and lo, it was all grown over with thorns, the face thereof was covered with nettles" (Prov. 24:30-31) form the source for the behavior of Idleness and the description Sloth gives of the results of her company. The biblical figure of Elias appears in connection with Sloth's axe. And a stock simile as well as an *exemplum* are reflected in Sloth's song "cras, cras" and in the figure of the netmaker. Yet beyond these easily traceable images, Deguileville has used others which very probably were his own invention. In addition to employing images that appear in description and monologue, the two allegorical pilgrimages of life we have analyzed visualize the psychology of temptation through dramatic action, such as: the pilgrim's being tied by the cords of Sloth, his being surprised by her as he stands in fear of physical hardship, or his falling into obliviousness as soon as *taedium vitae* shuts the door to sunlight and the quest for valor. With all these characteristics of a poetic imagination present, one may well ask whether these works do not really belong to genuine poetry rather than didactic literature and should therefore be rejected as sources for the iconography of sloth in popular teaching.

Certainly, these allegorical pilgrimages have a high claim to rank with works of truly imaginative literature. In them, the various molecules which in the catechetical handbooks were floating in solution have been, by the poet's pictorial imagination, crystallized, if not into a gem, at least into a precious stone of some value. However, their image of sloth contains one element which strongly links them with the simpler allegories and further with the common handbooks, and which shows clearly that their authors were more intent upon teaching than on creating a work of art. The ancient "daughters" or "species" of the vice, which appeared in the allegories of battle, marriage, and the journey to hell, by means of both moral and pictorial description, are still used in the allegorical pilgrimages and visualized as keepers of the tower (*Chemin de Vaillance*) or as the tools Sloth carries to destroy man (Deguileville-Lydgate). However successfully these "species" may have been transformed into well-integrated images (as in Deguileville and Lydgate), they betray their author's urge to pack as much traditional teaching matter into his poem as possible. They give his work an emblematic appearance which makes it, essentially, a piece of didactic literature.

VI

THE POETS

A lover of imaginative literature who has learned from Aldous Huxley and T. S. Eliot that *acedia* was the medieval forerunner of melancholy, *ennui*, and *Weltschmerz*,[1] and who then turns to medieval belles-lettres with the expectation of finding lyrical expressions comparable to the poetry of Keats, Baudelaire, or Matthew Arnold, will suffer much surprise and frustration. There is nothing like an Ode to Accidie or a Sonnet on Sloth nor even a Complaint against Idleness of great lyrical stature. Penitential lyrics often mention the seven deadly sins,[2] and the vast amount of didactic poetry contains descriptions of the vice which are often, as we saw in the case of extended allegories, not devoid of charm and wit. But one misses more intensive poetic explorations of a personal experience which, in its more "interesting" spiritual aspects, must have been shared by a large number of lettered men and women capable of expressing themselves in verse and imagery.

Writing a chapter on *acedia* in medieval poetry from the viewpoint of literary criticism is, therefore, rather like the old problem of sailing between Scylla and Charybdis. On the one hand, one could catalogue all the instances in romances, religious allegories, lyric poetry, and the drama where the sin of sloth is mentioned or dealt with. The result, undoubtedly, would be a little dull and not very profitable for a critical understanding of medieval literature. On the other hand, one could follow the more fashionable course of allegorical interpretation and look for the sin beneath the literal events narrated in a romance or dream vision. This method has its undoubted value if a careful analysis succeeds in showing that the poet has used a cluster of images conventionally referring to this concept and, what is perhaps more important, that the allegorized concept does not stand in a vacuum but is linked to other allegorized concepts in a fashion that corresponds with a clearly recognizable and coherent pattern of medieval thought. Otherwise, an analysis that can do no more than suggest that a lovesick romance hero is meant to symbolize *acedia* because he stays in bed and weeps abundantly,[3] seems rather pointless. But even if it can make a more solid and plausible case—and for such critical work I hope the preceding chapters have furnished a useful tool—, allegorical interpretation will remain somewhat speculative and consequently fail to provide concrete evidence for our investigation of what the notion of *acedia* meant to medieval man and how it was used by the poets.

There is, however, a *via media* which may avoid the two dangers and lead to some true insight and appreciation by means of selecting a few works of first importance in which the term "acedia" or "sloth" is used and asking what the poet has done with the inherited tradition. For such an analysis I have chosen four works: Dante's *Divine Comedy*, *Piers Plowman*, the English morality play *Mankind*, and Petrarch's *Secretum*. These works use the concept in different fashions, for different literary purposes, and with great originality.

Acedia in the *Divine Comedy* is quite easy to appraise because, following conventions of the allegorical pilgrimage to hell or paradise, Dante used it and the other deadly sins as consecutive stations on man's way of purgation. Yet discussing the vice is somewhat complicated, first, by the fact that the position of the deadly sins in *Inferno* is a matter of controversy,[4] and second, because even a slight knowledge of the sin tradition will discover familiar aspects of *acedia* scattered through all parts of the poem. For example, in fore-hell Virgil and the poet encounter the souls of the lukewarm, "the wretched souls of them who lived without blame and without praise" (*Inf.*, III, 35-36),[5] who are disdained by heaven and hell alike and forgotten by the world (49-50). In similar positions at the entrance of the other two realms are souls who *delayed* conversion because of *negligence* (*Purg.*, III-VIII) and who somewhat *neglected* their religious vows (*Par.*, III, 56-57), the latter fittingly inhabiting "the *slowest* sphere," that of the moon (III, 30.51). No wonder that critics are sometimes tempted to see in these and similar details and images the sin of sloth. But one should remember that in the *Summa theologiae* of St. Thomas *negligentia, tepiditas,*

and other features customarily belonging to the vice are likewise treated separately from *acedia.*

For a just understanding of Dante's *acedia* one must, therefore, turn to the place where the vice is pictured unequivocally and in detail: the fourth terrace of purgatory. As the two pilgrims arrive there, night falls, and by a general law of purgatory they are unable to move any farther. Virgil uses the enforced rest to expound to Dante the organization of the mountain. What follows (XVII, 91-139) is a Scholastic rationale of the seven capital vices in *terza rima* which deduces them from the principle of misdirected love. *Acedia* consists in loving a great good with less intensity (*vigore* or *cura,* ll. 96 and 100) than it deserves; it is "slow love" (*lento amore,* l. 130). This rational explanation of the seven vices is not, as has previously been believed, a creation of Dante's own thought but has its perfect model in the rationale developed by William Peraldus in his *Summa de vitiis.*[6] Dante's ingenuity lies not so much in creating his rationale for the seven vices as in selecting, from a number of existing schemes, the one that derives all sin from the singular principle of misdirected love, without relying on other principles, such as the powers of the soul or the psychological movements of attraction and flight.[7] How beautifully Peraldus' rationale fits into Dante's poetic cosmos where Love "moves the sun and the other stars" (*Par.,* XXXIII, 145) hardly needs to be pointed out.

The conception of *acedia* as "slow love" is unfolded and visualized in the scene Dante observes on the fourth cornice. To his question what offense is punished here, Virgil replies:

> "Love of the good," said he, "that once let slide
> Its proper duties, is restored up there."
> (XVII, 85-86)

In Scholastic Latin the offense (*amor del bene, scemo del suo dover*) would be expressed as "amare bonum minus quam est debitum," which echoes Peraldus' "parvus amor magni boni."[8] Virgil immediately adds an image: "Here the slackened oar is plied again" (l. 87). I have not found this metaphor in the standard treatments of *acedia,* but Dante's predilection for images of the sea voyage is well known, and rowing on the ocean of the world was a common medieval allegory for man's life on earth. The adjective *tardato* ("slackened"), of course, recalls a main aspect of *acedia.*

The pilgrim's contact with sloth is then interrupted by Virgil's exposition of the structure of purgatory, followed by his lecture on the psychology of love and on free will (XVIII, 1-75). When he has finished, it is deep night, the moon has risen, and Dante grows drowsy (ll. 85-88). But suddenly he is shaken out of his *sonnolenza* by a crowd that rushes past him with shouting and weeping like a throng of bacchantes. They are souls who once were slothful and are now in expiation driven by "good will and just love" to race along the cornice. In giving them this punishment Dante follows the principle of sacramental penance that *contraria contrariis curantur*:[9] slowness is healed by haste, lacking zeal by an orgy-like fervor in which their rectified good will and just love *ride* the souls (l. 96):[10] *buon voler,* because now the slothful wholeheartedly desire the good; *giusto amor,* because now they love the good justly, that is, with due intensity. Curiously enough, they run by night, whereas the two pilgrims cannot move one foot. Again, Dante's arrangement reflects commonplaces of medieval preaching: The slothful are doing penance by night because they failed to heed the example of Christ, who had to "work while it is day" (John 9:4), and because they neglected to follow His warning to wake and pray (Matt. 26:41).

As the souls hurry past, Dante hears an antiphony of shouts. Two voices proclaim *exempla* against the vice of sloth. The first praises the zeal of the Blessed Virgin: "Mary went in haste to the mountains" (l. 100). The idea of systematically using incidents from the life of Mary as examples against the seven vices may have come to Dante from Conrad of Saxony's *Speculum beatae Mariae Virginis.*[11] But the *Speculum* does not connect *acedia* with Luke 1:39 ("Maria abiit in montana cum festinatione"). That connection occurs in catechetical literature, notably in Peraldus (*Summa,* 1. 142). The second *anti-exemplum* recalls the eagerness of Julius Caesar:

> "Caesar, to subjugate Ilerda, thrust
> Hard at Marseilles and raced on into Spain."
> (ll. 101-2)

I have not encountered Caesar in connection with the vice elsewhere; but we have seen how theologians did sometimes illustrate Christian vices with classical figures and *exempla.* In response to these two examples of virtuous haste the rest of the crowd shouts,

"Quick, quick! let not the precious time be lost
For lack of love!" the others cried, pursuing.
(ll. 103-4)

The antiphonal character of this scene reminds us of the fact that negligence and drowsiness in saying the office, in reciting the Psalms in choir, was a dominant aspect of *acedia.* So was the waste of time, stressed in the crowd's reply. On the other hand, the image in the last line of this tercet: "Let zeal in doing good make grace green again" (*Che studio di ben far grazia rinverda,* l. 105), suggests the aridity of sloth, which in popular preaching was commonly expressed by biblical images such as the withered fig tree and the man with the dry hand.

Virgil addresses the running host as people in whom "sharp fervor . . . makes up for negligence and delay which you perhaps used through lukewarmness in doing good" (ll. 106-8). The equation of *acedia* with *tepiditas* occurs also in Peraldus, and *negligenza* and *indugio* ("delay") are common aspects of the vice. More interesting is the subsequent answer of the slothful: "We are so filled with the will to move/That we cannot take rest" (ll. 115-16). Although all the penitents on the mountain willingly accept the penance which God has imposed on them, there is a remarkable contrast between the former *accidiosi* and souls being cleansed of other vices: They are not pressed down by heavy loads, or blinded by having their eyelids sewn up, or deprived of food and drink, or suffering within hot flames, but they are impelled and even "ridden" (l. 96) by their own "will to move." Their penance thus appears less as a pain imposed from outside than as an act which rises out of their own will. This emphasis on the more active will of the erstwhile slothful (in contrast to patient suffering) accords neatly with the Scholastic notion that *acedia* is a disease of man's affect or will.

The following episode on the cornice of sloth is less clear because of our ignorance about the historical figure whom Dante now introduces as the unique representative of the slothful in purgatory. "I was abbot of San Zeno in Verona" (l. 118) he exclaims, adding that he lived during the reign of Barbarossa, and then Dante launches into an indirect attack on a nearly contemporary lord of Verona who had made his illegitimate and unsuitable son abbot of San Zeno. The latter attack does not concern us, but the figure of the twelfth-century abbot is puzzling because nothing is known about any such person who would provide a good example of *acedia.* Dante commentators have suggested that the poet used an abbot as a general symbol for the fact that *acedia* was primarily a monastic vice, or that the poet deliberately left this man a vague figure because, as an *accidiosus,* the abbot had given himself to "a life without fame" (cf. *Purg.,* XVIII, 138). Neither suggestion is very convincing, because this abbot is not really a general symbol but a sufficiently individualized figure, and because in fore-hell, the proper place for those who lived without praise or blame, Dante did indeed identify one of them quite clearly (Pope Celestine V; *Inf.,* III, 58-60). Surely, such explanations try to make a virtue out of necessity. Yet in the absence of further historical information nothing more can be said about the abbot.

The end of the hurried procession has arrived. Virgil calls Dante's attention: "See where two others come, giving *accidia* bites" (*dando all' accidia di morso,* ll. 131-32). Here the vice is for the first and only time called by its technical name. The curious image of "biting" *acedia* once more expresses the almost unseemly fervor of the penitents (like *cavalca* in l. 96) and continues the simile of bacchantes in their orgy-like frenzy.[12] The two penitents pointed at by Virgil proclaim two more *exempla,* this time of the vice itself. The first alludes to the tedium of the Hebrews in the desert, a standard example of spiritual sloth in popular literature, including Peraldus. The second comes from the *Aeneid*:

> "The folk whose faint endeavour
> Failed good Anchises' son, and did not last,
> Sank to a slothful life, disfamed for ever."
> (ll. 136-38)

The allusion is to Aeneas' companions who, weary of the hardships of the sea voyage, give up the quest for Rome and stay behind (*Aeneid,* V, 604ff.).

Finally, after the episode of Dante's dream of the Siren, the two wanderers hear the farewell song from the cornice of sloth: "Blessed are they who mourn" (XIX, 50). The connection between the blessings of the Sermon on the Mount and the seven vices formed part of the conventional practice of theologians and preachers to correlate various septenaries.[13] But Dante's choice of this particular blessing for *acedia* defies tradition, in which *acedia* was normally linked to the blessing of "those that hunger and thirst for righteousness." One might explain Dante's change as having been suggested by the Scholastic view that *acedia* ultimately consisted in *tristitia,* i.e., sadness or aversion of the mind because of the hardship which accompanies the exercise of virtue. But this would mean a divine approval of the vice instead of the virtue, or at least a very dubious equivocation in the use of *tristitia,* and I believe a different explanation must and can be found.

Let us return for a moment to the scene just before the slothful appear. Dante is quite drowsy, *sonnolento* (XVIII, 87-88), and although his somnolence may be nothing but the natural result of a hard day's climb and of paying close attention to Virgil's labored explanation of the seven deadly sins, love, and free will, it is a very fitting state for the pilgrim to suffer on the terrace of sloth. Significantly enough, Dante's somnolence returns as soon as the bacchantic procession is gone, and now he falls asleep and dreams (XVIII, end).

In this second dream on the mountain the poet is deeply disturbed by the figure of a siren who, at first ugly and stammering, revives under his glance and sings seductively, to be at last revealed by Virgil in all her revolting squalor. As Virgil explains to the poet later, this frightening creature symbolizes the last three sins which they will encounter on the mountain: avarice, gluttony, and lust (XIX, 58-60). In having the pilgrim pass in his prophetic dream from the realm of sloth to the sins of the flesh by turning his eyes upon a seemingly beautiful but essentially rotten object, Dante once more uses an old and common medieval tradition, the psychological concatenation of the seven chief vices, established by St. Gregory and fully developed by Hugh of St. Victor. According to this scheme, the soul who has lost her inner joy by *tristitia* or *acedia* turns to external goods from which she expects comfort (*avaritia*) and thence descends to the pleasures of the flesh (*gula* and *luxuria*).

Beyond this function in the general psychology of the vices, the Siren also has a very personal meaning for Dante. In the tense scene of his confession (*Purg.*, XXXI) Beatrice rebukes him for having after her death turned to false, earthly goods instead of following her immortal beauty with his whole mind and affections, and she warns him not again to follow "the sirens" (l. 45). Dante had already confessed that it was *le presenti cose* which turned his footsteps astray (ll. 34-36). Despite the difference in grammatical number, it seems logical to identify the Siren of Dante's dream with *le serene* of the confession. Does the dream thus not express a symbolic reliving of Dante's former experience, the progression from immense grief at Beatrice's death to a false turn towards the lures of external beauties, whatever precisely they may have been? If this is true, Dante has here added a personal dimension to the theological and moral meaning which *acedia* bears in his cosmos, a personal dimension which implies that for Dante *acedia* or *lento amore* sprang from the loss of good. This experience agrees very well with Hugh of St. Victor's concatenation of the vices: "When all is lost (viz., God, neighbor, and self, through the preceding three vices), there is nothing from which man's miserable mind can derive joy, and thus it is dashed upon itself through *tristitia*."[14] And St. Thomas similarly included grief as a secondary aspect of *acedia*: "Also the sorrow about a true evil is bad . . . if it depresses a man so much that it makes him withdraw entirely from a good deed."[15] We have thus penetrated from the doctrinal to a personal level of Dante's vision of *acedia*, and in doing so are able to see why the poet-pilgrim is sent from the cornice of sloth with the unconventional blessing of "those that mourn, for they shall be comforted."

The same fusion of tradition with personal experience is possibly indicated already at the very beginning of the *Commedia*. *Inferno* I shows the poet struggling to climb the mountain. He has extricated himself from the *selva oscura* and sees the sunlit heights that invite him, but he falters, "so that the firm foot was always the lower" (l. 30). Then he encounters the three beasts, of which the fiercest, the *lupa*, in all probability symbolizes avarice (I, 49-60. 93ff.; cf. *Purg.*, XX, 10). J. Freccero has shown, and I believe conclusively, that the *piè fermo* refers to the left foot, the *pes affectus* of medieval theologians and preachers.[16] What hinders Dante from ascending even before the appearance of the beasts is his spiritual lameness. We have noticed earlier that the discord between *pes intellectus* and *pes affectus* was used to characterize *acedia* by Peraldus and in the very influential *Compendium theologicae veritatis*. It is therefore probable that here again Dante expressed the psychological reality that man's soul, when captured by sin and incapable of rising before it gains true insight into sin, passes from *acedia* to avarice and the other sins of the flesh.

The concept which occupies such a central position in Dante's poem—literally as well as spiritually—agrees in both its doctrinal and its personal dimensions fully with medieval traditions as we have studied them so far. Dante's rationale for the seven sins, his definition of *acedia*, and the images by which he expresses the vice, have demonstrably grown out of Scholastic teaching and popular imagery. The poet combined traditional aspects of the concept with personal poetry, but he did not change it. There is only one slight exception. In *Purgatorio* XVIII the slothful proclaim four examples of the vice and its opposite virtue, of which two are taken from Scripture and are quite conventional (Mary and the Hebrews), and two from pagan literature and apparently Dante's conception (Caesar and the companions of Aeneas). Although the use of pagan examples for *acedia* has its models in catechetical works before Dante, such an equal proportion of pagan to biblical figures does not. Moreover, what Caesar and the companions of Aeneas illustrate is not zeal and sloth in the pursuit of virtue in general, but zeal and sloth in pursuing worldly glory (XVIII, 138) or, more specifically, in building the Roman Empire. In this respect Dante has widened the concept to include, in the neglect of religious duties, care for the temporal order. In harmony with the religious-political ideal set forth throughout the *Commedia*, Dante's *acedia* includes *lento amore* of the Eagle as well as of the Cross.

If Dante successfully integrated *acedia* in his poetic world and, retaining a firm theological definition, could harmoniously link it to his political theory as well as to elements of personal experience without disrupting the traditional concept, *Piers Plowman* in contrast shows a curious disintegration of the idea and indeed of Scholastic thought patterns. It begins with the use of the seven deadly sins, which in this poem no longer furnish an important structural principle. Whereas in other allegorical pilgrimages, such as the *Purgatorio* or Deguileville's *Pèlerinage de vie humaine* or the *Chemin de Vaillance*, the sins appear allegorized as stations or obstacles on the pilgrim's way, here they serve no major structural purpose but only form part of larger allegories which, in their turn, are parts of the poem's over-all allegory. There are five separate allegories of this kind in which Sloth appears, not otherwise linked to one another than by the poet's putative dream experience.

The first of these passages is the mock enfeoffment in Passus II of the B-text.[17] After Lady Holy Church has explained to the Dreamer his vision of the tower and the pit and her own nature, she answers his request to understand Falsehood with the long vision of Lady Mede's proposed wedding to False. As part of the wedding ceremony a charter is read by which Mede and False are given possession and lordship over the seven sins. After Pride, Wrath, Envy, Avarice, and Lechery, they receive Gluttony, which allows them to drink and eat, swear and "jangle,"[18] and then

> to sitten and soupen · til slepe hem assaille,
> And breden as burgh-swyn · and bedden hem esily,
> Tyl sleuth and slepe · slyken his sides;
> And thanne wanhope to awake hym so · with no wille to amende.
>
> (II, 96-99)

The next appearance of the seven sins is in the great confession scene of Passus V. Moved by Reason's *sermo ad status* and by Repentance, such figures as Peronelle Proudeherte, Lecchoure, Envye, and so on, appear on the scene and confess their guilt with varying degrees of thoroughness. Here Langland characterizes the sins by diverse methods: description, monologue (either self-revelation or accusation), and dramatic action (most memorably in the case of Gluttony). Again, Sleuthe—or Accidia, as the rubric explains—is the last and follows upon Gluttony. His confession is one of the longest and will engage our attention later.

The seven sins appear a third time as blemishes on Haukyn's coat in Passus XIII. On his pilgrimage to Truth the Dreamer witnesses Conscience and Patience wandering along as fellow pilgrims. They meet one who introduces himself as a "minstrel" and wafer-seller and is called Activa Vita. He represents the simple Christian layman in the world, doing his duties toward God, society, and fellowman—in many ways an ideal figure in Langland's world until the Dreamer discovers that his "coat of Christendom" is stained and soiled in many places with the seven deadly sins.[19] Sloth once more follows upon Gluttony, not only in the order of the poem but also in the psychological sequence of the sins, because the Glutton eats and drinks more than his nature can bear, so that he falls sick and fears to die:

> That in-to wanhope he worthe · and wende nauȝt to be saued,
> The whiche is Sleuthe so slow · that may no slithes helpe it,
> Ne no mercy amenden · the man that so deyeth.
>
> (XIII, 407-9)

The B-text then adds a passage on "the braunches that bryngeth a man to Sleuth" (ll. 410-21).

Later in the same scene with Haukyn, Patience makes a long speech, in the course of which she shows that (patient) poverty is a good protection against the seven deadly sins. She argues that the poor man, when he is pursued by Sloth and fails to serve God, falls into such "mischief" or adversity that his condition "maketh hym to thynke/That god is his grettest helpe · and no gome elles" (XIV, 254-55). In other words, when the poor are slothful, they become so miserable that they will cast their hopes on God—and this good hope saves them from sloth, whose final stage, we remember, is despair or wanhope, in the sense of not hoping for any good from God.

Finally, at least five of the seven deadly sins occur once more in the last passus of the poem. The Dreamer sees Antichrist come and tear up "the croppe of treuthe." In his army fight a number of abstractions, including Pride, Lechery, Covetousness, Sloth, and Envy. They fight against Conscience, which as Langland had earlier told us is one of the many names of Anima or the Soul (XV, 31-32, 39). Conscience has taken refuge in Unity, the Church, where the Dreamer eventually follows, and is besieged by seven great giants "that with Antecrist helden" (XX, 214-15). The poem ends inconclusively, with the battle as well as the search for Piers the Plowman continuing. The general allegory here used is that of the vices' assault upon man's soul, a commonplace in late medieval didactic literature.[20] Yet Langland introduced rather original details by making Sloth the offspring of Life and Fortune, himself married to Wanhope and going about with a sling throwing "drede of dyspayre · a dozein myle aboute" (XX, 163). I have not found this curious though plausible genealogy of Sloth outside *Piers Plowman*, but it is quite possible that Langland had seen it in some sermon or allegorical poem.

The most important of these five and the key passage for our examination of sloth is the confession scene. Sleuthe, "al bislabered with two slymy ciȝen," introduces himself as extremely drowsy and promptly falls asleep. Upon a brief warning from Repentance to awake and hasten to shrift, he confesses a number of individual faults: "I do not know the Lord's prayer very well . . . . I have made forty vows and forgotten them the following day. I never performed my penance," and so forth (V, 400-48). This confession of a slothful man can be easily divided into three sections according to the nature of the faults and the changing profession of the penitent. First, Sleuthe confesses faults that concern religious duties of Everyman: ignorance of prayers; failure to fulfill vows, to carry out the imposed penance, to be truly sorry for his sins; prayer without attention; idle occupations; failure to practice the works of mercy, to listen to the word of God, to observe vigils and fast days, to come to mass in time, to go to confession regularly, and to confess well. Next follow a series of faults that are proper to parish priests, and the change is indicated by Sleuthe's words, "I haue be prest and parsoun." The faults are those of ignorance: he cannot sing, read saints' lives and the canon law, or explain the Psalms to his parishioners (ll. 422-28). Finally, Sleuthe mentions a longer series of non-clerical faults, and although no shift of identity is explicitly marked, the speaker now seems once more to be a layman. This section comprises faults of negligence in the realm of social obligations, of justice between landlord and servant and vice versa. Sleuthe forgets to pay or to return borrowed goods (ll. 429-32); he withholds his servants' wages or pays them unwillingly (ll. 433-35); he is unkind toward benefactors and forgets favors received from his "even-Christians" (ll. 436-41); he spoils his master's goods by carelessness (ll. 442-45); he wasted his youth in idleness instead of learning a craft, and he is now a beggar (ll. 446-48).

Repentance asks Sleuthe to repent, but he swoons and has to be waked with some cold water from Vigilate, who exhorts him to beware of wanhope and to trust in God's mercy (ll. 449-55). Sleuthe rallies and promises to amend: He will henceforth never miss the church services again (ll. 458-62), and he will make restitution:

> And ȝete wil I ȝelde aȝein · if I so moche haue,
> Al that I wikkedly wan · sithen I wytte hadde.
> And though my liflode lakke · leten I nelle,
> That eche man ne shal haue his · ar I hennes wende:
> And with the residue and the remenaunt · bi the rode of Chestre!
> I shal seke treuthe arst · ar I se Rome!
>
> (V, 463-68)

At this point the C-version adds a passage on the branches of sloth, which in B occurs in the section on Haukyn's coat (B: XIII, 410-21). Although Langland uses the technical term "branches," he gives nothing like the progenies one finds in Peraldus or *The Book of Vices and Virtues* but simply lists a number of faults against religious duties: Sloth "is when a man does not mourn for his misdeeds . . . and performs his penance badly, gives no alms. . . . Each day is a holiday for him," and so forth. The last aspect of the series, hate against those who tell of "Penaunce and pore men · and the passioun of seyntes" (l. 419), evidently led Langland to add a passage on the evil of maintaining idle jesters and minstrels (ll. 422-57), but the section on the branches of sloth clearly ends with line 421.

The confession of Sleuthe has caused readers and critics two major difficulties: the apparent change of the speaker's identity from layman to priest and back to layman, and the incongruity of Sleuthe's promise to make restitution, followed by the curious passage on "Robert the robbere." Concerning the change of identity, G. R. Owst suggested that it was prefigured in a homily.[21] In fact, such a change is quite common in confessional instructions from the mid-thirteenth century on. Henry of Segusio ("Ostiensis"), for example, included a section on what questions the priest was to ask in his vast *Summa super titulis Decretalium* (1253). The questionnaire on *acedia* contains the following:

> Have you been tepid and remiss in doing well when you were able to? . . . Have you ever failed to go to church or to the sermon because of laziness and indolence? . . . Have you delayed your annual confession? Have you neglected to perform the given penance? Have you neglected to carry out with diligence the ecclesiastical duties imposed on you? . . . Have you been unwilling to say Mass or to hear confession in order to shun the hardship because you would rather rest? Have you withheld your advice or help from your needy neighbor because of laziness alone? Have you, out of negligence, delayed the restitution of others' goods? . . . Have you been negligent in the faithful service of your lord, from whom you receive food, clothes, and other goods? Have you neglected to keep your oath? Have you delayed in paying your hireling the wages you had agreed on, or to remunerate him for his work and service?[22]

This formula recurs in somewhat shorter form in the *Memoriale Presbiterorum,* a manual written in 1344 at Avignon but evidently designed for an English audience,[23] and with some additions in the alphabetical encyclopedia *Omnebonum,* written about 1350-1360 in England by a certain Jacobus who was perhaps a Cistercian monk.[24] A different questionnaire shows the same change of identity. It occurs in the *Modus confitendi* ascribed to Robert Grosseteste (and another formula also attributed to the Bishop of Lincoln) and appears frequently in fourteenth-century pastoral handbooks by Englishmen.[25] This type of questionnaire may have been the model for the confession of "Suerness" that occurs at the end of *Cursor mundi* in the Cotton Vespasian manuscript. Here again the identity of the speaker shifts back and forth between layman (who is guilty, among other things, of negligence to his wife, children, and household) and priest, the latter announcing his identity in a way similar to Sleuthe in *Piers Plowman*: "Where I was shepherd and had souls to keep" (ll. 28278) and again, "And I, priest, . . . have said Mass in deadly sin," and so forth (ll. 28360f.). I do not wish to suggest that Langland copied a confessional formula or followed a questionnaire slavishly; but for the shifting identity in his confession of Sleuthe he could have found several models in instructions on hearing or making confession.

Langland's concept of sloth thus appears closely akin to what I have called the "popular image" of the sin. It is presented within such allegorical frames as the stains on the coat of grace or the assault of vices, which were frequently used in contemporary sermons. It is developed in a confessional formula, and in connection with it Langland uses at least the term "branches"—both elements characteristic of the literature of popular instruction. Above all, the emphasis lies on external faults of neglect, not on such inner attitudes as insufficient love of the divine good or lack of spiritual courage. This emphasis also appears in the fact that in *Piers Plowman* many common aspects of sloth are not included in the five passages but are attacked separately, as for instance, idle words, failure to chastise unruly children, or "overhopping."[26]

Another popular trait of sloth given peculiar emphasis in *Piers Plowman* is its connection with gluttony. In fourteenth- and fifteenth-century sermons and didactic works the two sins were often linked together or further joined by lechery. The Oxford professor John Felton (fl. 1430), for example, constantly linked *gula* with *acedia* when he discussed the seven deadly sins in his sermons.[27] We have previously noticed that the two sins sometimes shared the same animal symbol, the pig, and Langland also uses the fattened hog as an image to link the two sins in the enfeoffment passage: Through gluttony Lady Mede and her husband will

> breden as burgh-swyn · and bedden hem esily,
> Tyl sleuth and slepe · slyken his sides.
>
> (II, 97-98)

This peculiar connection probably resulted from the fact that in late medieval popular literature *acedia* came to be reckoned among the sins of the flesh, a development which will be further discussed in the final chapter. *Piers Plowman* reflects this conception when it connects sloth with gluttony in four of the five passages that present the seven deadly sins. As outlined above, sloth follows upon gluttony in the order of their presentation in Passus II, V, and XIII, whereas in Passus XIV the two are linked because of their relation in human behavior: the poor man attacked by gluttony—"So for his glotonie and his grete scleuthe · he hath a greuous penaunce" (XIV, 234). A similar psychological sequence of cause and effect links the two in Passus II and XIII, and the Glutton of the confession scene makes the assertion that his excessive drinking bout leads to "an accidie" (V, 366)—a startling and unique use of the term.[28] It should be noticed that Langland's fondness for the connection of sloth and gluttony is more than a prosodic feature, since the two terms do not alliterate.

A final characteristic which relates Langland's sloth to fourteenth-century popular handbooks is the importance he gives to worldly or social faults. Neglect of social obligations between lord and servant or family head and household usually took up some space in manuals for confession. Such faults appear in *Piers Plowman* as the third section of Sleuthe's confession. But in contrast to the manuals, they occupy a proportionately much larger space (twenty lines out of forty-nine) and are neatly set off against strictly religious faults. This fact points to a peculiarity of Langland's conception which emerges as a main characteristic of his entire vision: the connection of sloth with the waste of worldly goods, which is strongly condemned throughout the poem. Although "wastours" are not explicitly included in the confession of Sleuthe, the last three faults there mentioned concern this very sin: "forsleuthing" the goods of one's master, failure to learn a trade in youth, and begging[29] because of "foule sleuthe" (V, 442-48). The same connection exists in the few lines where Langland uses the word *sleuthe* outside the five major passages. In the Dreamer's initial vision of the field full of people, which leads to moral criticism of different social groups, sloth is explicitly ascribed to "bidders and beggeres": "Slepe and sori sleuthe · seweth hem eure." (Prol., l. 45). In Passus III Conscience paints a picture of the future ideal society in which reason shall reign, Mede shall disappear, love shall bind men together, and the common laborer shall either plow, spin, spread dung, or else "spille hym-self with sleuthe" (III, 308). Passus VI, which is particularly concerned with the right ordering of worldly goods and manual labor, symbolized by Piers's plowing the half-acre, has the "wastoures" scolded because "In lecherye and in losengerye · ȝe lyuen, and in sleuthe" (VI, 145). It should be added that later in the same passus, during the discussion about manual work and the right attitude toward false beggars, four biblical passages are quoted which are standard companions of *acedia* in the handbooks for preachers (VI, 233-54), the last one actually being from the psalm which "Parson Sleuthe" had confessed he could not construe and teach very well (V, 425-26).[30]

In Langland's vision, therefore, sloth means negligence both in man's relations with God and in his dealings with his fellow man and society, particularly in the common laborer's attitude toward his work and his duty of providing the necessities of life. The latter aspect is peculiar to Langland's thought, at least in comparison with the treatment of *acedia* in theological literature, and in this sense one might well say that in Langland's vision the concept bears a strong secular or social emphasis.[31] But one must at once add that Langland simultaneously stresses the spiritual aspect of sloth by a singular emphasis on wanhope or despair. In four passages on the seven deadly sins wanhope is explicitly linked to sloth: In the allegories of the enfeoffment (Passus II), of Haukyn's coat (XIII), and of Poverty's struggle with the sins (XIV), sloth always leads to wanhope; in the final assault of the vices on Unity, Sleuthe gets married to Wanhope and flings about despair (XX; see the summary given above). The confession scene of Passus V, too, contains this connection, though by implication only, because upon Sleuthe's promise to restore ill-won goods there follows the controversial passage in which one "Robert the robbere," who does not have the means to make restitution, comforts himself with the thought of "Dismas my brother," the penitent thief who in popular catechetical literature appears as the standard exemplary figure against despair, the last consequence of *acedia*.

This heavy and consistent stress on the close connection between sloth and despair is quite understandable in the light of traditional views about *acedia*. But observing the equally heavy emphasis Langland lays on sloth as a sin of the flesh and as neglect of social duties, one begins to wonder about the logical clearness and consistency of "sloth" in Langland's thought. Why, among all sins, should negligence in fulfilling worldly duties particularly cause despair, especially if poverty—as Langland himself says—is apt to stifle the spiritual effects of sloth and lead to good hope? (XIV,

254-55)? It looks as if Langland had used the concept with emphases which, sooner or later, might lead him into great logical difficulties. And they did. The case in point is the end of Sleuthe's confession (Passus V), which has caused readers the second major difficulty alluded to earlier, all the more vexing because it has led to questioning the single authorship of the poem's three versions.

When Sleuthe has promised to amend his life, he goes on to promise restitution (V, 463ff., quoted above). Then follows a passage on Robert the Robber, who looks on "reddite" and begins to weep because he does not have wherewith to make restitution. But he comforts himself with the thought of his "brother" Dismas, the penitent thief on Calvary, who like him had no goods with which to make amends but besought Christ's mercy and found it. Some readers have experienced great difficulty in following the sudden transition in Sleuthe's promised amendment from religious duties to restitution of "wickedly won" goods, and in accepting the rather tenuous connection of Sleuthe with a thief. Robbery, and the Church's command that a thief must restore stolen goods if possible before he can receive absolution, belong to the sin of avarice, not to sloth.

Observing the apparent incongruity, J. M. Manly explained the "break" between lines 462 and 463 (corresponding to A: V, 235-36) by suggesting that here a leaf had been lost in the original text of the A-version, and that, in order to make sense of Sleuthe's connection with Robert and restitution, the author of the B-text—a different person from A—had added the confession of Sleuthe, which includes the section on returning borrowed and ill-won goods (B: V, 392-449, not in A).[32] Manly's "lost leaf theory" and his conclusion of multiple authorship of the three versions caused much controversy, which even in recent years has not come to a standstill.[33]

Against Manly's argument of a logical break between the confession and the idea of restitution, various attempts have been made to show that the two passages can be read as following each other quite logically. R. W. Chambers connected "Robert" with the "Robert's men," that is, professional vagabonds and thieves of Langland's time, and linked these in turn to the "wastours" so often attacked in *Piers Plowman* for their besetting sins of lechery, gluttony, and sloth. Since to Langland "a Robert's man or a Wastour would seem to convey the notion of vagabondage, leading to ribaldry, gluttony and theft," the confession of such a Robert would, indeed, not be "an unfit sequel to the confession of Sloth."[34] Thus, Robert may very well be a comprehensive figure representing, and repenting for, several or even all the seven deadly sins. A different explanation was advanced by T. P. Dunning, who takes Robert to represent Covetousness and shows that the connection between sloth and covetousness was quite orthodox, and that to associate these two sins is characteristic of Langland's concern with the abuse of exterior worldly goods.[35]

I believe an even better case can be made for reading the promise of restitution and the figure of Robert in close connection with sloth, indeed as a part of this sin. The observation which started Manly's theory: that the lines in which Sleuthe promises to restore ill-won goods (B: V, 463-68; A: V, 236-41) "are entirely out of harmony with his character,"[36] loses some of its force when we consider that such restitution occasionally was an aspect of *acedia* in some confessional questionnaires of the later Middle Ages. Several of the works quoted earlier as demonstrating the shift of identity also contain questions on restitution. Ostiensis and the derived *Memoriale presbiterorum* have the confessor ask: "Distulisti ex negligentia restituere aliena? . . . Distulisti mercenario reddere salarium de quo convenisti vel aliter considerato labore suo et servicio ipsum remunerare?" Although it is true that these questions do not specify stolen goods, that they speak only of delay in restitution, and that restitution is never a major aspect of the vice, the concept of restitution does occur in a fairly influential work on confession and is therefore not entirely out of harmony with sloth.[37]

Yet there is another reason for thinking of the Robert passage as a natural and logical sequel to the confession of Sleuthe. The main purpose of the passage (V, 469-78) is obviously to emphasize the need, not of making restitution, but of relying on Christ's mercy even when the sinner cannot make amends of his own. When Robert finds that he cannot fulfill his obligation of *reddere,* the thought of the penitent thief who symbolizes victory over despair arises in his mind and comforts him. Hence the passage under discussion expresses a very harmonious psychological sequence: from the confession of sloth to the promise of amendment, including the restitution of wickedly won goods, and thence to the possibility of despair, which is warded off by the saving thought of Christ's mercy. It may very well be that poor Robert stands for three or six or seven deadly sins and not for sloth alone; the point is that the experience he symbolizes at this moment is in complete agreement with traditional medieval teaching.[38]

That sloth is consistently related to wanhope in *Piers Plowman* has already been shown. Now we must add that wanhope is as consistently connected with restitution, a connection which is almost a hallmark of Langland's thought. This connection stands out best in the speech of the Good Samaritan, who represents Charity and Christ on His way to Jerusalem (Passus XVII). The Samaritan explains the nature of the Holy Trinity, especially the comforting and saving power of the Holy Ghost which brings grace to all except those who are "unkind" to their "even-Christians" (XVII, 203ff.). The Dreamer then raises the question of deathbed conversion: "Suppose I had sinned against my neighbor and should die this moment, but now am sorry that I offended the Holy Ghost and confess and call for God's grace, who made all things, and meekly ask for His mercy—can I not be saved?" (XVII, 293-96). The Samaritan replies yes, it is possible that through repentance God's justice be turned to pity; "yet it is but seldom seen, as truth bears witness," because in God's court Justice must be satisfied. The only satisfaction a sinner on his deathbed can make is to have true sorrow, and from this he is often prevented by despair:

> Thus it goes with people who falsely all their lives
> Lived in evil and did not cease from it until life forsook them;
> Then the fear of despair drives away grace
> So that the thought of mercy cannot come into their minds.
> Good hope, which should help them, turns into wanhope—
> Not that God has no power, not that He is not mighty enough
> To amend all that is amiss, or that His mercy is not greater
> Than all our wicked deeds, as Holy Writ says, *Misericordia eius super omnia opera eius,*—
> But before His justice can turn into mercy, some restitution is needed;
> Sorrow is enough satisfaction for the man who cannot repay God.
>
> (ll. 305-14)[39]

In other words, the thought that in the economy of salvation God demands restitution often causes despair.

In this passage "restitution" designates *satisfactio operis,* the third part of the sacrament of penance. However, in the confession of Covetousness (V, 232ff., 276ff.), "restitution" is used with the meaning of restoring ill-won goods to their legal owner (or the

Church). In Langland's use of this term, therefore, we observe what is very much a peculiarity of his poetry in general: that the lines between the concrete and the abstract, or between the individual and the universal, or between the temporal and the spiritual dimensions of a concept, are fluid, and that Langland apparently employed this fluidity as a device of poetic discourse. Just as "mede" in the poem means a good many things from a bribe to the use of temporal goods, so does "restitution" imply both the returning of stolen or borrowed objects and making satisfaction for man's debt before God.

These two different denotations of "restitution" are both utilized by Langland as causes of wanhope: once in the speech of the Good Samaritan, where the sinner despairs because his life is ending, and a second time in the earlier confession of Covetousness, where the penitent robber, confronted with the Church's demand to restore ill-won goods before he can be absolved and realizing that he has no means, falls into despair and "would have hanged himself" (V, 285). The latter situation—the confession of avarice —is of course the right place for the idea of restitution in the narrow sense. The truly startling fact about restitution in *Piers Plowman* is that the poet has used it within the sequence of required restitution leading to wanhope a third time at the end of the confession of Sloth. The reason for this unexpected appearance is, I believe, a double allegiance on Langland's part. On the one hand, he apprehended wanhope as the result of inability to make restitution, whereas on the other hand he accepted wanhope as the conventional result of sloth. Since in agreement with traditional teaching the confession of Sleuthe had to include despair as the last result of *acedia,* and since Langland was so fond of deriving despair from inability to make amends, he *had* to introduce the passage on Robert the Robber, wherein despair is warded off, by a reminder of restitution, here made in the form of the penitent's promise to amend.

The difficulty readers have experienced with Robert the Robber may, thus, be due not to a lost leaf but rather to unclarity in Langland's thought. Wanhope as he understood and incorporated it into his poem is not peculiar to sloth or to avarice but consequent upon any sin (especially when one understands "restitution" as *satisfactio operis*). His failure to take this into full account seems to derive from an unresolved tension between adherence to tradition and a conception, or at least an emphasis, of his own. The conflict evidently bothered Langland himself, as the rearrangement of the respective passages in the C-version shows. This unresolved tension is probably also to blame for the logical difficulties in his notion of sloth, as I stated earlier. Obviously, Langland's concept lacks a definition that would unify the aspects of sloth and the various associations with which he built the concept into his poem, a definition like Dante's *lento amore* which holds together all the poetic images of *Purgatorio* XVII-XVIII and fits so neatly into the *Divine Comedy* with its various levels.

The analysis of Langland's sloth shows that the poet attempted to use tradition in his own way, adapting it to characteristics of his vision, but that he did not succeed in detaching himself far enough from tradition to create a logically consistent work. One might add that in *Piers Plowman* the entire scheme of the seven deadly sins has lost the importance it held in other allegorical pilgrimages, including the *Purgatorio.* Not only did Langland discard them as insignificant for structural purposes, but he also used different and more germane patterns in evaluating good and evil. For example, the scheme of Dowell-Dobetter-Dobest has much greater importance in the pilgrim's progress to Truth, and evil is primarily judged and categorized in terms of *status,* of various social groups and their pertinent duties. Hence one can notice a certain breakdown of the dividing lines between several deadly sins: traces of wrath appear in the confession of Envy (and vice-versa), as do features of avarice in the confession of Sleuthe. Thus, in *Piers Plowman* tradition and the originality of a poetic vision appear side by side. Yet with respect to the seven deadly sins, Langland's often so astonishingly powerful imagination, his skill in fusing concepts and images, seems to have lacked the necessary freedom to create its own, consistent world.

In medieval morality plays the personification of the sins, which we analyzed in our earlier survey of extended allegorics (Chapter V), is carried one step further insofar as here the sins become true *dramatis personae* and appear, speak, and act on stage. Unfortunately, of the earlier English moralities only one, *The Castle of Perseverance,* really presents the sins as actors; yet, although the evidence is so scanty, it neatly shows how the full dramatization of the vices grew out of didactic literature. A brief glance at *The*

Castle is necessary in order to see how the later play *Mankind,* with which we shall be concerned, differs in technique from what historians of the English drama consider the pure type of medieval moralities, and how it uses the idea of spiritual sloth much more originally than the genuinely allegorical drama.

In *The Castle of Perseverance,* written in the first quarter of the fifteenth century, the seven deadly sins are distributed as helpers among the three enemies of man, the World, the Flesh, and the Devil, and in this conventional scheme "Syr Slawth" belongs with Lechery and Gluttony to Flesh. In the beginning of the play, its hero, Mankind, chooses to follow the persuasions of his Bad Angel and enters the service of the World. He is enfeoffed to Avarice and the other deadly sins, who now appear for the first time and, in taking leave from their respective masters, reveal their characters by a set of appropriate speeches. Later, Mankind is converted and brought into the Castle of Perseverance. The seven virtues appear, and we learn that Sloth is opposed by Solicitudo or "Besynesse" (ll. 1644-56). Eventually, all of man's enemies muster and besiege the castle. A verbal battle between vices and virtues for the possession of Mankind begins, surely accompanied by some appropriate stage action. Again, Sloth is pitted against Busyness. The vice carries a spade as his weapon:

> ACCIDIA. Ware, war! I delue with a spade;
> men calle me þe 'lord syr Slowe.'
> gostly grace I spylle & schade;
> fro þe watyr of grace, þe dyche I fowe. [clean]
> (ll. 2327-30)

This peculiar action of draining the ditch or moat of the water of grace occurred earlier in the allegorical battle of virtues and vices described in a fourteenth-century pastoral handbook, the second part of *Oculus sacerdotis* (written before 1343) by William of Pagula. Here the vices engage in a series of consecutive military operations:

> In the army of the devil, pride carries the banner. . . . Envy draws the arrows by backbiting other men. Wrath throws the stones, as it were, of cursing and scorn. Then Accidia empties the ditches of the water of grace; for "a sad mind dries up the bones" [Prov. 17:22]. Avarice fills the empty ditches with the lust for earthly goods. Lechery lights a fire. Gluttony throws the fire and kindles it with the wood of food and drink.[40]

In *The Castle of Perseverance* all these actions except that of Avarice are used dramatically, though in different order.

The character of "Syr Slawth" agrees closely with the popular image of the vice. Besides being a sin of the flesh, as in *Piers Plowman,* its main characteristic is to hinder man in God's service (ll. 990, 1238, 2344; cf. l. 69) by causing his bed, where he "takes a sweat" (ll. 1218, 1227), or the ale-house (l. 2335) to be more attractive than the church. The other religious obligation in which faults of sloth are most common—receiving the sacrament of penance—is similarly stressed: Sloth causes delay of confession (ll. 2348-52; see also ll. 1349-57) and leaves the imposed penance undone (ll. 1222f.). The sin rules men of religion as well as lords, ladies, and rogues (ll. 989-92).

In *The Castle* Man's antagonist is not so much the combined force of the seven deadly sins as it is World with his servant, Avarice.[41] As a matter of fact, the moral struggle of Mankind boils down to the choice between God and the World. For as soon as Mankind appears on the stage, poor and naked (ll. 285, 293), he is tempted by his Bad Angel to enter "the world's service" (l. 342). In perplexity, but clearly understanding the alternatives of his choice, Mankind turns to the World with the argument that he is young and death is far away (ll. 424ff.). It is only after this choice that the seven deadly sins approach the hero. Although they have been introduced to the audience before the true action begins (ll. 157-274), and although the sins together with the Three Enemies represent a formidable array of evil, the temptation proper of Mankind is realized in terms of avarice alone, that is, of undue desire for worldly goods, which are here materialized as rich clothes and money. In similar fashion, the great siege of the castle presents an impressive gathering of evil forces. But the vices fight only against personified virtues, whereas the true and decisive assault on Mankind himself is made by Avarice alone, who—unlike the vices that preceded him—refuses to debate with his opponent virtue and instead appeals to Mankind directly. I do not think it overly subtle to say that in the genuine moral action which the play dramatizes the seven deadly sins do not hold the center but act more as a filler or perhaps a means to create comic action.

In this play the psychological reality of man's fight against evil—his fall, conversion, and relapse—is thus dramatized by objectifying good and evil forces as personified abstractions who persuade, dispute, and occasionally engage in physical action. This technique of an allegorical battle for man's soul—customarily taken to be the essence of the English morality plays—is still used to some extent in a later play, *Mankind* (*ca.* 1475). But here the temptation of man is handled with a significant difference. The "hero" stands between Mercy and Mischief, the latter accompanied by three good-for-nothings (Newguise, Nowadays, and Nought) and aided by the devil Titivillus. After receiving spiritual advice from Mercy, Mankind sets to work in the field, where he is chaffed by the three scamps but remains firm in his proposal to work and drives them off with some well-aimed blows of his spade. His enemies call Titivillus to their aid, who eventually succeeds in inducing Mankind to give up his work and join their evil fellowship. His final ruin is imminent, but in the end Mankind is saved when Mercy appears with a scourge, drives off the enemies, and by a reminder of God's mercy dissuades him from ending his life in despair.

The temptation that leads to Mankind's eventual fall is of great interest to our study because, although the word "sloth" is not used in the play, the temptation curiously follows the psychology of this vice as developed in popular catechetical literature. Mankind appears as a peasant, carrying a spade and engaged in digging up his field to sow grain. He looks like any other farm laborer, until his reason for digging strikes a surprising note:

> Thys erth with my spade I xall assay to delffe;
> To eschew ydullnes I do yt myn own selffe.
>
> (ll. 321-22)

Manual labor in order to avoid idleness—precisely the spiritual, therapeutic value given to work as one of the chief remedies against *acedia* in monastic literature and in popular instruction. Man must work in order to fulfill God's injunction after the Fall; idleness not only opens the door to the Fiend but is in itself a grave offense to man's Creator, as medieval preachers and confessors never tired of emphasizing in their discussions of sloth.[42] Realizing this, Mankind can easily ward off the open attempts made by the three rogues to draw him away from his work.

In contrast, the assault of the Devil is less easy to repel, and in fact Mankind never suspects that it is the Fiend who now induces him to give up his service of God. This gradual recession from God forms the psychologically most interesting section of the play. Titivillus buries a plank in the ground that Mankind is digging up, with the purpose "to yrke hym of hys labur" (l. 525); in other words, the devil tempts Mankind to forsake "hys goode purpose" (ll. 519, 573) by making him feel the tedium and disgust of his work.

The temptation is a success. As soon as his spade strikes the plank, Mankind exclaims: "Thys londe ys so harde yt makyth wnlusty and yrke" (l. 538). Disgusted by a little hardship, Mankind decides to sow his grain in winter "and lett Gode werke" (l. 539). But the grain is gone—Titivillus has meanwhile done away with it. In consequence, Mankind not only delays his work but gives it up altogether, refusing to accept any hardship to his body. Yet he still clings to God and, although he will not go to church,[43] kneels down and recites the Pater Noster. But Titivillus is at hand again "to make this fellow yrke" (l. 549): He whispers in his ear that "a short prayer pierces heaven," that Mankind is already holier than the rest of his kin, and that in addition he must follow an urge of his nature (ll. 551-53). And Mankind indeed abandons his beads "for drede of the colyke and eke of the ston" (l. 555), so that Titivillus can rejoice at having diverted him from being "besy in his prayers" and "from hys dyvyn seruyce" (ll. 558-59).

When Mankind returns, he has further advanced in *acedia*: Now evensong seems much too long for him:

> I am yrke of yt: yt ys to longe be on myle.
> Do wey! I wyll no more so oft on the chyrche-style.
> (ll. 575-76)

Thus he gives up, not only his work, but also his prayer with the remark, "I am nere yrke of both" (l. 578). The final step: He lies down to sleep, leaving his mind open to evil instigations of the Devil. Of course, Titivillus is only too ready with the Devil's first and last ruse: a handful of lies which he whispers into Mankind's ear, denigrating the character of Mercy and leading Mankind to believe that his spirtual father is dead. As a result, Mankind bids his former master adieu and joins the company of the rogues.

The very plot of the temptation scene intimates that the author of the play has used the vice of *acedia* as the hero's fault through which he is turned away from good. Mankind falls through tedium in doing good work, which is caused by the bodily hardship that accompanies good works, both physical and spiritual. He gives in to sleep and thus becomes fully a prey to the Devil, who then leads him to all sorts of sins and to Mischief.[44] Yet the suggestion that Mankind's fall is motivated by *acedia* can be further substantiated by the terminology employed in this passage. Mankind's first reaction to physical hardship includes two very revealing key terms: "Thys londe ys so harde yt makyth *wnlusty* and *yrke*" (l. 538). The first, "wnlusty," is an equivalent for "slothful." In *Ayenbite* the noun "onlosthede," and in *Vices and Virtues* as well as the *Ormulum* the noun "vnlust" are used as synonyms of "sloth," in addition to which *Jacob's Well* defines: "Slowthe is whan þou art vnlustig of þi-self to seruyn god or þe world."[45] The second term, "yrke," which occurs five times in the temptation scene of some eighty lines, is the Middle English equivalent for Latin *taedere* or *fastidire,* both verbs commonly used to characterize the nature of *acedia.* "Yrken" and derivatives appear frequently in Middle English works in close connection with the sin of sloth. Thus, the prose *Mirror of St. Edmund* in the Thornton manuscript (1430-1440), for example, says of sloth that it "makes man's heart heavy and slow in good deeds, and causes man to irk in prayer or holiness, and puts man in the wickedness of wanhope, for it slackens the liking of ghostly love."[46] Similarly, Rolle admonishes the would-be lover of God "not to be noyd with irksumness [*tedio*], nor with ydilness to be takyn. . . . Cees not ȝit to rede or pray, or ellis some oder gude dede inward or outward do, þat not in-to idilnes or sleuyth [*ociositatem vel accidiam*] þou scryth [fall]. Many sothely irksomnes has drawen to idilnes, and ydilnes to necligens and wikkydnes."[47] And in some versions of the *Speculum Christiani* the verses on *Accidia* begin: "I yrke full sore with goddes seruyce."[48]

As in theological discussions of *acedia,* tedium in doing good leads Mankind to delay of confession and eventually to wanhope or despair. When Mercy tries to regain Mankind, his admonition is shrugged off, Mankind apparently being unaware of the warner's identity: "I xall speke with thee a-nother tyme; to morn, or the next day" (l. 720). But when Mercy approaches a second time, now with a scourge, Mankind falls into despair (ll. 793ff.) and is helped by his evil companions in his attempt to hang himself. He is saved, but remains in the state of not hoping for God's mercy for himself because he deems his sins greater than God's willingness to forgive, until Mercy finally succeeds in reviving his hope. It is noteworthy that in his lengthy speech Mercy attacks not only wanhope but also its opposite, overhope or vain trust (ll. 837-47), a combination occasionally also found in treatments of *acedia.*[49]

If the notion of *acedia* thus lies at the heart of Mankind's fall, it equally penetrates into other aspects of the play and gives them a peculiar slant. The first three tempters, for example, are shown to be allegorical figures by their names, Newguise, Nowadays, and Nought, but their precise meaning is uncertain and they cannot easily be fitted into standard medieval patterns of temptation and evil. Unfortunately, their introductory speeches have been lost. But near the end of the play, Mercy enlightens Mankind and us that in the familiar scheme of Flesh, World, and Devil as man's three enemies they represent the world (ll. 876ff.). Yet their own activities in the play make it a little hard to be identified as such at first sight. They tempt Mankind by idle speeches and songs to let go his work, and their further enterprises make them look very much like Langland's wastours, who were also closely related to sloth: they drink and steal, murder and fornicate. Could it be that in this play the conventional enemy World has been given predominantly those aspects that appeal to Man's penchant for idleness and sloth? In Lydgate's *Pilgrimage* Dame Ydelnesse reveals it as one of her functions to

> Studye ffor to ffynde off newe
> Devyses mad off many an hewe,
> ffolk to make hem fressh & gay,
> And hem dysguyse in ther array:
> Thys myn offys, yer by yere.
> (ll. 11,667-71)

This would make at least Newguise a blood brother to Idleness.

If the temptation from the World is thus curiously slanted toward idleness and sloth, the same is also true of the Devil. I am now not thinking of his approaches to Man, already analyzed, but of his name. The choice of "Titivillus"[50] for the subtle archenemy of Man in this play has puzzled critics, especially since a devil by the same name has, in the Last Judgment play of the Towneley cycle, only a very minor function. But the name fits the Devil's role in *Mankind* very well as soon as one sees here the temptation of *acedia*. It is well known that in medieval literature from the fourteenth century on the proper function of Titivillus was to watch out for idle talk in church and for the overskipping of syllables and words in the divine service. This is exactly the occupation by which he identifies himself in the Towneley cycle.[51] Also in the *exemplum* which narrates the vision of a fiend carrying a sack of overskipped syllables, the Devil is sometimes identified as Titivillus.[52] This *exemplum* was occasionally told as a warning against the sin of sloth.[53] Although I know of no text which mentions Titivillus himself in connection with *acedia,* the faults of jangling in church and of "syncopating" were standard aspects of the sin.[54] If, therefore, the author of *Mankind* did use the concept of *acedia* to motivate Man's fall, what devil's name would have suggested itself more naturally than that of Titivillus, traditionally associated with faults of sloth?

The motivation of Man's fall by *acedia* also fits very well into the over-all meaning or moral of the play. Whether or not Sister M. Ph. Coogan's thesis is correct—that the play is a dramatized invitation to confession and penance performed during Shrovetide[55]—the fact remains that *Mankind* is concerned with the instability of man whose spiritual integrity is endangered by the conflict between body and soul, and who needs firm reliance upon God's mercy in order to be saved. The play shows Man's absolute need for Mercy to teach, to guide and, ultimately, to save him, since his own nature proves untrustworthy and "unstabyl."[56]

> Mankend ys wrechyd; he hath sufficyent prowe; [proof]
> There-fore God kepe yow all *per suam misericordiam.*
> (ll. 904-5)

Thus the declared moral of the play. But reliance upon God's mercy is frustrated by despair, and the sin which traditionally opens the way to despair is *acedia,* beginning with boredom in the fulfillment of one's duties and leading to negligence, abandonment of God's service, and the turn to sinful delights.

The remarkable fact about *Mankind,* therefore, is its utilization of the medieval concept of *acedia* for dramatic purposes in a way that is quite unprecedented. Here is not the allegorical figure of Sloth approaching Mankind from the outside, as it does in *The Castle of Perseverance,* but sloth forms Mankind's inner disposition to which the three scamps and Titivillus appeal and which only gradually, after the Devil employs various kinds of deceit (invisibility, the buried plank, theft, and lies), responds positively. Man's fall is then presented as a gradual descent from grace to sin, or from Mercy to Mischief, and the steps on this descent correspond to psychological stages on the downward path of *acedia,* with despair at the end.

The notion of *acedia* thus employed combines popular elements of the sin of sloth with more spiritual features reminiscent of the Schoolmen. On the one hand, the play emphasizes man's obligation to physical labor, symbolized in Mankind's digging with a spade; and once Mankind has become spiritually slothful he enters the boisterous fellowship of idlers whose proper habitat is the tavern, and whose main vices are wenching, theft, and murder (ll. 695-710). On the other hand, if one were to define Mankind's besetting sin it would be with the scholastic *taedium* or *fastidium de bono*: the temptation scene focuses on man's inner attitude; his external acts are realized as consequences thereof. The cause of Mankind's irksomeness and of his desisting from further physical and spiritual efforts is the bodily hardship which accompanies such labor, here visualized in details such as the plank, kneeling on the ground, the supposed "colic," and others. We remember that some Schoolmen defined *acedia* as aversion against spiritual good on account of the accompanying physical hardship. And finally, throughout the play Mankind is preoccupied with the fact that his soul is burdened by a body, a fact which he laments as soon as he enters the stage (ll. 189ff.).[57] Again, we are reminded of St. Thomas' analysis, which located the ultimate psychological root of *acedia* in the opposition between spirit and flesh.[58] I am of course not suggesting St. Thomas as a source for *Mankind*, but it appears as if whoever was responsible for creating this morality play combined the Scholastic interest in the psychology of *acedia* with the very late medieval popular image of the sin to produce a quite remarkable drama of Mankind's fall where "sloth" is hardly mentioned but demonstrably informs the entire temptation scene.

The last work in our consideration of the poets, Petrarch's *Secretum* or *Discourses on the Contempt of the World*, is a self-analysis which easily ranks with the *Confessions* of St. Augustine and of Rousseau. Although it was written more than a century before *Mankind* and only a generation after Dante's *Purgatorio*, it reflects a consciousness that is closer to the Renaissance than to the medieval world.

The *Secretum* introduces Petrarch meditating upon the origin and end of his life, when he is visited by Lady Truth, who has come to help him raise his eyes from earthly to eternal things. In her company appears the venerable figure of St. Augustine, who engages Petrarch in three days' conversation about the sins of the world, in the course of which much is said with regard to Petrarch himself, and this, so he tells us, Petrarch has written down as his secret treasure, kept for future reading and meditation. The ensuing three dialogues between "Augustinus" and "Franciscus" start from Augustinus' proposition that nobody can be unhappy against his will; a sufficiently strong desire will necessarily lead to happiness. Franciscus denies the truth of this for some time but is finally compelled to admit that, although he has desired philosophical happiness, and although he has tried to train himself in the contempt of the world by meditating upon death, he has failed to reach this happiness because he has desired it but feebly. Augustinus now teaches him that he has not firmly enough grappled with the passions of his soul, the classic four affects, which unduly bind him to this world. "Hence that plague of phantasms which shatter and wreck your thoughts and, with their pernicious distractions, block the way to those illuminating meditations by which one ascends to the only one and supreme light" (pp. 64-66).[59] To recognize these ties is the first step toward overcoming them; under Augustinus' guidance, Franciscus will now have to examine his conscience.

The self-analysis is carried out in the following two dialogues. In Discourse III Augustinus shows Franciscus and attempts to bring him to reject his two deepest wounds, the two adamantine chains that fetter his soul: love and fame. But it is the discourse of the second day which touches upon *acedia,* because here the two speakers examine Franciscus' moral life in terms of the seven deadly sins. In pointing out the enemies that threaten Franciscus on all sides, Augustinus begins with pride, as if this were a matter of course; and just as naturally Franciscus follows the lead by passing on to envy. So the analysis continues through all seven vices. Of envy, gluttony, and wrath Franciscus is relatively free; pride and lust need some more attention; but the longest analyses are those of his avarice and *acedia,* the latter coming at the end of the series and occupying the most space in this discourse.

Augustinus introduces the subject as "a deadly plague of the soul which the moderns call *accidia,* the ancients *egritudo*" (p. 106). Franciscus has suffered from it sorely and for a long time. It renders all things hard, miserable, and horrible and leads to despair and ruin. Whereas other vices may attack the soul frequently but only for a brief moment, *acedia* is a "tenacious plague" which keeps him in its grip for whole days and nights. And worst of all, "I feed upon my tears and sufferings with dismal pleasure so that I am loath to leave them" (p. 106).

From this somewhat superficial description of Franciscus' "sickness" Augustinus presses on to the causes. Is Franciscus grieved by the passing of temporal things, or by bodily pain, or by an injury of Fortune? Franciscus replies that his grief comes not from any single blow of Fortune but from a concurrence of mishaps. It springs from the cumulative discouragement which the consideration of the miseries of the human condition, the memory of past hardships, and the fear of the future jointly produce. With such considerations Fortune besieges the Castle of his Reason until he is quite dejected—an image that Franciscus develops with fond eloquence (p. 108).

To heal Franciscus from such depression and general "hatred and contempt for the human condition," Augustinus proposes to pull up and examine its roots individually. Although Franciscus once more takes refuge in generality—it is *everything* that gives him displeasure, which Augustinus agrees is quite characteristic of *acedia*—, his mentor takes up a number of individual causes for dejection. First, Franciscus' complaint against his fortune or, to be more precise, his want of means (*inopia,* pp. 116, 118). Franciscus is not really ambitious to obtain a high place; on the contrary he has made it his goal to attain some modest sufficiency, the Horatian *aurea mediocritas* (pp. 112-14). But even this modest goal he has never reached, and that causes him grief. Augustinus retorts that what Franciscus has deemed modest is really above him and that he has long since achieved, nay even surpassed, the true *mediocritas.* If he would only look behind him, at the multitude of those who own less, he might be quite contented.

A second cause of Franciscus' grief is his *servitus,* the fact that he must "live for others," or more truly, that he cannot wholly "live for himself" (p. 116). Precisely what relations or duties have occasioned Franciscus' complaint at servitude is not indicated. But Augustinus consoles him with the thought that even Caesar, whom all mankind served, had to "live for others," namely, for the greed of Brutus and the Roman conspirators.

Another cause for depression is "the frailty or some hidden sickness of the body" (p.118). Franciscus agrees that the body is an unpleasant burden, with its heaviness, pains, and need for sleep but adds that this is the common condition and that, actually, he is better off than many others.

A fourth cause carries greater weight, although Augustinus passes over it quickly because Franciscus is still smarting from it keenly. It is a particular stroke of Fortune, who has "overthrown with her cruel blow myself, my hopes and all goods, my kindred and my house" (p. 118). Again, Augustinus counsels that Franciscus remember that such mishaps are common to all men.

In contrast to the preceding two, the last cause rouses Franciscus to more eloquent complaints. Living in a turbulent, crammed, incredibly dirty city nauseates him and produces weariness of life and daily disgust ("vite mee tedia et quotidianum fastidium," p. 120). Stinking streets full of dirty pigs and wild dogs, the clanging of wheels that shakes the walls, all types of people bartering and begging with shouts—it is like hell. Augustinus counters the outburst with the remark that Franciscus' complaint is leveled against a place unfit for studies; but if Franciscus could only calm the "inner disturbance of this mind," outward noises would not move him (p. 120).

To achieve inner tranquillity, Augustinus advises careful study of several stoic writings by Cicero and Seneca, an advice that leads to a longer digression on how to read with profit for one's moral growth, which is illustrated with reference to wrath (pp. 120-24). When Augustinus returns to the subject of *acedia* (p. 126), he adds further bits of Stoic wisdom in order to overcome "sadness of the mind" (*animi tristitiam,* p. 126), notably the untroubled contemplation of the miseries and complaints of other men as well as the thought that servitude and the tumult of city life are hindrances (*anfractus,* p. 126) from which Franciscus can extricate himself by his own will. And in the end Franciscus agrees that he might even become reconciled with his bad fortune (p. 128).

Petrarch's self-analysis, revealing the inner tensions of a man who measures his character, his deepest desires and emotions against the medieval ideal of ascetic contempt of the world, and whose "inner discord" (p. 68) between striving to reach a Stoic-Christian *imperturbatio* through otherworldliness and his urge for self-realization in this world remains in the end unsettled, has been justly hailed as the first, intensely vivid portrayal of the new *Lebens- und Weltgefühl* of modern man. In the words of G. Koerting, "one might call this book the foundation charter of Humanism and Renaissance, and the renunciation of the Middle Ages."[60] In particular, the analysis of what Petrarch calls "accidia" has been accepted as the first articulation of that bitter-sweet disgust with the world and with life which the Elizabethans were to call melancholy and the Romantics, *ennui* or *Weltschmerz.* To be even more specific, it is the *voluptas dolendi* in Petrarch's analysis, his feeding with great delight upon his own sorrows, which has been read as foreshadowing such figures as Goethe's Werther and Chateaubriand's René. In the light of such modern appraisals Petrarch's use of the concept *acedia* is of the greatest interest: In precisely what relation does it stand to medieval traditions?

I have shown elsewhere[61] that Petrarch's *acedia* follows the medieval concept rather closely: Petrarch not only used the technical term and considered it within the scheme of the seven deadly sins, but he gave it features that formed standard aspects of the vice, such as grief, tedium, joylessness and hatred of life, and a constant inclination to despair.[62] Moreover, as is evident from the summary of the *Secretum,* the voice of medieval asceticism in Petrarch's mind, objectified in the figure of "Augustinus," clearly considers *acedia* a vice, that is, a morally evil passion in Franciscus' soul that prevents him from reaching felicity.

This relation of Petrarch's *acedia* to medieval conceptions can be elucidated with greater precision on the basis of the preceding chapters. Careful analysis of the *Secretum* reveals that Petrarch understood *acedia* to mean grief, sorrow, depression, or (to use the Latin equivalent) *tristitia.* As a matter of fact, Augustinus eventually refers to it as *animi tristitia*[63] and distinguishes it from the salutary sorrow about one's sins, a customary distinction drawn whenever theologians discussed the sin of *tristitia saeculi.*[64] The close connection of *tristitia* with *acedia,* the eventual identification of the two in Scholastic thought, and the incorporation of *tristitia* among the branches of *acedia,* have all been discussed in earlier chapters. One main result of our historical investigation has been to point out the fact that by the early fourteenth century a variety of conceptions of *acedia* were available, from the Scholastic *tristitia de bono divino* to the popular neglect of religious duties. In the complex history of the vice, Petrarch's conception of *acedia* as *tristitia,* therefore, follows a component that is at once ancient and dominant.

That the term *acedia* covered a number of quite different moral faults, even different psychological attitudes, was not at all hidden to the view of Scholastic theologians. The Franciscan David of Augsburg, for example, who flourished about the middle of the thirteenth century, distinguished three species of the vice in a description which is interesting enough to be quoted at some length:

> The vice of *accidia* has three kinds. The first is a certain bitterness of the mind which cannot be pleased by anything cheerful or wholesome. It feeds upon disgust and loathes human intercourse. This is what the Apostle calls the sorrow of the world that worketh death. It inclines to despair, diffidence, and suspicions, and sometimes drives its victim to suicide when he is oppressed by unreasonable grief. Such sorrow arises sometimes from previous impatience, sometimes from the fact that one's desire for some object has been delayed or frustrated, and sometimes from the abundance of melancholic humors, in which case it behooves the physician rather than the priest to prescribe a remedy.
>
> The second kind is a certain indolent torpor which loves sleep and all comforts of the body, abhors hardships, flees from whatever is hard, droops in the presence of work, and takes its delight in idleness. This is laziness (*pigritia*) proper.
>
> The third kind is a weariness in such things only as belong to God, while in other occupations its victim is active and in high spirits. The person who suffers from it prays without devotion. He shuns the praise of God whenever he can do so with caution and dares to; he hastens to rush through the prayers he is obliged to say and thinks of other things so that he may not be too much bored by prayer. [More faults of monastic *acedia* follow.][65]

Of these three kinds, it is the first with which Petrarch's *acedia* agrees neatly and in detail. From David's description one can also see why this peculiar sickness of the mind was eventually to be called melancholy and no longer held to be sinful.

The question why Petrarch chose to apprehend the sin of *acedia* as grief rather than as indolence or neglect of spiritual duties can be tentatively answered in different ways. At the time he wrote the *Secretum*, Petrarch may have known *acedia* only as an equivalent to *tristitia*, for which there is some evidence (see the following paragraph). On the other hand, one need only consider that in the second discourse of the *Secretum* Petrarch did not follow the traditional matter of the seven sins, that is, the particular faults of pride, envy, sloth, and so on, as listed in theological handbooks, but instead adopted the inner dispositions of the vices and applied them to the matter of his personal life and experience, a procedure which characterizes especially the section on *acedia*. If Petrarch had chosen to think of this vice as neglect or as Dante's *lento amore*, *acedia* would in consequence have covered, not some specific aspects, but the entirety of his spiritual and emotional life. For the self-analysis of the *Secretum* is carried out when Franciscus realizes that he has made no progress in the pursuit of happiness *because he has loved the supreme good too little*—which, at least in Dante's conception, forms exactly the nature of *acedia.* In this case, there would have been no place for *acedia* as spiritual negligence in the second discourse.

One might ask why Petrarch then used the name "accidia" rather than *tristitia.* The answer is that apparently by the time he first composed the *Secretum* (1342-1343)[66] the particular vice within the scheme of the seven capital vices was known to him as "accidia" (as indeed it was called in fourteenth-century Scholastic and popular teaching) and meant grief.[67] Although it is dangerous to make chronological statements about the original form of Petrarch's writings,[68] some proof can be derived from his *De otio religioso,* written during Lent of 1347.[69] Here Petrarch enumerated the seven deadly sins twice, using "accidia" both times.[70] In a third passage he collected scriptural passages as admonition against a large number of vices, including the seven chief ones. After dealing with "people who are lazy in good works" he continues: "To people who are *accidiosi* and also sad, it is said . . ." and quotes a passage from Ecclesiasticus about *tristitia.*[71] At least in this instance, "accidia" for him meant evil *tristitia.*

It must be noted, however, that in a later work the vice appears as torpor, as bodily and spiritual inertia. The third book of *De remediis utriusque fortunae,* begun in 1354 or earlier and finished in first draft by 1360 but not receiving its completed form until 1366, contains seven successive chapters in which Petrarch treats the seven chief vices. What would correspond to the sin of *acedia* is here called *torpor animi,* and the speaker who is being consoled by Ratio complains of his malaise in such terms as, "I am listless in doing my duties. . . . I am numb and rise slowly to good works."[72] I cannot tell what reason lies behind the change: whether Petrarch learned of the aspect of physical torpor implied in *acedia* later,[73] or—which seems more likely—whether he discarded the name "accidia" with its strong theological flavor because, in contrast to *De otio religioso,* the later *De remediis* was conceived of as a compendium of prudential ethics, of moral philosophy. In any event, his use and conception of *acedia* in the *Secretum* is not an isolated phenomenon in his literary production during the 1340's.

Somewhat startling at first sight is Augustinus' introduction of *acedia* as "that plague of the soul . . . which the ancients called *egritudo*" (p. 106). But a brief glance at "the ancients"—which in this case means Cicero—immediately reveals that Petrarch was thinking of the Stoic term for one of the four main passions or affects, which Franciscus had already referred to in the first discourse of the *Secretum* (p. 64). Cicero classified the four affects according to their being caused in the soul by the thought of some good or some evil, either present or future. *Aegritudo* is "the thought of a great present evil."[74] This definition as well as the doctrine of the four affects was, of course, a commonplace among the Church Fathers and medieval theologians, but the Stoic term *aegritudo* came to be replaced by *tristitia*. The change was made by none other than St. Augustine: "Concerning *tristitia*, which Cicero would rather name *aegritudo* and Virgil *dolor*, but I prefer to call *tristitia* because *aegritudo* and *dolor* more commonly refer to bodily states . . . ."[75]

Petrarch's *acedia* in the *Secretum* is, therefore, conceptually a combination of the medieval chief vice and the Stoic main affect.[76] For his self-analysis Petrarch took the vice of *acedia* in the sense of "grief at some present evil," a psychological attitude usually included in the concept of *acedia* as it was used by medieval theologians. But instead of applying this psychological phenomenon to man's attitude toward God (as the Schoolmen had done), Petrarch searched his consciousness for any manifestations of sorrow. It is at this point that the Petrarchan transformation of *acedia* begins. Not only does Petrarch fill the traditional concept with an intensely personal, subjective experience, but this very experience has nothing to do with *tristitia de bono divino* or with the preachers' hundred-and-one faults in fulfilling religious duties. The Thomistic "grief at some true evil" (which formed part of *acedia* in the *Summa theologiae*)[77] is still in the background of Petrarch's concept, but the full portrait of his *acedia* is a very subjective lament at lack of means, lack of full personal independence, disgust at surroundings that hinder concentration—not on prayer but on writing poetry, history, moral philosophy—, and weariness of a world which seems disgusting and contemptible, but which it is so delightful to fret about.

What importance does this portrait have for the history of the vice? This question has always proved very attractive to Petrarch scholars and to students of the Italian Renaissance and of European *Geistesgeschichte,* whose answers vary from a flat denial that Petrarch's use of *acedia* was at all appropriate, to glowing praises of the idealization Petrarch effected of "the ancient monastic vice of indolent dullness" to "noble melancholy or *Weltschmerz.*"[78] That Petrarch's use of the term was not at all so unfitting as Voigt thought, and that the poet need not have received it from Dante (as Tatham suggested) but evidently knew contemporary Church teaching on the seven deadly sins, has been demonstrated by the preceding analysis. On the other hand, statements about Petrarch's transforming the traditional concept are frequently mistaken by apprehending medieval *acedia* too narrowly; "monastic disease" and "indolent dullness" were only segments of the whole concept. Moreover, such statements about the ennoblement of *acedia* obviously concern Petrarch's thought rather than the history of *acedia* in the fourteenth and fifteenth centuries. The transformation Petrarch unquestionably effected is an isolated phenomenon and concerns our study only insofar as in him we perceive the one thinker who, in the midst of medieval culture, had the boldness and originality to use the conventional scheme and concept for an exploration of his subjectivity, an exploration which indeed reveals a most fascinating mind between two worlds.

VII

THE DETERIORATION OF ACEDIA

Restat nunc agere de obitu acediae. The fate of the sin during the later Middle Ages is frequently thought to have been a process of deterioration from the interesting spiritual phenomenon it was in the accounts of the desert fathers to the much less interesting sin of laziness among ordinary folk. This view implicitly underlies older appraisals of Petrarch, in which "the first modern man of letters" is said to have restored the concept *acedia* to new heights of noble melancholy out of the depths of dullness and indolence into which it supposedly had fallen.[1] The most authoritative study of the seven deadly sins in a way substantiates this idea with regard to medieval *acedia.* Morton W. Bloomfield summed up the history of the vice as follows: "Gradually its spiritual meaning—dryness of the spirit—wears off, and more and more frequently it is used as a synonym for sloth. The intermediate step in this transformation is the common interpretation of sloth in the middle ages as laziness in performing one's duties to God in such matters as church attendance."[2]

Undoubtedly, some such change did occur in the history of the vice, yet its precise nature and course must be determined with greater penetration. The key idea in the quoted summary, evidently, is "loss of spiritual meaning," and by focusing on it I believe we shall be able to elucidate more fully the development of *acedia* during its medieval lifetime.

The notion of "spiritual dryness" as a synonym for the original meaning of *acedia* is rather misleading because it suggests connections with mysticism and the Dark Night of the Soul described by St. John of the Cross. To carry modern notions of mysticism which are based on the sixteenth-century Spanish mystics into medieval views on the contemplative life is a dangerous undertaking, for the "spirit of *acedia*" experienced by the desert monks,[3] and the notion of *acedia* as it was held by St. Bernard, Peraldus, and Thomas Aquinas, were clearly not the same as what is today understood by "spiritual dryness." It would, therefore, be better to use medieval terms instead and speak of the vice as spiritual disgust or inappetence, a notion designated by words like *taedium, fastidium, tepiditas,* or *tristitia* (in the Scholastic sense).

If one examines medieval definitions of the vice for the supposed gradual disappearance of its meaning of spiritual inappetence, one soon finds that the suggested pattern is disturbed by conflicting pieces of evidence. As early as the year 1000, for example, a monastic writer—Aelfric—is found to translate *acedia* as *slaewþ* and to consider it as unwillingness to do any good.[4] "It is obvious that Aelfric did not look upon this sin as the enemy of the mystical way."[5] On the other hand, in the 1440's, Antoninus of Florence, who dealt with all kinds of religious negligence in his treatment of *acedia,* obviously gave the sin a spiritual meaning when he defined it as "a certain spiritual coldness or lack of spiritual love and divine fervor, through which the soul is not moved—or is moved with difficulty—to do some good work."[6] Neither text is unique or exceptional for its period. Like Aelfric, several other early writers, such as Pirminius, Alcuin, Jonas, and Hrabanus, equated *acedia* with idleness in religious activities. And like Antoninus, hundreds of treatises on the vices produced during the fourteenth and fifteenth centuries began their discussion of sloth with a definition in which the vice is grasped as spiritual disgust or inappetence; thus we find "onlosthede" (*fastidium*),[7] "werynesse" (*taedium*),[8] "hevynesse" (*tristitia*),[9] "the angwissh of troubled herte" (*turbatae mentis anxietudo*),[10] or "hertly anger or anoye,"[11] to mention only some common definitions in Middle English documents.

It is therefore hardly possible to view the history of *acedia* as a gradual loss of its spiritual meaning, as a linear change of meaning from spiritual dryness or inappetence to plain laziness. But surely—it may be objected—during the later Middle Ages *acedia* passed from a "vice of the spirit" to a "vice of the flesh." Does this not sufficiently indicate its loss of spiritual meaning? Such a change did indeed occur. The vice shifted its position in two schemes where the seven capital vices were distributed among various categories: the scheme of the Three Enemies of Man (the Flesh, the World, and the Devil), and the other scheme of *vitia spiritualia* vs. *carnalia*. A closer look at each will teach us much about medieval writers' views on the vice during its period of culmination and about the suggested changes it underwent during its long history in general.

Although the *topos* of the Three Enemies is sometimes called "classic,"[12] it is not as ancient as that term may suggest. Of course, the World, the Flesh, and the Devil separately were considered man's adversaries from the beginnings of Christianity on, and many relevant statements occur in the New Testament. But the combination of all three into a commonplace was apparently not effected before the eleventh century and seems to have been a product of the new ascetic impulses in monasticism after the Cluniac reform. The earliest text I have found which uses the *topos* is by Jean de Fécamp (*ca.* 990-1078), who wrote: "The world fights against us with its aspirations (*concupiscentiis*), the flesh with its desires, and the devil with his continual temptations."[13]

But it is in the works of St. Bernard and of Hugh of St. Victor that the *topos* all of a sudden occurs again and again and is developed at greater length. "There are three that raise war against us: the devil, the world, and our flesh," says Hugh; and he explains: "The devil arrays the army of [sinful] suggestions against the faithful soul; the world offers prosperity and misfortune to overcome us; and the flesh rises in battle against us by bringing forth its hosts of carnal desires."[14] St. Bernard explained the triad of tempters similarly and is responsible for a formula which became ubiquitous in the following centuries: "The flesh offers me softness, the world vanities, the devil bitterness."[15] From these two writers on, the Three Enemies immediately became a commonplace in spiritual treatises, sermons, theological *summae,* and handbooks, and finally in didactic and allegorical poems and medieval drama. A Latin stanza expresses the topos with rhyme and rhythm:

> Mundus, caro, demonia
> Diversa movent proelia.
> Incursu tot phantasmatum
> Turbatur cordis sabatum.[16]

It was inevitable that the seven deadly sins should eventually be distributed among these Three Enemies. The earliest text which does this known to me is a sermon by Bernard's disciple Isaac of L'Étoile. He gives the following explicit scheme:

Caro: luxuria, gula.
Mundus: avaritia, tristitia.
Diabolus: ira, invidia, superbia.[17]

The distribution, although in a different fashion, was already implied in a sermon by St. Bernard, to which we shall return below. Again, to connect the sins with individual tempters became a favorite device in later sermons and the drama, although it is not found as frequently as the *topos* of the Three Enemies itself.

In this scheme the position of *acedia* varies. It may be best to indicate the evidence in detail. *Acedia* is connected with:

The Devil: Jacques de Vitry (1227-1240), various sermons (1575 edition, pp. 193, 217; ed. Pitra, p. 375).

Grosseteste, *Templum domini* (first half of thirteenth century; see Bloomfield, *Seven Deadly Sins*, p. 437); and the Middle English version (fifteenth century; ed. R. Cornelius, l. 538). *Chateau d'amour* (*ca.* 1230; ed. J. Murray, l. 808); its Middle English version *The Castel of Loue* (1350-1400; EETS 98, l. 900), but not *The Myrour of lewed men* of MS. Egerton 927 (see under "The Flesh").

Jean de Journi (1288), *La Dime de penitance* (ed. Breymann, ll. 2054f.; "pereche," i.e., *paresse*).

Cursor mundi (*ca.* 1300, l. 10095).

Speculum morale (early fourteenth century; col. 895).

The World: [Isaac of L'Étoile, see above. *Tristitia.*]
Wyclif, *Trialogus*, III, 9 (*ca.* 1382; ed. Lechler, pp. 160f.).

Nicholas Hereford, "On the Seven Deadly Sins" (*ca.* 1385; ed. Th. Arnold, *Select English Works of John Wyclif*, III, 121).

The Flesh: William Shoreham (*ca.* 1320), *De septem sacramentis* (EETS, es, 86, l. 353).

William of Pagula, *Oculus sacerdotis*, II (*ca.* 1320-1323; MS. BM. Royal 6.E.i, fol. 46r).

Fasciculus morum, V (before 1340; MS. Bodleian 332, fol. 149v).

Bromyard, *Summa praedicantium* (1348-1349), under "Avaritia" (A: XXVII, art. 14), and "Infirmitas" (I:III, art. 5).

Fitzralph, a sermon given in 1348 (MS. BM. Lansdowne 393, fol. 55v).

Thomas Brinton, Sermons 27 and 93 (1376 or 1381, and perhaps after 1378; ed. Devlin, I, 107f., and II, 432).

John Waldeby (middle of fourteenth century), *Expositio super orationem dominicam* (MS. BM. Royal 7.E.ii, fol. 27v).

Ranulph Higden (d. 1364), *Speculum curatorum* (MS. BM. Harley 1004, fol. 41r).

Grosseteste, *Chateau d'amour,* Middle English version of MS. BM. Egerton 927 (1350-1400), *Myrour of lewed men.*

Morgan MS. 861 (cf. J. H. Fisher, *Speculum,* XXVIII [1953], 864).

Middle English Sermon 7, from MS. BM. Royal 18.B.xxiii (ed. W. D. Ross, EETS 209, p. 32).

John Gregory (before 1404), Sermon "Per proprium sanguinem" (ed. H. G. Pfander, p. 59).

Poem "Jesu, Mercy for My Misdeeds" (ed. C. Brown, *Religious Lyrics of the Fifteenth Century,* p. 222, l. 12).

Garrett MS. (cf. Bloomfield, *Seven Deadly Sins,* pp. 215-16).

The Castle of Perseverance (1400-1425; EETS, es, 91, *passim*).

Mary Magdalene (1480-1490; EETS, es, 70, l. 350).

The evidence suggests that in the thirteenth century *acedia* was held to be a temptation of the devil and that in the following century it became a temptation of the flesh. Before discussing this change and its reasons further, we turn to the second scheme in which a similar shift occurred.

The division of the chief vices into carnal and spiritual ones was already made in Cassian's *Collationes.* Gregory the Great adopted it and included *tristitia* among the spiritual vices. What the distinction meant was explained by Cassian himself:

> Although the Apostle declared that in general all vices are carnal, . . . we distinguish them by a twofold division for the purpose of considering their cure and nature more diligently. For some of them we call carnal, others spiritual. Those we call carnal which especially belong to carnal movement and sense, by which the flesh receives such delight and nourishment that it also excites our quiet minds and often draws them reluctantly to the consent of the will. . . . But we call those spiritual which arise from the soul alone and not only do not give the flesh any pleasure, but also affect it with a most grievous languor, while they nourish only the diseased soul with a most miserable delight. . . . It is necessary to heal this double sickness with a double remedy. (*Coll.*, V, 4)

Later theologians would explain that through the Fall man had become corrupted in his whole nature, body and soul, and that all actual sins can be reduced to root sins or corruptions (the capital vices) which spring from either the body or the soul. This division occurs very frequently in Scholastic thought and forms the basis for many rationales of the seven sins which were surveyed in Chapter II, especially those by Grosseteste,[18] Alexander of Hales, and Albertus Magnus.

The texts which assign *acedia* a place in this scheme are, unfortunately, in their majority from the thirteenth century. Here, *acedia* is always considered a sin of the spirit,[19] with the single exception of *Ancrene Riwle,* where sloth is a sin of the flesh.[20] From the next century, I have found only a few texts. The *Dicta salutis* reckons *acedia* among spiritual vices.[21] Hilton, in his *Scale of Perfection,* includes it among the carnal desires, although one senses a certain uneasiness about this since he does not deal with the vice as extensively as he does with the others.[22] William of Shoreham, who in one poem on the Three Enemies included sloth among the sins of the flesh, in another poem distinguishes between "sins in the heart" and sins "in flesh." Here *acedia* is a sin of the heart.[23]

Although the evidence is too scanty to permit a valid generalization, it seems safe to state that in the second scheme, too, there was a tendency to include *acedia* among the sins of the flesh during the thirteenth and fourteenth centuries. The reason why there are fewer utterances to this effect than in the case of the Three Enemies is probably that the scheme of carnal vs. spiritual vices had the authority of Gregory (which the other, more recent scheme did not have), and that writers were reluctant to go so plainly against the Church Father's word.

On the other hand, the rational probing so characteristic of the thirteenth century was clearly not satisfied with Gregory's dichotomy. Several theologians divided the seven chief vices into three categories: sins of the spirit, of the body, and of both spirit and body. Caesarius of Heisterbach, in the *Dialogus miraculorum* (*ca.* 1220), included *acedia* in the last group.[24] Peter Quivil, however, thought of it as a *peccatum spiritus*.[25] Alexander of Hales and Albertus Magnus divided the seven sins among *spiritus, anima,* and *corpus,*[26] a scheme which combines the just mentioned division with St. Paul's blessing, "May your spirit and soul and body be preserved entire" (I Thess. 5:23). Here *acedia* appears as a sin of *anima,* that is, it holds the intermediate position between flesh and spirit.

Although this rationale for the seven sins, based on the division of human nature into flesh, spirit, and the intermediate "soul," was eventually replaced by Aristotelian psychology and an altogether different principle of division in Albert's later work and in St. Thomas, *acedia* remained a vice which curiously stands between body and soul, as we have seen in our earlier discussion of the Scholastic analysis.

However, the great Scholastic *summae* do not explain why in later popular literature *acedia* came to be looked upon as a vice of the body pure and simple. Certainly St. Thomas emphasized the spiritual nature of the vice. Was there no theological basis, then, for including sloth among the bodily sins?

There was indeed, as is shown in a passage by John of Wales. His *Summa justitiae,* seemingly written before St. Thomas' mature work was known to him, reflects a good deal of the theological uneasiness about *acedia* before the last quarter of the thirteenth century. John finally decides that *acedia* is principally a spiritual vice: "According to other authorities, *acedia* is sadness or tedium against spiritual good which we owe God—not in so far as it is spiritual good, nor in so far as it is owed to God (because this pertains especially to injustice), but in so far as it impedes bodily rest, yet not chiefly so but [rather] because it hinders the rest of the soul. Hence it is a spiritual vice—not simply carnal, but chiefly spiritual."[27] But before this he had discussed why *acedia* is at least partially a sin of the body, in a passage which reveals well the theology behind the change:

> After dealing with the four principal vices by which the inner man is corrupted, we now treat of the remaining three by which the outer man is deformed and disordered, viz., *acedia*, gluttony, and lust. For *acedia* seems partially to belong to the body. Chrysostom, in *Hom. imperf.* 18, says there are chiefly three natural passions which are proper to the flesh: first, eating and drinking; second, a man's love for a woman; and third, sleep. From no passion does abstinence sanctify our body so much as from these . . . , and no passion defiles our body so much as these three.[28]

In other words, *acedia* is a carnal vice because it is closely related to a basic need of the body. As gluttony springs from man's need for food, and lust from his sexual drive, so does *acedia* spring from the need for sleep and rest.

This connection explains immediately why *acedia* could become a sin of the flesh in the scheme of the Three Enemies. We only need to recall one of the earliest developments of the *topos*, in St. Bernard's *Sermones de diversis*:

> The spirit of the flesh always counsels softness, the spirit of the world vanities, and the spirit of malice bitterness. For whenever a fleshly thought assails the mind with its customary importunity: namely, when in human fashion we begin to burn with desire as we think of food, drink, sleep, or similar things that belong to the care of our flesh, we can be sure that it is the spirit of the flesh which speaks to us. . . . But when idle thoughts come into our hearts concerning worldly ambition, boasting, arrogance, and so on, it is the spirit of the world which speaks. . . . But the prince [of these] himself rises against us in his great anger, roaring like a lion, when we are stirred . . . to wrath, impatience, envy, and bitterness of the mind.[29]

Bernard in general seems to have set no store by the series of capital vices, and in the quoted passage it is not the traditional seven which he distributes among the three foes. But there is no doubt that *acedia* would stand among the sins "counseled" by the flesh, once it was apprehended as the inordinate desire for bodily rest, a meaning it certainly had in the thought of John of Wales.

The Bernardian passage can lead us a step further to understand the "deterioration" of *acedia* in another respect as well. Among the sins attributed to the Devil appears "bitterness of the mind," a synonym for *tristitia*. That in the scheme of the Three Enemies the temptation of unreasonable grief should accompany the Devil is fairly obvious. In the other scheme—*vitia carnalia* vs.

spiritualia—also, *tristitia* could not be anything but a vice of the spirit, while idleness or somnolence would belong to the flesh. The following quotation, which is quite representative of medieval thought in this matter, makes this clear: "For lust, drunkenness, voracity, idleness [*otiositas*] and similar vices dissolve men, so that by serving carnal desires they pass into mud; but envy and the sadness of this world [*tristitia saeculi*], which works death, and avarice, which is never satisfied with its gains, and the other spiritual vices that are similar to these, hold the minds of men bound with icy coldness."[30]

The examples which are here given for carnal and spiritual vices are, again, perfectly obvious, and it may seem a waste of space even to quote this passage. But the interesting question is: what would happen if a writer like the last-quoted distributed all the seven capital vices in this scheme?[31] Evidently, his placing *acedia* either among the spiritual or among the carnal vices would depend on whether he considered it as *tristitia* or as *otiositas.* As long as writers defined *acedia* as *tristitia* of some kind, the vice would have to be a spiritual one, and concomitantly, a temptation coming from the devil. That *acedia* was understood as *tristitia* has been shown at length before. Twelfth-century theologians were especially responsible for this identification, and thirteenth-century Schoolmen carried out the equation with full logical consequence. That this identification was indeed responsible for including *acedia* among the sins caused by the devil can be shown from instances in the sermons of Jacques de Vitry. When he speaks of the seven capital vices, he uses sometimes *tristitia,* sometimes *acedia,* and sometimes both,[32] as Hugh of St. Victor and others had done before him. In one sermon he distributes all seven among the Three Enemies. About the Devil he says: "The third yoke is hard and the heaviest, that is, the Devil's yoke, by which the soul is weighed down with envy and malice, with wrath and furor, with *acedia* and *tristitia.*"[33] The structure of this sentence makes it clear that Jacques considered *acedia* and *tristitia* as synonymous, a fact which also appears elsewhere in his sermons.[34]

On the other hand, if and when writers understood *acedia* as *otiositas,* the vice would naturally be included among the *vitia carnalia* and the temptations of the flesh. This, we know, happened in the fourteenth century. The question is now whether *acedia* came to be looked upon as a sin of the flesh about 1300, whether after this date it was a carnal vice and identical with *otiositas* whereas before 1300 it had been a spiritual vice and identical with *tristitia,* as the evidence especially of the Three Enemies scheme seems to suggest.

The answer to this question is negative. We have seen that *acedia* was included among the *vitia carnalia* and temptations of the flesh because it was conceived as *otiositas*—but this conception had been standard for many centuries before 1300. It goes back as far as Book X of Cassian's *Instituta,* where *acedia* and *otiositas* were verbally equated and, through several chapters, treated as synonymous. The equation recurred with regularity in the *libri poenitentiales* and in moral instructions for laymen written in the eighth and ninth centuries. Moreover, Scholastic theologians about the middle of the thirteenth century were fully aware that the notion *acedia* comprised two different aspects: idleness of the body (*otiositas*) and spiritual aversion of the mind (*tristitia* or terms like *taedium*). Robert Grosseteste furnished a perfect expression of this awareness when he divided the chief sin into the following two species:

1. Laziness of the soul, which is an inner grief of the mind [*interna mentis tristitia*], as when someone meditates without devotion and thus derives no profit, or prays without joy, or reads without savoring heavenly things.

2. Idleness of the body [*otium corporis*], which occurs when the body shrinks from holy works, such as helping, teaching, and giving good counsel. [Various species of *otium* follow.][35]

Quite similarly several Scholastic *summae theologicae* of the same period declared that "this vice has two names, scil., *tristitia* and *accidia,*" the former denoting a shrinking from some spiritual good which is deemed hard, the latter indicating a turning toward bodily rest.[36] Evidently, for the writers of these *summae* the term *acedia* proper was synonymous with *otiositas.*

This double nature of *acedia,* incidentally, manifested itself in various other contexts during the thirteenth century and after. The two schemes analyzed above are one instance. Another is the opposite virtue assigned to *acedia,* which may be either spiritual joy or fortitude, according to whether the vice is grasped as either *tristitia* or *otiositas.* Similarly, the vice was occasionally related to one of the four humors which may in part cause it. As one can expect, either melancholy or phlegm was held responsible, according to the vices's nature as either grief or indolence (see Appendix A).

On occasion, a theologian would be quite bothered by his awareness of this double nature when he assigned *acedia* its place in one of the two schemes discussed above. John of Wales has been quoted a few pages earlier as considering *acedia* partially a sin of the body but primarily a sin of the spirit. A similar example for the scheme of the Three Enemies can be found in *Fasciculus morum* (written before 1340), whose author puts *acedia* squarely among the temptations of the Flesh. But when he defines the vice, he makes this restriction: "*Acedia* is loathing of good or anguish. But the devil loathes all good—therefore the vice is justly attributed not only to the ministration of the flesh but also to the devil."[37]

Thus, to reflecting minds of the thirteenth and fourteenth centuries, *acedia* was a vice of neither spirit nor flesh exclusively but belonged to both; and it contained the aspect of mental aversion against spiritual goods as well as that of bodily indolence in performing external religious duties to God and man. Our evidence shows plainly that these two notions—spiritual inappetence and laziness—co-existed as integral elements of the vice, not only during the Scholastic period, but indeed from at least Cassian's *Instituta* on. Their mutual relation is nothing more than that between a state of mind (*taedium* or *tristitia* in the Scholastic sense) and external faults which flow from it as its effects (expressed as *otiositas* and covering sleepiness, roaming, and later all sorts of negligence). In the history of *acedia* the two notions did not follow upon each other, "laziness" eventually replacing the spiritual meaning of the vice, but instead were always present. Maybe at certain times and in certain works one or the other was more evident, but this I think was a matter of emphasis. One can indeed show that a given author, or an entire literary genre, or even a whole period, laid greater stress on either the inner attitude or the external faults expressed by *acedia*. The varied pattern of this development as well as its causes can be revealed in a brief review of the vice's history.

The concept of *acedia* as a vice originated in the milieu and the intense personal experience of the Egyptian desert monks of the fourth century. There it designated the temptation to quit religious exercises, to slacken one's wakefulness, or to leave the spiritual life altogether because of depression, physical weariness, boredom with the cell—inner experiences in part caused, and certainly aggravated, by such external factors as the desolate monotony of the desert, noonday heat, and the peculiar daily schedule as well as the ascetic ideals of the hermits.

This peculiar temptation, which had already been included among the eight principal vices with which the monk had to struggle, was then transmitted to the Latin West by John Cassian. In his two main works, *acedia* preserved all its original local color. It was definitely a monastic vice "which attacks primarily those who live in the desert." Yet already Cassian's *Instituta* adapted the notion to different conditions, most notably by emphasizing, in connection with *acedia,* that idleness (*otiositas*) had been condemned by the Apostle Paul and that monks must engage in manual labor for their sustenance as well as for spiritual protection against the attacks of the Devil.

Cassian's doctrine exerted an enormous influence until the very end of the Middle Ages, and the various forms *acedia* was to take in the long course of its history, its transformations and extensions, can all be regarded as a continuous exfoliation of the Cassianic concept. For many centuries *acedia* remained a monastic vice, that is, a temptation that was primarily, if not exclusively, experienced by persons who cultivated an intense spiritual life in seclusion. Yet attempts to apply it to the layman appeared among the earliest post-Cassianic treatments in which *acedia* is mentioned. Four works of the eighth and ninth centuries adapted the vice to the moral life of Christians outside the monastery and thus mark the beginning of a "laicization" of the concept which was to be fully realized in the thirteenth century. These four works explicitly understood *acedia* to mean *otiositas.*

Before this complete adaptation to the moral life of layfolk was realized, however, other developments had taken place and had added new components in the fully grown concept as we know it from the later Middle Ages. Most important in this respect was the twelfth century with its profound interest in the psychology of the spiritual and moral life and the new tendency to systematize inherited theological doctrines and harmonize differing traditions. The new interest in psychology led to an "interiorization" or "spiritualization" of *acedia.* In contrast to previous centuries, when the stress had lain on such external aspects as indolence or drowsiness, discussions of *acedia* now emphasized its internal states, such as boredom, tepidity, or disgust. Hence a variety of new definitions characterizing the vice as spiritual inappetence sprang up and remained in use to the end of the fifteenth century. At the same time, the desire to systematize traditional knowledge effected a reconciliation between the two different schemes of capital vices, those by Cassian and by Gregory the Great, which since the seventh century had lived in a state of somewhat uneasy co-existence. From the beginning of the twelfth century on, one witnesses a conceptual identification of *acedia* with *tristitia* in spiritual writers, systematic theologians, and early catechetical handbooks, and this peculiar feature was to determine speculative discussions about *acedia* throughout the Scholastic period, culminating in the system of Thomas Aquinas. It is thus no exaggeration to say that in this period *acedia* stood under the far-reaching influence of Gregory the Great; in the history of *acedia,* the twelfth and thirteenth centuries may well be called its *aetas Gregoriana.*

The most important contribution of the Schoolmen to the history of *acedia* was, then, to give the historical fusion of *acedia* and *tristitia* a sound logical and psychological basis. In this process *acedia* came to be understood as man's culpable aversion against the divine good—a conception with which the emphasis on the vice's mental aspects and the more "spiritualized" view reached its culmination. At the same time the concept was totally stripped of its original local color. For the *summae theologiae* of the thirteenth century, *acedia* was no longer a monastic vice but a moral perversion of human nature which could manifest itself in any profession, state of life, or locality.

At exactly the same time the adaptation of *acedia* to the lay world was carried out *totaliter.* In the immediate wake of the reform movement officially decreed by the Fourth Lateran Council (and prescribed already earlier by diocesan legislation), with the new impulse given to penance and the regular preaching of the catechism, *acedia* became popularized as the sin of sloth, as negligence in the performance of religious duties. Here the ancient monastic vice turned fully into a sin of Everyman.

This "popular" *acedia* is strikingly characterized by its emphasis on external faults, on detailed instances of neglect in the fulfillment of religious duties to God and man. The aspect of spiritual inappetence is preserved, usually in the form of one or several of the definitions developed during the twelfth century; but this aspect is greatly overshadowed by attention to the effects of *acedia,* to its manifestations of spiritual and physical indolence. The difference of the popular image from Scholastic discussions of the vice, or from the use twelfth-century spiritual writers had made of the term *acedia,* is undoubtedly due to the practical purposes of the literature in which this image appears. Confessional instructions, handbooks, sermons, and encyclopedias for preachers were written to give the clergy practical guidance in their work of instructing penitents in the confessional and of teaching common Christians from the pulpit. The confessor and the penitent in examining his conscience had to do with concrete faults, not with abstract states of mind. It is this application of the scheme of seven chief vices in the practice of confession and penance which I would claim to be responsible for the emphasis in treatments of *acedia* on the vice's external faults of indolence. This emphasis is so prominent as almost to determine the essence of the vice in the popular image after 1200; but it had occurred already earlier, in the works written for laymen during the eighth and ninth centuries.

That it was the practical intention of a given work rather than its audience (monastic vs. lay) which must be held responsible for the emphasis on external faults can be readily seen from the early *libri poenitentiales,* created for eminently practical purposes. Here the section on *acedia* apparently has monastic penitents in mind, yet it is concerned with such un-spiritual phenomena as idleness, somnolence, and instability. In similar fashion, the emphasis on external faults after 1200 appears not only in treatises directed to secular folk but equally in strictly monastic contexts. For example, *De perfectione vitae ad sorores,* attributed to Bonaventure, specifies: "*Acedia* is strong in a religious person when he is lukewarm, drowsy, idle, late (to choir service), negligent (in singing), slack (in fighting his torpor), dissolute (in conversation), undevout (at mass), sad (in countenance), and bored (in his cell)."[38]

The various tendencies which were thus at work in the discussion of *acedia* at the beginning of the thirteenth century—partly intellectual (reconciling Cassian's term with Gregory's list) and partly social or pastoral (concern with confession)—can be seen very clearly in the following passage from Thomas of Chabham's *Poenitentiale* (*ca.* 1222).

> *Acedia* is a most grievous sin, and yet it is hardly known to anyone. Man must attend to God's service with devotion and diligence. But when man is affected by tedium so that he loses

> his diligence in serving God and withholds his devotion in divine services, then it is the sin of *acedia* and he sins much. For he who prays without devotion calls his judgment upon himself. The sin of *acedia* is called by the Apostle "the sorrow of the world which works death" [II Cor. 7:10]. On account of this sin many have killed themselves when they are so absorbed that they have no joy in God or in divine services. Often *acedia* springs from laziness or negligence. Hence princes must be admonished with diligence and care, when they come to confession, that they should be diligent and not idle in honest works. As the Apostle says, "let them be hospitable without murmuring" [I Peter 4:9] and make all their deeds pleasing to God through their good devotion. For otherwise no human service pleases God. *Acedia* is the worst sin because through tedium and weariness it deprives man of his good works with which he might merit eternal life. Therefore a penitent must be anxious that the devil never find him idle, for "idleness teaches much evil" [Ecclus. 33:29]. From idleness come somnolence and laziness, which turn man's heart away from all divine service and from all joy of working for God.[39]

This passage reads very much like one of the earlier descriptions by Alcuin, Jonas, or Hrabanus, with its emphasis on idleness and somnolence and its quotation of Ecclus. 33:29. Yet its author leaves no doubt that in essence *acedia* means lack of devotion and zeal in religious exercises. This is the spiritualization of *acedia* newly introduced by twelfth-century spiritual writers. In addition, Thomas of Chabham equates *acedia* with evil *tristitia*—another result of twelfth-century theology. Yet the general orientation of the passage is toward external behavior, such as suicide, laziness, inhospitality, and somnolence. From here it is but a short step to the questionnaires, confessional formulas, and descriptions of sloth that became common from the middle of the thirteenth century on.

It therefore appears that the different tone which distinguishes descriptions of *acedia* after 1200 from earlier ones was due to the practical purposes for which the scheme of seven chief vices was used, or to be more specific, to its connection with confession and penance. Hence, the common view that in the later Middle Ages *acedia* "deteriorated" from spiritual dryness into plain laziness should be corrected to the effect that, first, what appears as a change of the meaning of *acedia* was really no more than a shift of emphasis caused by practical concerns; second, that this shift became complete and dominated the picture of *acedia* in the thirteenth but had been heralded and indeed partially effected as early as the ninth century;[40] and third, that it apparently was the result not so much of the rise of the bourgeoisie, as of the descent of systematic moral theology to the common people, because of the new impulses in confessional practices.

The most distinctive feature of *acedia*'s history between 400 and 1400 is, therefore, not the gradual loss of its spiritual meaning or its deterioration, but rather a continuing process of de-monasticization or secularization in the sense that the concept was carried from the monastery to the *saeculum*, the world outside the cloister. This process reached its climax in the popular image of the thirteenth and fourteenth centuries, but it had begun much earlier. In fact, it would seem that this development, in which *acedia* was understood as idleness and negligence in spiritual deeds, formed the unbroken mainstream in its history, whereas the spiritualization we found in the twelfth century was an innovation made by contemplative and systematic theologians under the influence of Gregory's *tristitia*. Thus, the ordinary notion of "sloth in God's service" should not be considered as a result of the deterioration of the lofty concept which *acedia* was in Scholastic *summae theologiae*, but rather as representing the true main line of the concept's development, from which the Scholastic analysis branched off into an area of refined theory, of logical and psychological penetration made with the help of Aristotelian thought.

In looking over the whole medieval period, one can therefore distinguish three types of *acedia*: monastic, Scholastic, and popular, which can be localized with some accuracy in time and, even more so, in literary genres. But never did a later form completely replace an earlier one. The laicization or de-monasticization of the vice in the twelfth and thirteenth centuries did not entail the total loss of monastic elements. Originally monastic faults such as lack of devotion in saying the office or sleepiness in choir continued to be listed in popular descriptions of the vice, and corresponding *exempla* which report the experience of the desert monks were told again and again in sermons and handbooks addressed to laymen. In other words, the concept of *acedia* one meets in the longer treatments of the fourteenth and fifteenth centuries is a comprehensive one, embracing elements from all stages of *acedia*'s past life. One must be aware of those stages and the just-mentioned forms of the vice. Especially in the fields of literary or art criticism it will not do to consult a single source (such as Cassian or Thomas Aquinas) or a few selected texts which contain only a segment of the total and rich picture of *acedia*. I believe I have been able to show that poets like Dante, Petrarch, and Langland were much closer to the total tradition of the vice as it was reflected in popular literature than has been understood by critics who, in commenting upon their works, usually rely on a few exclusively Scholastic treatises.

The complexity which the notion *acedia* had gained in medieval thought by approximately 1250 was well enough realized by medieval authors themselves. We have referred to the "double face" of *acedia* earlier and quoted Grosseteste's two species and other theologians' remarks that the vice has two names. A near contemporary of Grosseteste, the Franciscan David of Augsburg, even spoke of three kinds: "bitterness of the mind," which represents the old *tristitia saeculi* in a spiritual sense and is very similar to melancholy; "torpor of laziness," which reflects bodily idleness and negligence in performing spiritual duties; and boredom with things that belong to God, in which survives the ancient monastic vice of lacking fervor.[41]

After approximately 1300 the concept remained static. What one finds in the literature of the next two centuries is the popular image of "sloth in God's service." Longer descriptions of the vice usually define it in terms of a state of mind and then indicate a host of external faults for which it is responsible. We noticed some tendencies to be all-inclusive and to extend the concept to worldly faults during this period, but we had to add that such tendencies did not reach very far and that the vice continued to be condemned for *theological* reasons. Here and there an individual trait was included. Henry of Lancaster, for example, accused himself of negligence in his activities as a judge,[42] and a fourteenth-century French confessional formula added to the eighteen branches of Frère Lorens the following bit of local color: "Also, I have sinned by *acedia* that I have had myself treated by a Jewish physician where I could have had a Christian one."[43] But by and large such peculiarities are extremely rare. Finally, *acedia* is not characteristic of any particular profession or social class but attacks everyone. *The Castle of Perseverance* names "men of relygyon, . . . lordys, ladys, and lederounnys [rogues]" (ll. 989, 992). Questionnaires and confessional formulas list faults that may be committed by any Christian, with only a few traits peculiar to priests and to landlords and workers. The clergy, of course, remained a special prey to *acedia*, and "negligence of priests" takes up a long chapter in the *Summa theologica* by Antoninus of Florence. Otherwise, one finds princes,[44] burghers,[45] and peasants[46] occasionally singled out in discussions of the sin. Quite interesting from the sociological point of view is the long section on sloth in the poem *C'est des seculers* by Abbot Gilles li Muisis (d. 1350).[47] He criticizes the clergy, the knighthood, merchants, and the lower classes (workers and servants), the latter indeed arousing the abbott's longest tirade. There is definitely a tendency in the later Middle Ages to scold laborers for their laziness, but I do not find that this is an important feature in treatments of the sin of sloth.

The fate of *acedia* after 1500 lies outside the scope of this study and cannot be investigated here. Yet a few suggestions may be made to elucidate why the vice lost its significance in Renaissance and later analyses of moral behavior.

The main reason for this disappearance, obviously, was the replacement of an essentially theological system or *Weltanschauung* by various non-theological systems. This profound change affected, first of all, the scheme of the seven vices itself. Although the seven deadly sins still survive today in some catechisms, the scheme has played no important part in the analysis of human behavior since the Renaissance, when it was replaced by ethical systems based on Aristotle, by characterological analyses based on the humors, or by other thought patterns. Although this replacement was, *prima facie*, the result of the combined attack of humanism and the Reformation on the authority of Cassian, Gregory, and Scholastic theology, one should not forget that theological texts from the last medieval century before 1500 had already shown traces of dissatisfaction with the sin scheme. Such thinkers as Wyclif and Reginald Pecock were very critical of it,[48] and Langland apparently felt the scheme to be insufficient for a moral evaluation of his society. Indeed, one even finds that some of the greatest and most original medieval thinkers seem to have thought of the scheme very lightly. Bernard of Clairvaux did not expand on it and apparently did not even mention it. Thomas Aquinas, although he treated it in *Prima secundae,* discarded it in *Secunda secundae* as the structural scheme for dealing with moral acts in particular. Even St. Gregory, though he established the tradition of the seven chief vices, did not further apply the scheme in his vast work outside the very section in which he introduced it.

Yet despite the complete secularization of ethics and of character analysis, most chief vices nevertheless have survived through the centuries after 1500. Pride, envy, wrath, lust, and so on, are still in current use as concepts denoting individual vices, whereas the notion of *acedia* in its peculiar medieval meaning has certainly disappeared. I believe two considerations can explain why this particular vice suffered such a fate.

First, throughout its medieval history, even to the late fifteenth century, *acedia* had been fundamentally a theological concept. In contrast to pride, wrath, and the others, the sin of *acedia* included in its definition a reference to the *divine* good or to *religious* duties. Both the Scholastic analysis and the popular image were quite clear in this respect. Although *acedia* was often defined simply as *taedium boni,* as weariness with or aversion against *any* good, vernacular handbooks made it clear that the vice meant sloth *in God's service.* We discussed the question of its secularization during the period of 1200-1450 at some length earlier and concluded that, even where in a discussion of *acedia* the sin comprised many worldly faults and looked very much like plain laziness, it was condemned for strictly theological reasons. This theological aura surrounds *acedia* also in non-theological contexts, such as treatises of prudential ethics. When such works include the seven vices, they either treat them as a piece of religious instruction (as does the *Menagier de Paris,* written about 1393, for example[49]), or they refer the reader to a proper religious manual. "I am neither monk nor friar," says the author of the fifteenth-century *Ratis Raving* and sends his readers to "the book of confessions."[50]

There is, however, an area where the conceptual secularization of *acedia* may indeed have been carried out to some extent. This is moral philosophy proper, that is, the attempt to build a system of ethics on natural philosophy (under the guidance of "pagan" philosophers) rather than on revealed religion. In contrast to Scholastic theologians who preserved the scheme of Christian vices and virtues and demonstrated its rationale and coherence with the help of Aristotelian principles, some thinkers preserved the Aristotelian scheme of ethics and showed how the Christian vices and virtues agreed with it. The entire subject of secular ethics in medieval thought, especially as it was expressed in thirteenth- and fourteenth-century commentaries on the *Nicomachean Ethics,* needs much further study. But one example may be given here to show how *acedia* was fitted into the Aristotelian pattern and how, in consequence, it became partially secularized. In commenting on Dante's *Inferno* (Canto VII, the souls in Styx), Boccaccio speaks of *acedia* as "the vice opposed to wrath"; that is, he considers *acedia* as the vice caused by a deficiency of *iracundia* (cf. *Nic. Eth.*, IV, 5). He explains:

> In the Fourth Book of his *Ethics* Aristotle shows that he is *accidiosus* who does not get angry when necessary, and says that it is the reaction of a foolish man not to get angry when, and as much as, and against whom it is necessary. Therefore it appears that such a person lacks human feeling, because he does not grieve at anything and become vindictive [in the sense of reacting with force against an evil he has received]. Aristotle adds that bearing with a person who inflicts injury, and not holding one's friends in esteem, is the behavior of a slave. . . . For what else should we think of the mental slackness of an *accidiosus* but that it proceeds from a certain torpor, vileness, idleness of mind, by which he bears with injuries without getting excited?

Boccaccio immediately differentiates this insensitivity from the humility of saints. Then he continues and distinguishes between two areas of behavior in which *acedia* is found: moral acts and spiritual acts. The latter are the common faults of negligence in performing religious duties. But the *atti morali* contain the following interesting details:

> The management of household affairs grows worse and worse in his hands; he does not look after, nor is he solicitous about his possessions, his workers, or his servants; and if the productivity of his estate decreases, he does not care because of his negligence. He would never burn with zeal for public affairs. . . . His bed, prolonged nights, and equally long sleep are to him the most pleasant and desirable good: he prefers solitude, darkness, and silence to any sort of delightful company.[51]

Further search in ethical treatises and in allegorical poems inspired by Aristotle (such as Spenser's *Faerie Queene* and Phineas Fletcher's *Purple Island*) would undoubtedly bring to light similar passages in which the vice of *acedia* is conceived of as inappetence, insensitivity, or lack of fortitude per se, without necessary reference to the divine good. Yet even the discovery of a large number of passages like Boccaccio's would not alter the fact that from the sixteenth century on the word and notion *acedia* no longer played an important part in the moral assessment of human behavior. Apparently the word *acedia* had acquired such a strong theological flavor as to be deemed unsuitable in the terminology of secular ethics.

A second reason for its disappearance may have been the aura of artificiality which surrounded *acedia* from at least the twelfth century on. A number of observations suggest that for medieval man *acedia* always retained the air of a stranger. This applies to its Greek name as well as to the concept itself. We have noticed earlier how relatively seldom the word is found outside discussions of all seven chief vices, and that in its place one often encounters *desidia, torpor,* or *taedium,* not only in Augustine and Gregory but also in much later authors.[52] In the 1220's, Caesarius of Heisterbach furnished an explicit remark about the strangeness of the vice's name when he had his novice observe, "the name of this vice sounds a bit foreign."[53] It may very well be this linguistic difficulty which was at least partially responsible for its replacement, in vernacular languages, by native words. Beyond the strangeness of the original name, we have seen how in the thirteenth century theologians would still observe that the vice itself was not very well known.[54]

There is a second aspect of this artificiality. This derives from the complexity which the concept had acquired by 1300. We noticed that late medieval treatments of the vices display a strong tendency toward all-inclusiveness. In the case of *acedia,* this tendency helped to shape a concept which by 1300 had grown so bulky that it simply could no longer be conceptually held together and must eventually fall to pieces. This state of affairs becomes conspicuous as soon as one takes a critical look at the sixteen "species" of the vice established by Peraldus. In what relation to *acedia* do they stand? Traditionally, the "daughters" or "branches" of the vice were considered particular effects or symptoms of the root sin. But from the early thirteenth century on one notices much confusion about this relationship, which appears as early as Peraldus' *Summa de vitiis.* In this work, the first species, *tepiditas,* is certainly not an effect of *acedia,* but rather its cause and actually synonymous with it, since the two share the same definition ("parvus amor boni"): "Tepidity is small love of good, and it seems to be the first root in the sin of *acedia.* From it seem to spring the other vices that have been mentioned. For tepidity causes many evils in man" (2.01).

Similarly, Peraldus included *tristitia* and *taedium* among the species of the vice—both concepts which were commonly used to define *acedia* itself at the very moment when he wrote his *Summa de vitiis*. The Peraldian "progeny," therefore, is no longer a list of vices that genetically "spring from" *acedia*, as they had in Cassian's and Gregory's conception (*nascuntur*), but instead a more or less comprehensive collection of vices that somehow "belong" to the chief vice (*pertinent*). This difference was clearly enough grasped by later theologians. Jordan of Quedlinburg (d. 1378?), for example, after enumerating the six Gregorian "daughters," explained: "The species of this vice are assigned differently by different authors. But they comprise everything that belongs to this vice beyond its daughters, whether they are species or distinctive characteristics or effects. These are: [twenty-three aspects follow] . . . . To this vice may also be reduced everything that is caused by a lack of fortitude, such as fear, pusillanimity . . . ."[55]

It seems that for Jordan *acedia* meant lack of fortitude; nevertheless, he had earlier defined it, with John Damascene and Hugh of St. Victor, as a form of *tristitia*. This urge to list a variety of definitions is quite characteristic of longer discussions after and outside the Scholastic analysis of the vice. To be sure, thoughtful theologians would attempt to find a conceptual center around which they could group the many aspects that had come to be looked upon as "species" of *acedia*. Thus, Peraldus saw the root of all the various phenomena in spiritual tepidity, and two hundred years later Antoninus of Florence did the same by defining *acedia* as "a certain spiritual coldness or a lack of spiritual love and divine fervor, through which the soul is not moved—or is moved with difficulty—to do some good work" (*Summa theologica*, ii, 1). But the more encyclopedic handbooks, which reflect the totality of tradition much better, lack this conceptual center. They merely juxtapose a number of definitions, from "Augustinus" to St. Thomas, without an attempt to harmonize the often bewildering variety. One is frequently compelled to think that *acedia* has become a mere name, a label stuck on a cage whose inhabitants live rather uneasily together and are ready to break out and defect into different directions.[56]

I believe this condition accounts for the infeasibility of secularizing *acedia* in the same way in which the other vices could be secularized, that is, by being made to designate psychological phenomena or character attitudes without reference to the divine good. Proof can be derived from Petrarch's dealing with the concept. He did indeed conceive of *acedia* as, purely, the phenomenon of grief, of sadness of mind, and then looked for the objects he was sad about. These included a variety of things except what for Scholastic theologians would have been essential: the *bonum divinum*. Hence we can say that Petrarch secularized the vice, just as Boccaccio did in the quoted explanation. In this process of reducing the concept to a psychological phenomenon per se (*tristitia*), however, Petrarch's notion of *acedia* has lost such aspects as lack of devotion, boredom with religious acts, neglect of spiritual duties, all of which were essential components in the genuine medieval vice. Thus, with Petrarch *acedia* has indeed become secularized, but it is no longer the complete concept as fourteenth- and fifteenth-century theologians knew it.

The case of Petrarch's *acedia* also shows what fate the medieval concept was to suffer with the Renaissance: Due to its comprehensiveness and the lack of a conceptual center, the term dissolved into its old components which the Schoolmen had tried to fuse. The ancient factor of *otiositas* survived as laziness or "sloth" in its modern sense—the meaning which "the sin of sloth" evokes in the common understanding today.[57] On the other hand, the original aspect of *taedium vitae* and *tristitia* was replaced in secular Renaissance thought by the notion of "melancholy."

The survival of medieval *acedia* in Renaissance melancholy is, of course, a hypothetical development which cannot be demonstrated to have happened in the same way as a plant grows or a chemical change takes place. The two terms are related only partially; they share some of the symptoms by which they are characterized, such as unreasonable sadness, dejection, a sad face, and so on. But although in medieval texts the melancholy humor was occasionally considered a natural cause for *acedia* (see Appendix A), I know of no text which equates the two verbally. A more convincing case for the replacement of the vice by the complexion has been made by E. Panofsky and F. Saxl, who showed that the late medieval iconography for *acedia* (or, at least one major aspect of it) was used to represent the melancholy type.[58] We may add that a literary document from the seventeenth century indicates that by then cultivated men of letters recognized *acedia* as the medieval forerunner of what they called "melancholy." Abbé Claude Fleury (1640-1723), disciple of Bossuet and friend of Fénelon, wrote a treatise on education in which at one point he argued for making religion the first part in one's course of studies. Religion, he says, does not engender depression and melancholy at all:

> On accuse encore la dévotion de rendre les gens tristes, et, si l'on osait le dire, malheureux, parce qu'on voit en effet beaucoup de ceux qui passent pour dévots être chagrins, critiques et plaintifs; mais rien n'est plus éloigné de l'esprit du christianisme. C'est un esprit de douceur, de tranquillité et de joie; et la mélancolie est comptée par les plus anciens spirituels, entre les sept ou huit sources de tous les péchés, comme la gourmandise et l'impureté.

In order to leave no doubt, Fleury added, in the margin of the page beside "mélancolie," the word "acedia."[59]

The demise of the concept *acedia* in the Renaissance can therefore be seen as the result of the strong theological flavor which the medieval concept had carried and of a certain artificiality the term had acquired during the last two or three centuries of the Middle Ages. This artificiality had posed no danger to its existence as long as the authority of Gregory the Great and Scholasticism, which backed the term, went unchallenged. But in the Renaissance attack on this authority, *acedia* could only be the loser. Its ultimate fate thus throws an interesting light on the concept and its long history. Clearly, the notion of *acedia* was intimately dependent on the God-centered world view of medieval culture, on the essentially religious aspirations of medieval man, at least as he thought of himself ideally. The growth of the concept makes a fascinating story, from the noonday demon of the desert monks to the whisperings of Titivillus, from Evagrius' and Cassian's combat with spiritual dejection to the confession of Sleuthe. Many chapters in that story were obviously written from a direct and intensive experience of spiritual struggle. But we must also realize that later phases, especially the analysis and description of *acedia* from the thirteenth century on, were heavily dependent on tradition. By the end of the Middle Ages, the history of the concept had become a process which may be called philological, rather than phenomenological. Thinkers and writers were content with handing on the word and the concept, with listing and—at best—harmonizing various traditions, instead of exploring and analyzing fresh insights into human nature or into the truths of revealed religion.

APPENDICES

Appendix A

ACEDIA AND THE HUMORS

Medieval documents occasionally connect *acedia* with one of the four humors or complexions. For the relation of the vice to melancholy, the following passages are of interest:

1. *Acedia* can be caused by melancholy:

   (a) Guillaume d'Auvergne, *De virtutibus*, 17: "Augetur interdum, et iuvatur istud vitium honore [*read*: humore] vel fumo melancolico" (*Opera*, I, 174).

   (b) Grosseteste (?), "Primo videndum est quid sit peccatum": "Iuxta terram etiam nascitur accidia, quia melan grece, terra latine vel nigrum. Inde malencolici, qui magis sunt accidiosi" (MS. BM. Royal 8.A.x, fol. 57r). This treatise divides the seven deadly sins among the three parts of the soul and the four elements of the body. The same division occurs in the treatise "Quoniam ut ait sapiens," sometimes attributed to Peraldus (e.g., MS. BM. Harley 3823. fol. 65v) and in Servasanctus, *Liber de exemplis naturalibus*, III, 21 (MS. Bodleian 332, fol. 230r).

   (c) Alexander of Hales, *Summa theologica*, II-II, 566: "In multis accidit qui sunt ad hoc [peccatum] dispositi, sicut in melancholicis. Unde multoties contingit ex infirmitate melancholiae vel etiam alia."

   (d) David of Augsburg, *Formula novitiorum. De interioris hominis reformatione*, 50: "Prima [species accidiae] est quaedam amaritudo mentis. . . . Haec aliquando nascitur . . . ex praedominantibus melancholicis humoribus" (Bigne, XXV, 893). For the whole passage, see above, chap. VI, p. 160 and n. 65.

   (e) Antoninus of Florence, *Summa theologica*, II, 9: "Impugnatur autem quis de accidia aliquando . . . ex corporis complexione. . . . Melancolici ex complexione inclinantur ex humore qui superabundat in eis melancolie, et partim flegmatici" (cap. i).

2. Less precise instances where melancholy is related to *acedia*:

   (a) *Rancor*, a branch of *acedia*, is caused by *atra bilis* in *De fructibus carnis et spiritus*, 7 (PL 176:1001).

(b) Bartholomaeus Anglicus, *De proprietatibus rerum* (Cologne, 1481), XVIII, 17, calls the ass (a traditional symbol for *acedia*) "animal melancholicum frigidum . . . et siccum" (fol. 361r). For the connection of animals with humors, see Klibansky, Panofsky, and Saxl, *Saturn and Melancholy* (London, 1964), pp. 105f.

(c) *Speculum morale,* III, vi. 4, compares [!] the branch *pusillanimitas* to melancholy: "Ad modum melancholicorum, qui solas imaginatas fantasias trepidant . . ." (col. 1216).

(d) Peraldus, *Speculum religiosorum* or *De eruditione religiosorum,* III, 12: Pusillanimity is often caused by melancholy —"saepe causa pusillanimitatis est complexio, quam etiam augent cibi, ex quibus humores melancholici generantur" (Bigne, XXV, 694).

(e) Gerson, Sermon on *acedia,* considers melancholy an effect of the vice: "Deinde est paupertas, mater latrocinii, comitata angustia et melancholia" (*Opera omnia,* III, 1037).

(f) *Fiore di virtù* considers melancholy a species of *tristitia* (with *tristitia* proper and *otiositas*): "La terça si é, quando per alcuna ymaginacione l'omo fa tropo grande pensiero e questa si é mellanconia" (ed. G. Ulrich [Leipzig, 1890], p. 11).

(g) Meffreth, *Sermo 1us dom. I Adv.,* compares the sapphire to penance, whose virtues drive out the seven deadly sins. "Septimo saphirus habet virtutem cordis letificativam. Unde valet contra cordiacam passionem et melancoliam. Et hoc penitentie competit inquantum accidiam expellit que animam tristem et gravem facit" (1487 edition, A.1).

3. *Acedia* is caused by, or related to, phlegm:

(a) John of Wales, *Moniloquium*: *Pigritia* is caused by the cold and moist disposition, according to Seneca, *De ira,* II, 19 (MS. Cambridge Peterhouse 200, fol. 32v); "si enim est accidia ex composicione naturali frigida et fluida, sicut loquitur Seneca libro 2° de ira . . ." (*ibid.*, fol. 35v). Similarly, Ranulph Higden (?), *Speculum curatorum* (MS. Balliol College 77, fol. 36r).

(b) Frère Lorens, *Somme le Roi*: The devil inquires into the condition of each man and his complexion and which vice he is most disposed to; then he tempts "le flematique de gloutonnie et de peresce, le melencolieus de envie et de tristesce." Ed. E. H. Allen (M.A. thesis, University of North

Carolina, 1951), p. 36 (from MS. BM. Royal 19.C.ii). The same in *The Book of Vices and Virtues,* p. 156; *Ayenbite of Inwit,* p. 157.

(c) Gower, *Mirour de l'omme*:

> Si fleumatik soie attemprée,
> Lors Gloutenie et *Lacheté*
> Me font tempter en chascune hure.
> (ll. 14707-9)

In *Confessio Amantis,* VII, 413ff., Gower calls the phlegmatic man,

> Foryetel, slou and wery sone
> Of every thing which is to done.

(d) Antoninus of Florence: see (1.e) above.

4. "Melancholy" is related to wrath:

(a) *The remedy ayenst the troubles of temptacyons,* 4: "The fende our ghostly enemy aspyeth in euery man what wyse he is dysposed by his compleccyon, and by that disposicyon he tempteth hym. For there as he fyndeth a man full of malencoly he tempteth hym moost with ghoostly temptacyons of Ire" (*YW,* II, 109). This statement derives from Frère Lorens; see (3.b), above. But the idea that the sin of wrath is sometimes caused by melancholy occurred already in Hugh Ripelin's *Compendium theologicae veritatis,* III, 24 (p. 116). Hence, "malencoly" appears frequently in company with anger and envy in writings of fourteenth-century English mystics: Hilton, *The Scale of Perfection,* I, 15.69; II, 38; *The Goad of Love,* 19; "Against Boasting and Pride" (*YW,* I, 123); "Discerning of Spirits" (ed. E. G. Gardner, *The Cell of Self-Knowledge* [London, 1910], p. 122); *Piers Plowman,* B: XIII, 334.

(b) "Melancholy" appears as a "daughter" of Wrath in Gower, *Mirour de l'omme,* ll. 3853ff., and *Confessio Amantis,* III, 27ff.

That *acedia* is sometimes related to melancholy (1), sometimes to a phlegmatic disposition (2), illustrates the fact brought out repeatedly in our survey of its history: that by 1200 *acedia* comprised two essentially different vices, grief and indolence (cf. chap. vii). The following statement from Guillaume d'Auvergne, *De vitiis,* on the effects of original sin, leaves no doubt: "Adjuvatur autem illud seminarium, ut foetus maledictos vitiorum germinet, et gignat tribus modis. Et primum ab ipsa complexione corporis, in quo est, sic ut iracundiam vel iram gignat a colerica complexione, ut pigritiam vel desidiam a flegmatica, ut solicitudinem superfluam at tristitiam a melancolica, ut inanem laetitiam risumque superfluum atque luxuriam a sanguinea" (*Opera*, I, 272).

It should also be noted that, for medieval theologians, linking the vices to the complexions was a matter of practical concern. The new directions in the practice of confession and penance around 1200 recognized that some men are predisposed to certain vices by their physical constitution, and therefore advised priests to take the temperament of their penitents into consideration: "Complexio etiam consideranda est, secundum quod signis exterioribus perpendi potest; quia secundum diversas complexiones, unus magis impellitur ad aliquod peccatum quam alius, quia si cholericus est, magis impellitur ad iram, si melancholicus, magis ad odium, si sanguineus, vel phlegmaticus, ad luxuriam." (Alanus of Lille, *Liber poenitentialis*, PL 210:287.). Similarly in Praepositinus, *Summa de penitentia iniungenda* (*ca.* 1190), MS. Vienne, Bibl. de l'État, 1413, fol. 131v (see P. Anciaux, *La Théologie du Sacrement de Pénitence au XII*[e] *siècle* [Louvain, 1949], p. 124, n. 1); Peter Quivil, *Summula*, 35 (*Councils*, II, 1075).

Appendix B

THE TREATMENT OF *ACEDIA* BY PERALDUS

The following structure clearly underlies the discussion of *acedia* in the *Summa de vitiis et virtutibus,* although it is often obscured in later printed editions. In order to facilitate reference to this section, I shall give my own division in Arabic numerals on the left and indicate folio and column of the Antwerp 1587 edition on the right.

Part V, "On *acedia.*"

1.	What can help man to detest *acedia*:	
1.1	Various examples—	77c
1.11	of inanimate things,	
1.12	of plants,	
1.13	of animals,	
1.141	of men, bad,	
1.142	good,	
1.2	Words of Holy Scripture;	78c
1.3	Showing how much this sin—	79a
1.31	displeases God,	
1.32	pleases the Devil,	79b
1.33	harms man—	79c
1.331	by inflicting in him evils—	80a
1.3311	of pain (poverty, vileness, affliction),	
1.3312	of guilt;	
1.332	by depriving him of goods;	80b
1.333	eight reasons for making good use of time;	80d
1.4	Six further reasons.	81c
2.	The vices which belong to *acedia*:	
2.01	*Tepiditas*	82b
2.02	*Mollities*	82c
2.03	*Somnolentia*	82d
2.04	*Otiositas*	83c
2.05	*Dilatio*	85d
2.06	*Tarditas*	93b
2.07	*Negligentia*	93c
2.08	*Inconsummatio* (or *imperfectio* or *imperseverantia*)	94b
2.09	*Remissio*	94c
2.10	*Dissolutio*	94d
2.11	*Incuria*	95a
2.12	*Ignavia*	95a
2.13	*Indevotio*	95c
2.14	*Tristitia*	95d

2.15	*Taedium vitae*	96b
2.16	*Desperatio*	96b
2.2	*Acedia* of seculars and of religious; the twelve evils in religious people.	96d
3.	Remedies	97c
4.	On indiscreet fervor	98b

Ends on fol. 100b

Appendix C

A QUESTIONNAIRE ON *ACEDIA*

From John de Burgo, *Pupilla oculi* [1385] (Paris, 1510), lib. V, cap. 8 (fol. xl, r). (Spelling slightly normalized.)

> De accidia inquiratur: Si nesciens simbolum aut orationem dominicam ea neglexerit addiscere vel filios spirituales si quos habuerit docere. Si in divino servitio negligens aut tepidus [fuerit]. Si ad ecclesiam ire tempore debito aut orare neglexerit, aut alios ne irent impedierit. Si officium divinum in ecclesia turbaverit vel impedierit. Si verbum dei predicatum parvipenderit. Si per ipsos aliquos defectus in officio divino vel sacramentorum administratione contigerit. Si infra sacros ordines constitutus vel etiam beneficiatus horas canonicas non dixerit. Si dies solemnes aut dominicos et festas sanctorum in debita reverentia non servaverit. Si in his caste et mundo non vixerit. Si verbum otiosum exercuerit frequenter. Si opus domini sui negligenter fecit vel omiserit. Si tempus suum male expenderit. Si parentes non honoraverit. Si vir uxorem suam secundum facultates suas non debite exhibuerit, corripuerit quando oportuit, aut instruxerit. Vel si prolem non debito modo et affectu educaverit, instruxerit, vel cum oportuit non corripuerit. Si aliquando nimia tristitia absortus fuerit ita quod desperaverit aut vitam suam parvipenderit. Si in infirmitate vel tribulatione aliqua impatiens fuerit. Si in prosperis ac etiam adversis deum non honoraverit ei gratias referendo, quoniam diligentibus deum omnia cooperantur in bonum. Si confiteri peccata sua distulit ultra tempus debitum, vel si forte peccata sua celando vel simulando confessionem diminuerit vel si confessionem suam non bene previdebat de peccatis suis per confessionem detegendis penes se et sic peccata sua per negligentiam oblivioni tradidit et sic in confessionionibus suis non expresserit circumstantias requisitas. Item si penitentias iniunctas non plene, seu indevote peregisset, vel per negligentiam et oblivionem pretermisisset. Si alicuius legati negligens fuerit executor. Si domus et familie negligens dispensator extiterit. Si animarum rector in docendo, corrigendo, subveniendo, vel orando remissus fuerit. Si in missa ignem, aquam, vinum, stolam, vel aliquid huiusmodi vel aliquid de canone omiserit. Si peccata sua ante confessionem per negligentiam oblivioni tradiderit.

Appendix D

A CONFESSION OF *ACEDIA*

The following confessional formula occurs in *Confessionale*, MS. BM. Harley 211, fol. 106*r-v*. For discussion see above, chap. iv, pp. 83-84.

> Confiteor insuper me per Accidiam multum peccasse. Negligens enim fui symbolum et orationem dominicam addiscere et spirituales [filios] docere. Opus domini mei negligenter feci. Neglexi eciam orare pro meipso et pro aliis quibus tenebar. Ad ecclesiam ire neglexi debito tempore et alios ne irent impedivi. Multa similiter feci per que officium dei impediebatur. Pro me nichilominus offense multe acciderunt in officio divino et in sacramento altaris. Infra sacros constitutus vel beneficiatus, horas canonicas sepe non dixi. Iniunctam mihi penitenciam non perfeci. Verbum eciam predicacionis audire parvipendi et quandoque perverti. Sepe tedium boni habui. Ociosus frequenter fui, et ocium ex affectu amavi. Tempus meum male expendidi cum essem studens vel alias. In officio domini et aliorum sompnolentus et torpens sepe fui. Ffesta statuta in ecclesia non custodivi, sed opera servilia aut peccata in eis feci. Parentes meos et superiores non honoravi. Uxorem eciam meam ego maritus minus sufficienter exibui ut eam prout debui instruxi. Eam et iuracionibus et vanitatibus assuescere permisi, nec corripui, nec instruxi. Discipulos et meos minus fideliter instruxi, et moribus informavi cum eorum magister essem. Domus eciam vel familie negligens dispensator fui. In cura animarum nimis remissus fui. Ecclesiarum rector, negligens fui in docendo, corripiendo, et monendo parochianos meos. Minus in temporalibus eis subveni. Negligenter eis divina ministravi et pro eis minus oravi quam deberem. Curam animarum suscepi sine proposito curandi, et ideo male intravi. Illicita sepius novi et illorum executor fui. Vota nichilominus licita non solvi, aut nimis distuli. Ffrequenter nimia tristicia absortus fui. Quandoque/ [fol. 106v] forte desperavi et animam vel vitam parvipendi. Consilia et alia secreta mihi coniuncta indiscrete alijs revelavi. Multa frequenter dicenda non dixi, et facienda facere omisi. Confiteri post lapsum parvipendi et quandoque nimis distuli. In confessione mea peccata quandoque aut peccatorum circumstancias scienter silui. Simulate ad confessionem quandoque accessi, scil. ut viderer ab hominibus. In confessione aliquando mentitus sum. Penitenciam mihi iniunctam facere frequenter vel in parte vel in toto omisi. Tempore debito quandoque non communicavi. Communicavi quandoque ex-

communicatus vel in mortali peccato existens. Sentenciam excommunicacionis innodatus vel in mortali peccato existens ordines recepi. Existens preterea in mortali peccato sacerdos celebravi vel ministerium ministravi. Celebravi eciam in irregularitate ante dispensacionem. Indevote eciam ad altare accessi et confeci, ministravi et oravi. In fide similiter erravi, quandoque unum, quandoque plures articulos non credens. Sortilegia sectatus sum, similiter et eriminaciones [?]. Beneficiis divinis et humanis, vel deo et hominibus ingratus extiti. Dei graciam sepe repuli. In bono inchoato constans et progressus non fui. Quosdam a bono proposito quandoque retraxi. Multis malum exemplum prebui. Ego eciam multa bona omisi que facere potui et debui. Bona frequenter et minus pure feci. Malum eciam peccati non ita detestatus sum ut debui, aut in me aut in alio. Testamentorum exsecucionem quandoque neglexi aut contra voluntatem defunctorum exsecutus sum. Presens fui ubi aliquis sine viatico et confessione vel testamento condicione decessit. Cogitaciones frivolas et inanes sepe admisi et permisi animum in talibus vagari. Verbis vanis et scurrilibus vel turpibus assuetus fui. De ludis mimicis et theatralibus aut venacionibus me nimis intromisi. Ad aleas et scaccos ut huiusmodi ludere consuevi et in hijs nimis delectatus sum.

Appendix E

THE FIFTH CIRCLE IN DANTE'S HELL

Toward the end of *Inferno* VII, Dante and Virgil enter the fifth circle of hell, the swamp of Styx. Virgil points out that the souls Dante sees in the swamp—"genti fangose . . . Ignude tutte con sembiante offeso" (ll. 110-11)—are "the souls of those whom wrath has overcome" (l. 116). Then he speaks of a second group of sinners submerged in the swamps, who make the water bubble with a hymn that rises curtailed from their throats:

> Fitti nel limo dicon: "Tristi fummo
> Ne l'aere dolce che dal sol s'allegra,
> Portando dentro accidioso fummo.
> Or ci attristiam ne la belletta negra."
> (ll. 121-24)

After wandering on, the two pilgrims are carried across the muddy water in a boat piloted by Phlegyas. During the crossing they witness more sinners in the swamp, particularly Filippo Argenti who once was "persona orgogliosa" (VIII, 46) and whom they finally leave turning "upon himself with his teeth" (l. 63). Then they arrive at the City of Dis and the sixth circle of hell.

The various answers given to the question what type or types of sinners are punished in the fifth circle can be reduced to three major groups, which may be roughly summarized as follows.

(1) The fifth circle contains sinners punished for *ira* and for *acedia*, the latter being the submerged souls. This answer was given by most of the fourteenth-century commentators on the *Divine Comedy*. Why Dante should have placed two types of sinners in this circle, in contrast to only one type for each of the preceding circles, is usually not considered. Francesco da Buti, however, thought that Dante placed wrath and sloth together because both sins "cause sadness in mind and body" and therefore are fittingly punished in Styx, whose name means *tristitia*.[1] The "Anonimo Fiorentino" thought that the two vices are together because they flank the virtue of temperance.[2] Among the moderns, Pietrobono, whose analysis of the moral structure of Dante's *Commedia* on the basis of parallel images is most noteworthy, similarly sees *ira* and *acedia* in this circle, the two vices being defects of *fortitudo* (with reference to *Convivio*, IV, vi, 43).[3]

(2) In the fifth circle are punished, not two but four deadly sins: *ira, acedia, superbia,* and *invidia.* This interpretation, already voiced by Pietro Alighieri,[4] found its strongest defender among modern scholars in Pio Rajna.[5] The main reason for finding four sins here is the assumption that Dante included all seven sins in upper hell, parallel with the seven capital vices in *Purgatorio.* Although there is no evidence for *invidia* in the fifth circle, Rajna maintains that the vice could not possibly be absent.

(3) Like the preceding circles, the fifth contains sinners punished for only one sin, and that is *ira.* The submerged souls can be explained in either one of two ways, by reference to Aristotle's ethical system: (a) They may be one of three types of *iracundi* distinguished by Aristotle, namely the sullen (*amari*) who repress their fury and smolder inwardly; or (b) they may be those who have sinned by lack of the virtue whose excess is *iracundia,* that is, the Aristotelian ἀόργητοι. Both explanations were offered as alternate suggestions by E. Moore and previous scholars,[6] and have been adopted by more recent critics and commentators.[7]

Concentrating for a moment on the text, we cannot escape the very definite impression that in lines 121-24 of *Inferno* VII Dante describes souls punished for *acedia.* The adjective *accidioso* had too precise, too technical a meaning in the twelfth and early thirteenth centuries to have been used lightly by a poet like Dante, with a general meaning of "sad." The surrounding images strengthen this impression: the smoke which these unhappy souls carry within them, their past sadness at "the sweet air that rejoices in the sun," and above all their punishment of "gurgling a hymn" because—like the somnolent monks or the clippers and overskippers of popular preaching—they cannot say it "con parola integra."

Yet Dante did not make an explicit statement that these submerged souls indeed represent the sin of *acedia,* and although I find it hard to do so it must be admitted that the just-mentioned details *may* be interpreted differently. It appears therefore that any fully convincing identification must proceed from circumstantial evidence. The main piece of circumstantial evidence for identifying *acedia* in a work of literature is the context of the seven deadly sins. But did Dante use that scheme in *Inferno*? For the second through fourth circles (lust—gluttony—avarice) the answer seems positive, but then any such plan disappears. Hence the split between explanations (2) and (3) I have outlined above: Group 2 assumes that Dante included all seven sins in hell and consequently has to detect four in the fifth circle; whereas Group 3 denies that the deadly sins appear in schematic form in *Inferno* at all and, therefore, can (and must) explain the *accidiosi* as somehow belonging to the vice or passion of *ira*.[8]

Neither position is absolutely convincing, and one can feel sympathy for the modern critic who sidesteps the issue altogether. Perhaps the fault is not so much the scholar's as Dante's own. In discussing the swamp of Styx, Pio Rajna had to conclude that here Dante, "invece di parlare, ha bisbigliato." Also, there still remains the possibility of a change in Dante's plan for the *Inferno* after Canto VII. In any event, it is clear that the identification of the submerged souls depends on finding a convincing answer to the larger question of the moral structure of Dante's hell, a question which by far transcends the subject of this study. I would surmise, however, that further search in Scholastic treatises on ethics, especially in commentaries on Aristotle, may produce fresh light on this problem. On the basis of my analysis of *Purgatorio* XVII, I strongly suspect that Dante used a single model for his structure of hell instead of borrowing bits and pieces from Aristotle, Cicero, St. Thomas on Aristotle, St. Thomas against Aristotle, and selected Doctors of the Church, as most critics seem to imply. We have seen earlier that Scholastic theologians tried to combine Christian traditions with Aristotelian psychology and ethics. It is not improbable that Dante's *Inferno* was shaped after some attempt to relate human evil (whether the seven deadly sins or some other scheme) with the parts of the soul,[9] or the chief passions, or the cardinal virtues, or some such "pagan" scheme.

ABBREVIATIONS

Anal. hymn.	*Analecta hymnica medii aevi.* 55 vols. Leipzig, 1886-1922.
ASNS	*Archiv für das Studium der neueren Sprachen.* Braunschweig.
Beiträge Baeumker	Beiträge zur Geschichte der Philosophie des Mittelalters. Texte und Untersuchungen. Ed. C. Baeumker. Münster.
Bigne	Marguerin de La Bigne. *Maxima Bibliotheca Veterum Patrum et Antiquorum Scriptorum Ecclesiasticorum.* 28 vols. Lyon, 1677; Genoa, 1707.
CCSL	Corpus Christianorum, Series Latina. Turnhout, Belgium.
CSCO	Corpus Scriptorum Christianorum Orientalium. Louvain.
CSEL	Corpus Scriptorum Ecclesiasticorum Latinorum. Vienna.
Councils	F. M. Powicke and C. R. Cheney. *Councils and Synods with other documents relating to the English Church.* Vol. II, *A.D. 1205-1313.* Two parts. Oxford, 1964.
DTC	*Dictionnaire de Théologie Catholique.* 15 vols. in 30. Paris, 1930-1950.
EETS	Early English Text Society. Original Series.
EETS, es	Early English Text Society. Extra Series.

GCS — Die griechischen christlichen Schriftsteller der ersten drei Jahrhunderte. Ed. Kirchenväterkommission der Preussischen Akademie, Berlin.

MGH — Monumenta Germaniae historica. Hannover.

MLR — *The Modern Language Review.*

MP — *Modern Philology.*

OED — *The Oxford English Dictionary,* 12 vols. and Supplement. Oxford, 1933.

PG — J.-P. Migne. Patrologiae Cursus Completus. Series Graeca. 161 vols. Paris, 1857ff.

PL — J.-P. Migne. Patrologiae Cursus Completus. Series Latina. 221 vols. Paris, 1844ff.

PMLA — *Publications of the Modern Language Association of America.*

RBén. — *Revue Bénédictine.* Abbaye de Maredsous, Belgium.

RHE — *Revue d'Histoire Ecclésiastique.* Université Catholique de Louvain.

RMAL — *Revue du Moyen Age latin.* Lyon: Facultés catholiques.

RTAM — *Recherches de Théologie ancienne et médiévale.* Louvain: Abbaye du Mont César.

SATF — Société des anciens textes français. Paris.

SP — *Studies in Philology.*

STC — Scottish Text Society. Edinburgh.

YW — C. Horstman. *Yorkshire Writers. Richard Rolle of Hampole, an English Father of the Church, and His Followers.* 2 vols. London, 1895-1896.

ZKG — *Zeitschrift für Kirchengeschichte.* Gotha.

ZKTh — *Zeitschrift für katholische Theologie.* Innsbruck.

NOTES

For principles of documentation followed in the Notes, see pages viii-ix of the Preface.

PREFACE

1. F. Paget, "Introductory Essay concerning Accidie," in *The Spirit of Discipline* (4th ed.; London, 1892), pp. 1-50 (written in 1890); a historical survey of the sin from Cassian to Paget's contemporaries. Noteworthy among the encyclopedias are: E. Vansteenberghe, "Paresse," DTC, XI[2] (Paris, 1932), cols. 2023-30, a good historical and doctrinal survey; G. Bardy, "Acedia," *Dictionnaire de Spiritualité ascétique et mystique*, I (Paris, 1937), cols. 166-69, a rich survey with emphasis on spiritual writers.

2. For example, J. O. Hannay, *Christian Monasticism* (London, 1903), pp. 153-57; O. Zöckler, *Askese und Mönchtum* (2nd ed.; Frankfurt, 1897); and many subsequent studies.

3. M. Lot-Borodine, "L'Aridité ou *Siccitas* dans l'antiquité chrétienne," *Études carmélitaines mystiques et missionaires*, XXII (1937), 191-205, and G. Truc, "Les états mystiques négatifs (La tiédeur—l'acédia—la sécheresse)," *Revue philosophique*, LXXIII (1912), 610-28, both important for distinguishing *acedia* from "spiritual dryness."

4. Especially, R. Caillois, "Les démons de midi," *Revue de l'histoire des religions*, CXV (1937), 142-73; CXVI (1937), 54-83, 143-86, who relates the "noonday demon" of *acedia* with such myths as the Sirens, the Lotos Eaters, and Plato's grasshoppers.

5. A. de Martonne, "Recherches sur l'acédia," *Annales de le Société académique de Saint-Quentin*, IX (1852), 187-99; P. Alphandéry, "De quelques documents médiévaux relatifs à des états psychasthéniques," *Journal de Psychologie normale et pathologique*, XXVI (1929), 763-87, an interesting analysis of medieval texts from the psycho-pathological viewpoint; W. Sombart, *Der Bourgeois. Zur Geistesgeschichte des modernen Wirtschaftsmenschen* (München, 1923), pp. 311-12, who briefly discusses the socio-economic aspects of *acedia* in his reply to Max Weber's *The Protestant Ethic and the Spirit of Capitalism*; J. Pieper touches on *acedia* in his *Leisure, the Basis of Culture*, trans. A. Dru (New York, 1952), pp. 48ff.

6. Especially H. Cochin, *Le Frère de Pétrarque et le Livre "Du repos des religieux"* (Paris, 1903), Appendix "Accidia," pp. 205-21, who surveys the word *acedia* from Greek texts to Petrarch; for other discussions of the term by Petrarch scholars, see chap. vi. A. Huxley, in *On the Margin. Notes and Essays* (London, 1923), pp. 18-25, analyzes modern forms of *acedia*, such as Renaissance melancholy, Romantic *mal-du-siècle*, and nineteenth-century *ennui*.

7. M. W. Bloomfield, *The Seven Deadly Sins. An Introduction to the His-*

tory of a Religious Concept with Special Reference to Medieval English Literature ([East Lansing,] 1952).

8. Special mention should be made of Father M. A. Connell's unpublished doctoral dissertation, "A Study of *Accidia* and Some of Its Literary Phases" (Cornell University, 1932). The study roughly follows the outline and tendency of Bishop Paget's essay and presents a great wealth of material, mostly from theological texts. It does not investigate the Scholastic rationale of the vices, nor does it distinguish between the various "types" of *acedia* (monastic, Scholastic, popular) or analyze its supposed change of meaning. In general, Father Connell uses a broader basis than I do, by including passages which describe states similar to *acedia* but do not use the term. Of medieval poets, he considers only Dante at some length.

CHAPTER I

1. The form *acedia* is the exact transliteration of the Greek ἀκηδία. *Accidia,* however, which is found in manuscripts from at least the ninth century on, became the normal form in the later Middle Ages. Intermediate forms *accedia* and *acidia* also occur. In my text, I have chosen to use the form *acedia* consistently except in direct quotations. For the phonetic change, see A. Ernout, "Accidia," in *Mélanges Desrousseaux* (Paris, 1937), pp. 161-63.

2. W. Bousset, *Apophthegmata, Studien zur Geschichte des ältesten Mönchtums* (Tübingen, 1923), p. 92. For Evagrius' life see J. Quasten, *Patrology,* III (Utrecht, etc., 1960), 169.

3. For Evagrius' works see Quasten, *Patrology,* III, 169-76; J. Muyldermans, *Evagriana Syriaca* ("Bibliothèque du Muséon," No. 31 [Louvain, 1952]); and the convenient list in R. Draguet, "L'*Histoire lausiaque,* une oeuvre écrite dans l'esprit d'Evagre," *RHE,* XLI (1946), 323-25, n.1.

4. *De octo vitiosis cogitationibus,* 7 (hereinafter cited as *DOVC*; PG 40: 1273). A similar description appears in *De octo spiritibus malitiae,* 13-14 (hereinafter cited as *DOSM*; PG 79:1157-60), attributed to Nilus. See also Ps.-Nilus, *De octo vitiosis cogitationibus* (PG 79:1456-60), which is attributed to Nilus, but in reality is a combination of excerpts from Nilus, Evagrius, and Cassian; and Antiochus of Saba, *Homilia* 26, "De acedia" (PG 89:1513ff.), based on Nilus' (?) *DOSM.*

5. Relevant passages are:

Capita practica, I, 14.18.19.25 (PG 40:1226ff.);
Tractatus ad Eulogium, 6.8.12.28 (PG 79:1101ff.);
Antirrheticus (in Syriac; see the following note); with an additional fragment published by J. Muyldermans, "Evagriana de la Vaticane," *Muséon,* LIV (1941), 6-7;
De oratione, 75 (PG 79:1184);
De malignis cogitationibus, 12.18.25 (PG 79:1213ff.);
Institutio ad monachos (PG 79:1236);
Speculum monachorum, 55 and 56, edited under the title "Mönchsspiegel" by H. Gressmann ("Texte und Untersuchungen," No. 39 [Leipzig, 1913]);
Speculum virginum, 39 ("Nonnenspiegel," ed. *ibid.*);
Rerum monachalium rationes, 8 (PG 40:1260);
Capita cognoscitiva, 28 (ed. J. Muyldermans, "Evagriana," *Muséon,* XLIV [1931], 54).

6. In the *Antirrheticus,* which exists only in a Syriac translation edited by W. Frankenberg (*Abhandlungen der königl. Ges. d. Wiss. zu Göttingen,* philol.-hist. Klasse, neue Folge, XIII, 2 [Berlin, 1912]) and provided by him with a Greek retranslation. Book VI contains 57 "spiritual words" against ἀκηδία, of which the following are three good examples:

"28. Against the λογισμός of ἀκηδία which throws away the work of one's hands and makes the body lean in slumber against the wall: 'How long wilt thou sleep, o sluggard . . .' [Prov. 6:9ff.].

"34. To the soul in *ἀκηδία* which reasons that there is no limit to its sufferings: . . . .

"16. To the mind that does not understand that the *λογισμοί* of *ἀκηδία*, when they tarry in it, disturb its fixed state and at the time of prayer dim the holy light in its eyes: . . . ."

7. For passages in pre-Christian authors, see: A. Vögtle, "Acedia," in *Reallexikon für Antike und Christentum*, ed. Th. Klauser, *et al.*, Vol. I (Stuttgart, 1950), cols. 62-63; H. G. Liddell and R. Scott, *A Greek-English Lexicon*, rev. H. S. Jones (Oxford, [1925]); H. Estienne, *Thesaurus Graecae Linguae* (Paris, 1831).

8. *Ad Atticum*, XII, 45, 1.

9. *Hermotimus, or the Rival Philosophies*, 77 (ed. H. W. Fowler and F. G. Fowler, *The Works of Lucian of Samosate*, II [Oxford, 1905], 85-86).

10. E. Hatch and H. A. Redpath, *A Concordance to the Septuagint and the other Greek versions of the Old Testament (including the apocryphal books)* (Oxford, 1897; reprint, 1954).

11. The excellent entry in G. W. H. Lampe, *A Patristic Greek Lexicon* (Oxford, 1961ff.), provides a rich and detailed survey of *ἀκηδία* in patristic literature. Cf. S. Wenzel, "'Ἀκηδία. Additions to Lampe's Patristic Greek Lexicon," *Vigiliae Christianae*, XVII (1963), 173-76.

12. *Visio* III, 11, 3 (ed. M. Whittaker, GCS, XLVIII [Berlin, 1956], 17).

13. *Philocalia*, XII, 2 (ed. J. A. Robinson [Cambridge, 1893]; trans. G. Lewis [Edinburgh, 1911]). Cf. a similar passage in Origen's commentary *In Jesu Nave*, XX, 1 (ed. W. A. Baehrens, GCS, XXX [Leipzig, 1921], 418), preserved in Latin translation (with *taedio fatigatus*); notice however that the respective sentences in the two passages carry different meanings.

14. *In Lucam*, hom. 29 (ed. M. Rauer, GCS, XXXV [Leipzig, 1941], 182); in the second edition, Rauer placed this passage among the dubious fragments (p. 265).

15. *Selecta in Psalmos*, PG 12:1552.

16. J. B. Pitra (ed.), *Analecta Sacra Spicilegii Solesmensis* (8 vols.; Paris, 1876ff.), III, 170f.

17. Pitra, *Analecta Sacra*, III, 263f.

18. R. Cadiou (ed.), *Commentaires inédits des Psaumes. Étude sur les textes d'Origène dans le manuscrit "Vindobonensis 8"* (Paris, 1936), p. 106.

19. *Selecta in Psalmos*, PG 12:1664. The same scholium appears in an ascetic florilegium at the Vatican library under the name of Evagrius; see J. Muyldermans, "Evagriana de la Vaticane," *Muséon*, LIV (1941), 10. Muyldermans was unable to identify the verse.

20. *Selecta in Psalmos*, PG 12:1593.

21. See above, n. 19.

22. H. U. von Balthasar, "Die Hiera des Evagrius," *ZKTh*, LXIII (1939), 86-106, 181-206. Von Balthasar's findings are accepted in the recent handbooks on Patrology by Altaner (*Patrology* [New York, 1960], p. 307) and Quasten (*Patrology*, III, 175). They are further strengthened by the scholium on Ps. 139:3 attributed to Evagrius, which was discovered and edited by Muyldermans (see above). See also M.-J. Rondeau, "Le commentaire sur les Psaumes d'Évagre le Pontique," *Orientalia Christiana Periodica*, XXVI (1960), 307-48.

23. Von Balthasar, "Die Hiera des Evagrius"; and M. Rauer, in his edition of *In Lucam*, GCS, IX, 225 (2nd ed.).

24. *Vita s. Antonii*, 36 (PG 26:896); also, trans. R. T. Meyer ("Ancient Christian Writers," No. 10 [Westminster, Md., 1950]).

25. *Ibid.*, 17 and 19 (PG 26:869 and 872).

26. On Ps. 60:2 (PG 27:272), 85:5 (376), 90:6 (401).

27. Basil, *Regulae fusius tractae*, XXXVII, 5 (PG 31:1016).

28. *Sermo asceticus* (PG 31:881).

29. *Constitutiones asceticae,* 7 (PG 31:1368). The origin of this work is uncertain.

30. Cf. *Sermo de ascetica disciplina,* 2 (PG 31:652).

31. John Chrysostom, *In II Tim.,* homilia 1: "*Quench not the spirit* [I Thess. 5:19]. The spirit is quenched by ἀκηδία and negligence, but roused by vigilance and attentiveness" (PG 62:603). Cf. *In Col.,* hom. 2 (PG 62:310) and hom. 10 (368).

32. Macarius, *Homilia* 56 (ed. G. L. Marriott, *Macarii Anecdota. Seven Unpublished Homilies of Macarius* ["Harvard Theological Studies," No. 5 (Cambridge, Mass., 1918)], p. 46). There seems to be agreement that these homilies are not by Macarius (Quasten, *Patrology,* III, 162ff.). In recently published homilies attributed to Macarius, ed. E. Klostermann and H. Berthold, *Neue Homilien des Makarios/Symeon. I. Aus Typus III* ("Texte und Untersuchungen." No. 72 [Berlin, 1961]), ἀκηδία appears in Nos. IX (pp. 43, 44, 50) and XIII (p. 68).

33. Nilus, *Epistulae,* III, 254 (PG 70:509).

34. *Ibid.,* I, 67 (PG 79:112).

35. *Ibid.,* III, 319 (PG 79:537).

36. *Ibid.,* III, 142 (PG 79:449).

37. E. C. Butler, *The Lausiac History of Palladius,* I (Cambridge, 1898), 3. In addition to using ἀκηδία in monk stories (see the passages indicated in the following notes), Palladius also employs the term with a more general meaning in his Prologue to Lausus (PG 34:1003 and 1009) and the *Dialogus de vita Joannis Chrysostomi* (PG 47:59, 60, 74, 75; also, ed. P. R. Coleman-Norton [Cambridge, 1928], pp. 106, 108f., 133).

38. Cf. Bousset, *Apophthegmata,* p. 66; J.-C. Guy, *Recherches sur la tradition grecque des "Apophthegmata Patrum"* ("Subsidia hagiographica," No. 36 [Brussels, 1962]), pp. 231f.

39. The recluse Alexandra has to "fight (like a boxer) with ἀκηδία and evil thoughts," *Historia Lausiaca,* 5 (PG 34:1017f.).

40. Mother Theodora teaches: "As soon as one applies oneself to the quiet life, the evil one approaches and depresses the soul with ἀκηδία, cowardice, and evil thoughts"; *Apophthegmata,* "Theodora," 3 (PG 65:201).

41. A young man, who is ordered to keep his cell until the Sabbath, becomes affected by ἀκηδία after two days, leaves his cell, and sees an Ethiopian who gnashes his teeth against him; *Apophth.,* "Heraclius" (PG 65:186).

42. See the preceding note. Similarly: When Cronius was young and a novice, he fled the dwelling of his archimandrite "because of ἀκηδία," *Hist. Laus.,* 25 (PG 34:1068; ed. Butler, chap. 21); according to Abba Poemen, ἀκηδία always comes in the beginning (?), *Apophth.,* "Poemen," 149 (PG 65:360).

43. Abba Poemen: "No passion is worse than ἀκηδία," *Apophth.,* "Poemen," 149 (PG 65:360).

44. See the reference to Cronius, n. 42. Nathanael, in the beginning of his ascetic life, was mocked by the devil so that "he seemed to feel ἀκηδία for his first cell and went off and built another nearer a village," *Hist. Laus.,* 18 (PG 34:1041; the text in Butler's ed., chap. 16, is somewhat different).

45. Other stories which contain the temptation: (a) "The saintly Abba Anthony once sat in the desert and fell into ἀκηδία and much darkness of evil thoughts"; to his prayer for enlightenment as to what he should do, he is granted a vision which teaches him to alternate prayer with manual work; *Apophth.,* "Antonius," 1 (PG 65:76). (b) Mother Syncletica: ἀκηδία is unreasonable grief; Guy, *Recherches,* p. 35; also in Ps.-Athanasius, *Vita s. Syncleticae,* 40 (PG 28:1512) and *Vitae Patrum,* V, 71 (PL 73:924). (c) A brother asks Abba Silvanus for advice concerning ἀκηδία and sleepiness he suffers when he gets up at night to recite his psalms; ed. F. Nau in *Patrologia Orientalis* (ed.

R. Graffin and F. Nau; Paris, 1903ff.), VIII, 180. (d) Palladius is affected by ἀκηδία (i.e., sad and grumbling) when he receives what appears to him a slight; *Hist. Laus.*, 43 (PG 34:1113).

46. The relation of Evagrius and monastic traditions in Lower Egypt to ascetic ideals pursued in Upper Egypt and in Syria is extremely hard to gauge, because of the lack of sufficient evidence. Pachomius speaks of a "spirit [πνεῦμα] of sloth," in Coptic: L. Th. Lefort, *Oeuvres de S. Pachôme et de ses disciples,* CSCO, Scriptores Coptici, 23-24 (Louvain, 1956), p. 2; and E. A. W. Budge, *Coptic Apocrypha in the Desert of Upper Egypt* (London, 1913), "Instructions of Apa Pachomius," pp. 148 and 354. No further description is given. The Coptic word is not etymologically related to ἀκηδία. For Ephraem the Syrian, see n. 65.

47. The use of πνεῦμα instead of δαίμων or λογισμός (see below) has been suggested as characteristic of Nilus (Bloomfield, *Seven Deadly Sins,* p. 60). But Evagrius, too, uses πνεῦμα ἀκηδίας occasionally: *Tractatus ad Eulogium,* 6 and 8 (PG 79:1101, 1104); *Speculum monachorum,* 55 and 56.

48. J. Daniélou, "Démon. II-Dans la littérature ecclésiastique jusqu'à Origène," *Dictionnaire de Spiritualité ascétique et mystique,* III (Paris, 1957), cols. 152-89.

49. III, 18-IV, 26 (ed. P. Boccaccio and G. Berardi, *Regula Unionis seu Manuale Disciplinae* [3rd ed., Rome, 1958]).

50. *Pastor Hermas, Mandatum* VI. Cf. M. Dibelius, *Der Hirt des Hermas,* in Lietzmann's *Handbuch zum Neuen Testament* (Ergänzungsband IV [Tübingen, 1923]), pp. 518ff.

51. "Testament of Reuben," II, 1; III, 2ff. (ed. R. H. Charles, *The Greek Versions of the Testaments of the Twelve Patriarchs* [Oxford, 1908]).

52. I have relied on the following studies: K. Heussi, *Der Ursprung des Mönchtums* (Tübingen, 1936); P. de Labriolle, "Les débuts du monachisme," in A. Fliche and V. Martin, *Histoire de l'Église depuis les origines jusqu'à nos jours,* III (Paris, 1950), 299-369; O. Chadwick, *John Cassian. A Study in Primitive Monasticism* (Cambridge, 1950).—For Origen: W. Völker, *Das Vollkommenheitsideal des Origines* (Tübingen, 1931); J. Daniélou, *Origène* (Paris, 1948); G. Teichtweier, *Die Sündenlehre des Origines* (Regensburg, 1958).—For Gregory of Nyssa: J. Daniélou, *Platonisme et théologie mystique. Essai sur la doctrine spirituelle de saint Grégoire de Nysse* (Paris, 1944); W. Völker, *Gregor von Nyssa als Mystiker* (Wiesbaden, 1955).—For Maximus the Confessor (in whose work "many roads converge," M. Viller and K. Rahner, *Aszese und Mystik in der Väterzeit* [Freiburg, 1939], p. 242); *Four Centuries,* trans. P. Sherwood ("Ancient Christian Writers," No. 21 [Westminster, Md., 1955]); H. U. von Balthasar, *Kosmische Liturgie. Das Weltbild Maximus' des Bekenners* (2nd ed.; Einsiedeln, 1961).

53. Evagrius, *Admonitio paraenetica,* 4 (ed. Muyldermans, *Evagriana Syriaca,* p. 158 [with French translation]).

54. For ἀπάθεια see: P. de Labriolle, "Les débuts du monachisme," pp. 336-38; G. Bardy, "Apatheia," *Dictionnaire de Spiritualité ascétique et mystique,* I (Paris, 1937), cols. 727-46; Th. Rüthner, *Die sittliche Forderung der Apatheia in den beiden ersten christlichen Jahrhunderten und bei Klemens von Alexandrien. Ein Beitrag zur Geschichte des Vollkommenheitsbegriffs* ("Freiburger Theologische Studien," No. 63 [Freiburg, 1949]); A. Dirking, "Die Bedeutung des Wortes Apathie beim hl. Basilius dem Grossen, "*Theologische Quartalschrift,* CXXXIV (1954), 202-12.

55. Evagrius, *Capita practica,* 2 (PG 40:1221); cf. *ibid.*, 53 (1233).

56. Cf. A. and C. Guillaumont, "Démon. III-Dans la plus ancienne littérature monastique," *Dictionnaire de Spiritualité ascétique et mystique,* III, cols. 201-2.

57. Evagrius, *Tractatus ad Eulogium,* 15 (PG 79:1113). Athanasius calls the

λογισμοί "stumbling-blocks" put by the demons in the monk's way, *Vita Antonii*, 23.

58. *Four Centuries*, II, 31; cf., PG 90:993.

59. For a survey of the various theories, see A. Vögtle, "Woher stammt das Schema der Hauptsünden?" *Theologische Quartalschrift*, CXXII (1941), 217-37; much summarized in "Achtlasterlehre," *Reallexikon für Antike und Christentum*, I (Stuttgart, 1950), cols. 75-76.

60. Bloomfield, *Seven Deadly Sins*, chap. 1 and 2; and "The Origin of the Concept of the Seven Cardinal Sins," *Harvard Theological Review*, XXXIV (1941), 121-28.

61. The distinction between λογισμός, temptation, and sin is clearly drawn by Evagrius, *Capita practica*, 46 and 47 (PG 40: 1233): "The temptation of the monk is the λογισμός rising from the passible (sensitive, παθητικός) part of the soul and darkening the mind. The sin of the monk is the consent of thought to a forbidden delight."

62. "De doctrina spirituali Christianorum orientalium quaestiones et scripta. 3. L'origine de la théorie orientale des huit péchés capitaux," *Orientalia Christiana*, XXX (1933), 164-75.

63. Vögtle, "Woher stammt," p. 237.

64. *Historia monachorum*, XX, 15; Cassian, *Coll.*, V, 18; *Inst.*, praef. (p. 6), V, 2.3; VI, 1, etc. (the absence of Evagrius' name from Cassian's works may be due to the anti-Origenist persecutions); Gennadius, *De viris illustribus*, XI.

65. Bloomfield, *Seven Deadly Sins*, p. 60. There is an interesting list of sins in a work by Pachomius or his disciples, published after the appearance of Bloomfield's book: ed. Lefort, CSCO, Scriptores Coptici, 23-24 (Louvain, 1956), pp. 2-3.—J. Stelzenberger claimed that the list of eight vices was already used by Ephraem the Syrian, who died in 373 (*Die Beziehungen der frühchristlichen Sittenlehre zur Ethik der Stoa* [München, 1933], p. 398). But the passages Stelzenberger cites are hardly by Ephraem; see A. Baumstark, *Geschichte der syrischen Literatur* (Bonn, 1922), pp. 36 and 45.

66. Horace uses the adjective *iners*, *Epistulae*, I, 1, 38.

67. Servius, *In Vergili carmina commentarii*, on *Aeneid*, VI, 714 (ed. G. Thilo and H. Hagen [Leipzig, 1881-1887], II, 98). For a discussion of this and the previous passage, see Bloomfield, *Seven Deadly Sins*, pp. 45-50.

68. See esp. S. Schiwietz, *Das morgenländische Mönchtum*, II (Mainz, 1913), 72-84.

69. *Manual of Discipline*, IV, 9. S. Wibbing has pointed out that the phrase "slackening of hands" (in Hebrew) occurs also in Eccles. 10:18 and similarly in the Qumram commentary on Habacuc; *Die Tugend- und Lasterkataloge im Neuen Testament und ihre Traditionsgeschichte unter besonderer Berücksichtigung der Qumram-Texte* ("Beihefte zur Zeitschrift für die neutestamentliche Wissenschaft und die Kunde der älteren Kirche," No. 25 [Berlin, 1959]), pp. 52-53. Cf. also the "slackened hands" of Heb. 12:12, quoting Is. 35:3. To the cited analogues to sloth one might add the "esprit de lâcheté" in Pachomius' list; see above, n. 65.

70. PG 12:1552 and 27:401.

71. On the midday demon see esp. the rich studies by R. Caillois, "Les démons de midi," *Revue de l'histoire des religions*, CXV (1937), 142-73; CXVI (1937), 54-83, 143-86; and by R. Arbesmann, "The *Daemonium Meridianum* and Greek and Latin Patristic Exegesis," *Traditio*, XIV (1958), 17-31.

72. PG 12:1593 and Cadiou, *Commentaires inédits des Psaumes*, p. 106.

73. Cf. H. Jonas, *Gnosis und spätantiker Geist*, I (2nd ed.; Göttingen, 1954), 114ff.

74. A good example of this mythological significance of sleep is furnished by the "Hymn of the Soul," verses 34-35, of the *Acts of St. Thomas*, ed. M. R. James, *The Apocryphal New Testament* (Oxford, 1924), pp. 411-15; see also

the psychologico-moral symbolism of "sleep" and "awakening" in Philo, *De congressu eruditionis gratia,* 15, 81ff. (ed. L. Cohn and P. Wendland, *Philonis Alexandrini Opera quae supersunt* [Berlin, 1896-1930], III, 88-89).

75. *Homilia paschalis,* 18 (PG 77:816).

76. Antiochus of Saba, *Homilia* 26 (PG 89:1513-20); John Climacus, *Scala Paradisi,* 13 (PG 88:857-61).

77. O. Chadwick, *John Cassian. A Study in Primitive Monasticism* (Cambridge, 1950).

78. Cassian's transliteration of ἀκηδία into Latin was preceded by an ancient translation of Athanasius' *Life of St. Anthony,* which dates from the third quarter of the fourth century; see G. Garitte, *Un témoin important du texte de la Vie de S. Antoine par S. Athanase. La version latine inédite des Archives du Chapitre de S. Pierre à Rome* (Brussels, 1939), p. 7.

79. *Inst.,* X, 1 (E. C. S. Gibson [trans.], *A Select Library of Nicene and Post-Nicene Fathers,* 2nd ser., XI [New York, 1894], 266).

80. The most comprehensive recent study of Cassian's sources is H.-O. Weber, *Die Stellung des Johannes Cassianus zur ausserpachomianischen Mönchstradition* ("Beiträge zur Geschichte des alten Mönchtums und des Benediktinerordens," No. 24 [Münster, 1961]). For *Inst.* X, see pp. 82-83. Cf. also S. Marsili, "Giovanni Cassiano ed Evagrio Pontico. Dottrina sulla carità e contemplazione," *Studia Anselmiana,* V (Rome, 1936).

81. Besides *Inst.,* X, 1, the formula is used *Inst.,* V, 1, and *Coll.,* V, 2.

82. *Coll.,* V, 11; see also *Inst.,* X, 3 and 5.

83. *Coll.,* V, 23. Apparently an innovation, for among Greek writers the virtue opposed to the vice had usually been patience; cf. especially Evagrius, *Tractatus ad Eulogium,* 4 (PG 79:1144); *Institutio ad monachos* (1236); *De malignis cogitationibus,* 12 (1213); Nilus (?), *DOSM,* 14 (1160); *De vitiis quae opposita sunt virtutibus* (1144).

84. *Coll.,* V, 3. Weber, *Johannes Cassianus,* pp. 24-25, has shown the dependence of Cassian's division on Evagrius, *Capita cognoscitiva,* 56. Another division occurs in *Coll.,* XXIV, 15, where eighteen vices are distributed among the classical three parts of the soul; *acedia* belongs to the irascible part. In contrast, several Greek writers emphasized that *acedia* attacks *all* parts of the soul: Evagrius, *Capita cognoscitiva,* 28 (ed. J. Muyldermans, "Evagriana," *Muséon,* XLIV [1931], 54); Ps.-Nilus, *De octo vitiosis cogitationibus* (PG 79: 1460); Maximus, *Four Centuries,* I, 67 (PG 90:973); Ps.-Ammonius Alexandrinus, on Matt. 24:13 (PG 85:1385). See also the scholium on Ps. 118:28 quoted above, p. 18.

85. *Coll.,* V, 9 and *Inst.,* X, 1.

86. *DOVC,* end (PG 40:1278).

87. A similar chain of vices appears in hom. 40 attributed to Macarius (PG 34:764), where ἀκηδία comes from impatience and leads to laziness; and in the so-called Great Letter of Macarius (ed. W. Jaeger, *Two Rediscovered Works of Ancient Christian Literature: Gregory of Nyssa and Macarius* [Leyden, 1954], p. 268), where ἀκηδία comes from impatience and leads to negligence.

88. "Rogamus autem vos, fratres, ut abundetis magis, et operam detis ut quieti sitis, et ut vestra negotia agatis, et operemini manibus vestris" (I Thess. 4:10-11), cf. ed. Petschenig, p. 179, ll. 5, 7, and 16, and *passim.*

89. II Thess. 3:6; cf. *ibid.,* p. 181, ll. 9-10.

90. "Et ut honeste ambuletis ad eos qui foris sunt" (I Thess. 4:12), cf. *ibid.,* p. 180, ll. 1-4.

91. *Coll.,* praef., p. 4, ll. 13-23.

92. Cf. the contemporary treatment of the same subject in St. Augustine's *De opere monachorum.*

93. Again, the relation between the two vices occurred already in Evagrius:

"The demon of ἀκηδία is close to laziness (ἀργία), and 'he [the slothful] lies in desires', as they say [Prov. 13:4]," *Rerum monachalium rationes*, 8 (PG 40: 1260).

CHAPTER II

1. Gregory the Great, *Moralia in Job*, XXXI, 45 (PL 76:620ff.).
2. Bloomfield, *Seven Deadly Sins*, pp. 72ff.
3. *In I Regum*, V, 9 (PL 79:364).
4. M. de la Taille, "Le Commentaire de saint Grégoire le Grand sur le Ier Livre des Rois," *Recherches de Science Religieuse*, VI (1916), 472f.; cf. *ibid.*, XVIII (1928), 322f.
5. P. Verbraken, "Le Commentaire de S. Grégoire sur le premier Livre des Rois," *RBén.*, LXVI (1956), 159-217; also, *ibid.*, 39-62.
6. R. Gillet, "Spiritualité et place du moine dans l'Église selon saint Grégoire le Grand," in *Théologie de la vie monastique* (Lyon, 1961), p. 326.—Also, K. Hallinger, "Papst Gregor der Grosse und der heilige Benedikt," *Studia Anselmiana*, XLII (1957), 241, n. 31.
7. A quick check of passages on spiritual depression in the *Moralia* reveals that Gregory used such terms as *taedium* (X, 18; PL 75:939), *gravitas cordis* (I, 36; col. 551), *desidia* (IX, 34; col. 888), *torpor negligentiae* (IV, 23; col. 657; V, 31; cols. 708-9), and others, but not *acedia*.
8. R. Gillet, Introduction to *Grégoire le Grand, Morales sur Job*, ed. A. de Gaudemaris ("Sources chrétiennes," No. 1 [Paris, 1952], pp. 89ff.). Dom Gillet's arguments have been accepted by Hallinger, "Papst Gregor," p. 295, n. 202.
9. O. Zöckler, *Die Tugendlehre des Christentums geschichtlich dargestellt in der Entwicklung ihrer Lehrformen* (Gütersloh, 1904), pp. 99-100; Bloomfield, *Seven Deadly Sins*, p. 72.
10. An example is J. Stelzenberger, whose insistence on Gregory's fascination with the holy heptad led him to believe that each of Gregory's seven sins has *seven* daughters: *Die Beziehungen der frühchristlichen Sittenlehre zur Ethik der Stoa* (München, 1933), p. 384. In fact, envy and gluttony have five, sadness and wrath six, lechery eight. Bloomfield (*Seven Deadly Sins*, p. 73) repeats the error.
11. Gillet, Introduction to *Grégoire le Grand* . . . , p. 91.
12. Evidence that *acedia* was considered a physical disturbance comes only from the Scholastic period. See below, chap. iii, p. 59. An excellent analysis of the pathological aspects of *acedia* is the study by P. Alphandéry, "De quelques documents médiévaux relatifs à des états psychasthéniques," *Journal de Psychologie normale et pathologique*, XXVI (1929), 763-87.
13. *Inst.*, IX, 1 (E. C. S. Gibson [trans.], *A Select Library of Nicene and Post-Nicene Fathers*, 2nd ser., Vol. XI [New York, 1894]).
14. Already in the works of the Egyptian monks, ἀκηδία follows the attacks of λύπη: Evagrius, *Tractatus ad Eulogium*, 6 (PG 79:1101); Ps.-Nilus, *De octo vitiosis cogitationibus* (PG 79:1456); Ps.-Athanasius, *Epistula II ad Castorem*, 5 (PG 28:897).
15. The fiend "injects a quite irrational sadness, which by some is called ἀκηδία"; J.-C. Guy (ed.), *Recherches sur la tradition grecque des "Apophthegmata Patrum"* ("Subsidia hagiographica," No. 36 [Brussels, 1962]), p. 35 (listed as S. 10). The saying recurs in *Vitae Patrum*, V, 71 (PL 73:924), and *Vita s. Syncleticae* (PG 28:1512).
16. Cassian, *Inst.*, IX, 10, and *Coll.*, V, 11; other examples: Evagrius, *Tractatus ad Eulogium*, 7 (PG 79:1101f.); Nilus (?), *DOSM*, 11-12 (PG 79:1156f.); the apophthegm of Mother Syncletica, referred to in the preceding note, which equates *acedia* specifically with the evil kind of sorrow.

17. Nilus (?), *DOSM,* 11 (PG 79:1156): "Sadness consists in the frustration of carnal desire; but desire is joined to every passion."

18. Aristotle, *Nicomachean Ethics,* II, 4, 1105b.

19. He may have rejected *acedia* because of its Greek origin (just as he rejected similar Greek terms such as *gastrimargia* and *cenodoxia* in his sin list) or because the word had no biblical authority. But in either case he could have used Cassian's translation *taedium.*

20. Cf. Gillet, *Grégoire le Grand,* p. 102.

21. The author is referring to the scheme of eight vices given by Isidore, *Differentia,* II, 40 (PL 83:96ff.). See below, n. 29.

22. *De vitiis et virtutibus,* III, 54 (PL 112:1377f.). The "reason" adduced is of course verbally taken from Cassian, *Inst.,* X, 1. The attribution of Book III of this treatise to Hrabanus is uncertain. See Peltier, *DTC,* XIII (1937), 1615.

23. The very old claim that Gregory was the first Benedictine monk on the papal cathedra has been recently shaken by the Benedictine scholar Dom Kassius Hallinger, "Papst Gregor," pp. 231-319.

24. "Ut ad eum per oboedientiae laborem redeas, a quo per inoboedientiae desidiam recesseras," *Regula,* 1 (ed. R. Hanslik, CSEL, 75 [Vienna, 1960]). Notice the connection of the Fall with sloth, negligence (*desidia*), which is strangely reminiscent of Origen, *De principiis,* II, 9, 2 (ed. P. Koetschau, GCS, XXII [Leipzig, 1913], 165). Origen considered the Fall a receding from the Good through sloth. The aspect of inobedience, which is not in Origen's passage, derives from St. Paul (Rom. 5:19) and Augustine, *De natura et gratia,* XX, 22 (PL 44:257); cf. also *Vitae Patrum,* V, 15 (PL 73:950-51, "oboedientiae labor").

25. "Post sexta autem surgentes a mensa pausent in lecta sua cum omni silentio aut forte, qui uoluerit legere sibi, sic legat, ut alium non inquietet," *Regula,* XLVIII, 5. The *Regula Magistri* is even more specific in this respect: the monks "are to spend the noon hours and the burning heat in slumber, and in the bodies of the brethren which are worn out from fasting and work the shortness of the nights during that season must be supplemented with some sleep at noon," so that the monks may rise sufficiently awake for their prayers at night. Chaps. 50 and 29 (PL 88:1012 and 999). Cf. V. Stebler, "Die *Horae competentes* des benediktinischen Stundengebetes," *Studia Anselmiana,* XLII (1957), 17.

26. The individual's living under the eyes of others seems to have been an important principle in early Western cenobitism; cf. Hallinger, "Papst Gregor," p. 269.

27. Cf. R. Gillet, *Grégoire le Grand,* pp. 101-2; repeated in "Spiritualité et place . . . ," in *Théologie de la vie monastique* (Lyon, 1961), p. 328.

28. For a detailed account of the seven vices during that period, see Bloomfield, *Seven Deadly Sins,* pp. 70-104; cf. S. Wenzel, "Acedia, 700-1200," *Traditio,* XXII (1966), 73-102.

29. Isidore, *Differentia,* II, 40 (PL 83:96ff.). Elsewhere, however, Isidore speaks of "septem spiritus vitiorum" (*Allegoriae,* 164; PL 83:120, without either *tristitia* or *acedia*) or says, "septem istae gentes sunt principalia vitia" (*In Deut.,* 16; PL 83:336; listing the Cassianic eight vices). The "third scheme" (i.e., eight vices without *acedia*) occurs in the penitentials of Egbert (Wasserschleben, *Die Bussordnungen der abendländischen Kirche,* p. 233), Theodore of Canterbury (PL 99:941), the *Ordo* of Noyon (E. Martène, *De antiquis ecclesiae ritibus,* I, 799), Ps.-Theodore (Thorpe, *Ancient Laws and Institutes of England,* I, 279), Halitgar (PL 105:657), Burchard of Worms (PL 140:976f.), *Poenitentiale ecclesiarum Germaniae* (Schmitz, *Die Bussbücher und die Bussdisciplin der Kirche,* II, 452). See also Theodulf of Orléans (PL 105:201, 217).

30. *Capitula ad presbyteros parochiae suae,* 31 (PL 105:201).

31. Hugh of Saint Victor, *Expositio in Abdiam* (PL 175:400, 403); concerning

the authorship of this work, see below, n. 84.—Peter Lombard, *Sententiae*, II, xlii, 8 (PL 192:753).

32. Peter Lombard's *Sententiae* received the official approbation of the Church at the Fourth Lateran Council; see J. de Ghellinck, *Le mouvement théologique du XII*e *siècle* (2nd ed.; Bruges, 1948), p. 266.

33. Cassiodorus, *De institutione divinarum litterarum*, 29 (PL 70:1142).

34. Guibert of Nogent, *Moralia in Genesim*, I (PL 156:27).

35. Cassian was heavily used, for example, by Henry Suso in his *Horologium sapientiae* and by Johannes Nider in his *24 guldin harpfen* (fourteenth century).

36. S. Wenzel, "Acedia, 700-1200," pp. 100-2.

37. "Accedia te vel somnolentia deprimit" (PL 145:355).

38. *De institutis ordinis eremitarum* (PL 145:349).

39. *De perfectione monachorum*, 23 (p. 322; also, PL 145:325).

40. *Vita beati Romualdi*, p. 21.

41. *Vita sancti Rodulphi*, 2 (PL 144:1010).

42. Cf. the conclusions of A. Rousselle-Estève's study of the *Concordia regularum* and Benedict of Aniane: "La méditation et l'oraison pour lesquelles Cassien pouvait servir de maître . . . étaient très réduites, pour ne pas dire supprimèes. . . . Il ne restait pas même une véritable orientation à la contemplation." *Annales du Midi* [Toulouse], LXXV (1963), 160.

43. *Tractatus de ordine vitae*, 30 (PL 184:579).

44. Aelred, *Sermo in festo S. Benedicti*, in *Sermones inediti*, p. 69.

45. Aelred, *Sermones de oneribus*, XVI (PL 195:424).

46. Bernard, *In psalmum "Qui habitat,"* sermo XII (PL 183:235).

47. Isaac de Stella, *Sermo XIV, in dom. IV post Epiph.* (PL 194:1735).

48. See the list in chap. iii, n. 17.

49. Adam of Perseigne (fl. 1190), *De institutione novitiorum* (PL 211:586).

50. Isaac de Stella, *Sermo XXXII, in dom. I Quadrag.* (PL 194:1796).

51. *Apophthegmata*, "Poemen," 111 (PG 65:349); *Vitae Patrum*, III, 204 (PL 73:805).

52. Bernard, *Super Cantica*, sermo XXI (I, 124).

53. Isaac de Stella, *Sermo XXIX, in dom. Quinquag.* (PL 194:1786f.).

54. Richard of St. Victor, *Explicatio in Cantica*, XXXIII (PL 196:498f.).

55. Basil, *Regulae fusius tractae*, XXXVII, 5 (PG 31:1016) and *Constitutiones asceticae*, 7 (PG 31:1368); quoted above, chap. i, p. 9.

56. Aelred, *De institutione inclusarum*, 9 (in *La vie de recluse*, p. 66; PL 32:1456).

57. Bernard, *Epistulae*, LXXVIII, 4 (PL 182:193).

58. Isaac de Stella, *Sermo XIV, in dom. IV post Epiph.* (PL 194:1735ff.).

59. PL 194:1736.

60. Adam Scot (*ca.* 1190), *De quadripartito exercitio cellae*, 24, "De taedio" (PL 153:841f.). This passage is very similar to St. Bernard's Sermon 54 *Super Cantica*, in word choice and structure; cf. below, chap. iii, pp. 61ff.

61. Pp. 60-63.

62. Benedict, *Regula*, 48.

63. *De fructibus carnis et spiritus*, 7 (PL 176:1000f.). The work is probably by Conrad of Hirsau; cf. R. Bultot, "L'auteur et la fonction du *De fructibus carnis et spiritus*," *RTAM*, XXX (1963), 148-54.

64. PL 176:1001.

65. The definition of the second *acidia* is verbally identical with Hugh's (except that this writer uses *nimia* for Hugh's *immoderata*); *De sacramentis*, II, xiii, 1 (PL 176:526), and elsewhere.

66. For Scholastic "etymologies" of *acedia*, see below, chap. iii, p. 54.

67. Cassian, *Inst.*, X, 1; Alcuin, *Liber de virtutibus*, 32 (PL 101:635); Radulphus Ardens, *Sermo* XXXI (PL 155:1426); Alanus of Lille, *Summa de arte*

praedicatoria (PL 210:126); Hugh of St. Cher, *Ad Isaiam,* 29 (IV, 61); Bonaventure (?), *Vitis mystica,* 66 (VIII, 197); "Narratio allegorica de vitiis," MS. BM. Harley 1294, fol. 89r (see chap. v, p. 120); Alvarus Pelagius, *De planctu Ecclesiae,* II, 75 (fol. 199r); Caesarius of Heisterbach, *Libri miraculorum,* I, 41, in A. Meister (ed.), *Die Fragmente der Libri VIII Miraculorum des Caesarius von Heisterbach* ("Römische Quartalschrift," No. 13. Supplementsheft [Rome, 1901]), p. 60. Cassian's original remark, of course, continued to be copied by writers after 1200.

68. "Ociositas inimica est animi." This quotation, a constant travel companion of *acedia,* derives from Benedict's *Regula,* 48.

69. Pirminius, *Scarapsus,* p. 45.

70. Alcuin, *Liber de virtutibus et de vitiis ad Widonem comitem* (PL 101:635). Cf. L. Wallach, "Alcuin on Virtues and Vices. A Manual for a Carolingian Soldier," *Harvard Theological Review,* XLVIII (1955), 175-95.

71. PL 106:122f.

72. PL 106:245f.

73. Cf. H. Peltier, *DTC,* XIII (1937), 1614.

74. Hrabanus, *De ecclesiastica disciplina,* Preface (PL 112:1191f.).

75. *Ibid.,* Book III, "De agone christiano" (PL 112:1251-53).

76. Cf. the further discussion of the *libri poenitentiales* in chap. iv, pp. 70f.

77. The technical name for this question seems to have been *De sufficientia vitiorum.* For example: Hugh Ripelin of Strassburg, *Compendium theologicae veritatis* (p. 104), and John of Wales, *Summa justitiae* (MS. BM. Harley 632, fol. 177v).

78. The dates of the authors referred to in this section are as follows:

1136-1141 Hugh of St. Victor, *Summa de sacramentis christianae fidei.*
1138-1141 Otho of Lucca (?), *Summa Sententiarum.*
after 1139 Peter Lombard, *Sententiae.*
1148-1152 *Ysagoge in theologiam.*
1245 d. Alexander of Hales.
1245-1250 Albertus Magnus, *In Sententias.*
before 1257 Bonaventure, *Breviloquium.*
ca. 1265 Hugh Ripelin of Strassburg, *Compendium theologicae veritatis.*
1266-1272 Thomas Aquinas, *Summa theologiae,* I, I-II, II-II.
1268-1272 Thomas Aquinas, *De malo.*

According to F. Stegmüller, *Repertorium Commentariorum in Sententias Petri Lombardi* (Würzburg, 1947), I and II, 709ff.

79. R. Seeberg, *Lehrbuch der Dogmengeschichte,* III (5th ed., Graz, 1953), 186.

80. *Summa de sacramentis,* II, xiii, 1 (PL 176:525).

81. Cf. Bloomfield, *Seven Deadly Sins,* pp. 84-85.

82. *Summa de sacramentis,* II, xiii, 1 (PL 176:525). The same sequence occurs in *De quinque septenis,* 2 (PL 175:405-7); *Expositio in Abdiam* (PL 175:401); "De septem vitiis" (MS. Vat. Reg. lat. 167), ed. R. Baron, *Études sur Hugues de Saint-Victor* (Bruges, 1963), p. 246; *Scala celi Magistri Hugonis* (*ibid.,* p. 235).

83. Hugh's usage of the name for this sin wavers. He calls it *tristitia* in: *Expositio in Abdiam* (PL 175:402), *De quinque septenis,* 2 (406), *Miscellanea,* I, 173 (PL 177:569), *De laude charitatis* (PL 176:976), "De septem vitiis" (ed. cit. [see n. 82], p. 246), *Scala celi* (*ibid.,* p. 236); *acedia* in: *De sacramentis,* II, xiii, 1 (PL 176:525-26), *Expositio in Abdiam* (PL 175:384), *Allegoriae in Novum Testamentum* (776, 782f.), *Sententiae,* 56 (ed. O. Lottin, *RTAM,* XXVII [1960], 62), "De septem vitiis" (ed. cit., p. 246), *Scala celi* (*ibid.,* pp. 234f.); and finally *acedia seu tristitia* in: *Expositio in Abdiam* (PL 175:400, 403).

84. *Expositio in Abdiam* (PL 175:401f.). The authorship of this treatise is a matter of debate: Hugh, Richard of St. Victor, and a third writer have been proposed. Yet the part under consideration, which contains the septenaries

and the metaphors for the concatenation of the seven vices, all of which occur in genuine works by Hugh, seems to come at least from Hugh's teaching. See R. Baron, *Études sur Hugues de Saint-Victor* (Bruges, 1963), pp. 53-58, and older literature listed there.—The authorship of *Allegoriae in Novum Testamentum* is similarly disputed; see Baron, pp. 58ff. J. Chatillon attributed the work to Richard, but excluded PL 175:775-88, where the septenaries and the seven vices are treated; "Le contenu, l'authenticité et la date du *Liber exceptionum* et des *Sermones centum* de Richard de Saint-Victor," *RMAL*, IV (1948), 23-52.

85. *Summa de sacramentis*, II, xiii, 1 (PL 176:525-26): "Per superbiam inflatur, per invidiam arescit, per iram crepat, per acidiam frangitur, per avaritiam dispergitur, per gulam inficitur, per luxuriam conculcatur, et in lutum redigitur." The same in "De septem vitiis" (ed. cit., p. 246), and with *tristitia* in *Scala celi* (*ibid.*, p. 236) and *Expositio in Abdiam* (expanded to "per tristitiam conteritur, et quasi in pulverem redigitur"; PL 175:402f.).

86. *Summa de sacramentis*, II, xiii, 1 (PL 176:525-26).

87. Formerly attributed to Hugh of St. Victor, but probably written by Otho of Lucca; PL 176:43-174.

88. *Tristitia* is used here, but in the preceding section on the vices the author speaks of *accidia*: pp. 105-6.

89. "Ad iniusticiam referuntur superbia, avaricia. Ad debilitatem vero tristicia, invidia. Ad intemperantiam ira, ingluvies, luxuria," p. 106.

90. The anonymous author is conscious of following Aristotle. He knows that four virtues were enumerated by "Socrates" and accepted by Cicero and Macrobius, but he rejects them, counting *prudentia* among the *scientiae*; p. 74.

91. See chap. i, p. 20, n. 84.

92. Alcuin, *De animae ratione liber ad Eulaliam virginem*, IV (PL 101: 640-41). Notice that *ira* is omitted from the vices because it is one of the three "powers" of the soul. For Alcuin's position in the history of medieval psychology, see K. Werner, "Der Entwickelungsgang der mittelalterlichen Psychologie von Alcuin bis Albertus Magnus," *Denkschriften der Kaiserl. Akad. d. Wiss.*, philos.-hist. Kl., No. 25 (Vienna, 1876), pp. 69-150. A similar distribution of the seven vices among the three parts of the soul occurs in a treatise *De confessione* ascribed to Grosseteste, "Perambulavit Judas . . . ." Here pride and vainglory belong to the rational part; wrath, envy, and *acedia* to the irascible; and lust, gluttony and greed to the concupiscible (MS. Bodl. Laud misc. 527, fol. 259r).

93. Often a theologian freely used models of various provenance. Bonaventure, for example, accepts the Aristotelian division of *potentia vegetativa, sensitiva,* and *intellectiva* together with the Platonic three (*rationalis, irascibilis, concupiscibilis*), which he applies to the *potentia intellectiva* (*Breviloquium*, II, 9). Elsewhere he divides the *anima rationalis* into three faculties: memory, understanding, and will (*Sent.*, I. d.3, p.2, a.1, qu.1)—a favorite doctrine of St. Augustine's (*De Trinitate*, X, 11, and elsewhere). See E. Lutz, *Die Psychologie Bonaventuras nach den Quellen dargestellt* ("Beiträge Baeumker," Vol. VI, 4-5 [Münster, 1909]), p. 141.

94. For example: *Republic*, IV, 439-42.

95. Aristotle, *De anima*, II, 2-3. I have used in part the terminology of Thomas Aquinas, in *Summa theologiae*, I, qus. 78-82.

96. Aristotle's *De anima* was translated from Greek into Latin before 1215, probably in the twelfth century. Around 1230 Michael the Scot translated the work from Averroes' Arabic version, and somewhat later William of Moerbeke made a new translation from the Greek. Ueberweg-Geyer, *Grundriss der Geschichte der Philosophie*. II. *Die patristische und scholastische Philosophie* (11th ed.; Berlin, 1928), pp. 347-48; F. van Steenberghen, *Aristotle in the West* (Louvain, 1955), pp. 63, 90ff.

97. In contrast to other Scholastic theologians, Alexander of Hales speaks of *peccata capitalia,* not *vitia.*

98. Alexander of Hales, *Summa theologica,* II-II, qu. 498 (III, 484). The sin that belongs to the *vis rationalis* is not mentioned. Alexander also rejects another scheme in which the sins are results of a misdirection given to the (Aristotelian) powers of the soul, *vegetabilis, sensibilis,* and *rationalis.* Here, *acidia* appears as the misdirected love of *ratio,* "when man loves his inner good less than the external good" (III, 484).

99. *Summa theologica,* II-II, qu. 498 (III, 486-87).

100. *Ibid.,* p. 487.

101. "Penes generalia moventia appetitum." *In II Sententiarum,* d.42, art. 6, ad 2 (XXVII, 663).

102. Hugh Ripelin of Strassburg, *Compendium theologicae veritatis,* III, 6 (in Albertus Magnus, *Opera omnia,* XXXIV, 93).

103. *Compendium theologicae veritatis,* III, 6 (pp. 104-5). The whole passage is verbally taken from Bonaventure, *Breviloquium,* III, ix (V, 238).

104. Bonaventure himself adopted a different and simpler scheme in his later commentary on the *Sentences.* Here all seven vices are reduced to the "inclination towards some apparent good," and "good" is subdivided into the good of the spirit in itself and the good of the spirit in the body. *Sententiae,* II, d.42, dub.iii. Notice that the Quaracchi ed. prints this article as dubious (II, 977-78).

105. Thomas Aquinas, *Summa theologiae,* I-II, qu. 84, a.4 (II, 308-9); similarly, *De malo,* qu. 8, a.1 (VIII, 339). Notice, however, Thomas' diverging view in his later II-II; see below chap. iii, pp. 49ff.

CHAPTER III

1. MS. Douai 434 contains several *quaestiones de accidia*: Vol. I, Nos. 120, 329, 390, 391; Vol. II, Nos. 419, 475. P. Glorieux dates them (on grounds of the content) 1231-1235: Glorieux, "Les 572 Questions du manuscrit de Douai 434," *RTAM,* X (1938), 123-52, 225-65. Also of the 1230's are the questions by Guiard de Laon (No. 66, *de acedia*); cf. F. Pelster, "Le *Quaestiones* de Guiard de Laon dans Assise Bibl. comm. 138," *RTAM,* V (1933), 369-90.

2. The dates given are according to O. Lottin, *Psychologie et morale aux XIIe et XIIIe siècles,* III, ii (Louvain, 1949), 681ff.

3. *Quaestio disputata de malo,* qu. 11 (VIII, 357-61); *Summa theologiae,* II-II, qu. 35 (III, 144-47).

4. These topics are also discussed, and their order is the same, in the respective treatments by the Scholastic theologians mentioned above. The longest and richest discussion of *acedia* appears in Alexander of Hales, *Summa theologica,* II-II, Nos. 559-69 and 636-37 (III, 551-60, 612-14). Alexander treats the following topics: The name "accidia" and its derivation; its definition; its genus; its cause and root; whether it is a capital vice; its opposite virtue; its relation to envy; its degree of sinfulness; whether it is a sin by excess or by lack; by which commandment it is forbidden; its effects; its offspring.

5. *Summa theologiae,* II-II, qu. 35, a.1, resp.

6. *Ibid.,* a.2.

7. *De malo,* qu. 11, a.2, resp.

8. *Summa theologiae,* II-II, qu. 35, a.2.

9. I-II, qu. 84, a.4, resp. See above, chap. ii, p. 45.

10. E.g., Guillaume d'Auxerre: "tedium boni prout est graue in consideratione infirmi siue difficile" (*Summa aurea,* fol. 90v); Alexander of Hales: "penes fugam eius quod aestimatur malum inferius, id est grave carni, sumatur acidia. . . . Taedium boni difficilis aut laboriosi . . . ; peccatum acidiae, cuius est fastidire laboriosum" (*Summa theologica,* II-II, qu. 498; cf. qu. 559); Albertus

Magnus: "acedia, quae fugit poenam quae est ex labore spiritualium" (*In II Sententiarum*, II, xlii, 6); Hugh Ripelin: "aversio a spirituali bono quod aestimatur grave" (*Compendium*, III, 18).

11. II-II, qu. 35, a.2, resp. The same contradiction appears in *De malo*, qu. 8, a.1, resp., and qu. 11, a.2, resp.

12. *De malo*, qu. 11, a.2, resp.

13. *Summa theologiae*, II-II, qu. 35, a.3.

14. *De malo*, qu. 11, a.3, ad 1. Cf. Albertus Magnus, *Summa theologica*, II, tract. xviii, qu. 118, membrum primum, art. secundus (XXXIII, 370-72). Christ's words in Matt. 26:38 express, not passion, but *propassio*, which does not carry away reason.

15. *Summa theologiae*, II-II, qu. 35, a.4.

16. Thomas omits *pervagatio* from Isidore's or Cassian's lists, in his quotation as well as the refutation (*Summa theologiae*, II-II, qu. 35, a.4, arg. 3 and ad 3). The idea of *pervagatio* is, of course, contained in Cassian's *inquietudo corporis* and *instabilitas*, as well as in Gregory's *evagatio* as interpreted by Thomas.

17. The following are characteristic definitions often found in treatises of the twelfth, thirteenth, and fourteenth centuries:

(a) "Interna mentis tristitia, per quam quis minus devote orat aut psallit." *Ysagoge in theologiam* ("interna tristitia"), p. 105. Thomas Aquinas attributes this to Gregory, *Moralia in Iob*, XI (*De malo*, qu. 11, a.1, arg. 7). Slightly expanded in Grosseteste, *Templum domini.*

(b) "Saeculi tristitia, quando damnis rerum, vel molestia corporum sic afficimur, ut etiam taedeat nos orare, vel legere, vel quidpiam hujusmodi agere." Petrus Cantor, *Distinctiones* (or, *Summa Abel*; MS. BM. Royal 10.A.xvi, fol. 110v); Petrus Comestor, *Sermo* XI (PL 198:1754).

(c) "Tristitia aggravans." From John of Damascus (see text, below); quoted by Jean de la Rochelle, Guillaume d' Auxerre, Alexander of Hales, Albertus Magnus, Thomas Aquinas, etc.

(d) "Ex confusione mentis nata tristitia, sive taedium et amaritudo animi immoderata; qua jocunditas spiritualis extinguitur; et quodam desperationis principio mens in semetipsa subvertitur." Hugh of St. Victor, *Summa de sacramentis fidei*, II, xiii, 1, and *Scala celi Magistri Hugonis.* Used in *De fructibus carnis et spiritus* and by Caesarius of Heisterbach.

(e) "Ex frustrato rebus contrariis voto turbatae mentis anxietudo, et rei bonae bene gerendae taedium." *De fructibus carnis et spiritus*, 7 (PL 176:1000).

(f) "Taedium interni boni." Attributed to Augustine, "on Psalm 106:18," by Jean de la Rochelle, Alexander of Hales, Albertus Magnus, and quoted by Guillaume d'Auvergne. Cf. definition (i) below. Probably a variant is: "Taedium boni," used by Guillaume d'Auxerre, Ostiensis, and Robert de Sorbon (*De confessione*). Similarly, "taedium de bono," used by Alexander of Stavenby (*Constitutiones*). The same definition occurs expanded as:

(g) "Taedium boni spiritualis, quo quis nec in Deo, vel ejus laudibus, aut bonorum operum exercitatione delectatur . . . ." Archbishop Peckham (Canons of the Council of Lambeth, 1281); a definition which became very influential on English catechetical literature.

(h) "Taedium animi, quod de fastidio interni boni nascitur, in qua animus amisso bono suo solitarius et desertus manens, sibi ipsi in amaritudinem et dolorem commutatur." Ps.-Hugh of St. Victor, *Allegoriae in Novum Testamentum*, II, 5 (PL 175:176). Not influential.

(i) "Fastidium interni boni." Ps.-Augustine, *Tractatus de septem vitiis et septem donis Spiritus Sancti* (PL 40:1089). Quoted by Hugh of St. Victor, Guillaume d'Auvergne.

(j) "Animi torpor quo quis aut bona negligit inchoare aut fastidit perficere." Alanus of Lille, *De virtutibus et de vitiis et de donis Spiritus Sancti* (p. 42).

Often attributed to Bernard, "in quodam sermone": Bromyard, *Omnebonum*, and Rypon.

(k) "Torpor mentis bona negligentis inchoare." Evidently a variant of (j). Quoted by Jean de la Rochelle, Alexander of Hales, Albertus Magnus, Thomas Aquinas.

(l) "Animi quidam languor, cum legere non libet et orare non delectat, meditationes sollicite non sentiunter." Attributed to Bernard by *Omnebonum* ond others. Cf. n. 65, below.

(m) "De virtutum laudabili exercitio utriusque hominis languida dejectio." Attributed to Gregory the Great. Quoted by Hugh Ripelin, *Omnebonum*, and others; sometimes appearing as "languida utriusque hominis dejectio."

(n) "Diffidentia implendi mandata." Guillaume d'Auxerre (*Summa aurea*, II, tr. 24, c. 1: fol. 90v). Quoted by Jean de la Rochelle, Alexander of Hales, Albertus Magnus. Expanded to, "Diffidentia de propriis viribus et de mandato dei implendo ardua tristitia," in Hugh Ripelin.

(o) "Amaritudo mentis ex displicentia spiritualis actionis proveniens." Reported as given by "quidam" (plural), by Guillaume d'Auxerre (*Summa aurea*, fol. 91v). Not influential.

18. Alexander of Hales, *Summa theologica*, II-II, 560 (III, 553).

19. Particularly *Summa theologiae*, II-II, qu. 35, a.1, resp., in the beginning.

20. See chap. ii, pp. 28f. and n. 31.

21. *Tropologiae in Osee*, II (PL 156:366).

22. S. Wenzel, "Acedia, 700-1200," *Traditio*, XXII (1966), 84-86.

23. *Ibid.*, Nos. 57-59.

24. *Summa de sacramentis fidei*, II, xiii, 1 (PL 176:526). See definition (d) above, n. 17.

25. E.g., *Florilegium morale Oxoniense*, p. 98, and definition (b) listed above, n. 17.

26. See above, p. 48 and n. 5.

27. "*Acci* grece, cura latine. Unde hec accidia, e, id est, tristitia, sublestia, anxietas vel tedium" (MS. BM. Addit. 27328, fol. 14r). The same definition reappears in the later *Catholicon* by Johannes Balbus of Genoa ("Januensis") and is occasionally found in theological works, such as the *Summa justitiae* by John of Wales (MS. BM. Harley 632, fol. 217v); the *Summa de casibus* by Astesanus ab Asti (Bk. II, tit. 63. Notice the observation: "Secundum vero grecum debet scribi cum aspiratione sicut *achidia*, ut dicit frater Johannes theutonicus," i.e., Johannes of Sterngassen); Antonius de Bitonto, *Sermones quadragesimales de vitiis*, sermo 35 (fol. 98v). In the *Derivationes* by Osbern this definition is shortened to "haec accidia, ae, i.e. tristitia" (ed. A. Mai, *Classicorum auctorum e Vaticanis codicibus editorum tomus VIII* [Rome, 1836], p. 40). In contrast, the dictionary of Papias gives, "accidia, quae est taedium animi vel anxietas vel contra" (Venice, 1485).—Notice that Alanus of Lille also equates *acedia* and *tristitia* in his theological dictionary, *Distinctiones dictionum theologicarum*: "Tristitia, proprie. Dicitur acedia . . ." (PL 210:980).

28. PG 94:931.

29. Burgundio's translation of John of Damascus has been edited by Fr. Eligius M. Buytaert ("Franciscan Institute Publications, Text Series," No. 8 [St. Bonaventure, New York, 1955]). For the influence of John of Damascus on Scholastic theology, see J. de Ghellinck, *Le mouvement théologique du XIIe siècle* (2nd ed.; Bruges, 1948), pp. 374-415.

30. Buytaert, cap. 28.

31. Albertus Magnus, *Summa theologica*, II, tract. xviii, qu. 118 (XXXIII, 369f.); Thomas, *Summa theologiae*, I-II, qu. 35, a.8, arg. 3, and resp. The phrase "tristitia vocem *amputans*" (used by Thomas) occurs in Burgundio's translation of Nemesius (see text above); the phrase "tristitia vocem *auferens*" (used by Albertus Magnus), however, is found in the marginal correction of Bur-

gundio's translation of John Damascene, made by Grosseteste: "In greco sic. [accidia ergo] est tristicia uocem auferens, achos . . ." (MS. BM. Royal 5.D.x, fol. 91v). In *Summa de bono*, however, Albertus Magnus uses "amputat" and translates ἄχθος as *anxietas* (*Opera omnia*, ed. B. Geyer, *et al.*, XXVIII [Münster, 1951], 205).

32. The Latin translation of Nemesius made by Burgundio was edited by Karl J. Burkhard, "Gregorii Nysseni (Nemesii Emeseni) περὶ φύσεως ἀνθρώπου liber a Burgundio in Latinum translatus," *Jahresbericht des K.K. Staats-Gymnasiums im XII. Bezirke von Wien* [Untermeidling], VIII (1891), IX (1892), XIII (1896), XVIII (1901), XIX (1902). The passage on *tristitia* appears in XIII (1896), 24. For Nemesius' sources and importance, see B. Domański, *Die Psychologie des Nemesius* ("Beiträge Baeumker," Vol. III. 1 [Münster, 1900]). As far as Burgundio's inconsistency in translating the Greek is concerned, it seems as though in translating Nemesius, Burgundio (or someone else) had mistaken *achthos* for the genitive of *achos*.

33. Albertus Magnus, *Summa theologica*, II, tract. xviii, qu. 118 (XXXIII), 370. The same word ἄχος, incidentally, was sometimes used to etymologize *monachus*: "cum enim monachi etymon sit solitudo et tristitia" (Bernard, PL 182:705); see J. Leclercq, "Études sur le vocabulaire monastique du moyen âge," *Studia Anselmiana*, XLVIII (1961), 21, 148.

34. For example: Petrus Comestor, *Sermo* XI (PL 198:1754): "quae, quia est proxima praecipitatio desperationis, acedia, quasi ad casum, id est juxta casum sita, nominatur." This etymology was later used by William de Montibus, *Speculum penitentis* (MS. BM. Cotton Vesp. D.XIII, fol. 63v) and *Numerale* (MS. BM. Harley 325, 75v); and John of Wales, *Moniloquium* (MS. Cambridge Peterhouse 200, fol. 32v).

35. Alexander Carpentarius, *Destructorium vitiorum*, fol. 173v. Similarly in Guillaume d'Auvergne, Hugh of St. Cher (III, 183, 1), Alexander of Hales, Hugh Ripelin, Thomas Aquinas, Caesarius of Heisterbach, and later theologians. As a curiosity it might be added that Jean Rigaud, in his *Compendium pauperis* (before 1311), gives this etymology: "Accidia vocatur ab attedine [!] quia per eam habet anima tedium de omni spirituali difficili" (VIII.X).

36. An excellent survey of Thomas' doctrine of the passions and its sources is M. Meier, *Die Lehre des Thomas von Aquinas "de passionibus animae" in quellenanalytischer Darstellung* ("Beiträge Baeumker," Vol. XI.2 [Münster, 1912]).

37. See chap. i, n. 83.

38. Cassian, *Coll.*, V, 23. See also: Isidore, *Sententiae*, II, 37 (PL 83:638); *In Deut.*, 16 (PL 83:367).

39. Cassian, *Coll.*, V, 23; Hrabanus, *De clericorum institutione*, 3 (PL 107: 417), using the Gregorian scheme.

40. Hugh Ripelin of Strassburg, *Compendium theologicae veritatis*, III, 18 (p. 110).

41. Nilus (?), *DOSM*, 14 (PG 79:1160); Cassian, *Coll.*, V, 23.

42. *Topics*, IV.5, 126a.10. Cf. M. Meier, *Die Lehre des Thomas von Aquinas*, pp. 39f. Thomas treats of the opposition in *Summa theologiae*, I-II, qu. 35, a.3 (*tristitia* and *delectatio*); cf. I-II, qu. 31, a.3 (*delectatio* and *gaudium*).

43. See J. de Ghellinck, *L'Essor de la littérature latine au XIIe siècle* (2nd ed.; Brussels, 1955), p. 235; Lottin, *Psychologie et morale*, III, i, 434-35; L. Ott, *Untersuchungen zur theologischen Briefliteratur der Frühscholastik* ("Beiträge Baeumker," Vol. XXXIV [Münster, 1937]), pp. 437ff. For the importance of these septenaries for popular teaching, see chap. iv, p. 74.

44. Especially Grosseteste, *Templum domini*; see the reproduction of the table in Bloomfield, *Seven Deadly Sins*, p. 437, n. 213. The explicit connection of *acedia* (and, for that matter, of the seven chief vices) with a planet is extremely rare in medieval literature. *Templum domini* links the vice *accidia*

with *Dies Saturni* (which is called a "coadiutor," without further explanation), and the derived Middle English poem of the same title establishes the same relation (ed. R. D. Cornelius, *The Figurative Castle* [Bryn Mawr, 1930], Appendix, ll. 571f.). Another relevant passage may be the Digby play *Mary Magdalene,* ll. 313ff. (cf. Bloomfield, *Seven Deadly Sins,* p. 234), where Saturn, whose characteristic metal is lead, is one of the seven "prynsys of hell." *Acedia* is connected with lead in Gower's *Mirour de l'homme* (see chap. v, p. 118) and Nicolaus Cusanus, *Excitationes,* IX (in *Opera* [Basle, 1565], p. 651).—On the other hand, *acedia* is occasionally linked to the moon. Servasanctus, *Liber de exemplis naturalibus,* III, 27 (linking all seven vices to the planets): "In luna aerem inspissante et quandam semper umbram vel obscuritatem in se habentem [sic], accidiam accipe que menti ingerit quandam nigredinem per quam inspissat et perturbat anime cogitacionem" (MS. Bodleian 332, fol. 231r). Bonaventure connects the moon with "pigri et accidiosi," *Commentarius in Sapientiam,* 13 (VI, 193).

45. In the *Summa* by Simon de Hinton (fl. 1250-1260), for example, the usual five septenaries are increased by the seven "vices of nature." *Acedia* corresponds with *timiditas.* Cf. A. Dondaine, "La Somme de Simon de Hinton," *RTAM,* IX (1937), 11.

46. Hugh of St. Victor, *De quinque septenis* (PL 175:405-14); *Expositio in Abdiam* (PL 175:400ff.); *Allegoriae in Novum Testamentum,* II, 3ff. (PL 175: 774-89). For the authenticity of the last two works, see chap. ii, n. 84.

47. Hugh, *De quinque septenis,* 4 (PL 175:409).

48. The same correspondences occur in Bonaventure, *Expositio orationis dominicae,* 9 (VII, 654).

49. *Summa theologiae,* II-II, qu. 35, a.3, ad 1.

50. *Ibid.,* I-II, qu. 23, a.4, resp. The attempt to harmonize the chief vices with the Ten Commandments was already made in earlier treatises on penance and confession, as for example in the *Poenitentiale* by Thomas of Chabham (*ca.* 1222), MS. BM. Royal 8.F.xiii, fol. 3v.

51. *Pigritia* is verbally identified with *acedia*: Alanus of Lille: "Piger, proprie. Dicitur etiam aliquis laborans accidia," *Distinctiones dictionum theologicarum* (PL 210:901); Hugh of St. Cher: "*pigredo,* i.e., operandi spiritualia, quae dicitur accdia," Commentary on Prov. 19:15 (III, 42); Alexander of Hales: "pigritia sive accidia," *Summa theologica,* II-II, 559 (III, 551); Robert de Sorbon: "est enim acedia taedium boni sive pigritia," *Supplementum tractatus novi de poenitentia* (in Guillaume d'Auvergne, *Opera,* II, 237); Bonaventure connects the moon with "pigri et accidiosi," *Commentarius in Sapientiam,* 13 (VI, 193).—Similarly in "popular" literature: Peraldus: "Post peccatum avaritiae dicendum est de peccato accidie: quia pigritia [!] interdum ex avaritia sequitur," *Summa de vitiis,* beginning of section on *acedia*; *pigritia* similarly appears in place of *acedia* in a series of the seven chief vices, in one of Peraldus' sermons (in Guillaume d'Auvergne, *Opera,* II, 392); Jacques de Vitry: "pigri et accidiosi," *Sermones in Epistolas et Evangelia Dominicalia* (pp. 826, 238); John of Wales: "ad cavendam accidiam sive pigritiam," *Moniloquium* (MS. Cambridge Peterhouse 200, fol. 34r); Guido de Monte Rocherii: "accidia vel pigritia," *Manipulus curatorum,* II, iii, 9.—*Pigritia* appears among the offspring of *acedia* in Alcuin and Hrabanus (PL 101:635 and 112:1252), Alanus (*De virtutibus et de vitiis et de donis Spiritus Sancti*), John of Wales (*Moniloquium,* fol. 32v: "sub ea comprehenditur pigricia, ociositas"), the *Speculum morale* (the second offspring is "segnities, ignavia vel pigritia," col. 1213).

52. *Summa theologiae,* I-II, qu. 41, a.4 (laziness is here called *segnities*), and qu. 44, a.4, ad 3: "cum pigritia sit timor de ipsa operatione, inquantum est laboriosa, . . ." Cf. H. D. Gardeil, *Saint Thomas d'Aquin, Somme Théologique* (Paris, 1957), pp. 289-90.

53. Cassian, *Coll.*, V, 4 (cf. above, chap. i, p. 20); Gregory, *Moralia in Job*, XXXI, 45 (PL 76:621). See the further discussion in chap. vii, pp. 168ff.

54. H.-D. Noble, "Passions," *DTC*, XI² (Paris, 1932), col. 2215.

55. Notice, however, that he does counter the objection that *acedia* cannot be a sin because, like a sickness, it occurs at certain fixed hours of the day: II-II, qu. 35, a.1, obj. 2 and ad 2.

56. John of Wales, *Moniloquium* (MS. Cambridge Peterhouse, 200, fol. 35v and 32v).

57. *De virtutibus*, 17 (I, 174). For further passages and discussion, see Appendix A, "*Acedia* and the Humors."

58. Alexander of Hales, *Summa theologica*, II-II, 566.

59. Roger Bacon, *Moralis philosophia*, III, vii, 8 (p. 181).

60. *De virtutibus*, 17.

61. *Moniloquium* (MS. Cambridge Peterhouse 200, fol. 35v). "Interesse dulcibus melodiis" is also recommended as one of four activities which diminish *acedia*, in Ps.-Thomas, *De vitiis et de virtutibus deque aliis numero quaternario procedentibus* (XVII, 398).

62. For further evidence of the Scholastic awareness that *acedia* belonged to both body and soul, see chap. vii, pp. 170ff., esp. 173f. Cf. definition (m) above, n. 17: "*utriusque hominis* languida dejectio."

63. For example: R. Daeschler distinguishes between *aridité*, *désolation*, and *tiédeur* (the equivalent of *acedia*); "Aridité," *Dictionnaire de Spiritualité ascétique et mystique*, I (Paris, 1937), cols. 845-46. Quite in contrast to this view, G. Truc considered *tiédeur*, *acedia*, and *sécheresse* as negative mystical states of increasing intensity. From the psychologist's point of view, he argues, the three states differ from one another only as nuances of the same emotional state: the felt absence of grace and spiritual comfort. "Les états mystiques négatifs (La tiédeur—l'acédia—la sécheresse)," *Revue philosophique*, LXXIII (1912), 610-28. However, it cannot be overlooked that moral and ascetic theologians do distinguish, at least between *acedia* and dryness.

64. Cf. Daeschler, "Aridité," col. 846.

65. "Hinc ista sterilitas animae meae, et devotionis inopia quam patior. Quomodo ita exaruit cor meum, coagulatum est sicut lac, factum est sicut terra sine aqua? Nec compungi ad lacrymas queo: tanta est duritia cordis. Non sapit psalmus, non legere libet, non orare delectat, meditationes solitas non invenio. Ubi illa inebriatio spiritus? Ubi mentis serenitas, et pax, et gaudium in Spiritu Sancto? Ideo ad opus manuum piger, ad vigilias somnolentus, ad iram praeceps, ad odium pertinax, linguae et gulae indulgentior, segnior obtusiorque ad praedicationem. Heu! omnes montes in circuitu meo visitat Dominus, ad me autem non appropinquat." Bernard of Clairvaux, *Sermones super Cantica Canticorum*, 54 (II, 107-8).

66. *Coll.*, IV, 3.

67. "Non sine causa sane ab heri et nudiustertius invasit me languor iste animi et mentis hebetudo, insolita quaedam inertia spiritus. Currebam bene; sed ecce lapis offensionis in via: impegi et corrui. Superbia inventa est in me, et Dominus declinavit in ira a servo suo. Hinc ista sterilitas . . . ."

68. Cassian, *Coll.*, IV, 2 (E. C. S. Gibson [trans.], in *A Select Library of Nicene and Post-Nicene Fathers*, 2nd series, Vol. XI [New York, 1894], 331). The whole paragraph describes a spiritual state which, in the following paragraph, is called *sterilitas mentis*.

69. Thomas Aquinas, *De malo*, qu. 11, a.1, obj. 7, and ad 7.

70. Peraldus, *Summa de vitiis et virtutibus* (2.13).

71. Notice that "not caring" or *incuria* is the literal meaning of ἀκηδία.

72. Cf. the fine analysis by M. Lot-Borodine, "L'Aridité ou *Siccitas* dans l'antiquité chrétienne," *Études carmélitaines mystiques et missionaires*, XXII, 2 (1937), 191-205.

73. *Noche Oscura*, i.9, in *Obras del Mistico Doctor S. Juan de la Cruz*, ed. Gerardo de San Juan de la Cruz (Toledo, 1912), II, 29. A good study of a seventeenth-century analysis of spiritual dryness is J. Heerinckx, "Ariditas spiritualis secundum B. Carolum a Setia," *Antonianum*, XI (1936), 319-50. Blessed Charles did apparently not use the term *acedia*, but the respective moral fault is clearly a possible moral cause of dryness, together with pride and inordinate desire for sensible consolation, just as in Peraldus (cf. Heerinckx, "Ariditas spiritualis," p. 335).

74. "Cassianus in libro De Institutis Coenob. distinguit tristitiam ab acedia; sed convenientius Gregorius acediam tristitiam nominat," *Summa theologiae*, II-II, qu. 35, a.4, ad 3.

75. *Acedia* hinders man from coming "ad celestia . . . quia vix ad locum quis veniet qui unum pedem hodie movet et post annum alium: sic et illi quorum motus est pes intellectus, et non pes affectus, cum tamen sit affectibus ambulandum." Hugh Ripelin of Strassburg, *Compendium theologicae veritatis*, iii, 18 (p. 111). Similarly, Peraldus, *Summa de vitiis et virtutibus*, under the branch of *ignavia* (2.12). Cf. Thomas Brinton, Sermon 54: "pes tuus, idest affectio mentis et deuocio cordis" (II, 243). Bernard of Clairvaux deals with the split between *intellectus* and *affectus* at some length in *Sermo V in Asc. Domini* and also uses a comparison with the two feet (PL 183:318). On the connection of *acedia* with the feet see below, chap. v, p. 108.

76. "Postquam posuit unum pedem, i.e., intellectus vel boni propositi, in via mundicie, alium tamen pedem, i.e. affectus vel operis, differt movere per duos annos vel amplius," Peraldus, *Summa*, 2.12.

77. On the *exitus-reditus* scheme see M.-D. Chenu, *Introduction à l'étude de saint Thomas d'Aquin* (Montréal, 1950), pp. 255-76; A. Hayen, *St. Thomas et la vie de l'Église* (Louvain, 1952); Th.-A Audet, "Approches historiques de la *Summa Theologiae*," in *Études d'histoire littéraire et doctrinale* (Université de Montréal, "Publications de l'Institut d'Études Médiévales," Vol. XVII [Montréal, 1962]), pp. 7-29; and P. E. Persson, "Le plan de la *Somme théologique* et le rapport *Ratio-Revelatio*," *Revue philosophique de Louvain*, LVI (1958), 545-72. The discussion is surveyed by I. Biffi, "Un bilancio delle recenti discussioni sul piano della *Summa theologica* di S. Tommaso," *La scuola cattolica*, Suppl. bibl., XCI (1963), 147*-76*, 295*-326*.

78. For example: Albertus Magnus, *In II Sent.*, d. 42, art. 6 [second objection] (XXVII, 662); Bonaventure, *In II Sent.*, d. 42, dubia, iii (II, 977); Thomas Aquinas, *In II Sent.*, d. 42, qu. 2, art. 3, 6 (VI, 769). See also Guillaume d'Auvergne, *De vitiis et peccatis*, 9 (I, 283).

79. Alanus of Lille, for example, in discussing "vices" distinguished between the *logicus* and the *theologus* and their respective conception of the term: *De virtutibus et de vitiis et de donis Spiritus Sancti*, II, 1 (p. 40). Also William of Doncaster, *Aphorismata philosophica*: "Penes theologos turpium precipuorum genus septenum esse constat . . ." (ed. M. Grabmann, in *Liber Floridus. Mittellateinische Studien, Paul Lehmann . . . gewidmet*, ed. B. Bischoff and S. Brechter [St. Ottilien, 1950], p. 314).

80. Definition (j) in n. 17, above.

CHAPTER IV

1. A good survey of the council, its reform tendencies, its influence on penitential and catechetical literature, and similar conciliary and synodal decrees that preceded and followed it, is given by E. J. Arnould, *Le "Manuel des Péchés." Étude de littérature religieuse anglo-normande (XIIIme siècle)* (Paris, 1940), pp. 1-59. See also H. G. Pfander, "Some Medieval Manuals of Religious Instruction in England and Observations on Chaucer's *Parson's Tale*," *JEGP*, XXXV (1936), 243-58.

2. MS. Douce 114, fol. 90 (ed. Horstmann, *Anglia*, X [1888], 328).

3. Standard treatments of the history of penance and of confession in the early Middle Ages are: É. Amann, "La pénitence privée," *DTC*, XII[1] (Paris, 1933), 845-948; B. Poschmann, *Die abendländische Kirchenbusse im frühen Mittelalter* (Breslau, 1930); A Teetaert, *La confession aux laïques dans l'Église latine depuis le VIIIe jusqu'au XIVe siècle* (Bruges, 1926); P. Galtier, "Les origines de la pénitence irlandaise," *Recherches de science religieuse*, XLII (1954), 58-85, 204-25; K. Rahner, *Tractatus historico-dogmaticus de poenitentia* (4th ed.; hectographed typescript, Innsbruck, 1960); O. D. Watkins, *A History of Penance* (London, 1920).

4. Egbert, *Dialogus*, XVI, 4, in Watkins, *History of Penance*, II, 636f.

5. *Poenitentiale Ps.-Egberti*, IV, 65 (Wasserschleben, p. 342).

6. P. Browe, "Die Pflichtbeicht im Mittelalter," *ZKTh*, LVII (1933), 337-83.

7. For example: "Instruendus est itaque peccatorum suorum confessor, ut de octo principalibus vitiis, sine quibus in hac vita difficile vivitur, confessionem faciat." Council of Chalon (A.D. 813), can. 32. Similarly, Council of Rheims (813), can. 13 (for both texts, see Watkins, *A History of Penance*, II, 675f.); Charlemagne, *Capitula ecclesiastica*, LXXXI, 15 (A.D. 810-813; MGH, Leges, sect. II, vol. I, pars prior, 179); Theodulf of Orléans, *Capitula ad presbyteros parochiae suae*, I, 31 (PL 105:201).

8. For the change from "chief vices" to "deadly sins," see Bloomfield, *Seven Deadly Sins*, p. 73 and *passim*.

9. The best survey of *libri poenitentiales* is G. Le Bras, "Pénitentiels," *DTC*, XII[1] (Paris, 1933), 1160-79. Important collections of texts were made by Wasserschleben, Schmitz, and Bieler; J. T. McNeill and H. M. Gamer, *Medieval Handbooks of Penance. A Translation of the Principal "Libri Poenitentiales" and Selections from Related Documents* ("Records of Civilization. Sources and Studies," Vol. XXIX [New York, 1938]).

10. For the wavering use of Cassian and Gregory, see Bloomfield, *Seven Deadly Sins*, pp. 97-99.

11. *Poenitentiale Bigotianum*, 6 (Bieler, pp. 234ff.) expands the three parts (*otiositas, somnolentia, vagatio*) by adding several *exempla* from the *Vitae Patrum. Poenitentiale XXXV capitulorum* (or, *judiciorum*; Wasserschleben, p. 524; Schmitz, II, 247) expands slightly the second part of the original (on the *somnolentus*). A penitential preserved in a manuscript from Bobbio adds other Cassianic branches; ed. O. Seebass, *Deutsche Zeitschrift für Kirchenrecht*, VI (1896-1897), 37.—For the appearance of *acedia* in *libri poenitentiales*, see S. Wenzel, "Acedia, 700-1200," *Traditio*, XXII (1966), 76-78.

12. On the relations between theology and canon law in the twelfth century, see J. de Ghellinck, *Le mouvement théologique du XIIe siècle* (2nd ed.; Bruges, 1948), chap. v, pp. 416-547; P. Michaud-Quantin, "A propos des premières *Summae confessorum*. Théologie et droit canonique," *RTAM*, XXVI (1959), 264-306; P. Fournier and G. Le Bras, *Histoire des collections canoniques en occident depuis les Fausses Décrétales jusqu'au Décret de Gratien* (2 vols.; Paris, 1931-1932), II, 314-52.

13. Also called *summae de casibus conscientiae*. The best recent attempt to survey this literature and to interpret it is P. Michaud-Quantin, *Sommes de casuistique et manuels de confession au moyen-âge (XIIe-XVIe siècles)* ("Analecta mediaevalia Namurcensia," No. 13 [Lille, 1962]), with extensive bibliographical information. Cf. also his article in *RTAM*, XXVI (1959); see the preceding note. Other important studies: P. Anciaux, *La théologie du sacrement de pénitence au XIIe siècle* (Louvain, 1949), pp. 121-31; J. Dietterle, "Die *Summae confessorum sive de casibus conscientiae* von ihren Anfängen bis zu Silvester Prierias," *ZKG*, XXIV-XXVIII (1903-1907).

14. Burchard of Worms, *Decretum*, XIX, 34 (PL 140:987); Ivo of Chartres,

Decretum, XV, 52 (PL 161:870); Bartholomew of Exeter, *Paenitentiale,* 37 (ed. A. Morey [Cambridge, 1937]), p. 203.

15. P. Michaud-Quantin, *Sommes de casuistique,* p. 21.

16. "De penitentia igitur dicturi subtilitates et inquisitiones theoricas praetermittemus, et operationes et considerationes practicas, que ad audiendas confessiones et ad iniungendas penitentias sacerdotibus necessarie sunt, diligentius prosequamur" (MS. BM. Royal 8.F.xiii, fol. 1r).

17. "Irregularities" are certain conditions, not necessarily sinful, which carry prohibitions established by canon law (such as, conditions which prevent a man from ordination).

18. Fol. 3r-5r.

19. "Quia pauci sunt qui confiteantur spiritualia paccata. Vix enim confitetur aliquis se habere invidiam, vel iram, vel avariciam, vel accidiam, vel superbiam. Multi etiam sunt qui numquam sciverunt vel audierunt quid esset accidia et tamen sepe peccaverunt per accidiam. . . . Similiter de accidia intimandum est ei quod esse pigrum in servitio dei et esse tedio affectum in bonis operibus, mortale peccatum est" (fol. 37v-38r).

20. William de Montibus, Chancellor of Lincoln (d. 1213), *Speculum penitentis,* "De peccatorum agnicione"; MS. BM. Cotton Vesp. D.XIII, fol. 60-74r. Cf. Hugh Mackinnon, S.J., "The Life and Works of William de Montibus" (Ph.D. dissertation, Oxford, 1959).

21. Robert of Flamborough, *Poenitentiale*; see F. Firth, "The *Poenitentiale* of Robert of Flamborough. An Early Handbook for the Confessor in its Manuscript Tradition," *Traditio,* XVI (1960), 541-56; and *ibid.,* XVII (1961), 531-32. Father Firth, who is preparing a critical edition, has kindly provided me with a transcription of the passage on *acedia.*

22. Now conveniently re edited in *Councils,* II, 214ff. (Alexander Stavensby), 268 (Grosseteste), 886ff. (Peckham), 982ff. and 1059ff. (Peter Quivil). The *Lambeth Constitutions* of John Peckham formed the basis for later works such as *The Lay-Folks' Catechism* (EETS 118) and William of Pagula's *Oculus sacerdotis.*

23. Book III, c. 34, par. 31 (Avignon, 1715), pp. 680f.

24. For example, the important canonical *summae* by Astesanus of Asti (1317), Bartholomew of Pisa (1338), Nicholas of Ausimo (1444), and Angelo di Clavasio (after 1475).

25. Some examples from England: the Synodal Statutes of William of Blois (Worcester, 1229), William Briwere (Exeter, 1225/37), Grosseteste (Lincoln, 1239?), Walter de Cantilupe (Worcester, 1240), Nicholas of Farnham (Durham, 1241/49), Ely (1239/56), Peter Quivil (Exeter, 1287), and the *Instituta* of Roger de Weseham (*ca.* 1250). See *Councils,* II, 172, 228, 268-69, 304, 423, 516, 1017-18; and C. R. Cheney, *English Synodalia of the Thirteenth Century* (Oxford, 1941), App. II, pp. 149-52.

26. *Inc.* "Qui bene presunt presbiteri"; also attributed to "Richard of Leicester" and others. I have used the text in MS. BM. Royal 4.B.viii, fol. 222r-243v (thirteenth century).

27. "Maxime vero ad fidem et ad mores pertinentia et frequentius predicanda sunt: simbolum fidei, duodecim articulos fidei continens; oratio dominica, septem habens petitiones; dona dei generalia et specialia, specialiter septem dona Spiritus que enumerat Ysaias . . . ; virtutes etiam cardinales quatuor . . . ; similiter gratuite et theologice . . . ; et precipue predicanda sunt septem capitalia vicia, que sunt superbia, avaritia, tristicia, invidia, ira, gula, luxuria; similiter innotescenda sunt septem sacramenta . . . ; similiter et duo mandata caritatis . . . ; predicanda sunt decem moralia legis . . . ; predicandum est etiam que sit iustorum merces in celo tam in corpore quam in anima, que sit malorum pena in inferno" (fol. 222r).

28. Fol. 224v, ff. The respective mnemotechnic verse is: "[P]a., fortis, sciciens,

saciatus tristicia[m] pellit" (fol. 225r). Notice the wavering in Richard's use of *accidia* and *tristitia* for the same vice.

29. *A Mirror to Lewed Men,* MS. BM. Harley 45, fol. 34v. Substantially the same in the metrical *Speculum vitae,* attributed to William Nassyngton (MS. BM. Cotton Tib. E.VII, fol. 21v-22r). The prose *Mirror* has been edited by Edna V. Stover (Ph.D. dissertation, University of Pennsylvania, 1952).

30. See above, chap. iii, pp. 56f.

31. Guillaume d'Auvergne, *De virtutibus,* 11 (I, 143). Joscelin of Soisson, on the contrary, thought the septenaries useless for the education of simple folk (PL 186:1496).

32. Some exceptions: *Acedia* is related to the fifth petition, "Dimitte nobis debita nostra," in a *rota vitiorum* in MS. BM. Arundel 507 (fol. 17r), and in Wyclif's English Sermon 114 (*Select English Works,* ed. Arnold, III, 108); to the sixth petition, "Et ne nos inducas in tentationem," in John Waldeby's *Expositio super orationem dominicam* (MS. BM. Royal 7.E.ii, fol. 26v). The just-mentioned *rota vitiorum* arranges seven septenaries in concentric circles. Here *acedia* corresponds with the fifth petition, the sacrament of penance, the gift of knowledge, the spiritual virtue of "alacritas," the deed of mercy of comforting prisoners (literal as well as spiritual), and the chief virtue of faith.

33. *Councils,* II, 1059ff.

34. A good example is William of Pagula's *Oculus sacerdotis.* Part I is a treatise of confessional instructions for priests and lists questions on the Creed, the Ten Commandments, and the seven deadly sins, followed by much canonical material ("pénitence tarifée"). Part II is a "catechetical handbook." A section entitled "Qualiter sacerdos debet predicare" (fol. 27v) presents a program similar to that by Richard of Wethershed but actually based on Peckham's *Lambeth Constitutions.* The seven sins are treated fol 34r-43r (MS. BM. Royal 6.E.i). This twofold treatment appears also in John de Burgo's *Pupilla oculi.*

35. Discussed by E. J. Arnould, *Le "Manuel des Péchés"* (Paris, 1940); Ch. Laird, "Character and Growth of the *Manuel des Pechiez,*" *Traditio,* IV (1946), 253-306; and D. W. Robertson, Jr., "The Cultural Tradition of *Handlyng Synne,*" *Speculum,* XXII (1947), 162-85.

36. Cf. E. Brayer, "Contenu, structure et combinaisons du *Miroir du monde* et de la *Somme le roi,*" *Romania,* LXXIX (1958), 1-38, 433-70.

37. For a complete listing of English translations of the *Somme,* see W. N. Francis, EETS 217 (London, 1942), pp. xxxii-xl.

38. A. Dondaine, "Guillaume Peyraut, vie et oeuvres," *Archivum Fratrum Praedicatorum,* XVIII (1948), 162-236. Fr. Dondaine conjectures that *De vitiis* was composed in 1236; *De virtutibus* much later, but not after 1248-1249; both parts were circulated together in 1250 (pp. 186f.).

39. Similar examples were given, before Peraldus, in the *Summa de arte praedicatoria* by Alanus (PL 210:127).

40. "Praeter istam divisionem peccatorum, cuius membra iam prosecuti sumus [i.e., the 16 branches], sunt multae aliae divisiones pertinentes ad peccatum acediae quas praetermittimus, nisi quod de una breviter tangemus. Notandum est ergo quod acedia potest dividi in acediam saecularium et acediam claustralium." The latter causes twelve evils, which are then discussed (2.2).

41. Like Peraldus, the French *Mireour de monde* deals with indiscreet fervor ("fole ferveur") after the remedies against sloth. In contrast, Frère Lorens' *Somme le roi* incorporates *fole ferveur* among the branches of the sin (branch 11). Middle English treatises derived from these works follow their respective model; see above, p. 80, and below, n. 57. *Indiscretus fervor* also appears in the questionnaire on *acedia* given by Andreas d'Escobar, *Modus confitendi.* Grosseteste, who considers the Christian virtues and vices from the Aristotelian viewpoint, places *acedia* and *curiositas* as the two vices which flank the virtue

of *occupatio*, by diminution and excess. Hence, *curiositas* is "immoderatum bonorum operum exercitium" ("Deus est quo nihil melius cogitari potest," MS. BM. Royal 7.F.ii, fol. 91v). Cf. Gerson's *labor immodicus*, n. 119, below.

42. Various dates for John's death are given: *ca.* 1260, "perhaps 1285" (A. G. Little, *Studies in English Franciscan History* [Manchester, 1917], p. 175), and *ca.* 1303 (P. Glorieux, *Répertoire des maîtres en théologie de Paris au XIIIe siècle* [Paris, 1933], II, 114. The title of his work seems to appear as "Moriloquium" in MS. Berlin 448.—The most recent appraisal of John of Wales is W. A. Pantin, "John of Wales and Mediaeval Humanism," in *Mediaeval Studies Presented to Aubrey Gwynn, S.J.* (Dublin, 1961), pp. 297-319.

43. MS. Cambridge Peterhouse 200, fol. 1r. Cf. *Regula secunda*, c. 9.

44. See G. R. Owst, *The "Destructorium vitiorum" of Alexander Carpentarius* (London, 1952).

45. B. L. Ullman, "A Project for a New Edition of Vincent of Beauvais," *Speculum*, VIII (1933), 312-26, esp. 319. Still of value is Gass, "Zur Geschichte der Ethik. Vincenz von Beauvais und das *Speculum morale*," *ZKG*, I (1877), 365-96; II (1878), 332-65, 510-36.

46. Written near London by a certain Jacobus, perhaps a Cistercian monk; see A. Gwynn, *Proceedings of the Royal Irish Academy*, XLIV (1937), 15. The entry on "Accidia" contains a questionnaire, several definitions, material from Peraldus (only fifteen branches) and Thomas Aquinas. MS. BM. Royal 6.E.vi, Vol. I, fol. 37v-39v.

47. MS. BM. Royal 7.F.xi. The chapter on *acedia* has a monastic orientation, gives the Gregorian progeny, and uses some material from Peraldus (especially the *remedia*) and Thomas Aquinas (on gravity of sin); fol. 5r-6r.

48. Written about the middle of the fourteenth century. Cf. W. A. Pantin, *The English Church in the Fourteenth Century* (Cambridge, 1955), p. 147, n. 2.

49. Notice that many treatises contain both modes of discussing the sins: William of Pagula and John de Burgo, the *Summa rudium, Omnebonum*, and others.—This and the following section in this chapter are an expansion of my article "Sloth in Middle English Devotional Literature," *Anglia*, LXXIX (1962), 287-318.

50. The Gregorian scheme is used, for example, by Guillaume d'Auxerre, Alexander of Hales, Hugh Ripelin, Albertus Magnus, Simon de Hinton, John of Wales, Bartholomew of Chaimis (*Interrogatorium sive Confessionale*), and the *summae de casibus* mentioned in n. 24.

51. St. Edmund, *Speculum ecclesiae* (Bigne, XIII, 358). Four branches in *The Spore of Love* (EETS 98, ll. 349-58). Five in *The Myrour of the Chyrche*, ed. Wynkyn de Worde (London, 1521), chap. 8; and *The Mirror of St. Edmund* (MS. Vernon, in *YW*, I, 246). Six in "Hou a man schal lyue parfytly" (MS. Vernon, EETS 98, ll. 599-604). Seven in the Anglo-Norman *Le Merure de Seinte Eglise*, p. 21.—The original version of this work may have been the Anglo-Norman one (cf. D. Legge, *Anglo-Norman Literature* [Oxford, 1963], p. 211, and Robbins, *Le Merure*).

52. Ed. O. Lottin, *Mediaeval Studies*, XII (1950), 20-56; see esp. p. 23.

53. "Incircumspectio est animi uitium quo quis minus caute discernit contrarietatem uitiorum, ut si quis ita uitat auaritiam quod incidat in prodigalitatem" (p. 42).

54. Pope Celestin V, *De vitiis et peccatis* (Bigne, XXV, 791), and esp. the *Summa de poenitentia* ("Quoniam circa confessiones") by Paul of Hungary (1220-1221), whose second part (of the longer version) on the vices and virtues is apparently borrowed from Alanus. See P. Mandonnet, "La *Summa de Poenitentia Magistri Pauli presbyteri S. Nicolai*," in *Aus der Geisteswelt des Mittelalters* ("Beiträge Baeumker," Suppl., Vol. III.1 [Münster, 1935]), pp. 525ff. All eight branches (as in Alanus) appear in MS. Monte Cassino 184 (ed. *Florilegium Casinense* ["Bibliotheca Casinensis," Vol. IV (Monte Cassino, 1880)], pp. 203-

4) and in MS. BM. Harley 4887, fol. 45r. The branch *incircumspecto* evidently proved a stumbling block to later scribes. In MS. Harley it appears as *interconscripcio* (although defined as above), whereas the version of the work in MS. Leiden, Cod. bibl. publ. lat. 191 C leaves it out altogether (ed. J. Lindeboom, *Nederlandsch Archief voor Kerkgeschiedenis,* N.S., XV [1919], 195-96).—Some of Alanus' terms also appear in the *Poenitentiale* by Robert of Flamborough. All eight plus *vaniloquium* in *Tractatus de VII peccatis mortalibus,* MS. BM. Harley 206, fol. 124r.

55. "Ih hân gesundet in trâcheite, in sûmichheiti, in semftigerne, in irricheite, in unfernunstige, in ungenuuizzidi . . . ," ed. K. Müllenhoff and W. Scherer, *Denkmäler deutscher Poesie und Prosa aus dem VIII.-XII. Jahrhundert* (3rd ed.; Berlin, 1892), I, 297. Similarly in the *Bamburger Glaube und Beichte, ibid.,* p. 303.

56. For example: Alvarus Pelagius, *De planctu ecclesiae,* II, 75; Wyclif, *Trialogus,* III, 16 (p. 183); *Omnebonum; L'Ottimo Commento* (on *Purgatorio* XVII). Sometimes the Peraldian offspring competed with the Gregorian: Jean Rigaud, *Compendium pauperis;* Alexander Carpentarius (see above); the oldest German *Beichtbüchlein,* Mainz, 1465 (ed. F. Falk, *ZKTh,* XXXII [1908], 768-69); Dionysius, *Summa vitiorum.* It is worth noting that some texts speak of *fifteen* branches (before enumerating sixteen) and refer to the 15 cubits of water that covered the mountains (Gen. 7:20); e.g., William de Lancea, *Dieta salutis* (MS. BM. Royal 7.C.i, fol. 37v). Jean Rigaud, *Compendium pauperis,* does the same but removes the contradiction by equating *dilatio* and *tarditas* (IX.B).

57. William Nassyngton's *Speculum vitae* and the prose *Mirror to Lewed Men* have the same progeny as *DR.*—Close attention to names and order of the branches reveals that *A* and *BVV* depend on *S,* whereas *JW, DR,* Nassyngton, the prose *Mirror,* and Caxton's *Royal Book* depend on *M.*—Notice that these eighteen branches also appear in Latin treatises: e.g., *De oratione dominica,* MS. BM. Burney 356 ("Flos florum"), fol. 13v-14r.

58. *The Kalender of Shepardes,* chap. 7. *Speculum morale* also has at least 25 species of *acedia.*—Notice that the Tree of Vices which appears frequently in pictorial representation often has, on the branch of *acedia,* seven smaller branches: *mentis vagatio, pusillanimitas, otiositas, error in fide, tristitia* (or *singularitas*), *bonorum omissio,* and *desperatio.* Thus in MS. BM. Arundel 507, fol. 19r; MS. Monte Cassino 207, p. 328; *The Kalender of Shepardes,* chap. 21 (plate); MS. BM. Arundel 83, fol. 128b (O. E. Saunders, *English Illumination* [Florence-Paris-Philadelphia, 1928], Vol. II, Plate 105).

59. MS. BM. Royal 8.A.xv: "Species accidie. Quod si neglexerit symbolum vel orationem dominicam addiscere vel filios spirituales docere. Quod si orare tempore debito et loco neglexerit. Quod si ad ecclesiam ire neglexerit debito tempore vel alios ne irent impedierit. Quod si verbum predicationis audire parvipendit vel pervertit . . ." (fol. 121v). For other versions, see G. F. Warner and J. P. Gilson, *British Museum. Catalogue of Western Manuscripts in the Old Royal and King's Collections* (London, 1921), I, 214. I have found this formula with some variations in other confessional treatises in MSS. BM. Arundel 52, fol. 66v; Additional 24660, fol. 4v; William of Pagula, *Oculus sacerdotis,* I (Royal 6.E.i); John de Burgo, *Pupilla oculi,* and the MSS. of the following note.

60. MS. BM. Harley 211, fol. 102-3; Additional 6716, fol. 63-65 (ascribed to Grosseteste).

61. EETS 31, ll. 1049-1106. Another Middle English questionnaire, in Northern dialect, occurs in the treatise *Points of Religion Properly to Be Known by Priests,* MS. BM. Cotton Vesp. A.XXV, fol. 51v.—For a different type of questionnaire on sloth, see chap. vi, p. 139 and notes.

62. "Ic synȝode ȝelome þurh asolcennysse þa þa me ȝod ne lyste don ne ȝan to ȝodes huse ne nan ellen niman to aeniȝum ȝodan weorce. ac ic leofode

min lif lanȝe on asolcennysse butan ȝodum weorcum and ȝodum biȝȝenȝe." *Confessio et oratio,* MS. BM. Royal 2.B.v, fol. 197v. Also in MS. BM. Cotton Tib. A. III, fol 45r.

63. *Vices and Virtues* (EETS 89, pp. 3-5); *St. Brendan's Confession,* ed. R. H. Bowers, *ASNS,* CLXXV (1939), 42-43; *Table of Confession,* ed. W. A. Craigie, STC, N.S., 14, pp. 71-72; *Forma confitendi, YW,* II, 341; MS. BM. Harley 172, fol. 12v (fifteenth century).

64. Unique MS. Bodl. 923, part II, chap. 7, fol. 80v-86r.

65. EETS 68, ll. 28236-373 (only in MS. BM. Cotton Vesp. A.III). A Latin formula based on Grosseteste's questionnaire, but much expanded, appears in *Confessionale,* MS. BM. Harley 211, fol. 106.

66. Ed. E. Brayer, "Un manuel de confession en ancien français conservé dans un manuscrit de Catane (Bibl. Ventimiliana, 42)," in *Mélanges d'archéologie et d'histoire publiés par l'École française de Rome, 1947* (Rome, 1948), pp. 155-98. Cf. chap. vii, p. 180.

67. EETS 68, ll. 27762-821.

68. The following portrait of sloth is composed of features from many treatises. To keep documentation within reasonable proportions, I have identified only features which are not commonplace.

69. Apparently, the Sunday obligation in the later Middle Ages included more than just attending mass. Diocesan statutes from twelfth-century England are rather vague in this respect and speak of "vacare cultui divino," "audire divina obsequia," "audire divinum officium," "divinis officiis interesse," "celebrationi divinorum interesse"—which may include attendance at matins, vespers, and so forth. Cf. *Councils,* II, 35, 194, 204, 465, 902, 1021, 1117. Hence remarks like the following, from the section on sloth: "Ffor men scholde to chirche gonge, To here Matins, Masse, and Euensonge." "A disputison betwene a god man and þe deuel," ll. 708-9, cf. l. 805 (EETS 98).

70. "Terlyncel" seems to occur only in *Manuel des pechiez* (EETS 119, l. 4117), *Handlyng Synne* (ll. 4263ff.), *Peter Idley's Instructions,* II, 904 (based on *Handlyng Synne*), Bromyard, *Summa praedicantium,* "Anima" (A.XXIII, xviii), and Gower, *Mirour de l'Omme* (ll. 5198ff.).

71. A sad or dark face characterizes *acedia* in: Guillaume d'Auvergne, *De virtutibus,* 17 (I, 174); John of Wales, *Moniloquium,* 8 (MS. Cambridge Peterhouse 200, fol. 35r; from Guillaume d'Auvergne); the questionnaire "Ad habendum salutiferae confessionis ordinem" ("tristitia vultus"; ed. P. Michaud-Quantin, *RTAM,* XXXI [1964], 61); the questionnaire in "Fratres dilectissimi, plenius noverit" ("si . . . gravis vultus atque ponderosi fuisti?" MS. BM. Royal 9.A.xiv, fol. 234v); Gower, *Mirour de l'Omme,* l. 899 ("de mate chere"). The *Speculum perfectionis* reports of St. Francis: "Ideoque nolebat in facie videre tristitiam quae accidiam et indispositionem mentis atque inertiam corporis ad omne bonum opus saepius repraesentat" (c. 96; ed. P. Sabatier [Manchester, 1928]).

72. "Dan Jon Gaytryge's Sermon," EETS 26, p. 14. A commonplace in the later Middle Ages, based on such proverbial sayings as "otiositas inimica est animi" (St. Benedict, *Regula,* 48); "otiositas mater nugarum, noverca virtutum" (St. Bernard, *De consideratione,* II, 13; PL 182:756); "otiositas . . . est enim omnium malorum parens, . . . nutrix vitiorum" (Aelred of Rievaulx, *De institutione inclusarum,* 9; PL 32:1455); "idleness teaches all evil" (St. John Chrysostom, PG 62:112 and 580); etc.

73. Chaucer, *Second Nun's Tale,* l. 1. Cf. R. Hazelton, "Chaucer and Cato," *Speculum,* XXXV (1960), 365-67.

74. Presumption is not usually included in the species of *acedia.* It occurs, however, in *Cursor mundi* and elsewhere; see chap. vi, n. 49.

75. *The Clensyng of Mannes Sowle* (II, 7) mentions other faults of spiritual wilfulness under sloth: "Also for my more likynge I haue preferred singular

deuocions to fore þat I was bounde to sey"; preference given to reading over meditation, etc. (MS. Bodleian 923, fol. 81v-82r).

76. This aspect of *acedia* receives an unusual amount of attention in the *Moniloquium* by John of Wales: "Primo ociosos vocas quibus ad tonsorem multe ore transmittuntur, dum dissecta coma restituitur et aut deficiens hinc atque illinc in frontem compellitur. Secundum hos tu ociosos vocas inter pecten speculumque occupatos. . . . Similiter illos vocas ociosos qui in componendis, audiendis, discendis canticis operati sunt" (MS. Cambridge Peterhouse 200, fol. 35r).

77. "Si fructus decimarum et oblaciones pure et integre ecclesie sine diminucione vel peioracione fecisti vel reddisti," in a confessional formula, "Qualiter sacerdotes . . . seipsos regere debent," contained in *Flos florum,* MS. BM. Burney 356, fol. 35v.

78. *The Clensyng* systematically discusses sloth in the works of bodily and spiritual mercy (MS. Bodleian 923, fol. 84v-85v).

79. *The Myroure of oure Ladye,* EETS, es, 19, pp. 42-43.

80. "In cura animarum nimis remissus fui. Ecclesiarum rector, negligens fui in docendo, corripiendo, et monendo parochianos meos. Minus in temporalibus eis subveni. Negligenter eis divina ministravi et pro eis minus oravi quam deberem" (*Confessionale,* MS. BM. Harley 211, fol. 106r). Cf. *Cursor mundi,* ll. 28278-83.

81. This concern with the relative gravity of faults by sloth appears more typically in later *summae theologiae.* Jean Gerson devoted much space to it: *Regulae morales,* 51 (III, 87f.); *Compendium theologiae* (I, 350); *De cognitione* [or, *differentia*] *peccatorum venialium et mortalium,* 9 (II, 494).

82. *Councils,* II, 217.

83. For *pigritia* as a synonym of *acedia,* see chap. iii, n. 51.

84. For a fuller discussion of *acedia* as a "sin of the flesh," see chap. vii.

85. The Middle English terms for the sin are most fully discussed by H. Käsmann, *Studien zum kirchlichen Wortschatz des Mittelenglischen, 1100-1350. Ein Beitrag zum Problem der Sprachmischung* ("Anglia, Buchreihe," No. 9 [Tübingen, 1961]), pp. 298-300. For Old English equivalents of *acedia,* see G. Tetzlaff, "Bezeichnungen für die Sieben Todsünden in der altenglischen Prosa. Ein Beitrag zur Terminologie der altenglischen Kirchensprache" (Ph.D. dissertation, Berlin, Freie Universität, 1954), pp. 111-18. This study has to be used with some caution, since Tetzlaff considers *acedia* and *tristitia* as one sin, apparently unaware of the co-existence of two or three different sin lists in the Old English period. He also includes equivalents for *pigritia, desidia, torpor,* etc., in his discussion.

86. *Asolcennys*: Aelfric, *Second Letter to Archbishop Wulfstan,* "Quando dividis chrisma," 164, ed. B. Fehr, *Die Hirtenbriefe Aelfrics in altenglischer und lateinischer Fassung* ("Bibl. der angelsächsischen Prosa," No. 9 [Hamburg, 1914]); Letter "To Wulfyet at Ylmandun," ed. B. Assmann, *Angelsächsische Homilien und Heiligenleben* ("Bibl. der ang. Prosa," Vol. III [Kassel, 1889], l. 224); Wulfstan, Homilies X.c and VIII.c (ed. D. Bethurum, *The Homilies of Wulfstan* [Oxford, 1957], pp. 203 and 184); Theodulf of Orléans, *Capitula* (EETS 150, p. 107); *Vices and Virtues* (EETS 89, p. 3); *Vespasian Homilies,* 7 (EETS 152, p. 17); Sermon "De natale Domini" (EETS 29, p. 83). *Asolcennys* was the most frequent English term for *acedia* before 1200.

87. *Unlust: Vices and Virtues* ("unlust," EETS 89, p. 3); *Ormulum* (ll. 2633, 4562, 4746); *Ayenbite* ("onlusthede," EETS 23, pp. 31, 163). For later passages, see chap. vi, n. 45.

88. *Sleacmodnes*: for example, *Bodleian Homilies,* 5 (EETS 137, p. 40).

89. *Aemelnes*: for, example, *ibid.,* 9 (p. 88).

90. The *Middle English Dictionary* (ed. H. Kurath and S. M. Kuhn, Part A.1 [Ann Arbor, 1956], pp. 61-62) lists ten documents where *accidie* and variant

forms appear (an eleventh text has *accidious*). Additional texts are *BVV* (EETS 217), p. 163; *The Mirror of St. Edmund* (*YW*, I), p. 246; "A Treatise of a Galaunt" (ed. W. C. Hazlitt, *Remains of the Early Popular Poetry of England,* Vol. III [London, 1866], 154); Hilton, *Scale of Perfection,* II, 39 and *passim* (Wynkyn de Worde's text [London, 1494]). The earliest example appears in *Ancrene Riwle* (beginning of thirteenth century?), the latest in texts from around 1400 (*DR,* Hilton). But notice that Caxton still used "accydye" in the *Royal Book* (chap. 27), i.e., his translation of the *Somme le Roi,* made in 1484.

91. *Sloth* (and variants), *slowness* (and variants; e.g., "Dan Jon Gaytryge's Sermon," *The Lay Folks' Catechism, Handlyng Synne*), and *sloghthehede* (*Handlyng Synne*). The earliest translation of *acedia as slaewþ* occurs in Aelfric. *Sermo de memoria sanctorum,* EETS 82, p. 356, l. 296 ("asolcennys oþþe slæwþ"); the same text appears in the "Vespasian Homilies," of the twelfth century (EETS 152, p. 17). Aelfric's *Sermo de memoria sanctorum* is dated "992-1002" by P. A. M. Clemoes, "The Chronology of Aelfric's Works," in *The Anglo-Saxons,* ed. P. Clemoes (London, 1959), p. 244. "Slæwþe" for "accidiam" occurs also in the Old English glosses to a Latin confessional formula, in MS. Lambeth 427 (first quarter of eleventh century; ed. Förster, *ASNS,* CXXXII [1914], 330).

92. Thus in Frère Lorens, the *Mireour,* the *Manuel des pechiez,* etc. The Gallicized form *accide* seems to have been used about as often—or as rarely—as *accidie* in Middle English. For a list see Tobler-Lommatzsch, *Altfranzösisches Wörterbuch,* I (Berlin, 1925), and A. de Martonne, "Recherches sur l'acédia," *Annales de la Société académique de Saint-Quentin,* IX (1852), 192. Additional occurrences of *accide* not listed in Tobler-Lommatzsch: Frère Lorens, *Somme le Roi* (beginning of section on *acedia*); *Mireour de monde* (pp. 117, 127, 132); "Manuel," ed. Brayer, pp. 179f. (see above, n. 66); *Ancrene Riwle,* French text, MS. BM. Cotton Vit. F.VII (EETS 119, p. 137); *Compileison* (MS. Cambridge Trinity Coll., R.14.7, fol. 13v, ff.; and EETS 240, pp. 9-10, 39, 271); St. Edmund, *La Merure de Seinte Eglise* ("accidie," pp. 16f., 25); Peter of Peckham, *Lucidaire* (MS. BM. Royal 15.D.ii, fol. 26r); J. Giclé, *Renard le nouvel* (ed. H. Roussel, SATF [1961], ll. 1169, 1279, 3784); *Roman du riche homme et du ladre*; *Le Songe du Castel* (ed. R. D. Cornelius, ll. 209, 227); Robert de l'Omme, *Le Miroir de Vie et de Mort* (ed. A. Langfors, *Romania,* XLVII [1921], 511ff., ll. 31, 126, 303); N. Bozon, *Contes moralisés,* No. 127 (ed. L. T. Smith and P. Meyer, SATF [1889], I, 149); Gilles li Muisis, *C'est des séculers* (ed. Baron Kervyn de Lettenhove [Louvain, 1882], II, 79); Rutebeuf, *La Voie de Paradis* (I, 353ff.); *Le Bataille des Vices contre les Vertus* (I, 299ff.).

93. Forms of *Trägheit* are standard, although forms of *Verdruss* (displeasure, disgust) and *Unlust* (listlessness, unwillingness) also occur frequently. See L. Diefenbach, *Glossarium Latino-Germanicum mediae et infimae latinitatis* (Frankfurt, 1857), and W. van Ackeren, *Die althochdeutschen Bezeichnungen der septem peccata criminalia und ihrer filiae* (Dortmund, 1904). The original meaning of *träge* seems to have been concrete, such as "firm, dense, viscous." Cf. J. and W. Grimm, *Deutsches Wörterbuch,* XI,i.1 (ed. M. Lexer, D. Kralik, *et al.* [Leipzig, 1935]), s.v. "träge" and "Trägheit."

94. Besides these two virtues, occasionally one encounters prudence as the opposite to *acedia*: Servasanctus, *Liber de exemplis naturalibus,* III, 23 (MS. Bodleian 332, fol. 230r); Malachy, *Venenum Malachiae,* 10 (fol. 14r); the treatise "Remedium et tiriaca contra superbiam" (MS. Bodl. Laud. misc. 206, fol. 126v).

95. Zeal and persistence in good works had been recommended as remedies against *acedia* before 1200, but the identification of "busyness" or similar terms with the virtue that is opposed to sloth is characteristic of the early thirteenth century. Cf. Richard Wethershed, *Summa brevis*: "Fortitudo, hoc est strenuitas operandi et huiusmodi, est contra accidiam" (MS. BM. Royal 4.B.viii, fol. 225v). *Strenuitas* is also given by John of Wales (?), *Tractatus de viciis* (MS. BM.

Royal 4.D.iv, fol. 239v); Conrad of Saxony, *Speculum beatae Mariae Virginis*, 15 (p. 213); a short, catechetical treatise in MS. Bodleian 440, fol. 59r; Gerson, *De mystica theologia*, II, 8 (p. 181). Robert Grosseteste gives *acedia* as the vice by diminution of the virtue *occupatio: Templum domini* (MS. BM. Burney 356, fol. 26r); and "Deus est quo nihil melius cogitari potest" (MS. BM. Royal 7.F.ii, fol. 89r). The same opposition to *occupatio* in *Fasciculus morum* (MS. Bodleian 332, fol. 108r); *De septem peccatis mortalibus* ("good occupacion," MS. BM. Harley 211, fol. 69v). See further chap. vii, n. 40.

96. "Busyness" occurs as the opposite to sloth in: William Shoreham (*ca.* 1320), "De septem mortalibus peccatis," st. 94 (EETS, es, 86); Wyclif, on the Pater Noster (ed. Arnold, *Select English Works*, III, 108); Mirk, *Festial*, Sermon 30 (EETS, es, 96, p. 130); Audelay, "De septem peccatis mortalibus," l. 20 (EETS 184); *Cato's Distichs*, III, 5 (EETS 117, p. 588); *Peter Idley's Instructions*, II, 1156-57, 1537 (pp. 177 and 184); *The Mirror of the Periods of Man's Life*, ll. 209, 217ff. (personified); *The Castle of Perseverance* (see chap. vi).

97. Chaucer, *Gentilesse*, ll. 8-11. But in the *Parson's Tale*, the opposite virtue is "*fortitudo* or strengthe."

98. On the matter of "restitution" see the discussion of *Piers Plowman*, chap. vi.

99. *De septem peccatis mortalibus*, MS. BM. Harley 211, fol. 80v.

100. "[A-solknesse, vnlust] me haueþ ofte idon eten oþermannes sare swink all un-of-earned." *Vices and Virtues*, EETS 89, p. 3. Cf. "De alieno labore accidiosus reficitur, et quod alii duro labore fortiter lucrabantur tales devorant ociose"; in this, the slothful are like the cuckoo. *Fasciculus morum*, V, 1 (MS. Bodleian 332, fol. 150r).

101. "I haue synned in slewth. . . . ffor I haue not occupied my bodily wittes on werk daies in bodily werkes ne trauailed after my degree in such werkes þat weren behouely to me and to myn. . . ." *Clensyng*, Bodleian 923, fol. 82v-83r.—"Panem meum laboribus non quesivi," Andreas d'Escobar (bishop of Ciudad-Rodrigo, d. 1427), *Modus confitendi*.

102. *Select English Works of John Wyclif*, ed. Th. Arnold, III, 119-67.

103. Thus in the Vulgate: "Homo nascitur ad laborem, et avis ad volatum." The verse is quoted in the section on *acedia* by Peraldus (under *otiositas*, *Summa*, 2.04), *Compileison* (MS. Cambridge Trinity College R.14.7, fol. 14v), *Lay Folks' Catechism* (ll. 537f.). A similar scriptural quotation frequently given in discussion of *acedia* is the divine injunction after the Fall, "In sudore vultus tui vesceris pane" (Gen. 3:19), quoted by Peraldus, Hugh Ripelin, the *Mireour du monde*, *Speculum morale*, etc.

104. Brinton, *Sermo* 20 (I, 83). Cf. *Sermo* 59 (II, 269), 56 (II, 259).

105. On the fourteenth-century attitude toward "work" and the *status*, see G. R. Owst, *Literature and Pulpit in Medieval England* (Cambridge, 1933), pp. 548ff.

106. *Moralia in Job*, VI, 15-16 (PL 75:737f.).

107. *De civitate Dei*, IV, 16. The translation is from *The City of God*, trans. M. Dods (New York, 1950), p. 124. The ascetic-monastic conception of *quies* (as freedom from disturbing thoughts) and its relation with *acedia* was very neatly expressed by Aelred of Rievaulx (1110-1167): "Ad spiritualium ergo contemplationem suspirantibus, primum quies necessaria est, quam impugnans accidia, animum reddere nititur inquietum" (*Sermo in festo Sancti Benedicti*, in *Sermones inediti*, ed. C. H. Talbot, p. 69); cf. *Sermones de oneribus*, 16 (PL 195:424). William Peraldus, however, wrote in a sermon: "Sexta promissio est Apoc. 3, *Qui vicerit dabo ei sedere in throno*, quod potest referri ad vitium acediae. Hic non est locus quiescendi, sed in futuro. . . . Hic est locus laborandi," *Sermo II de Beato Vincentio* (*Sermones*, p. 402).

108. "Dicit Augustinus libri IV capitulo 16 de civitate dei, quod multos deos qui credebantur impellere homines ad motum receperunt in civitate Romani et

eos inter deos publicos, id est, inter illos deos qui curam rei publicae habebant, templis eorum constructis in Roma cum diligentia coluerunt. Verumtamen dea quies in urbe non fuit recepta; sed extra urbem templum ipsius est constructum. Noluerunt enim aliquem deum habere secum qui posset quietem aut desidiam procurare." Berchorius, *Dictionarius* ("A, a, a"), fol. 30r, sub "Accidia."

109. *Inc.* "Gregorius in cura pastorali sic dicit: Non est canis qui nescit latrare" (MS. BM. Addit. 24660, fol. 39v).

110. *De septem peccatis mortalibus,* MS. BM. Harley 211, fol. 80v.

111. EETS, es, 96, p. 285. Thus also in John of Wales: "Item debet cavere accidiam in hac vita ob penurie et egestatis in *utraque vita* devicionem [devitationem?] et ob affluencie execucionem," *Moniloquium,* MS. Cambridge Peterhouse 200, fol. 34v.

112. *St. Brendan's Confession,* ed. Bowers, *ASNS,* CLXXV (1939), 42. Similarly in *The Clensyng,* MS. Bodleian 923, fol. 82v; Andreas d'Escobar, *Modus confitendi*: "Nam bona quae tenebar facere, non feci nec procuravi. Mala autem quae tenebar fugere, nec fugi, sed plus facere curavi et opere complevi." Robert Rypon, the fourteenth-century preacher from Durham, gives the following comprehensive characterization: "Species [accidiae] sunt . . . ; et generaliter quando quis facit quod non debet, vel aliter quam debet, vel non providet quid et qualiter debet facere, aut indiscrete facit, cogitat, aut loquitur, peccat in accidia. Et sic generaliter accidia concomitatur quodcumque peccatum" (a view explicitly denied by St. Thomas). *Sermo IX in dom. II Quadr.,* MS. BM. Harley 4894, fol. 88v.

113. "In confessione mea peccata quandoque aut peccatorum circumstancias scienter silui. Similate [read: simulate] ad confessionem quandoque accessi, scil. ut viderer ab hominibus. In confessione aliquando mentitus sum." *Confessionale,* MS. BM. Harley 211, fol. 106v.

114. "Sciendum quod [negligentia] ex quattuor vitiis oritur": *imprudentia, accidia, avaritia, inordinatus amor* (Part II, tit. ix, cap. iii, par. 2). He includes *pigritia, desidia, inconstantia, torpor,* and *omissio* in *negligentia sensu lato.* The discussion of *negligentia* occupies ten of the sixteen chapters on *accidia* (or over 67 of the 112 columns in the 1480 edition).

115. The seventh species in Peraldus' offspring.

116. Another good example of the same inclusiveness is John of Erfurt's canonistic *Summa de poenitentia* (1302). Here the branch of *pusillanimitas* leads to long discussions of correction, war, excommunication, absolution, interdict, and the like, and finally to *negligentia praelatorum* (MS. Oxford Oriel 38, fol. 22-55). For the breakdown of the traditional sin scheme toward the end of the Middle Ages, and attempts to discuss Christian ethics in new or different frames, see Bloomfield, *Seven Deadly Sins,* pp. 224-26.

117. Like the *summae de casibus* by Astesanus, Bartholomew of Pisa, Nicholas of Ausimo, and Angelo di Clavasio, St. Antoninus combines the speculative theology of St. Thomas with practical concerns of canon law and popular instruction.

118. *Summa,* Part II, tit. ix, chap. 13, par. 6.

119. The most "progressive" treatment of *acedia* in this sense which I know is a sermon on the sin by Jean Gerson. The sermon, which was probably delivered in French, is addressed to citizens and declares that work (*labor*) is an honor, "melius quam regium servitium" (*Opera omnia,* III, 1035). *Acedia* is said to pervert true and vigorous work into *labor languidus* (too little), *labor vitiosus* (work of evil), and *labor immodicus* (too much work, the correlative to indiscreet fervor; see esp. *ibid.,* col. 1040). The main part of the sermon roughly follows these three perversions. In it Gerson takes up such questions as whether one should try to work better than one can, how much sleep a *bourgeois* needs (*ibid.,* col. 1038), whether a wealthy citizen is obliged to work himself (this question was already treated by Peraldus in his *Summa de vitiis,*

under branch *otiositas*), whether a healthy man may beg (*ibid.*, col. 1039), if feigned work is sin (*ibid.*, col. 1039), whether the status of laborers is better than of those who are occupied in God's service (*ibid.*, col. 1040; the discussion is omitted), etc. P. Glorieux, who is preparing a new edition of Gerson's works, promises to edit the French text.

CHAPTER V

1. Ps.-Nilus, *De octo vitiosis cogitationibus* (PG 79:1457); Evagrius, *Antirrheticus*, VI; Cassian, *Inst.*, X, 22-25; Gregory, *Regula pastoralis*, III, 15 (PL 77:74).

2. PL 210:126.

3. A good example is the *Dictionarius pauperum* by Nicholas de Byard. This alphabetical encyclopedia on theology and morals contains sections on all the chief vices except *acedia*. Instead, there are entries for *otiositas*, *tepiditas*, *negligentia*, and *pigritia*, which contain much of the homiletic material (mostly similes) Peraldus had gathered against *acedia*. See MS. BM. Royal 8.C.viii, fol. 34-178.

4. In the following, I am not considering material which in Peraldus is quite marginal. For example, under the branch of *dilatio* (delay of conversion) Peraldus discusses eight reasons why one should turn to God early in life. All of these reasons are accompanied by biblical passages, exemplary figures, *exempla*, both Christian and pagan, and so forth. Obviously, such material illustrates *conversio* directly, but *acedia* only very indirectly, and does not further our understanding of the popular image of sloth.

5. There is a second passage using the verb: "Non acediaberis in stultitia illius [viz., stulti]," Ecclus. 22:16, but I have never met this verse in medieval discussions of the vice.

6. Peraldus (*Summa*, 1.2): "Vincula sapientiae sunt divina praecepta quibus ligatus est homo qui ex morsu pomi prohibiti quasi venenati incidit in spiritualem insaniam." Notice that references to Peraldus are according to the division I have adopted in Appendix B.

7. Cassian, *Inst.*, X, 4.

8. For example: Cassiodorus (PL 70:846, with reference to Cassian), Gerhoch of Reichersberg (PL 194:754), and Peter Lombard (PL 191:1058f.); Hugh of St. Victor, *Sententiae*, 56 (ed. O. Lottin, *RTAM*, XXVII [1960], 62) and Bonaventure (?), *Vitis mystica*, 66 (VIII, 197); Antoninus of Florence, *Summa*, "Accidia," ii. Notice that references to Antoninus' *Summa* are by chapter and paragraph as given in the 1480 edition; *acedia* is there treated in *pars* II, *titulus* ix.

9. Bonaventure (?), *Vitis mystica*, 66 (VIII, 197).

10. In Alanus as well as Peraldus. For the medieval and later exegesis of this passage, see the study by J. Alonso, "El estado de tibieza espiritual en relación con el mensaje del Señor a Laodicea (Apoc. III, 14 ss.)," *Miscelánea Comillas* [Comillas, Santander], XXIII (1955), 263-326. Cf. chap. vii, pp. 184f.

11. *Dialogus miraculorum* IV, 38 (p. 206).

12. Antoninus, i. Similarly on Num. 21:4, *coepit populum taedere*; *ibid.*, ii, 1.

13. It seems that *acedia* was usually connected with the Hittite (Hethaeus), "qui interpretatur stupor vel formido": Jacques de Vitry, *Sermones in Epistolas et Evangelia Dominicalia*, p. 724; Holcot, *Super Sapientia Salomonis*, lectio 204. But Hugh of St. Victor links *acedia* with the Amorrhaeus, which stands for "amaricatus vel amaricans"; *Expositio in Abdiam* (PL 175:384).—Notice that the vice is also related to the demon Baal (Jacques de Vitry, *Sermones in Epistolas*, p. 255) and to Abadon of Rev. 9:11 (in the Wycliffite *Lantern of Light*, EETS 151, p. 60).

14. Gower, *Mirour de l'Omme*, ll. 5659-62.

15. This exegesis goes back to Gregory, *Moralia in Job*, I, 35 (PL 75:549).

It was specifically applied to *acedia* by Alanus (PL 210:126), Bonaventure (see following note), *Ancrene Riwle* (pp. 121-22), and later authors.

16. Bonaventure, *Sermo de sancto Nicolao* (IX, 477).

17. Petrus de Limoges, *De oculo morali*, viii.

18. Thus because the king said, "Ligatis manibus et pedibus eius mittite eum in tenebras exteriores," which refers to those "who will not take pains in good work . . . nor walk good ways"; *Compileison*, MS. Cambridge Trinity College R.14.7, fol. 15r.

19. Antoninus, ii and ii, 2.

20. Peraldus' *Summa*, 1.32; *Jacob's Well*, p. 114; Wyclif, *Trialogus*, p. 185; etc.

21. "Otiositas est mater vitiorum et noverca virtutum," usually attributed to St. Bernard, and found as "otiositas mater nugarum, noverca virtutum" in *De consideratione*, II, 13 (PL 182:756). Cf. chap. iv, n. 72.

22. For this image, see below, p. 109.

23. *Sermo IV dom. III in Quadrag.* (*Sermo* LVI, in *Sermones*, p. 227).

24. Wyclif, *Select English Works*, II, 129. Cf. also the thirteenth-century Cistercian treatise *Die heilige Regel*, p. 37.

25. Developed at length in *Compileison*, MS. Cambridge Trinity College R.14.7., fols. 15v-16v.—Notice that Wyclif, in explaining the parable, says that the words "he wasted his goods" refer to "slouthe of Goddis service." Sermon 159, *Select English Works*, II, 71.

26. The two are mentioned together, for example, in *Handlyng Synne*, ll. 5187-234.

27. In Peraldus' section on *acedia*, Seneca is quoted seventeen times.

28. In *De arte praedicatoria*, 7 (PL 210:126) and *Summa theol.*, II, xviii, 118 (XXXIII, p. 373), respectively.

29. "Classical" quotations are, of course, not as ubiquitous in popular catechetical literature as biblical ones. In this respect, writers like Peraldus and John of Wales were not imitated by subsequent makers of handbooks.

30. Bromyard, *Summa praedicantium* A.VIII, art. 5. The last two also in Hugh Ripelin, *Compendium theologicae veritatis*, III, 18 (p. 117). The stagnating water was already used by Peraldus, *Summa*, 1.3312, who also quoted: "Et capiunt vitium ni moveantur aquae," from Ovid, *Epistulae ex Ponto*, I, 5, 6.

31. Berchorius, *Dictionarius*, fol. 30r.

32. Farinator, *Lumen animae*, tit. XIV.D; also in F: "Slow water is muddy or putrid or full of worms"; and L: in running water frogs (i.e., demons) sit on the edges, whereas in slow water they sit right in the middle. See also tit. LIX.D.

33. Gritsch, *Quadragesimale*, XXIII.M.

34. Metrical *Modus confitendi*, st. 21 (*Anal. hymn.*, XXXIII).

35. *Tabula exemplorum*, p. 1.

36. Hugh Ripelin, *Compendium theologicae veritatis*, p. 117.

37. Also in Hugh Ripelin, Bromyard (art. 5), the metrical *Modus confitendi* (st. 19), Gower (*Mirour*, ll. 5395-400, and *Confessio amantis*, IV, 1108ff., as a symbol of Idleness).

38. *Asinus* or *asina* signifies lechery, impurity, etc., in Gregory (PL 79:412), Eucherius (PL 50:752), Garnerius of St. Victor (PL 193:88, 90; but see PL 205: 702), and others. On the contrary, the ass on which Jesus entered Jerusalem on Palm Sunday is moralized as a very good animal; Radulphus Ardens, for example, calls it "animal mansuetum, brutum, laboriosum [!], et utilitati deditum" (PL 155:1832).

39. The ass is *segnis ac stupidus*, in Boethius, *Consolatio*, IV, pr. 3; *torpens* in Bernard Silvester, *Commentum super VI libros Eneidos Virgilii*, V, 179 (ed. W. Riedel [Greifswald, 1924]); stubborn in *Fulgentius metaforalis* (ed. H. Liebeschütz ["Studien der Bibl. Warburg," No. 4 (Leipzig, 1926)], p. 73); *segnis* in

Gregory of Tours (PL 71:829); *negligens et segnis* in Brinton, Sermon 64 (II, 289; from Peter Damiani, PL 45:438); "rude" in the *Buke of the Governaunce of Princis* (STC 62, p. 157); etc.

40. *Compendium*, II, 16 (p. 105). Cf. below, n. 69.

41. Jacques de Vitry states that *acedia* transforms man into a wild ass, *onager* (*Sermones in Epistolas*, p. 246), though in another sermon he connects the vice with the more common *asinus* (*ibid.*, p. 432).

42. *Ancrene Riwle*, p. 86. *The Buke* says man is "lythir and heuy, suere as a bere" (STC 62, p. 157). Although the *Buke* is not speaking of the seven sins exclusively here, *suere* stands for "slow" or "slothful." *Suereness* seems to have been the Northern and Scottish equivalent for *acedia*: cf. *The Buke of Knychthede* (STC 62, pp. 55ff.); Dunbar, *The Dance of the Sevin Deidly Synnis*, in *Poems*, ed. W. M. Mackenzie (2nd ed.; Edinburgh, 1950), p. 121; *Cursor mundi* (EETS 68, l. 28236: the confession of "Suernes"); the poem "The Seven Words from the Cross" (ed. C. Brown, *Religious Lyrics of the Fifteenth Century* [Oxford, 1939], p. 142). Already Aelfric had explained *asolcennyss* as "modes swærniss" (ed. B. Fehr, *Die Hirtenbriefe Aelfrics in altenglischer und lateinischer Fassung* ["Bibl. der angels. Prosa," No. 9 (Hamburg, 1941)], p. 208).

43. "Mercy passes all things," EETS 117, ll. 163f. Notice that Middle English *harlotrie* means "idle talk and occupation."

44. Mirk, *Festial*, Sermon 69 (EETS, es, 96, p. 285).

45. "Syne Sweirnes, at the second bidding, Come lyk a sow out of a midding" (ll. 67-68).

46. Edgar in *King Lear*, III, iv.

47. *Modus confitendi*, st. 17 (*Anal. hymn.*, XXXIII). Also in Hugh Ripelin, *Compendium*, p. 117.

48. Bloomfield, *Seven Deadly Sins*, pp. 247-48.

49. Evagrius, *Capita practica*, 14 (PG 40:1226).

50. Bromyard, *Summa praedicantium*, art. 4; *Jacob's Well*, p. 113; *Tabula exemplorum*, p. 1 (cf. Bloomfield, p. 248); the *exempla* collection in MS. Bibl. Municipale d'Auxerre, 35 (J.-Th. Welter, *L'Exemplum dans la littérature religieuse et didactique du moyen âge* [Paris, 1927], p. 301, n. 38).

51. Peraldus, *Summa*, 2.05, referring to Sophonias 2:14, *Vox cantantis, in fenestra, et corvus in superliminari.* Also in Gerson's sermon on *acedia.* For the pun on *cras* as *vox corvina*, see D. and E. Panofsky, *Pandora's Box* (New York, 1962), pp. 28ff., with references to Caesar of Arles, Eucherius of Lyons, Alcuin, and Hrabanus.

52. Bromyard, *Summa praedicantium*, art. 4. Hugh of Folieto, in his bestiary, calls the *milvus* "desidiosus" and "mollis" (PL 177:41-42).

53. *Omnebonum*, MS. BM. Royal 6.E.vi, fol. 38v. Also in Farinator (XIV.A), though his idea of the animal is a very strange one; Felton, *Sermo* XI (MS. BM. Addit. 22572, fol. 51v). The tortoise was still used for the sin of sloth in a nineteenth-century devotional book where, in an engraving, the seven deadly sins are shown as animals inside a human heart: J. E. Gossner, *Herzbüchlein*; see the excellent study of the connection between animals and passions or sins by R. Eisler, *Orphisch-dionysische Mysteriengedanken in der christlichen Antike* ("Vorträge der Bibl. Warburg," 1922-1923, Teil II [Leipzig-Berlin, 1925]), p. 85.

54. For example, Hugh of St. Cher, Commentary on Is. 29 (IV, 61, col. 4).

55. Bonaventure, *Sermo de sancto Nicolao* (IX, 477).

56. Peraldus, *Summa*, 1.3311 and 2.14 (*tristitia*). Antoninus of Florence calls this worm "carollus" (*Summa theologica*, cap. i). The moth, *tinea*, of the same verse is also applied to *acedia* (*ibid.*, cap. ii, 2).

57. Petrus Cantor, *Summa de sacramentis*, 118. "De cantu ecclesiastico," ed. J.-A. Dugauquier, II, 231-32 ("Analecta Mediaevalia Namurcensia," No. 4 [Louvain, 1957]).

58. Malachy of Limerick, *Venenum Malachiae*, cap. ix.

59. *Mireour du monde* (p. 126); Frère Lorens, *Somme le Roi* (branch of pusillanimity); *Jacob's Well* (p. 107); *Book of Vices and Virtues* (p. 27).

60. The ant as an example against sloth is ubiquitous. The bee is mentioned by John of Wales, *Summa justitiae*, VI, 3 (MS. BM. Harley 632, fol. 218r), and in the popular treatise "Primo videndum est quid sit peccatum" (MS. BM. Royal 8.A.x, fol. 72v).

61. Some additional animals to which *acedia* is occasionally likened: The lizard (*stellio*) is quick only to run into fire or the sword (Farinator, *Lumen animae*, XIV.B); the mother hen keeps her chickens (the other sins) under her wings (Henry of Lancaster, *Livre de seyntz medicines*, p. 63); the unprofitable mole (A. Barclay, *Ship of Fools*, fol. CCVIv); the idle grasshopper (Gower, *Mirour*, l. 5834); the cuckoo lives on other birds' labor (see chap. iv, n. 100); the ostrich has wings but does not fly (John of Wales, *Summa justitiae*, VI, 3; MS. BM. Harley 632, fol. 218r); the salmon shies away from the turbid water of river mouths (i.e., penance; Holcot, *Heptalogus*).

62. Ps.-Peraldus, "Quoniam ut ait sapiens," MS. BM. Harley 3823, fol. 66v.

63. For example: Peraldus, *Summa*, 2.02; Grosseteste, *Templum domini* and its Middle English version (l. 582); Bonaventure, *Collationes in Joannem*, xi (VI, 587); Holcot, *Super Sapientiam Salomonis*, lectio 179; *Mireour du monde*, p. 121; *A Treatise of Ghostly Battle* (*YW*, II, 432); A German sermon of the thirteenth century which sees *acedia* in "die betterisen und die ligerlinge," healed by Jesus (Grieshaber, *Deutsche Predigten des dreizehnten Jahrhunderts* [Stuttgart, 1844-1846], p. 116); etc. The "man with the withered hand" occurs as an example of *acedia* in Peraldus, *Summa*, 1.4; Bromyard, *Summa praedicantium*, art. 5 and 6; etc.

64. Hilton, *Scale of Perfection*, I, 85.—In a vision of damned souls, the slothful "had fete al to gnawyn and bun as þai wer brokyn and bolnyd leggys," MS. BM. Additional 37049, fol. 74 (cf. Bloomfield, *Seven Deadly Sins*, p. 221).—Notice also that *piger* is "etymologized" as *pedibus aeger*: Isidore, *Etymologiae*, X, 213 (PL 82:389f.).

65. "Jesus Appeals to Man by the Wounds," ed. C. Brown, *Religious Lyrics of the Fourteenth Century* (2nd ed.; Oxford, 1952), p. 227. The same poem in a Cambridge MS., see H. A. Person, *Cambridge Middle English Lyrics* (2nd ed.; Seattle, 1962), p. 10. Other examples: "Jhesu, for þi precious blod," ed. C. Brown, *Religious Lyrics of the Fourteenth Century*, p. 219; and "Jhesu, for thi blode," ed. C. Brown, *Religious Lyrics of the Fifteenth Century* (Oxford, 1939), pp. 96f.

66. I have found the exegesis of *affectus* or *affectiones* for *pes* in Alanus, Garnerius, Richard of St. Victor, Bernard of Clairvaux, Anselm of Canterbury, Isaac of L'Étoile, Aelred of Rievaulx, Guibert of Nogent, Jacques de Vitry, Radulphus Ardens, Brinton, and Wyclif. This interpretation seems to derive from Augustine: for example, *In Joannem*, 48, 3 (CCSL, XXXVI, 413). See also J. Freccero, "Dante's Firm Foot and the Journey without a Guide," *Harvard Theological Review*, LII (1959), esp. 256ff.

67. Jacques de Vitry, *Sermones in Epistolas et Evangelia Dominicalia*, p. 792.

68. Metrical *Modus confitendi*, st. 27 (*Anal. hymn.*, XXXIII). Cf. Hugh Ripelin and Peraldus, above, chap. iii, pp. 64f. and nn. 75-76.

69. The correspondences are: The vice of *acedia* is likened to the *asinus* and to the disease of *lethargia*; it is healed by Christ's carrying the cross. Hugh Ripelin, *Compendium*, II, 16 (p. 105); the treatise "Qualiter se habere debeat sacerdos" (W. van Ackeren, *Die althochdeutschen Bezeichnungen der septem peccata criminalia und ihrer filiae* [Dortmund, 1904], p. 22). This table is different from the one in *Templum domini*, where *acedia* is likened to *paralysis* and *caro mortua* (see Bloomfield, *Seven Deadly Sins*, p. 437, n. 213).

70. "Qualiter se habere debeat sacerdos," in Ackeren, *Die althochdeutschen Bezeichnungen*, p. 22. Cf. Gower, *Mirour*, ll. 6158-59.

71. *Omnebonum*, MS. BM. Royal 6.E.vi, fol. 38v.

72. *Ship of Fools*, fol. CCVIr.

73. The poem "As I walkyd vppone a day" calls it "a sowkyng blayne," ed. Brown, *Religious Lyrics of the Fifteenth Century*, p. 275.

74. "Accidia . . . est similis morsui rabidi canis . . . ," in *Hortulus reginae* (ed. 1487), by Meffreth, *Sermo in dom. in medio Quadrag.* The entire passage is used in the seventeenth-century work by Aegidius Albertinus, *Luzifers Königreich und Seelengejaidt*, ed. R. Freiherr von Liliencron ("Deutsche National-Litteratur," No. 26 [Berlin, n.d.]), p. 390.

75. Writers who give animal images for the vices, such as Farinator or Malachy of Limerick, undoubtedly relied on books on natural history. An analogue is a Latin sermon which likens the effects of the seven vices to stones: *Sermo quod septem vicia capitalia assimilat* [*sic*] *hominem peccatorem septem generibus lapidum*, MS. BM. Cotton Faust, A. V, fol. 5v-8. *Acedia* makes man like a coral, which grows while it is in water (i.e., worldly tribulations), but dries up and hardens (i.e., loses the love of God) as soon as it is out of water (fol. 6v).

76. The "authority" seems to be a saying of the desert fathers, in *Apophthegmata*, "Poemen," 111 (PG 65:350). After Peraldus the simile was used by Hugh Ripelin, the metrical *Modus confitendi* (st. 18), *Mireour*, etc.

77. Peraldus uses *culcitra* (*Summa*, 2.02); Hugh Ripelin and *Omnebonum*, *pulvinar*; Frère Lorens, *coute*; *Book of Vices and Virtues* and *Jacob's Well*, *featherbed*.

78. Malachy, *Venenum Malachiae*, fol. 13r; *Omnebonum*, MS. BM. Royal 6.E.vi, fol. 38r.

79. Gower, *Mirour*, l. 296; Bromyard, *Summa praedicantium*, art. 4. Under "Anima" Bromyard develops the image of the castle which the devil builds in the souls of the impious; here, too, *acedia* is the *camerarius* ("Anima," xvii).

80. The basic study of the medieval *exemplum* is J.-Th. Welter, *L'Exemplum dans la littérature religieuse et didactique du moyen age* (Paris, 1927).

81. In this section I restrict myself to *exempla* which explicitly illustrate *acedia*. Most of these stories also occur in medieval collections of short stories or moralized tales which do not specify what particular vice or virtue, and so forth, is to be illustrated. Modern students of medieval folklore and narrative have collected parallels and analogues to a good many tales, and almost any critical edition points out sources and occurrences of a given *exemplum*. I refrain from doing the same, as this study concerns itself only with the popular conception of the vice and its iconography.

82. John Herolt, *Promptuarium* (in *Sermones Discipuli*), No. 15.

83. Peraldus, *Summa*, 3-3; *Alphabetum narrationum*, MS. BM. Arundel 378, fol. 4r; *Speculum exemplorum*, II, 54 (in the index given as *exemplum* for *acedia*); Petrus de Limoges, *De oculo morali*, viii.

84. *Poenitentiale Bigotianum*, VI, iii, 4, from *Vitae Patrum*. Other monk stories to the same effect in par. 3, 5, 6 (Bieler, pp. 234ff.).

85. *Liber exemplorum*, No. 62, told to the author by the woman's sister.

86. *Die heilige Regel*, pp. 37f., a thirteenth-century Cistercian work in German.

87. *Jacob's Well*, pp. 115f.

88. *Apophthegmata*, "Antonius," 1 (PG 65:76); Peraldus, *Summa*, 3.1; *Liber exemplorum*, No. 61; Gobius, *Scala caeli*, fol. 5v.

89. Peraldus, *Summa*, 1.142; *Omnebonum*, MS. BM. Royal 6.E.vi, fol. 39r.

90. Both in Peraldus, *Summa*, 2.03, under *somnolentia*, because "*laziness sends the sleep* of contemplation [cf. Prov. 19:15] into those who hide their laziness under the name of contemplation and are unwilling to do any work."

91. Cassian, *Inst.*, X, 24.

92. Jacques de Vitry, *Exempla*, 195.

93. *Poenitentiale Bigotianum,* VI,i,2.

94. Gobius, *Scala coeli,* fol. 5r.

95. Gobius, *ibid.*; *Speculum morale,* col. 1207.

96. The man fallen into the swamp or river is alluded to in Peraldus, *Summa,* 2.04 and 2.12; he occurs in *Tabula exemplorum,* p. 1 (with a brief discussion of analogues and sources, p. 87). The charioteer is used for *acedia* by Gobius, *Scala coeli,* fol. 5v.

97. Gobius, *Scala coeli,* fol. 6r; Jacques de Vitry, *Exempla,* 204. A different *exemplum* has the lazy servant talk back to his master and refuse to lock the doors at night because he has to open them again in the morning, etc.: *Fasciculus morum* (MS. Bodl. 410, fol. 48r) and *Liber accidiae* (MS. Bodl. Can. Misc. 368, fol. 1v), from Petrus Alphonsus.

98. Bromyard, *Summa praedicantium,* art. 5; alluded to in Gower, *Mirour,* l. 5811.

99. Peraldus (*Summa,* 2.12) merely refers to the three follies, without telling the story; the *exemplum* is told under *acedia* by Alexander Carpentarius, *Destructorium vitiorum,* fol. 176r; Bromyard, *Summa praedicantium,* art. 6; Petrus de Limoges, *De oculo morali*; Felton, Sermo XIX (MS. BM. Additional 22572, fol. 86v, f.); and is used in part by the metrical *Modus confitendi,* st. 25, and Barclay, *Ship of Fools.*

100. Caesarius of Heisterbach, *Dialogus miraculorum,* IV, 28 (pp. 197f.); John Herolt, *Promptuarium* (in *Sermones Discipuli*), No. 13; *Alphabetum narrationum,* MS. BM. Arundel 378, fol. 4r; Gobius, *Scala coeli,* fol. 6r; Bromyard, *Summa praedicantium,* art. 5.

101. In Caesarius, *Dialogus,* chaps. 28-38 of Bk. IV contain ten *exempla* of sinful sleep.

102. Chap. 38 (p. 206). A similar reaction of the crucifix in *Jacob's Well,* p. 110, where at the funeral services for a man who always slept during mass and disturbed others the Crucified stops His ears: "Pray no more for him, for he is damned." Some of Caesarius' stories on sinful sleep are repeated in the *Alphabet of Tales* (EETS 126-127, Nos. 263, 284, 285) and John Herolt's *Promptuarium* (Nos. 10-12).

103. Caesarius, *Dialogus,* chap. 36 (p. 205); similarly in *Liber exemplorum,* No. 64 (but without King Arthur). Gower has the slothful dream of Troilus and Criseyde in church (*Mirour,* ll. 5245ff.).—Other *exempla* on *acedia qua* somnolence in *Poenitentiale Bigotianum,* VI,ii,3; and Bonaventure, *Sermo I in feria VI in Parasceve* (IX, 261).

104. Petrus de Limoges, *De oculo morali,* viii. From here the story passed to Alexander Carpentarius (*Destructorium vitiorum,* fol. 173v). Source: Hélinand of Froidmont, *Chronica,* VIII (now apparently lost); *De cognitione sui,* IX (PL 212:730).

105. The tale is very widespread, see Jacques de Vitry, *Exempla,* p. 141; it is applied to *acedia* in *Jacob's Well,* pp. 114-15.

106. *Jacob's Well,* p. 115; Caxton, *Doctrinal of Sapyence* (London, 1489), chap. 35.

107. Both in Peraldus, *Summa,* 1.141; *Speculum morale,* col. 1208.

108. *Liber exemplorum,* No. 63.

109. *Handlyng Synne,* ll. 4701-38; notice that, in contrast to its French source, *Handlyng Synne* immediately adds an *exemplum* about Bishop Grosseteste which shows that music *can* be used for good purposes (ll. 4739-75).

110. *Ibid.,* ll. 4863ff; 4927ff.—The second *exemplum* is also used by Jacobus de Theramo, *Belial* (Venice, 1506).

111. Caesarius, *Dialogus,* chaps. 46-51. The parish priest occurs in chap. 49.

112. Blasphemy in chaps. 52 and 40; "apostasy" in chaps. 53-56.

113. Chaps. 39-45 (the last case of despair was caused by indiscreet fervor). There is a story of temptation to irrational sadness and suicide in a pious lay

couple, in a late fifteenth-century German *Beichtspiegel*, ed. F. X. Thalhofer, in *Festgabe Alois Knöpfler* (München, 1907), p. 300.

114. *L'epistre Othea* tells one hundred classical fables, giving for each a "Glose" (pointing out the chivalric virtue exemplified) and a "Moralyte" (pointing out the Christian lesson contained in it). No. 19, the story of Polyphemus, offers on the chivalric level the warning that "the good knight should not, by his sloth, be supplanted with the engines and crafty work of malicious people," the eye representing his "worship," land, rights, and so on. On the Christian level the fable reveals "þe synne of slouth." In the fifteenth-century version ed. by J. D. Gordon (Philadelphia, 1942).

115. *Dictionarius*, fol. 30r. See above, chap. iv, p. 92.

116. John of Wales, *Moniloquium*, MS. Cambridge Peterhouse 200, fol. 34r. The (acknowledged) source is Augustine, *De civitate Dei*, I, 30.

117. Antonius de Bitonto, *Sermones quadragesimales de vitiis*, 35, fol. 99r.

118. This *exemplum* occurs in both Sebastian Brant's and Barclay's version; printed in the 1509 edition by Pynson, fol. CCVv (Latin) and CCVIIr (English). As authorities are quoted in the margin "Augustinus de Roma," "Appianus," and "Ovidius I Fast."

119. Aldhelm, *De octo principalibus vitiis* (PL 89:285); cf. Cassian's "Our sixth fight is with what the Greeks call ἀκηδία . . . ," at the beginning of *Inst.*, X,1.

120. Ed. R. D. Cornelius, *PMLA*, XLVI (1931), 321-32. The allegory is rather undeveloped. "Accide" is the fourth king and comes with "'Malisse, Rancune, Desperance" (ll. 208-11).

121. Jacques Bruyant, *Le Chemin de Povreté et de Richesse* (1342), incorporated in *Ménagier de Paris* (1392-1394) and in Pierre Gringore's *Le Chasteau de Labour* (1499). The latter work was translated by Alexander Barclay and printed by Wynkyn de Worde (1506; reprinted with the French text of 1501, by A. W. Pollard, London, 1905). The *Ménagier* was edited by J. Pichon for the Société des Bibliophiles françois (Paris, 1846) and in part translated by E. Power, *The Goodman of Paris* (London, 1928). F. W. Bourdillon printed the *Livre du Chastel de Labour*, from a MS. in the Widener Library (Philadelphia, 1909). See also A. Langfors, *Romania*, XLV (1918-1919), 49-83.

122. EETS 24, pp. 58ff.

123. Similarly in Rutebeuf's poem entitled *La Bataille des Vices contre les Vertus* (*ca.* 1261-1263), the seven are briefly paired off, *Accide* being overcome by *Proesce* (l. 30); but not all individual fights are developed. See *Oeuvres complètes*, I, 299-312.

124. The first part of the *Moralité* contains a series of dialogues between Pride and the seven vices, who are his princesses. This is taken over, with some slight additions, from *Le Miroir de Vie et de Mort* by Robert de l'Omme (1266), a dream vision of a tree, whose roots are Orgoil with six princesses (including "Accide").

125. *Romania*, XXIX (1900), 54-72. Cf. Bloomfield, *Seven Deadly Sins*, pp. 142, 136, and notes. It should be added that Petrarch refers to "haud inelegans fabella" according to which the devil begets seven daughters with the sinful soul. These are the seven deadly sins (including *accidia*), which he then marries to "singulis populis" (no further specified). Cf. *De otio religioso*, ed. G. Rotondi (Città del Vaticano, 1958), p. 78.

126. MS. BM. Royal 8.A.xv, fol. 122r. This item is not separately described in the manuscript catalogue by Warner and Gilson.

127. In *Oeuvres complètes*, I, 336-70, with a brief survey of allegorical pilgrimages to hell or heaven in French (p. 337).

128. Unique MS.: BM. Royal 14.E.ii. For full contents, see H. L. D. Ward, *Catalogue of Romances in the Department of Manuscripts in the British Museum* (London, 1883), I, 900-902.

129. This is the first of three *Pèlerinages* written by the Cistercian Guillaume Deguileville. It exists in two versions, the earlier one of 1330-1332 (ed. by J. J. Stürzinger for the Roxburghe Club [London, 1893]) and the revision of 1355 (ed. by B. and J. Petit, *Le Romant des trois pelerinaiges* [Paris, *ca.* 1500]; and by Verard, 1511). Lydgate's English version was made from the revision and has been edited by Furnivall in EETS, es, 77, 83, 92 (London, 1899-1904).

130. Equally balanced statements in ll. 5359-62; 5590-92; 5596-97; 5701-5; 5773-76; 5816-17; 5837-38; 5849; 6121ff.

131. *Narratio allegorica de vitiis.* MS. BM. Harley 1294, fol. 89r: "Cui ille aiunt: Quidnam tantopere habeas dicere? Nihil, inquit, habeo, sed quibuslibet sermunculis tempus occupare quero. Nisi enim vel confabulando vel deambulando diem duxero, tedio morior."

132. Thus far also in Robert de l'Omme, *Le Miroir de Vie et de Mort*, except that there Accide carries a banner with God's name on it. The following detail is an addition in the *Moralité*, as is the later disputation. Notice that Robert called the sin *Accide*, whereas the other added portions of the *Moralité* call it *Pareche* (ll. 69, 651, 1569ff.).

133. Ed. J. F. Royster, *SP*, VI (1910). The quoted passage appears on p. 22.

134. "Thais," Queen of Carthage, having no hope in "Serpio," kills herself and her two sons. Plato's saying that one should never despair.

135. *Exempla* of *Paresce*: (1) "Dometrien," King of Athens; (2) Sardanapalus; (3) "Adrienne," daughter of "Minox," King of Crete, who worked very slowly.

136. *Exempla* of *Diligence*: (1) Joseph in Egypt; (2) Brutus; (3) Orpheus (in his search for "Erudice").

137. The whole episode of the Tower of Accide covers fol. 155v-167v of MS. BM. Royal 14.E.ii.

138. Thus, Lydgate makes Idleness say she is "Douhter to Dame Ydelnesse" (l. 11636)!—Despite Miss Locock's analysis of the differences between D I, D II, and L, the changes and especially L's "hopeless maze" of paths mentioned in this entire episode need more detailed study.

139. Undoubtedly a visualization of Prov. 26:15, "abscondit piger manum sub ascellam."

140. The emblem of the glove may have been taken from *Roman de la Rose* also (cf. ll. 560-61 in the ed. by F. Lecoy, "Les classiques français du moyen âge" [Paris, 1965]). As to her occupation with mirror and comb, compare ll. 6847-50 in D I (or ll. 11640-44 in L) with ll. 555-57, 566 in *Roman.*

141. The following account is somewhat composite of all three versions. For an important change in D II against D I, see below, n. 144.

142. In D I she calls herself "fame . . . au bouchier d'enfer" (l. 7120).

143. Again, L is confused: he adds a line to D H II, "Off custom callyd Ydelnesse" (l. 13829).

144. Thus in D II and L. In contrast, D I speaks of several cords but names only one, Desperation. The other four, added in D II are conventional hindrances to confession by mouth. They are called *spes longioris vitae, malus timor, mala pudicitia,* and *hypocrisis* and presented as four advocates of the devil in the Court of Mercy, in *De tribus dietis* by Robert of Sorbon, ed. F. Chambon ("Collection de textes pour servir à l'étude de l'histoire" [Paris, 1902]), pp. 35-61.

CHAPTER VI

1. A. Huxley, "Accidie," in *On the Margin: Notes and Essays* (London, 1923), pp. 18-25; T. S. Eliot, "Baudelaire," in *Selected Essays, 1917-1932* (New York, 1932), p. 339 (this essay appeared first in 1930).

2. The occurrence of the sin scheme in penitential lyrics and other didactic poetry has been sufficiently surveyed in M. W. Bloomfield, *The Seven Deadly*

Sins. An Introduction to the History of a Religious Concept ([East Lansing,] 1952).

3. As an example, see D. W. Robertson, Jr., "The Doctrine of Charity in Medieval Gardens: A Topical Approach through Symbolism and Allegory," *Speculum,* XXVI (1951), 44: Damyan, in Chaucer's *Merchant's Tale,* "sees May and takes to his bed with the lover's malady, an extreme form of *accidia.*"

4. See the summary in Appendix E.

5. For Dante's text I have used the revised edition by C. H. Grandgent (Boston, etc., 1933). The translations are my own except for those in verse, which are taken from the translation by D. L. Sayers (Harmondsworth, Middlesex, 1955).

6. See my article "Dante's Rationale for the Seven Deadly Sins (*Purgatorio,* XVII)," *MLR,* LX (1965), 529-33.

7. The Scholastic rationales are discussed in chap. ii, pp. 38ff.

8. Peraldus, *Summa de vitiis,* fol. 100r; cf. his *Sermo in dom. II post Oct. Epiph.*: "acedia, quae magna bona modicum curat" (*Sermones,* p. 191).

9. The idea of curing moral faults by practicing their opposite virtues appears in: Cassian, *Coll.,* XIX, 14-15; Columban (PL 80:260); Vinnian (Bieler, p. 84); Cummean (*ibid.,* p. 110); Pirminius (*Scarapsus,* pp. 60f.); Bartholomew of Exeter (ed. A. Morley, *Bartholomew of Exeter, Bishop and Canonist* [Cambridge, Engl., 1937], p. 202); and later writers.

10. The image of riding, *cavalcar,* also occures in *Convivio,* IV, ix, 10, and xxvi, 6, where reason or reasonable laws made by the Emperor are said to "ride" the human will.

11. Relevant passages in *lectio* IV, XV, and XVII. Though Conrad exemplifies the Virgin's *sedulitas* by her three months' stay with Elizabeth, he does not quote Luke 1:39. See the (erroneous) commentary by H. Gmelin *Dante Alighieri, Die Göttliche Komödie—Kommentar* (Stuttgart, 1954-1957), II, 179-80 and 295-96.

12. The bacchantes used to practice omophagia, that is, to tear the flesh off live sacrificial animals with their own teeth; see E. Rohde, *Psyche* (3rd ed.; Tübingen, 1903), II, 10; P. Nilsson, *Geschichte der griechischen Religion* (2nd ed.; München, 1955), I, 570.

13. See above, chap. iii, p. 56, and chap. iv, p. 74.

14. Hugh of St. Victor, *Expositio in Abdiam* (PL 175:401-10). See chap. ii, pp. 39ff. and notes.

15. *Summa theologiae,* II-II, qu. 35, a.1, resp. Cf. chap. iii, p. 48.

16. J. Freccero, "Dante's Firm Foot and the Journey without a Guide," *Harvard Theological Review,* LII (1959), 245-81.

17. My analysis of sloth in *Piers Plowman* is based on the B-version of the poem. The text used is that printed by W. W. Skeat in the three-texts edition (Oxford, 1886).

18. Swearing and jangling appear as aspects of gluttony because they are sins of the tongue; see the same connection in Lydgate, *The Pilgrimage of the Life of Man,* ll. 12999ff., and earlier in Frère Lorens' *Somme le Roi* and derived works. Cf. Bloomfield, *Seven Deadly Sins,* p. 125.

19. The image of a coat or garment representing man's soul, or innocence given at baptism, or sanctifying grace, is very frequent in medieval literature from early Christian writers on. With regard to Haukyn's coat one may point specifically to a sermon by Jacques de Vitry on the wedding garment of Matthew 22. Jacques admonishes that "we must daily examine our conscience to see whether on the coat of our soul [*in stola animae nostrae*] we find anything unstitched by negligence, or soiled by lust, or singed by wrath, or torn by envy, or smudged by greed" (*Sermones in Epistolas et Evangelia Dominicalia,* p. 867). That Langland had the parable of the wedding feast in mind is likely because,

at the beginning of Passus XIV, Haukyn quotes a line from the similar parable in Luke 14: *Uxorem duxi, et ideo non possum venire.*

20. For the allegory see chap. v, p. 116, and below, p. 148.

21. G. R. Owst, *Literature and Pulpit in Medieval England* (Cambridge, 1933), pp. 88-89 and notes.

22. Ostiensis, *Summa super titulis Decretalium,* V, 38 (fol. 497v). The questionnaire begins, "Fuisti umquam tepidus et remissus ad bene agendum cum posses?"

23. Cf. W. A. Pantin, *The English Church in the Fourteenth Century* (Cambridge, 1955), pp. 205-6. In the *Memoriale,* the confession of *acedia* occurs in chap. 17; MS. BM. Harley 3120, fol. 11.

24. See A. Gwynn, "The Sermon-Diary of Richard Fitzralph, Archbishop of Armagh," *Proceedings of the Royal Irish Academy,* XLIV (1937), 15. The questionnaire on *acedia* occurs MS. BM. Royal 6.E.vi, fol. 37v.

25. The questions on *acedia* in this formula begin with, "Si per accidiam neglexerit symbolum et orationem dominicam addiscere [vel filios spirituales docere]. Si orare vel ire ad ecclesiam tempore debito neglexerit." Grosseteste, *Modus confitendi,* MS. BM. Addit. 6716, fol. 63v. Similarly the questionnaire that appears very frequently, e.g., MSS. BM. Royal 8.A.xv, fol. 122; Arundel 52, fol. 66; Royal 8.B.x, art. 5; 8.E.xvii, art. 5; 8.C.vii, art. 15; 11.B.iii, art. 20; and others. In some of these versions it is ascribed to Grosseteste. The same formula with some alterations was used by William of Pagula, *Oculus sacerdotis,* part I (MS. BM. Royal 6.E.i, fol. 4-5); and John de Burgo, *Pupilla oculi,* fol. 40r. The text of the latter version is reproduced here, Appendix C.

26. Idle words: IV, 115; VI, 54; XIII, 225ff.; 422ff.; XIX, 281.—Chastising unruly children: IV, 117; V, 34ff.—Overhopping: XI, 296ff.; XIII, 68; XV, 379f.

27. Felton, *Sermones dominicales,* MS. BM. Additional 22572: *Sermo* 6 (fol. 28v); in the same sermon he compares the seven deadly sins to animals: "Some follow the pig, namely the gluttons and the *accidiosi*" (fol. 32r); in *Sermo* 17 he moralizes the story of Atalanta, explaining the first apple as gluttony, which is the mother of *acedia* and lechery (fol. 69r).

28. There is, however, a precedent for the use of "accidia" as "a (concrete) case of neglect in performing some spiritual duty": Peckham's Lambeth Constitutions, *Councils,* II, 894 (par. 1): "inter quorum dampnabiles accidias . . . ."

29. In theological literature, begging is usually *not* a symptom of *acedia.* Only in Gerson's sermon on the vice is the question discussed "whether a strong person who is able to earn his living may beg." The answer is no, unless it be for a noble purpose (III, 1039). *Fasciculus morum,* V, 1, merely compares the *acediosi* to beggars: "Unde tales bene comparantur trutannis contra solem tota die sedentibus et nichil boni operantibus, sed onus bonarum operacionum recusantibus" (MS. Bodleian 332, fol. 150r). Gower does include beggars among the retinue of Lady Idleness, daughter of *Acedia* (*Mirour,* ll. 5797-808).—Of course, poverty is an effect of *acedia,* in Peraldus (*Summa,* 1.3312) and derived literature.

30. In addition, the word *sleuthe* appears in VIII, 51, where it is opposed to man's "working" with his reason and free will to keep himself out of mortal sin; and in XIV, 76, where it translates *otiositas* of the Vulgate (cf. Exech. 16:49).

31. See Owst, *Literature and Pulpit,* chap. IX, "A Literary Echo of the Social Gospel."

32. J. M. Manly, "The Lost Leaf of *Piers the Plowman,*" *MP,* III (1906), 359-66.

33. D. C. Fowler's study, *Piers the Plowman: Literary Relations of the A and B Texts* (Seattle, 1961), has caused G. Kane to re-examine the whole question of authorship and to write a lucid analysis of the conflicting arguments and their logic: *Piers Plowman. The Evidence for Authorship* (London, 1965).

Kane concludes that there is "no ghost of a reason for believing in the multiple authorship of *Piers Plowman*" (p. 72).

34. R. W. Chambers, "The Authorship of *Piers Plowman*," *MLR*, V (1910), 3-6.

35. T. P. Dunning, *Piers Plowman: An Interpretation of the A-Text* (London, 1937), pp. 84-85.

36. Manly, "The Lost Leaf," p. 362.

37. The *Summa* by Antoninus of Florence (1440's) also includes a remark on restitution in its section on *acedia*. A paragraph on "pigritia seu tarditas in persequendo bonam operationem inchoatam" specifies: "Sed permaxime sunt homines tardi ad restitutiones faciendas et adimplenda legata ad pias causas facta a testatoribus . . ." (xiii, 6).

38. Regarding Langland's choice of a robber as demonstrating the attack of despair, one may compare a curious passage preserved in an incomplete treatise on the vices in MS. Oxford Hatton 26, fol. 205-11 (written 1234). Here Accidia marries her offspring and servants to various social and professional classes. "Despair-of-divine-mercy" she has given to "raptoribus et sacrilegis et incestuosis" (fol. 209r).

39. Notice also the Latin verse before l. 304: "Numquam dimittitur peccatum, donec *restituatur* ablatum." My translation is somewhat free.

40. William of Pagula, *Oculus sacerdotis*: "Superbia in exercitu diaboli vexillum portat. . . . Invidia sagittas trahit detrahendo aliis. Ira quasi petra iactat lapides blasphemie et improperii. Accidia fossa tum evacuat ab aquis gratie. 'Spiritus enim tristis exsiccat ossa' [Prov. 17:22]. Avaricia implet fossata per terrenorum cupiditatem. Luxuria ignem succendit. Gula hunc ignem incutit et accendit apponendo ligna cibariorum [sic] et potuum" (MS. BM. Royal 6.E.i, fol. 46r). In *The Castle*, the vices appear under the leadership of Devil, Flesh, and World in this order: Pride (ll. 2070-82), Wrath (ll. 2109-21), Envy (ll. 2148-60); Gluttony (ll. 2249-61), Lechery (ll. 2288-2300), Sloth (ll. 2327-39); Covetousness (ll. 2428-40). W. K. Smart noticed parallels between the siege of the vices in *The Castle* and those in the *Reply of Friar Daw Topias* and *Piers Plowman*, B.XX, but was unable to find a source; "The *Castle of Perseverance*: Place, Date, and a Source," in *The Manly Anniversary Studies in Language and Literature* (Chicago, 1923), pp. 42-53.

41. Cf. J. W. McCutchan, "Covetousness in *The Castle of Perseverance*," in *English Studies in Honor of James Southall Wilson* ("University of Virginia Studies," Vol. IV [Charlottesville, 1951]), pp. 175-91.

42. See above, chap. iv, pp. 93f. and notes.

43. Richard Fitzralph, Archbishop of Armagh, says in a sermon given on Ash Wednesday of 1346 that one must pray in church because there prayer is more *laboriosa* (and thus more pleasing to God), "because it is more toilsome to go to church than to rest at home, and it is said to man, 'In the sweat of thy face . . . ,' and, 'Man is born to work . . .' " (MS. BM. Lansdowne 393, fol. 37r).

44. The name Mischief for the antagonist to Mercy has caused some perplexity. See the ingenious suggestion by Sister M. P. Coogan, *An Interpretation of the Moral Play, "Mankind"* (Washington, 1947), pp. 59ff. But in the play this figure clearly represents something like wickedness or the state of sin and functions as the spiritual counterpoint to Mercy. The word bears this meaning of "wickedness" in Malory ("By thy meschyef and thy vengeaunce thou hast destroyed the mooste noble knyght") and in Coverdale's translation of Gen. 6:5 ("Ye earth was corrupte in ye sight of God and full of myschefe"; both quotations from *OED*); and in *Ludus Coventriae* the verb *myscheven* seems to denote "to fall into sin" (e.g., "on man þat is myschevyd haue compassyon." EETS, es, 120, p. 100, l. 76; see also p. 127, l. 100). Sister Coogan also recognized this meaning (p. 59 and note).

45. *Ayenbite*: "Onlosthede þet is sleuþe" (p. 31; cf. p. 163); *Vices and Virtues*, p. 3; *Ormulum*, ll. 2633, 4562, 4746; *Jacob's Well*, p. 103. In the poem "Jesus appeals to Man by the Wounds," sloth is called *vnlust* (C. Brown, *Religious Lyrics of the Fourteenth Century* [2nd ed.; Oxford, 1952], p. 227). *The Cloud of Unknowing* defines "slewþ" as "a weriness and an vnlistiness of any good occupacion" (EETS 218, p. 37).

46. EETS 26, p. 25.

47. Rolle, *Incendium amoris*, in the translation of Richard Misyn (1435), Bk. I, chap. xi (EETS 106, p. 23).

48. *Speculum Christiani*, EETS 182, p. 65. Cf. Mary's words, "In Goddys servyse I xal nevyr irke!" in the Purification play of *Ludus Coventriae* (EETS, es, 120), l. 194. The *Promptuarium parvulorum* gives "Hirkyn: ffastidio . . . , accidior . . . " (EETS, es, 102, col. 245).

49. For example: *Cursor mundi*, 27784ff. and 27800ff.; and esp. 28341-50 (wanhope) and 28351-59 ("presumpciun"); *Ménagier de Paris*, fifth and sixth branch of sloth (pp. 40ff); Brunetto Latini, *Il Tesoretto*, ll. 165-80.

50. The existing studies on Titivillus are not very clear on which *exempla* identify the fiend by name, nor even describe and classify relevant *exempla* very accurately. Good collections of relevant *exempla* are given by T. F. Crane, *The Exempla of Jacques de Vitry* (London, 1890), pp. 141 and 233; and J. Bolte, "Der Teufel in der Kirche," *Zeitschrift für vergleichende Literaturgeschichte*, N.F., XI (1897), 249-66. For occurrences of "Titivil" in English works, see *OED*, XI, 78. Some pictorial representations from medieval England are listed in M. D. Anderson, *Drama and Imagery in English Medieval Churches* (Cambridge, 1963), pp. 173-77. Sister Mary Emil Jennings in her MA. thesis, "A Study of the Literary Career of the Devil Tutivillus" (University of North Carolina, 1966), has collected a large number of passages from medieval and Renaissance sources which refer to Titivillus and the two *exempla*.

51. Play XXX, ll. 249-52 (EETS, es, 71). But notice that already in the Towneley play Titivillus' role is expanded: He captures souls "at the alehouse" and at plundering (l. 217), and others that are too much interested in new fashions (ll. 233ff.). Originally, however, his province were people who talked in church and who syncopated their prayers. See the following example:

> Janglers cum Jappers, Nappers, Galpers, quoque Drawers,
> Momlers, Fforskippers, Over*r*enners, sic Ov*er*hippers,
> Ffragmin*a* verboru*m* Tutivillus colligit horum.

(MS. BM. Lansdowne 763, fol. 60r; printed in *A Catalogue of the Lansdowne Manuscripts in the British Museum* [London, 1819], p. 170). See also item 179 in C. Brown, *Religious Lyrics of the Fifteenth Century*.

52. MS. BM. Arundel 506, fol. 46v; Bromyard, *Summa praedicantium*, "Ordo clericalis," II, xxvi; a somewhat different vision of the same devil, *ibid.*, "Ferie," VII, xxi; *The Mirror of Our Lady*, I, xx (EETS, es, 19, p. 54); *Sermones quadragesimales Thesauri Novi*, sermo 13 (Augsburg, 1487). See chap. v, p. 113.

53. Thus in *Jacob's Well*, pp. 114-15.

54. One text for many: "Accidia quidem est displicentia boni. . . . Si est clericus, si negligens est in officio suo. . . . Item, laicus si venit ad ecclesiam in festis et loquitur in eclesia cum alliis." Raymundus of Pennaforte (?), *Summa de vitiis*, MS. University of North Carolina 5 (written 1459), cap. xv.

55. *An Interpretation of "Mankind," passim*, following a suggestion made by W. K. Smart, "Some Notes on *Mankind*," *MP*, XIV (1916), 45ff.

56. The theme of instability is stated in ll. 207, 274ff., 739 (see Coogan, *An Interpretation of "Mankind,"* p. 107), (?902-903). Notice that in Play 24 of *Ludus Coventriae*, "The Woman Taken in Adultery"—a play similarly concerned with Mercy—, "vnstable" is synonymous with "sinful" (p. 208, l. 261; p. 201, l. 27).

57. The conflict between body and soul is mentioned in ll. 189-201, 220 and ff., 306, 890.

58. *De malo,* qu. 11, a.2, resp.; see above, chap. iii, pp. 49f.

59. Page references are to the Latin text of *Secretum,* ed. E. Carrara, in *Francesco Petrarca, Prose,* ed. Martellotti, *et al.* (Milan, 1955).

60. *Petrarca's Leben und Werke* (Leipzig, 1878), p. 646.

61. "Petrarch's *Accidia,*" *Studies in the Renaissance,* VIII (1960), 36-48.

62. *Ibid.*, pp. 44-45.

63. P. 126; *tristitia,* p. 128; *in hac autem tristitia,* said by Franciscus, p. 106.

64. Based on II Cor. 7:10; see the discussion above, chap. ii, pp. 25f.

65. David of Augsburg, *Formula novitiorum,* 51 (Bigne, XIII, 438). This passage also occurs in Henry of Balnea (?), *Speculum spiritualium,* I, xvi (Paris, 1510), fol. xiiir; and in the fifteenth-century *Summa vitiorum et virtutum* by the Carthusian Dionysius de Leuwis (p. 115).

66. For the chronology of Petrarch's writings I have relied on E. H. Wilkins, *Life of Petrarch* (Chicago, 1961).

67. Notice that the two very important *Summae de casibus* by Astesanus of Asti (1317) and by Bartholomew of Pisa (1338), both written by Italians during Petrarch's youth, call the vice *accidia* and follow St. Thomas in relying upon the definition of Damascenus, "quaedam tristitia aggravans quae ita deprimit animum hominis ut nihil ei libeat agere" (Astesanus, II, 63). Another important work written at Avignon in 1329-1330, *De planctu ecclesiae,* by the papal canonist Alvarus Pelagius, deals with *accidia* as "a secret vice of the religious of our times" but calls *tristitia* a "profana filia accidie" (II, 75). Alvarus' treatment is an interesting expansion of that given by Peraldus, especially in the branch of *tristitia.*—Notice also that the Latin glossary of Uguiccio da Pisa (*ca.* 1200), which Petrarch quoted several times (cf. P. de Nolhac, *Pétrarque et l'humanisme* [2nd ed.; Paris, 1907], II, 213 and elsewhere, see Index), defines *accidia* as "tristitia, sublestia, anxietas vel tedium" (MS. BM. Additional 27328, fol. 14r). John Balbus of Genoa, *Catholicon,* which appears in Petrarch's list of favorite books (made perhaps in 1333), has the same definition (but with *molestia;* MS. BM. Arundel 110, fol. 69v); cf. B. L. Ullman, *Studies in the Italian Renaissance* (Rome, 1955), chap. iv, "Petrarch's Favorite Books" (pp. 117-37).

68. Cf. H. Baron, "The Evolution of Petrarch's Thought: Reflections on the State of Petrarch Studies," *Bibliothèque d'Humanisme et Renaissance,* XXIV (1962), 7-41; and "Petrarch's *Secretum*: Was It Revised—And Why?" *ibid.*, XXV (1963), 489-530.

69. Ed. G. Rotondi (Città del Vaticano, 1958). For the two "editions" or rather forms of the text, see the "Introduzione" by G. Martellotti.

70. On pp. 14 ("deprimebat accidia") and 78 (a mere enumeration).

71. Ecclus. 30:22-26. Ed. Rotondi, pp. 11-12.

72. "Torpeo in agendis. . . . Torpeo et ad bona opera lentus assurgo." II, 109 (Rotterdam, 1649). A similar series of the seven chief vices, with *torpor ingenii,* occurs in II, 10.—A different series appears in *Rerum memorandarum libri,* III, 84, 2 (completed before February, 1345; *Opera* [Venice, 1501]). Here Petrarch lists a number of evils, such as ill fortune, old age, sickness, death, external commotions, and internal movements of the mind (*motus*). Among the last he specifies ten, in which one can recognize the seven chief vices and the four affects, with *dolor* representing both the affect and the vice of *acedia.*

73. Notice that *torpor animi* was also a current Scholastic definition of *acedia;* see chap. iii, n. 17, (j) and (k).

74. Cicero, *Tusculanae disputationes,* III, xi, 24-25; also in x, 23; xiii, 28.

75. *De civitate Dei,* XIV, 7. Notice that St. Jerome, in contrast, uses *aegritudo: Dialogus adversus Pelagianos,* Prol. (PL 23:517); *Epistulae,* XXII, 27 (PL 22:413, "aegrescit").

76. This conclusion was also reached by K. Heitmann, *Fortuna und Virtus.*

Eine Studie zu Petrarcas Lebensweisheit ("Studi Italiani," No. 1 [Köln-Graz, 1958]), pp. 202-4. Heitmann (p. 94) relates Petrarch's equation of Christian vice and Stoic affect to the hypothesis that the seven vices originated from the Stoic affects (Stelzenberger's theory; see above, chap. i, pp. 14f.). But he is apparently quite unfamiliar with the Scholastic interpretation of *acedia* as a form of the passion *tristitia.* Surely, Petrarch could not help being influenced by the Scholastic analysis of *acedia,* no matter how much he may have hated the Schoolmen.

77. *Summa theologiae,* II-II, qu. 35, a.1, resp.; discussed in chap. iii, p. 48.

78. For a series of learned opinions, see "Petrarch's *Accidia,*" pp. 36-37. The quotation is from O. Zöckler, *Die Tugendlehre des Christentums geschichtlich dargestellt in der Entwicklung ihrer Lehrformen* (Gütersloh, 1904), p. 279.

CHAPTER VII

1. See above, pp. 162f.

2. Bloomfield, *Seven Deadly Sins,* p. 96; similar statements occur on p. 415, n. 178; p. 416, n. 187; p. 226.

3. Cf. M. Lot-Borodine, "L'Aridité ou *Siccitas* dans l'antiquité chrétienne," *Études carmélitaines mystiques et missionaires,* XXII (1937), 191-205.

4. Aelfric, *Sermo XVI, de memoria sanctorum* (EETS 82, p. 356).

5. Bloomfield, *Seven Deadly Sins,* p. 113.

6. Antoninus, *Summa theologica,* lib. II, tit. 9, ii, 1.

7. *Ayenbite of Inwit,* p. 31.

8. *The Book of Vices and Virtues,* p. 26.

9. *The Clensyng of mannes sowle,* II, 6 (MS. Bodleian 923, fol. 65r). This definition appears as "tristess of spiritual goods" in the extremely "popular" *Kalender of Shepherds,* chap. 8.

10. Chaucer, *The Parson's Tale,* l. 677.

11. *Lay Folks' Catechism,* l. 525.

12. Bloomfield, *Seven Deadly Sins,* p. 394, n. 64. R. Brouillard, in *DTC,* XV (1946), 122-25, speaks of "la doctrine traditionelle" but gives no historical survey.

13. Jean de Fécamp, *Confessio theologica,* 3 (ed. J. Leclercq and J.-P. Bonnes, *Un maître de la vie spirituelle au XI*e *siècle, Jean de Fécamp* [Paris, 1946], p. 143).

14. Hugh of St. Victor, *In Ecclesiasten homiliae XIX,* hom. 16 (PL 175:235).

15. "Caro suggerit mihi mollia, mundus vana, diabolus amara," *De cognitione humanae conditionis,* 12 (PL 184:504). This is evidently based on the genuine Bernardian passage in *Sermo XIII de diversis,* "De discretione spirituum" (PL 183:601).

16. Odo of Cheriton, *Flores sermonum ac evangeliorum dominicalium* (Paris, 1520), fol. xxiiii; see P. Meyer, *Romania,* XVI (1887), 4-5.

17. Isaac, *Sermo VI in festo omnium sanctorum* (PL 194:1710).—The reason for attributing *tristitia* to the world is probably St. Paul's condemnation of *tristitia saeculi* (II Cor. 7:10).

18. Grosseteste seems to have been responsible for the rationale which distributes the seven vices between the three powers of the soul and the four elements of the body; see his treatise "Deus est quo nihil melius cogitari potest" (MS. BM. Royal 7. F.ii).

19. Thomas of Chabham, *Liber poenitentialis* (MS. BM. Royal 8.F.xiii, fol. 38r); Jacques de Vitry, *Sermones in Epistolas et Evangelia,* p. 258; John of Wales, *Summa justitiae* (MS. BM. Harley 632, fol. 217v; but see below, quotation in text); Bonaventure, *Commentarius in Evangelium Lucae,* XV, 25 (VII, 391; Simon de Hinton, *Summa theologica,* cf. A. Dondaine, *RTAM,* IX (1937), 218; Roger Bacon, *Compendium studii philosophiae,* ed. J. S. Brewer, *Opera*

quaedam hactenus inedita (London, 1859), p. 410; *Compileison*, MS. Cambridge Trinity College R. 14.7, fol. 3v.

20. *Ancrene Riwle*, p. 86. In the Middle English poem *The Owl and the Nightingale*, the position of sloth is uncertain; see Bloomfield, *Seven Deadly Sins*, p. 146.

21. William of Lancea, *Dieta salutis*, I, 2 (MS. BM. Royal 7.C.i, fol. 33v). Personality and date of the author are very uncertain; the cited manuscript is of the fourteenth century.

22. Hilton, *Scale of Perfection*, I, 72.

23. William of Shoreham, *De VII mortalibus peccatis*, ll. 297ff. (EETS, es, 86).

24. Caesarius of Heisterbach, *Dialogus miraculorum*, IV, 2 (p. 173): "In so far as *acedia* refers to pain (fear) of the heart, it is a spiritual vice; in so far as it refers to sluggishness of the body, it is a bodily vice."

25. Peter Quivil, *Summula*, 34 (*Councils*, II, 1074).

26. See chap. ii, p. 43.

27. *Summa justitiae*, MS. BM. Harley 632, fol. 217v: "Item secundum alios, Accidia est tristicia vel tedium boni spiritualis deo debiti: non in quantum est bonum spirituale, nec in quantum deo debitum (quia hoc specialiter convenit iniusticie), sed in quantum impedit quietem corporis non principaliter sed quia impedit quietem anime. Unde est vicium spirituale, non carnale simpliciter, sed spirituale principaliter."

28. *Ibid.*, fol. 217r: "Dictum est de quatuor viciis principalibus quibus corrumpitur homo interior. Sequitur de tribus residuis quibus deformatur et deordinatur etiam homo exterior, viz., de accidia, gula, et luxuria. Accidia enim pro parte ad corpus pertinere videtur. Crisostomus, Homilia 18 imperfecta: 'Tres sunt precipue passiones naturales intime et proprie carnis. Primo esca et potus, deinde amor viri ad mulierem, tertio loco sompnus. Nullius ergo passionis abstinencia sic sanctificat corpus quomodo abstinencia ab istis, ut sis castus, ieiunus, et vigiliis perseverans; et nulla passio sic coinquinat corpus sicut iste passiones.' "

29. Bernard, *Sermo XIII de diversis* (PL 183:601).

30. Gerhoch of Reichersberg, *Liber de laude fidei*, ed. P. Classen (Rome, 1955), I, 245.

31. Notice that, as in the quoted passage by Gerhoch, very often not all the seven chief vices are distributed, but only a few. One finds very many instances in which especially *acedia* is lacking—which may be another sign of the uneasiness experienced by theologians in having to place the vice into a flesh-vs.-spirit category.

32. Jacques de Vitry uses *tristitia* in: pp. 172, 196 (quoting Hugh of St. Victor); *acedia* in: pp. 43, 102, 217, 237f., 246, 432; both in: pp. 150, 182, 193, 195, 255, 258, 428, 452, 584, 724 (*Sermones*, 1575).

33. *Ibid.*, p. 193.

34. In this "spiritual" sense of grief or inappetence, *acedia* still appears among the temptations of the devil in *Speculum morale*: "[Diabolus] tentat simplices, quando scilicet diabolus applicans se humano intellectui, cum quadam obscuritate umbrosa, obscurat eum et obnubilat, ut in maximam tristitiam veniat, vel accidiam, vel nimium timorem, vel oblivionem eorum quae scivit vel quae scire debet; sicut fit in energumenis qui mente patiuntur," III, i, 6 (col. 895).

35. *Templum domini*, MS. BM. Burney 356, fol. 25r: "Accidie species. Desidia anime, que est interna mentis tristicia, ut cum sine devocione meditatur quis non proficiendo, orat non affectando gaudia, legit non sapiendo celestia. Ocium corporis, quod fit cum a laboribus sanctis corpus retrahitur, ut ab auxiliis, doctrinis, et consiliis bonis." Cf. Grosseteste's treatise "Deus est quo nihil melius cogitari potest": "Accidia dividitur in accidiam mentis et accidiam corporis.

Accidia [mentis] est interna mentis tristicia, et dicitur desidia. Accidia corporis est que primo se corporis affectibus carnalibus [? que se pro corporis affectibus carnalibus?] a laboribus sanctis retrahit, et dicitur ocium" (MS. BM. Royal 7.F.ii, fol. 91r).

36. E.g., Hugh Ripelin, *Compendium theologicae veritatis*, III, 18 (p. 110); Jean Rigaud, *Compendium pauperis* (VIII.X) and *Formula confessionis* ("duas habet facies," MS. BM. Arundel 379, fol. 12v). Jean de la Rochelle said that *tristitia* and *acedia* are different "secundum rationem" but identical "secundum rem." They designate the same movement of the will, but distinguish opposite directions: aversion from some difficult good (*tristitia*) and conversion to bodily rest (*acedia*); *Summa de vitiis*, MS. Bodl. Laud. misc. 221, fol. 33r.

37. The *Fasciculus morum* contains seven parts, one for each deadly sin. These are divided into sins of the Devil (pride, wrath, envy), the World (greed), and the Flesh (*acedia*, gluttony, lust), this larger division being consistently borne in mind throughout the rather long work. In MS. Bodleian 332, fol. 149v, the definition of *acedia* appears thus: "Tedium boni sive anxietas. Sed diabolum tedet omne bonum. Ergo non tamen carnis sed eciam sibi ad ministerium iuste deputatur."

38. Bonaventure, *De perfectione vitae ad sorores*, 1 (I, 109). The explicatory phrases in parentheses occur only in one manuscript.

39. Thomas of Chabham, *Poenitentiale*: "Accidia autem est gravissimum peccatum et fere tamen omnibus ignotum. Debet enim homo devote et diligenter divinis obsequiis intendere. Quando enim homo tedio affectus diligentiam aufert serviendi deo et tollit devotionem in obsequiis divinis, peccatum accidie est, et tunc multum peccat homo. Qui enim indevotus orat, iudicium suum implorat. Peccatum autem accidie ab Apostolo vocatur *tristicia seculi que mortem operatur*. Ex tali etiam peccato multi occiderunt se ipsos quando homines ita absorbentur quod nullam habent iocunditatem in deo nec in obsequiis divinis. Oritur autem accidia sepe vel ex pigricia vel ex negligencia. Unde diligenter et caute monendi sunt principes penitentes quando veniunt ad confessionem ut diligentes sint et non ociosi in operibus honestis. Et sicut ait Apostolus, *sint hospitales sine murmuratione* et omnia opera sua faciant deo sapida per bonam devotionem. Aliter enim nullum obsequium hominis placet deo. Pessimum ergo peccatum accidie quod per tedium et fastidium aufert homini bona opera sua, quibus posset mereri vitam eternam. Sollicitus sit ergo penitens ut numquam inveniat eum diabolus otiosum; quia *multa mala docuit ociositas*. Ex otio enim proveniunt sompnolentia, pigritia, que avertunt cor hominis ab omni obsequio divino et ab omni hylaritate laborandi pro deo." MS. BM. Royal 8.F.xiii, fol. 62r.

40. Further evidence can be derived from a similar change in the virtue opposed to *acedia*. Whereas in Cassian this was *fortitudo*, some texts of the ninth and following centuries specify *instantia boni operis*. Thus: *Florilegium ad Alagum*, MS. Reims 443 (ninth century; see H. M. Rochais, *RBén.*, LXVII [1957], 143); Aelfric, *Sermo de memoria sanctorum* (EETS 82, pp. 360-62); *Florilegium Oxoniense* (ed. Ph. Delhaye [Louvain, 1955], p. 98); a treatment of the eight principal vices in a tenth-century manuscript from Fleury (Martène, III, 246); similarly in MS. Cologne, Dombibliothek 106 (ninth century; cf. W. van Ackeren, *Die althochdeutschen Bezeichnungen der septem peccata criminalia und ihrer filiae* [Dortmund, 1904], p. 9). The "new" virtue of *instantia boni operis* foreshadows terms like *strenuitas*, *occupatio*, and *busynesse*, which became current in the thirteenth century. See above, chap. iv, p. 89 and nn. 95-96.

41. David of Augsburg, *Formula novitiorum. De interioris hominis reformatione*, 50. Quoted above, p. 160.

42. Henry of Lancaster, *Livre de seintz medicines*, p. 23.

43. "Encores je ay peché par acside et m'a fait meger a mege juif, la ou je pooit aver crestien mege." E. Brayer (ed.), "Un manuel de confession en ancien

français conservé dans un manuscrit de Catane (Bibl. Ventimiliana, 42)," in *Mélanges d'archéologie et d'histoire publiés par l'École française de Rome, 1947* (Rome, 1948), p. 180.

44. Princes are mentioned in connection with *acedia* by Thomas of Chabham, quoted above. Cf. Jacobus de Theramo, *Liber Belial de consolatione peccatorum*: "Hoc vitium extirpatur per sollicitam curam regentium" (Venice, 1506).

45. Gerson, in his sermon on *acedia*, raises the question, "whether a burgher is obliged to work, especially if he has some other means of livelihood" (III, 1038). The same point had already been made by Peraldus, *Summa*, under *otiositas* (2.04).

46. Frater Ludovicus, OFM, specifies *acedia* as one of the four sins for which many peasants are damned: "Primo in acidia, quia minus curant ire ad divinum officium et in festis subterfugiunt dicentes se laborasse per totam hebdomadam." Ed. A. Franz, *Drei deutsche Minoritenprediger aus dem XIII. und XIV. Jahrhundert* (Freiburg i, Br., 1907), pp. 88-89.

47. *Poésies de Gilles li Muisis*, ed. Baron Kervyn de Lettenhove, II (Louvain, 1882), pp. 71-125.

48. Cf. Bloomfield, *Seven Deadly Sins*, pp. 188ff. and 224-26.

49. A treatise on the duties of a wife, written about 1393 by an aging lawyer for his much younger spouse and containing moral and practical advice on how to make the husband feel at home, on gardening, on cooking, and so forth. One chapter speaks of the love of God and deals with the seven deadly sins. Here *paresse* is quite the theological concept with six common branches (though not the Gregorian progeny; included is vanity in the sense of unrepentance) and a confessional formula which contains nothing that cannot also be found in standard handbooks.

50. Ed. R. Girvan, STC, 3rd ser., Vol. XI, ll. 719ff.

51. Boccaccio, *Il Comento sopra la Comedia di Dante Alighieri*, ed. G. Milanesi, II (Florence, 1863), 124-26. A similar adaptation to the Aristotelian scheme occurs in the philosophical encyclopedia *Margarita philosophica* by Gregor Reisch (Strassburg, 1504), who considers *acedia* a passion of the concupiscible part of the soul and defines it as *displicentia boni proprii absentis*, "which neglects to reach for such good" (II, 4). Later, however, Reisch gives the standard theological definition (II, 55).

52. *Desidia* appears instead of *acedia* in an English sermon *De octo viciis et de duodecim abusivis huius seculi*: "þeo sixte [chief sin] is ihaten *Desidia*, þet is slewþe on englisc" (EETS 34, p. 103).

53. *Dialogus miraculorum*, IV, 27 (p. 197).

54. Chap. iv, p. 72 and n. 19.

55. Jordan of Quedlinburg, *Sermo* 441 (Strassburg, 1483).

56. A different indication of the same tendency to comprehensiveness appears in the very strange treatment of *acedia* in an incomplete treatise preserved in MS. Bodl. Hatton 26, fol. 205-11. Here the sin is defined as "omissio cuiuscumque boni faciendi," which comprises the commandments of God as well as the precepts (and, conversely, the prohibitions) of the rulers of Church *and state* (*prelati regni et ecclesie*, fol. 208v). In other words, *acedia* is the sin of not fulfilling what is demanded by, and of transgressing what has been forbidden by, God and spiritual as well as temporal rulers.

57. Notice, however, that in French authors *paresse* often retains a profoundly spiritual quality. See, for example, La Rochefoucault, "Maximes supprimées," 630, in *Oeuvres complètes* ("Bibl. de la Pléiade" [Paris, 1957]).

58. E. Panofsky and F. Saxl, *Dürers "Melencolia I," eine quellen- und typengeschichtliche Untersuchung* ("Studien de Bibliothek Warburg," No. 2 [Leipzig, 1923]); E. Panofsky, *Albrecht Dürer* (3rd ed.; Princeton, 1948), I, 156-71. More fully developed in R. Klibansky, E. Panofsky, and F. Saxl, *Saturn and*

Melancholy. Studies in the History of Natural Philosophy, Religion and Art (London, 1964), pp. 300ff. and *passim.*

59. Claude Fleury, *Traité du choix et de la methode des études* (Paris, 1686), p. 126.

APPENDIX E

1. Francesco da Buti, *Comento sopra la Divina Comedia,* ed. C. Giannini (3 vols.; Pisa, 1858ff.), I, 219.

2. Anonimo Fiorentino, *Commento alla Divina Commedia,* ed. P. Fanfani (3 vols.; Bologna, 1866-1874), I, 185.

3. L. Pietrobono, *Dal Centro al Cerchio. La struttura morale della Divina Commedia* (2nd ed.; Turin, 1956), chap. VI and *passim*; and his annotated edition (Turin, 1962), I, 76 and 85.

4. Pietro Alighieri, *Super Dantis . . . Comoediam Commentarium,* ed. V. Nannucci (Florence, 1846), pp. 107-9.

5. P. Rajna, *Il canto XVII del Purgatorio* ("Lectura Dantis" [Florence, 1901; revised, 1920]), p. 32.

6. E. Moore, *Studies in Dante. Second Series* (Oxford, 1899), chap. 3, esp. pp. 173-78. Position (b) is of course implied in the interpretation by "Anonimo Fiorentino," mentioned under (1) above.

7. Position (a) is taken, for example, by Grabher (Milan, 1950); position (b) by Gmelin (Stuttgart, 1954), Porena (Bologna, 1961), and Pietrobono (Turin, 1962), in their commentaries on the *Divine Comedy.*

8. In support of their theory that the *accidiosi* belong to the vice of *ira,* several modern Dante scholars have quoted some lines from Brunetto Latini's *Tesoretto,* beginning with "In ira nasce e posa Accidia niquitosa." These scholars fail to realize, (a) that Brunetto has all the deadly sins, after pride, originate in this fashion from the preceding vice, using the verb "nasce" with regard to envy, wrath, *acedia,* and covetousness; (b) that in this Brunetto followed the traditional medieval view that the seven chief vices are genetically concatenated, a view set forth by Cassian ("de ira tristitiam, de tristitia acediam necesse est pullulare," *Coll.*, V, 10) and by Gregory the Great ("ex ira quoque tristitia oritur," and similarly with the other four "spiritual" vices; *Moralia in Job,* XXXI, 45; PL 76:621) and further developed by Hugh of St. Victor (see above, chap. ii, pp. 39f.).

9. Cf. the suggestion made by C. A. Trypanis, "Dante and a Byzantine Treatise on Virtues and Vices," *Medium Aevum,* XIX (1950), 43-49.

LIST OF PRINTED SOURCES

The following are published sources of major importance I have used, whose publication data are given only here in order to simplify references in the text and the notes. Excluded are works that have appeared in certain collections, such as PG, PL, Bigne, etc. (see "Abbreviations").

Aelred of Rievaulx. *Sermones inediti,* ed. C. H. Talbot. ("Series Scriptorum s. ordinis Cisterciensis," No. 1.) Rome, 1952.

———. *La vie de recluse. La prière pastorale,* ed. Ch. Dumont. ("Sources chrétiennes," No. 76.) Paris, 1961.

Alanus of Lille. *De virtutibus et de vitiis et de donis Spiritus Sancti,* ed. O. Lottin, *Mediaeval Studies,* XII (1950), 20-56. Re-edited in O. Lottin, *Psychologie et morale aux XIIe et XIIIe siècles,* Vol. VI (Louvain, 1960), 41-92.

Albertus, Magnus. *Opera omnia,* ed. A. Borgnet. 38 vols. Paris, 1890-1899.

Alexander Carpentarius. *Destructorium vitiorum.* Nuremberg: Anton Koberger, 1496.

Alexander of Hales. *Summa theologica.* 4 vols. Quaracchi, 1924-1948.

An Alphabet of Tales. An English Fifteenth-Century Translation of the Alphabetum Narrationum once Attributed to Etienne de Besançon, ed. M. M. Banks. EETS 126-127. London, 1904-1905.

Alvarus Pelagius. *De planctu ecclesiae.* Lyons, 1517.

[*Ancrene Riwle.*] *The English Text of the "Ancrene Riwle,"* ed. M. Day. EETS 225. London, 1952.

Andreas d'Escobar. *Modus confitendi.* Paris, [*ca.* 1495].

Angelo de Clavasio. *Summa angelica.* Nuremberg: Anton Koberger, 1488.

Antoninus of Florence. *Summa theologica.* Venice: Nicolaus Jenson, 1480.

Antonius de Bitonto. *Sermones quadragesimales de vitiis.* Venice: G. Herzog, 1499.

Astesanus ab Asti. *Summa de casibus.* Nuremberg: Anton Koberger, 1482.

Ayenbite of Inwyt. See under Michael of Northgate.

Bacon, Roger. *Moralis philosophia,* ed. F. Delorme and E. Massa. Turin, 1953.

Barclay, Alexander. *The Ship of Fools.* London, 1509.

Bartholomaeus de Chaimis. *Interrogatorium sive confessionale.* Strassburg, [*ca.* 1476/78].

Bartholomaeus of Pisa (or, of San Concordio). *Summa de casibus conscientiae* [or, *Summa pisana,* etc.]. Venice: Girardengus, 1481.

Berchorius, Petrus. *Dictionarius* ("A, a, a"). Nuremberg, 1517.

Bernard of Clairvaux. *Opera,* ed. J. Leclercq, C. H. Talbot, and H. M. Rochais. 3 vols. Rome, 1957-1963.

Bieler, Ludwig (ed.). *The Irish Penitentials.* ("Scriptores Latini Hiberniae," No. 5.) Dublin, 1963.

Bonaventure. *Opera omnia.* 10 vols. Quaracchi, 1882-1902.

The Book of Vices and Virtues. A Fourteenth-Century English Translation of the Somme le Roi . . . , ed. W. N. Francis. EETS 217. London, 1942.

Brinton, Thomas. *Sermons, 1373-1389,* ed. Sister Mary Aquinas Devlin. ("Camden Third Series," Nos. 85-86.) London, 1954.

Bromyard, John. *Summa praedicantium.* Basel: Johann Amerbach, 1484.

Brunetto Latini. *Il Tesoretto e il Favoletto,* ed. G. B. Zannoni. Florence, 1824.

Caesarius of Heisterbach. *Dialogus miraculorum,* ed. J. Strange. 2 vols. Cologne, 1851.

Cassian, John. *Conlationes XXIIII,* ed. M. Petschenig. ("Corpus Scriptorum Ecclesiasticorum Latinorum," No. 13.) Vienna, 1886.

———. *De institutis coenobiorum et de octo principalium vitiorum remediis libri XII,* ed. M. Petschenig. ("Corpus Scriptorum Ecclesiasticorum Latinorum," No. 17.) Vienna, 1888.

The Castle of Perseverance, in *The Macro Plays,* ed. F. J. Furnivall and A. W. Pollard. EETS, es, 91. London, 1904.

Caxton, William. *Royal Book.* London, [1488?].

Conrad of Saxony. *Speculum beatae Mariae Virginis.* ("Bibliotheca franciscana ascetica medii aevi," No. 2.) Quaracchi, 1904.

Cursor mundi. A Northumbrian Poem of the Fourteenth Century, ed. R. Morris. EETS 57, 59, 62, 66, 68, 99. London, 1874-1892.

Dante Alighieri. *La Divina Commedia,* ed. and annot. C. H. Grandgent. Rev. ed., Boston, 1933.

Deguileville, Guillaume. *Le Pèlerinage de l'homme* [i.e., *Le Pèlerinage de vie humaine,* 2nd version], ed. A. Verard. Paris, 1511.

———. *Le Pèlerinage de vie humaine* [1st version], ed. J. J. Stürzinger, for the Roxburghe Club. London, 1893.

The Desert of Religion, ed. W. Hübner, *ASNS*, CXXVI (1911), 58-74; 360-64.

Dionysius de Leuwis, O. Carth. *Summa vitiorum et virtutum*, in *Opera omnia*. Montreuil, 1896ff. Vol. XXXIX.

Edmund Rich, of Pontigny. *Le Merure de Seinte Eglise*, ed. H. W. Robbins. Lewisburg, Pa., 1925.

Farinator, Matthias. *Lumen animae*. Augsburg: G. Zainer, 1477.

Florilegium morale Oxoniense, ed. Ph. Delhaye. ("Analecta Mediaevalia Namurcensia," No. 5.) Louvain, 1955.

Gerson, Jean. *De mystica theologia*, ed. A. Combes. Lugano, 1958.

———. *Opera omnia*, ed. Ellies Dupin. 5 vols. Antwerp, 1706.

Gobius, Johannes. *Scala coeli*. Louvain: Johannes de Westfalia, 1485.

Gower, John. *The Complete Works*, ed. G. C. Macaulay. Oxford, 1899-1902. *Mirour de l'omme* in Vol. I, *The French Works; Confessio amantis* in Vols. II-III, *The English Works*.

Gritsch, Johannes. *Quadragesimale*. Nuremberg: Anton Koberger, 1483.

Guido de Monte Rocherii. *Manipulus curatorum*. Strassburg: Martin Flach, 1499.

Guillaume d'Auvergne. *Opera*. 2 vols. Orléans and Paris, 1674.

Guillaume d'Auxerre. *Summa aurea*. Paris, 1518.

Handlyng Synne. See under Robert Manning of Brunne.

Die heilige Regel für ein vollkommenes Leben, ed. R. Priebsch. ("Deutsche Texte des Mittelalters," No. 16.) Berlin, 1909.

Henry of Lancaster. *Livre de seyntz medicines*, ed. E. J. Arnould. ("Anglo-Norman Text Society," No. 2.) Oxford, 1940.

Herolt, Johannes. *Sermones Discipuli*. [London, 1510.]

Hilton, Walter. *The Scale of Perfection*, ed. E. Underhill, London, 1923.

Holcot, Robert. *Heptalogus*. Paris, [1517].

———. *Super Sapientiam Salomonis*. Speyer: Peter Dach, 1483.

Hugh of St. Cher. *Opera omnia in universum Vetus et Novum Testamentum*. 8 vols. Venice, 1732.

Hugh Ripelin of Strassburg. *Compendium theologicae veritatis*, in *Alberti Magni opera omnia*, ed. A. Borgnet, Vol. XXXIV (Paris, 1895), 1-306.

Huon de Mery. *Tournoiemenz Antecrit*, ed. G. Wimmer. ("Ausgaben und Abhandlungen aus dem Gebiet der romanischen Philologie," No. 76.) Marburg, 1888.

Jacob's Well. An Englisht Treatise on the Cleansing of Man's Conscience, ed. A. Brandeis. Part I: EETS 115. London, 1900.

[Jacques de Vitry.] *The Exempla or Illustrative Stories from the*

Sermones Vulgares of Jacques de Vitry, ed. Th. F. Crane. ("The Folklore Society," No. 26.) London, 1890.

——. *Sermones in Epistolas et Evangelia Dominicalia*. Antwerp, 1575.

——. *Sermones vulgares*, ed. J. B. Pitra, in *Analecta novissima Spicilegii Solesmensis*, altera continuatio, Vol. II (Tusculana, 1888).

Jean de Le Mote. *La Voie d'Enfer et de Paradis*, ed. Sister M. A. Pety. Washington, D.C., 1940.

John de Burgo. *Pupilla oculi*. Paris, 1510.

The Kalender of Shepardes. [1518?].

[Langland, William.] *The Vision of William concerning Piers the Plowman, in three parallel texts*, ed. W. W. Skeat. 2 vols. Oxford, 1886.

The Lay Folks' Catechism, ed. Th. F. Simmons and H. E. Nolloth. EETS 118. London, 1901.

Liber exemplorum ad usum praedicantium, saeculo XIII compositus a quodam fratre minore Anglico de provincia Hiberniae, ed. A. G. Little. Aberdeen, 1908.

Lorens, Frère. *Somme des vices et des vertus* [i.e., *Somme le Roi*]. Part I: ed. A. B. Tysor, unpublished M.A. thesis, University of North Carolina, 1949. Part II: ed. E. H. Allen, unpublished M.A. thesis, University of North Carolina, 1951.

Lydgate, John. *The Assembly of Gods: or, The Accord of Reason and Sensuality in the Fear of Death*, ed. O. L. Triggs. EETS, es, 69. London, 1896.

——. *The Pilgrimage of the Life of Man*, ed. F. J. Furnivall. EETS, es, 77, 83, 92. London, 1899-1904.

Malachy of Limerick. *Libellus septem peccatorum mortalium venena eorumque remedia describens: qui dicitur Venenum Malachiae*. Paris, 1518.

Mankind, ed. J. Q. Adams, in *Chief Pre-Shakespearean Dramas* (Boston, 1924), pp. 304-24.

Martène, E. *De antiquis ecclesiae ritibus*. Editio novissima. 4 vols. Bassano, 1788.

Le Ménagier de Paris, ed. J. Pichon, for the Société des bibliophiles françois. 2 vols. Paris, 1846.

Michael of Northgate. *Ayenbite of Inwyt, or, Remorse of Conscience*, ed. R. Morris. EETS 23. London, 1866.

Mireour du monde, ed. F. Chavannes. ("Mémoires et documents publiés par la Société de l'histoire de la Suisse Romande," No. 4.) Lausanne, 1845.

Mirk, John. *Instructions for Parish Priests*, ed. E. Peacock. EETS 31. London, 1868; rev. 1902.

Modus confitendi (metrical), ed. C. Blume. *Analecta hymnica medii aevi,* vol. xxxiii (Leipzig, 1899), no. 239.

Moralité des sept péchés mortels et des sept vertus, ed. G. Cohen, in *Mystères et Moralités du manuscrit 617 de Chantilly* (Paris, 1920). Re-edited in *Nativités et Moralités liégeoises du moyen-age.* ("Académie Royale de Belgique. Classe des Lettres. Mémoires. Collection in 4°. 2e série," XII.1.) Brussels, 1953.

Nicolas d'Osimo. *Summa casuum conscientiae* [or, *Supplementum Summae Magistrutiae,* i.e., *pisanae*]. Venice: Franc. Renner, 1477.

The Ormulum, ed. R. M. White. Oxford, 1878.

Ostiensis (i.e., Henry of Ostia, or of Segusio). *Summa super titulis decretalium.* Lyons, 1517.

Peraldus, William. *Sermones,* in Guillaume d'Auvergne, *Opera,* Vol. II (Orléans and Paris, 1674).

———. *Summa de vitiis et virtutibus.* Antwerp, 1587.

Peter Idley's Instructions to His Son, ed. Ch. d'Evelyn. ("The Modern Language Association of America, Monograph Series," No. 6.) Boston, 1935.

Petrarch. *Secretum,* ed. E. Carrara, in *Francesco Petrarca, Prose,* ed. G. Martellotti, *et al.* ("La letteratura italiana. Storia e testi," No. 7.) Milan, 1955.

Petrus Damiani. *"De divina omnipotentia" e altri opuscoli,* ed. P. Brezzi. Florence, 1943. Includes *De perfectione monachorum.*

———. *Vita Beati Romualdi,* ed. G. Tabacco. ("Fonti per la Storia d'Italia," No. 94.) Rome, 1957.

Petrus de Limoges. *De oculo morali.* [1475?].

Pirminius. *Scarapsus,* ed. G. Jecker, in *Die Heimat des hl. Pirmin, des Apostels der Alamannen.* ("Beiträge zur Geschichte des alten Mönchtums und des Benediktinerordens," No. 13.) Münster, 1927.

The Pricke of Conscience, ed. R. Morris, in "The Philological Society's Early English Volume." London, 1863.

Rigaud, Jean. *Compendium pauperis.* Paris, 1501.

Robert Manning of Brunne. *Handlyng Synne,* ed. F. J. Furnivall. EETS 119 and 123. London, 1901-1903.

Robert de l'Omme. *Le Miroir de Vie et de Mort,* ed. A. Langfors, *Romania,* XLVII (1921), 511-31, and L (1925), 14-53.

Rutebeuf. *Oeuvres complètes,* ed. E. Faral and J. Bastin. 2 vols. Paris, 1959-1960.

Schmitz, H. J. *Die Bussbücher und die Bussdisciplin der Kirche. Nach handschriftlichen Quellen dargestellt.* 2 vols. (Vol. II bears the title, *Die Bussbücher und das kanonische Bussverfahren*). Mainz, 1883, and Düsseldorf, 1898.

Le Songe du Castel, ed. R. D. Cornelius, *PMLA,* XLVI (1931), 321-32.

Speculum exemplorum. Cologne: Johannes Koelhof, 1485.

Speculum laicorum. Édition d'une collection d'exempla, composée en Angleterre à la fin du XIIIe siècle, ed. J.-Th. Welter. Paris, 1914.

Speculum morale, in Vincent of Beauvais, *Bibliotheca mundi.* Vol. III. Douai, 1624.

Summa rudium (*Inc.* "Quoniam diversa dicta"). Reutlingen: Johannes Otmar, 1487.

Tabula exemplorum secundum ordinem alphabeti, ed. J.-Th. Welter. ("Thesaurus exemplorum," No. 3.) Paris, 1926.

Thomas Aquinas. *Opera omnia.* 25 vols. Parma, 1852-1873.

Thorpe, B. *Ancient Laws and Institutes of England.* 2 vols. London, 1840.

Vices and Virtues, being a Soul's Confession of its Sins, with Reason's Description of the Virtues, ed. F. Holthausen. EETS 89 and 159. London, 1888 and 1921.

Wasserschleben, F. W. H. *Die Bussordnungen der abendländischen Kirche.* Halle, 1851.

Wyclif, John. *Select English Works,* ed. Th. Arnold. 3 vols. Oxford, 1869-1871.

———. *Trialogus,* ed. G. Lechler. Oxford, 1869.

Ysagoge in theologiam, ed A. Landgraf, in *Écrits théologiques de l'École d'Abélard.* ("Spicilegium sacrum Lovaniense," No. 14.) Louvain, 1934.

LIST OF MANUSCRIPTS CITED

For references to these manuscripts in the text, see the General Index under the author's name or title of the work contained in the respective manuscript.

Cambridge.
- Peterhouse 200 (John of Wales, *Moniloquium*).
- Trinity College R. 14. 7 (*Compileison*).

Chapel Hill.
- University of North Carolina 5 (Ps.-Raymundus de Pennaforte, *Summa de vitiis*).

London. British Museum.
- Additional 6716 (*Fasciculus morum*; Grosseteste, *Modus confitendi*).
- Additional 22572 (Felton, *Sermones dominicales*).
- Additional 24660 (Questionnaire).
- Additional 27328 (Huguitius de Pisa, *Derivationes*).
- Arundel 52 (Questionnaire).
- Arundel 110 (Joannes Balbus, *Catholicon*).
- Arundel 378 (*Alphabetum narrationum*).
- Arundel 379 (Jean Rigaud, *Formula confessionis*).
- Arundel 506 (Cf. Chapter IV, note 52).
- Arundel 507 ("Rota vitiorum"; Tree of Vices).
- Burney 356 (*Flos florum*; Grosseteste, *Templum domini*; Questionnaire).
- Cotton Faust. A. V (*Sermo quod septem vitia assimilant hominem peccatorem septem generibus lapidum*).
- Cotton Tib. A. III (Confessional formula).
- Cotton Tib. E. VII (Nassyngton, *Speculum vitae*).
- Cotton Vesp. A. XXV (*Points of Religion*).
- Cotton Vesp. D. XIII (William de Montibus, *Speculum penitentis*).
- Harley 45 (*A Mirror to Lewed Men*).
- Harley 172 (Confessional formula).
- Harley 206 (*Tractatus de VII peccatis mortalibus*).

Harley 211 (*De septem peccatis mortalibus*, English; Questionnaire; *Confessionale*).
Harley 325 (William de Montibus, *Numerale*).
Harley 632 (John of Wales, *Summa justitiae*).
Harley 1004 (Ranulph Higden, *Speculum curatorum*).
Harley 1294 (*Narratio allegorica de vitiis*).
Harley 3120 (*Memoriale presbyterorum*).
Harley 3823 (Ps.-Peraldus, "Quoniam ut ait sapiens").
Harley 4887 (Paul of Hungary, *Summa de penitentia*).
Harley 4894 (Rypon, *Sermones*).
Lansdowne 393 (Fitzralph, *Sermones*).
Lansdowne 763 (Verses on Titivillus).
Royal 2.B.v (Confessional formula, Old English).
Royal 4.B.viii (Wethershed, *Summa brevis*).
Royal 4.D.iv (John of Wales [?], *Tractatus de vitiis*).
Royal 5.D.x (John Damascene, *De fide orthodoxa*).
Royal 6.E.i (William of Pagula, *Oculus sacerdotis*).
Royal 6.E.vi-vii (*Omnebonum*).
Royal 7.C.i (William de Lancea, *Dieta salutis*).
Royal 7.E.ii (Waldeby, *Expositio super orationem dominicam*).
Royal 7.F.ii (Grosseteste, "Deus est quo nihil melius cogitari potest").
Royal 7.F.xi (John of Mirfield, *Florarium Bartholomaei*).
Royal 8.A.x (Grosseteste [?], "Primo videndum est").
Royal 8.A.xv (Questionnaire).
Royal 8.C.viii (Nicholas de Byard, *Dictionarius pauperum*).
Royal 8.F.xiii (Thomas of Chabham, *Poenitentiale*).
Royal 9.A.xiv (Questionnaire).
Royal 10.A.xvi (Petrus Cantor, *Summa Abel*).
Royal 14.E.ii (Jean de Courcy, *Le Chemin de Vaillance*).
Royal 15.D.ii (Peter of Peckham, *Lucidaire*).

Oxford.

Balliol College 77 (Ranulph Higden, *Speculum curatorum*).
Bodleian 332 (Servasanctus, *Liber de exemplis naturalibus; Fasciculus morum*).
Bodleian 410 (*Fasciculus morum*).
Bodleian 440 (Cf. Chapter IV, note 95).
Bodleian 923 (*The Clensyng of Mannes Sowle*).
Bodl. can. misc. 368 (*Liber Accidiae*).
Bodl. Laud. misc. 206 ("Remedium et tiriaca contra superbiam").
Bodl. Laud. misc. 221 (Jean de la Rochelle, *Summa de vitiis*).
Bodl. Laud. misc. 527 (Grosseteste [?], "Perambulavit Judas").
Hatton 26 (Incomplete treatise on vices; cf. Chapter VII, note 56).
Oriel College 38 (John of Erfurt, *Summa de poenitentia*).

INDEX OF SUBJECTS

INDEX OF AUTHORS AND TITLES